Late on a summer evening—prime feeding time for bass—Paul Chamblee of
Raleigh, N.C., works a topwater silver Rapala on Lake Texoma.

Roland Martin's
one hundred and one
Bass-catching Secrets

Roland Martin's
one hundred and one
Bass-catching Secrets

by Roland Martin

Edited by
LARRY MAYER

WINCHESTER PRESS
TULSA, OKLAHOMA, 74114

Library of Congress Cataloging in Publication Data

Martin, Roland, 1940–
    Roland Martin's 101 bass-catching secrets.

    1. Black bass fishing. I. Title. II. Title:
101 bass-catching secrets.
SH681.M37   799.1'758   80-10481
ISBN 0-87691-309-5

Published by Winchester Press, Inc.
1421 South Sheridan
Tulsa, Oklahoma 74114

Printed in the United States of America

Book Design by Nancy Steinmeyer

1 2 3 4 5 — 84 83 82 81 80

To my wife Mary Ann,
for her encouragement and patience,
this book is dedicated.
It has been written in the hope
that sound conservation practices will
ensure good fishing for
our son Scott and his generation—
and that all those anglers will have the
skill to make the most of it.

Acknowledgments

I would like to acknowledge the assistance of a great many people in the preparation of this book. I've learned much from my fellow fishermen, and in a sense they've all contributed to the pages that follow. Quite a few of them are mentioned in the text. There isn't space to list them all, but I do thank them.

Several of the successful rigs and techniques shown in these pages originally appeared, in slightly different form, as illustrations for articles I wrote for *Fishing Facts* Magazine. My thanks to the editorial and art departments of that publication for their able cooperation. The diagrams illustrating flipping techniques are based on material provided by Fenwick, a pioneer in the design of flipping rods, and I want to thank that company, too.

Finally, a special note of thanks goes to Ron Gentzen, President of Marketing Communications Associates of Tulsa, Oklahoma. Ron served as consultant and editorial coordinator in the preparation and production of this book. His special qualifications for this post—long experience and expertise in communications and in outdoor recreation, particularly fishing—were vital to the completion of this work.

Contents

Introduction

There we stood casting heavy arm-tiring plugs trying to entice a muskellunge in that small lake near Hayward, Wis., this past August. Roland Martin was operating the trolling motor, and I was on the front deck of his bass boat fishing next to him. At our feet beside his fish locator was my small tape recorder. We were talking about fishing 8- to 12-inch shiners up under the hyacinth beds in Florida.

Three months later I was sitting at the table in a cottage near Salt Springs, Fla., looking out the window at Little Lake Kerr and listening to Roland discuss shiner fishing above the hum of his locator. Also, I typed his thoughts on fishing in the natural lakes in states like Wisconsin. It sort of reminded me of a definition of a modern business executive—you know, a guy who talks fishing with his buddies at the office and then talks business with them Saturday morning when they're on the lake.

This book might have set a record for having been taped at more locations than any other literary endeavor. We taped chapters in Roland's air-conditioned den in Broken Arrow, Okla., on 107-degree July days. Parts of it were done in a room on the ninth floor of a fashionable Atlanta hotel during a fishing-tackle trade show. Other segments were done at the side of a motel pool at Jackson, Miss., following the 1978 BASS Masters Classic. Some work was done in a boat stall at a marine on Georgia's West Point Lake, and a few chapters were done in various parts of Florida.

What makes Roland Martin so successful as a bass fisherman? That's a question I frequently was asked during my years working as a newspaper outdoor writer in South Carolina. Judging from what other good fishermen say about him and my own experience fishing with him, the answer is a combination of factors all connected by hard work and enthusiasm.

"Nobody works harder than Roland does," commented Billy Westmorland, one of Martin's friends and a fellow tournament competitor.

"What put Roland Martin ahead of the rest of us at Santee was the fact that he was out taking water temperatures and studying the water when we didn't pay any attention to those things," a Santee-Cooper bass guide once remarked.

Westmorland and that guide are right. Roland Martin approaches his fishing conscientiously, and his inquisitive, investigative mind seeks out the reasons why bass behave as they do. Not satisfied merely with catching a limit of good bass, he wants to figure out why they were there and why they hit and fought as they did. If he caught that limit out in the middle of a fifty-mile-long lake and didn't fish there again until five years later, it's a safe bet he could go right to that spot like a hound dog to a buried bone. Maybe it was the attention to detail Martin learned years ago when he was becoming an army lieutenant which makes him aware of everything possibly significant in fishing.

The all-time money winner in Bass Anglers Sportsman Society tournaments with more than $94,000, Martin also leads in total B.A.S.S. tourney victories—ten. He has earned more than $150,000 in a bass tournament fishing career which started in 1970. Martin also has qualified for the most prestigious bass tournament—the annual BASS Masters Classic—in six out of the seven years in the event's history. He also has captured the coveted B.A.S.S. point championship five times.

There is one key aspect to Roland Martin's success, something that sets him apart from the majority of guys such as me who also enjoy the sport: versatility. Instead of being able to fish one or two types of lures well, such as crank baits or topwater plugs, he can use a wide variety of lures and techniques under a wide variety of conditions. Versatility is something he's been stressing for years, and this is precisely what he and all the top pros have in common. Simply because the bass don't hit our one or two pet lures when we fish them in the one or two ways we know how, we often do poorly. Experts such as Roland Martin can usually come up with some method or pattern which will pay off. Hence this book: Roland Martin's clear, comprehensive explanation of his own secrets—of what it takes to catch bass consistently. You may never be a tournament winner like Roland (or maybe you will), but you'll catch a lot more bass next season.

LARRY MAYER

Salt Springs, Fla.

Foreword

Years ago, my goal in life was to be an outdoor photographer specializing in fish and wildlife. Back then fishing didn't have much prestige, though there were a few famous and highly respected fishing writers, such as Jason Lucas, Ray Bergman, Ted Trueblood, Al McClane, and Robert Page Lincoln. My father was a hydraulic engineer for the U.S. Geological Survey, and he designed hydroelectric dams all over the world. He and my mother couldn't see any future in my trying to make a living from fishing or the outdoors, and they were dead set against my working as a fishing guide. My father came fishing with me a couple of times, but he hated the sport. They wanted me to be a professional person such as a doctor or a lawyer.

My parents were tragically killed in an automobile accident in Europe. I didn't want to ignore their hopes and plans for me, but I stuck with bass fishing, though this was long before there were any professional bass fishermen who were able to make a living at their favorite sport. I did get a college education, but I never went to medical school or law school. I guided for seven years and then went to work doing seminars for Ray Scott and the Bass Anglers Sportsman Society in 1970. Then I did product research and design and promotion for Lowrance Electronics. Later I turned to making fishing movies for television and finally started my own TV fishing show. In addition to fishing for fun and money, finally I was able to get into something else I really like and always wanted to do professionally—outdoor photography.

Today, I'm convinced that if my parents were here to see how bass fishing has progressed to a well-respected plateau, they would be behind me and would respect what I've done in the sport—and also the success my wife, Mary Ann, has had in bass fishing. Within the past six or seven years, bass fishing has truly become a profession—one which I've been very pleased and honored to be associated with.

Five years ago I would have been most hesitant to have written this book. Even though my bassin' friends such as Bill Dance, Tom Mann, Billy Westmorland, and Al Lindner had written bass-fishing books, I was afraid to write a book for fear of divulging secrets or patterns which might be known only to me. Not many years ago, most of us believed that to try to keep an edge in tournament competition, we had to be rather close-mouthed and not reveal much to each other. Looking back, I can see that my attitude about this was a little immature.

The professional way is to reveal to others what we're doing and have a free exchange of information. We are pretty open with each other, the outdoor writers and the average fishermen today, and this has benefited all of us. We learn from each other.

Also, five years ago I didn't have 101 "secrets" I could recommend to you with confidence. I've learned many new patterns in recent years from this free exchange of information with other tournament anglers, guides, writers, and other good fishermen. Until 1970 my bass fishing was rather limited to a few specific geographic regions. But because of the wide scope needed for a nationally syndicated TV fishing show, my sponsors have almost demanded—and rightly— that I fish virtually everywhere and for a wide variety of fish. In tournament competition we've now fished for bass in more than thirty states. Now that versatility has been forced on my profession, I'm a 200 percent better fisherman than I was when I was guiding at Santee-Cooper in South Carolina.

I would never have known how to run a shiner 20 feet back under a big clump of water hyacinths in Florida if I hadn't been taught by Dennis Rahn, a central-Florida guide. At the warmup for a tournament at Table Rock in Missouri, Bill Dance showed me a better way to hold the rod for jig and eel fishing. Dee Thomas of California showed me how to flip a jig in the delta region of the Sacramento River. Al Lindner showed me a good way to buzz a spinnerbait for Minnesota largemouths after I'd shown him how to buzz up big Kentucky bass in Arkansas. Clifford Craft of Georgia showed me I really needed to learn deep-water structure fishing with a spinnerbait (he showed what could be done with this method one day in a tournament when I was paired with him). Marty Friedman of New York City taught me how to catch St. Lawrence largemouths from gunk—something I'd hardly ever bothered to fish.

Five years ago I'd never even thought about catching big smallmouths in August—much less ever fishing with a live leech, until I met Grant Hughes on Lake Vermilion in Minnesota. So since I left my regional fishing behind at Santee-Cooper in 1970, my bass-fishing horizons have been broadened by the many fine acquaintances I've made in my hobby-job as a fisherman.

This is a book on bass patterns and how to fish them. By "patterns" I don't mean what's on the end of the line. I've been given credit for coining and defining the concept of pattern fishing. I wrote the definition first in 1969 while preparing a bass-fishing map of Santee-Cooper. What I wrote back then was:

"A pattern is the exact set of water conditions such as depth, cover, structure, temperature, clarity, currents, etc., which attracts fish to that specific spot and to other similar spots all over the same body of water."

One day I was talking with Tom Mann and he said I hadn't discovered patterns because he'd been fishing patterns for thirty years. I asked him what he thought a pattern was, and he replied, "That's just a good place to fish." John Powell used to tell me that patterns are found in dress shops, but despite his whimsical definition, I've still learned a lot of good tricks from John, which are in this book too.

I admit that 101 pattern-fishing "secrets" seem like a large repertoire, but in fact I know at least 101 more. A lot of these latter I'm not well versed in, but I do know they exist. A statement Jerry Gibbs makes in his book *Bass Myths Exploded* points out why so many bass patterns exist:

"Bass populations, like other animal populations, are made up of individuals. What we are faced with is *many* types of bass behavior. There is absolutely no substitute for learning how bass react in the specific lake or river that you will regularly fish. Even after you have established patterns of behavior, the fish will occasionally throw you a curve. There's that matter of individuality. . . ."

Bass are the same great sportfish whether they're found in Connecticut or California. Therefore, some of these patterns I don't think are as remote as they might seem at first glance. Most can be adapted to similar conditions in other parts of the country. A Minnesota angler might wonder why he should bother reading about a cypress-tree pattern at Santee-Cooper—yet he might well discover small submerged scrub bushes in a lake close to his home, and he'd be apt to find that this pattern would work almost identically. You might never fish a feeder creek in a tidewater stream, but that little ditch which dumps in near the boat dock right behind your cottage might have the same pattern.

I've organized the book in five basic parts, covering bass behavior, lures and live bait, techniques with different kinds of tackle and in different special locales, shallow-structure fishing, and deep-structure fishing. The parts are subdivided into sections, and each section contains one or several of my 101 "secrets." Obviously there's some overlap from part to part and section to section—just because I discuss plastic worms in detail in the part on lures doesn't mean I'm going to forget about them in the parts on structure and techniques. But in each of the 101 discussions in the book, I've focused on a particular thing I've noticed about patterns and have taken advantage of; I've tried to break that thing out of my overall experience and enable the reader to pick up on it quickly and use it to increase his understanding of a given pattern or to solve a problem he's had with it. A pattern is just a good place to fish, all right—if you can recognize it and know how to fish it.

In my quest for more knowledge about this grand old sport, I'd like to know if you, the reader, have any bassin' patterns which differ from or contrast with any I discuss in this book. If you're willing to share your knowledge, be sure to drop me a line and let me know what you've found. My address is Suite 134, 6216 South Lewis, Tulsa, Okla. 74136. Meanwhile, good bassin'!

ROLAND MARTIN

Salt Springs, Fla.

Nine Behavioral Reasons Why Bass Strike

---

1 Feeding

We'd fished Florida's Lake Okeechobee hard that November day, and the bass didn't hit well at all. We were trying to do a film segment for my TV fishing show, but the largemouths gave us very little cooperation. We'd thrown Johnson Spoons and plastic worms to the edges of the grass as well as back in the thick vegetation, and turned half a dozen fish. I was fishing with John Petre, who was my cameraman back then. His duties were to film, and if the fish were hitting and the sun was out bright, he didn't have time to fish.

John really enjoyed fishing, and he didn't say much about not getting to cast, but when the sun finally started dipping down below the horizon, he let out a little warwhoop and said it was his turn to fish. He was a light-tackle enthusiast, and he picked up his favorite little spinning rod and started throwing a small Rapala to the edge of the grass. What he was trying seemed a little ridiculous to me, because I thought his tackle was too light for Florida bass.

We came up to a main lake point leading back into a cove, and John flipped out and let the Rapala lie there for several seconds. A slight sucking sound was audible, and he set the hook and a bass bored down and headed out deep. With his light tackle, I took it for granted that he'd hooked nothing more than a 2-pounder. Suddenly a 5-pounder blew out of the water. He battled it and finally landed it. That was the biggest one we'd caught all day.

Five or six casts later he repeated this episode and got another one about the same size. That one also hit at the edge of the grass. We continued back in the cove, and I was still throwing Johnson Spoons and worms to the thick grass. John spotted a patch of submerged

1

Feeding bass will strike just about anything, but surface plugs like this No. 13 gold Rapala, here attached to a 9-pounder, are favorites of mine.

milfoil, and he threw in there and on three consecutive casts he got sucking strikes. He hooked and landed the bass, all of which were in the 2-to-6-pound range. He had five bass and I hadn't had a strike since he'd started fishing, and he'd got ten, all of 'em in less than ten minutes.

He was using a No. 11 gold Rapala on 8-pound line and a spinning rod. I happened to have an identical rig in my rod-storage locker, so I got it out and tied it on. We stayed in the back of that cove and for the next forty-five minutes we really slaughtered the bass. Richard Stunkard was in my backup boat. This was his first filming trip with us, and we were using him as a bird dog. He was the world's worst, most horrible fisherman, and he'd never caught any bass. All week long he was using a rod and reel I'd lent him, and I'd send him over to different points and tell him to cast a worm or a Johnson Spoon around, and if he got any sort of a strike he was to come back and report it. If he got one strike, it meant we could go to that spot and get probably thirty. Richard is a cousin to Jim Stunkard, my executive producer.

Anyhow, Richard put on a Rapala just before I did, and quickly he caught three bass. When I tried a Rapala I too started catching bass. I was getting them on an average of every other cast. I got to noticing there wasn't any wind that night, and Okeechobee was mirror-calm. This was very unusual, because the lake is forty miles wide.

We ended up catching twenty-five bass from 2 to 8 pounds. John caught the eight-pounder, and I ended up catching one about 6½. I know bass sometimes go on heavy feeds during the evening, but this was twenty-five bass in an hour. We had another fifteen strikes we didn't get. What we'd experienced was a feeding frenzy.

Most fishermen think that most bass strike because they're hungry. Actually I find that hunger accounts for maybe no more than a third of my strikes—but that third is a very important part of the bass I catch. Maybe 35 percent of the time early in the morning or late in the evening the bass are on the feed.

In major slow periods the bass will feed for a short period of time. Another condition that causes bass to feed quite often is a weather change, such as a barometric drop or an approaching storm or possibly some cloud cover which has moved in—all of which affect atmospheric pressure and temperature. Another thing that could influence bass to feed would be a warming trend after a cold front.

There are several reasons bass feed. Feeding bass are the easiest to catch. You can catch them on almost any lure in your tackle box, because basically all lures at one time or other will catch feeding fish.

My favorite, most basic pattern for catching feeding fish would be a dawn-and-dusk surface-plug pattern. I call this pattern—remember, I'm using the word "pattern" to mean the sum total of all the variables in the fishing situation—my topwater treat. It involves getting out before the sun rises or in the twilight hours of the morning or after the sun is setting in the evening and that magical hour begins, because there's no direct sun on the water.

My largest topwater bass—11½ pounds—taken early one morning from an unnamed pond in the Ocala National Forest in Florida.

It's the time of day when generally the convection currents are low and there is very little sun to move the air around, producing almost a slick or mirror-calm surface. Another condition that is very important to this type of surface action is water temperature. You need warm water, in the 70-degree zone; 70 and up for your best surface-bait fishing.

The best depth would be the shallow depths less than 5 feet. The best cover would be any kind of an ambush point in the form of a stump or a rock or any type of a grass point. The best structure is a point—basically a main-lake point.

2 Reflex Action

Reflex action is the second most important reason fish strike, particularly why bass strike, and it accounts for 20 to 25 percent of the bass I catch in a year's time. A bass's reflex action is like the behavior of any predator—like a cat pouncing on a mouse.

A lurking bass is seeking two things. He's seeking shade for his non-eyelidded eyes. He can't stand direct sunlight, at least not for very long, so he's going to try to shade his eyes in the shadow of a boulder or a bush or a boat dock. Second, and probably more important, is that, being a predator, he is seeking concealment to hide or camouflage his body from the wary eyes of small baitfish of some description. So the bass is in the shadows of an object, in this case an ambush point.

To get a reflex strike you need one of two types of lures: either a crank bait or a spinnerbait. If you don't know what these are, you'll find sections in Part II on both. They are fast-moving lures which

Reflex action brought a strike from this 7-pounder, lurking in the shade of an old dock piling. Over-and-under-the-surface photos like this—and several others in this book—are tricky. These were shot by a "simple" method: The photographer lowered a waterproof camera, inside a big glass tank, halfway into the water. Since a bass won't hold still for a portrait, I sometimes had to work a fish back in front of the camera tank for a second or third try.

come whipping through there. The concept of reflex-action fishing is to try to throw the lure right on the fish instead of just throwing past the bush, past the stump, or past the ambush point and quickly cranking the spinnerbait or crank bait right down to where you think he is. I think about which way the sun's shining so I can fish on the shady side. I think about which way the wind is blowing, because the wind will automatically position the fish on these shallow cover areas. If the wind is blowing from the north, the fish will be facing the wind because of the current it creates. They can't swim backward, and they face the current. I conjure up a mental image of exactly where that bass is positioned. Then I theoretically try to snag the fish—I'm trying to get right to his eyes. And really the lure is coming right at the fish, right at his eyes, and at the last second he can do one of two things. He can either move out of the way or he can strike it in self-defense, and quite often, since bass are fairly bold and pugnacious,

A fast-moving spinnerbait or a crank bait is the best lure to coax a reflex strike. This is one of my new Roland Martin spinnerbaits; the 6-pound largemouth was hiding under a fallen tree in a flooded field after a 10-foot rise on a Kentucky lake.

they will strike at that lure simply out of reflex action. Taking advantage of the reflex action requires a very experienced fisherman with an eye or feel for the right kind of spot, and a little bit of analytical thought concerning the sun and which way the wind is blowing.

Another condition which is better for reflex-action fishing is a cool water temperature, because that means the lure can get just a little bit closer to the bass before he knows it's there. This is kind of an advantage. Water between 45 and 65 degrees is probably best for the spinnerbait and crank bait, because the fish does not detect the presence of the lure until it is pretty much right on top of him. Then he can see it and strike it.

When the water is muddy, it is the hotter water temperatures that are better for reflex-action strikes. When the water is below 50 degrees and muddy, you hardly ever get strikes on these kinds of lures. If the water temperature is from 60 to 90, and the water is real muddy, you'll get a lot of good reflex strikes. Here the fish doesn't see the lure well, but his lateral sensitivity is such that he detects its presence at the last second and he strikes it.

The pattern most representative of reflex-action strikes is bumping the stump with a crank bait. This is simply a great pattern because that's just a natural feeding spot. The best cover might be a stump on an exposed point, where the wave action has eroded under the roots so that there are some areas beneath that stump which the fish can use as his lair.

The best depth probably is less than 6 feet, because, remember, you need to make visual contact with these ambush points. You need to be able to identify where they are, and the best way is to spot them with Polaroid sunglasses. So look for stumps in about two to six feet of water.

3 Anger

The third most important reason bass strike is out of anger. Quite often the first cast you make to a spot produces a reflex strike or a hunger strike. But if you just keep throwing into the same spot and the fish isn't hungry, or the fish wasn't quite close enough to the lure, maybe after six, eight, or even ten casts he just gets thoroughly upset

**It took twenty casts to get this 10-pound, 2-ounce
Santee-Cooper bass angry enough to hit my spoon.**

at that lure swimming through there. Any lure can invoke an anger
strike if it is fished persistently enough.

There is a story I like to tell about when I really got onto the concept of anger fishing and started using it as a regular way to catch
fish. This was in 1967 at Santee-Cooper Reservoir. I had just fished
the evening before along this one grass point and had caught a couple
of pretty good bass there, so early the next morning I told my guide
party, a Mr. Smith, that I'd been catching a lot of fish on a Johnson
Spoon by sweeping it across these grass points, particularly early in
the morning.

So on the very first cast Mr. Smith made on this point in the grass,
a tremendous bass makes a big wave and sucks up that spoon. He
halfway sets the hook and the fish wiggles and right away is gone. The
fish really didn't get a chance to feel the hook, so I said, "Throw back!
Mr. Smith, he might hit again!"

Well, Mr. Smith threw back about three or four times, and I'm holding the boat with the trolling motor trying to keep him in good casting range. After six or seven casts he said, "Boy! That's the biggest fish I've ever had strike in my life. I bet that fish went 8 to 10 pounds."

I told him not to give up and that he might be able to catch him yet. He said, "No, after six or eight casts, he's not hitting now."

I suggested we anchor, and said I'd bet we could catch that fish if we just kept at it. He suggested we both cast. So I picked up my spoon. We had heavy 20-pound line and heavy casting rods. We made alternate casts to the grasspoint.

Finally, after about thirty casts, Mr. Smith began looking down the lake and he said, "What about those other grass points down there?" I said we'd go hit 'em—they were good spots and I was confident we could catch a fish or two off them—but I knew that there was a monster right here. He reminded me we'd made forty casts, and he said the big one was not going to hit. So he actually started throwing the other way. He acted kind of disgusted waiting for me to get tired of fishing this part of the lake, because he wanted to go try to get another one.

When I started fishing, I started counting. On the seventy-sixth cast, a 9-pound, 6-ounce largemouth bass launched himself through the canopy of the thick grass and skyrocketed right through my Johnson Spoon, actually clearing the water.

I've had bass hit on repeated casts, but undoubtedly this one hit with the most vengeance, the most anger, and the most power that I've ever seen. This was undoubtedly the angriest fish in the whole lake.

Since then on many occasions when I've located a bass I've made repeated casts. Quite often I will pull up to a spot which looks good and has all the depth, all the cover, and all the structure that is perfect for fish, and I'll tell my partner I know there's got to be bass here. Quite often I'll bet five dollars on it.

And sometimes the guy will say he'd bet a dollar against it. In a normal situation when I'm real positive, I'll just stop and anchor and cast from ten to fifteen times. Maybe on the first cast he'll hit, but after ten to fifteen casts in the same spot, I'll make him mad.

Probably the best lure for this is a crank bait or a buzz bait, which enables you to make a lot of casts. It's not the lure that's important, but recognizing a situation that demands repeated casts.

4 Protective Instinct

Protective instinct involves the spawning season. Largemouth bass spawn when the water temperature reaches 62 degrees, and smallmouth bass spawn when it reaches 59 degrees. No matter where you live, this is true. Generally the majority of bass spawn at or near a full moon. So in the southern United States—say in Florida, Alabama, and Georgia—quite often that first full moon in February or even late January might be a good spawning moon. In North Carolina and Virginia quite often they will spawn on the full moon in March and April. Up in Pennsylvania and Ohio, they spawn in May, and in the southern part of Canada and in the northern part of the U.S., they spawn as late as June. Theoretically, if you travel the country as I do, you have a six-month spawning season.

Another characteristic of spawning fish is that they never all spawn at the same time. Maybe 60 percent of the bass will spawn on the first good moon. On Santee-Cooper I learned my ABC's of bass fishing during seven years as guide, and every spring I would utilize my spawning patterns. Santee is a 171,000-acre reservoir, and you hit a lot of different water temperatures around the lake. In the warmer

A male largemouth guards the bed. Largemouth beds, usually 2 to 4 feet in diameter, are similar the world over.

After the eggs are laid, the smaller male bass protects the bed for the next three weeks. I always return any of these males I catch; otherwise bluegills and carp would eat all the eggs or fry.

My favorite for spawners is an unweighted plastic worm crawled through the bed, sometimes repeatedly to provoke the larger but less aggressive female.

parts they spawn earlier than they do in the colder areas of Santee.

Bass often spawn for a six-week period on a large reservoir.

The best pattern and the best way to catch a spawning bass involves crawling a plastic worm through the spawning bed. People who catch spawning bass often are unaware that the fish are spawning. They're throwing plastic worms by bushes and little stick-ups and in the backs of the coves. They're not watching, and they don't have Polaroid glasses. They're not looking to see if there's a spawning bed there. They just feel a strike, set the hook, and catch a bass.

I look for the north or northwest coves, and there's a reason for this. On most lakes in the northern hemisphere, the cold winds come from the north. When the cold fronts come down from the north, they push cold water to the south side of the lake, so they are often 10 degrees colder in the spring than the north shores. Also, when a warm front hits, it blows generally from the south, and these are warm winds. Again, the warm winds push the water, so when they push from the south, warm water is piled up against the north bank.

There's another reason I like to look for north banks. That is because of the southern sun exposure. The sun is still in the southern quadrant, and there's less shade created on the northern bank. The southern banks have the tall pine trees and a lot of shade. Bass seek sunny places for spawning areas. Bass also seek a hard bottom—they'll spawn on a mud bottom, too, but when they can find it, they will look for a sand bar. So quite often the pattern you're looking for involves finding a firm bottom on a north bank.

When they spawn they have a protective instinct. They hit not because of hunger or anger but merely because they're trying to guard the bed. They try to kill the intruder.

The male is the more aggressive fish. He builds the nest and goes out and rounds up the female. She is on the bed usually for only seventy-two hours, and then stays around for another two or three days. So she's there only for four or five days. The male guards the nest for an additional two to three weeks. He is there nearly a month. You're going to catch a lot more bass at spawning time, since the female is there a much shorter period.

When a male bass is caught, the biggest mistake many bass fishermen make is to move off the area and try somewhere else. Sure enough, they catch another male bass, but they don't catch any female bass—the trophies—because they're not fishing for them. They're just fishing for the males that hit first. To catch the females, you have to stop and make repeated casts to the spot. Possibly you're making them mad or angry. So maybe the big female doesn't hit the first couple of casts. Maybe she gets mad as well as having the protective instinct.

While the fish are spawning they are also hungry in the early-morning hours, so your best time to catch a spawner would be at dawn with your very first cast, which might cause a reflex strike or provoke a protective instinct. If that doesn't work, make a lot of repeated casts and provoke the anger.

---

5   Curiosity

A minor reason bass strike is out of curiosity. This amounts to only about 2 percent of the time, but it's still worth considering. Occasionally you see fish cruising around in clear water, such as in a gravel pit

This largemouth is just cruising, not actively feeding
—but don't ignore it; maybe you can make it curious.

I spotted this one cruising under
the willows on Lake Texoma, and
got his attention by twitching a
small surface plug.

or a small pond. I've caught these fish because they were curious. They're not hungry. It's the middle of the day and they're out sunning themselves or just cruising around.

One of the best ways to catch them is by twitching a small surface plug. I take a small topwater bait and sneak up on them where the fish can't see me. I don't cast right on the top of the fish because that might scare them. I throw within 8 to 10 feet of them so I know they'll see the lure floating there. When the bait splats down, instantly you'll see the fins raise on the fish, and next you see him turn and look at the plug. Most of the time the fish is not going to do anything.

When he starts to turn away, I barely twitch that lure, and the little bit of movement gets him interested again. Invariably he moves in just a little bit closer. He'll look at it and maybe half-circle it.

The plug lies there for ten to fifteen seconds, and again the fish turns to move away slightly. Then I twitch it again, and the bass circles right up beneath it. Again the plug is still, and he's up there pretty close, just inches away. And then again at the last minute he starts to sink or turn. I twitch it once more, and he'll suck it in.

Many of these kinds of strikes are merely gentle sucking strikes with no more ripple than a popping bug makes when it's taken by a bluegill. A plastic worm fished on the bottom can produce the same type of strike; it's the same concept.

---

6 Competition

When you're structure fishing in deep water, you're fishing for bass schooled up in numbers. When they're schooled up like this and one fish hits, other bass hit out of competition. When this creates a frenzy, quite often you'll catch a limit in one spot. This is a condition which exists mostly in deep water structure on the creek channels and dropoffs. Occasionally the competition is so severe and so fierce you'll see the fish breaking and surfacing as a school.

A lot of anglers have caught "doubles"—two at once—on a lure. Most of them think two bass just zoomed in and tried to get the lure, but that very seldom is the case. Those fish really got caught out of competition. What almost always happens is you throw out, and one of the fish is a little more eager and grabs the bait first. Fish are so

A school of largemouths like this can erupt into a feeding frenzy when conditions are right.

competitive that they try to pull the lure out of the other fish's mouth. Often bass actually tear a plastic worm like two dogs pulling on a towel or rug.

Often with a large topwater plug 4 to 6 inches long, enough of the lure is hanging out of the fish's mouth that the second fish tries to grab it and gets caught. I've caught a tremendous number of doubles because I do a lot of structure fishing on points where there are concentrations of fish. I'll throw most any type of lure and when I get a strike and hook the fish, many, many times on these structural places I'll see other fish following the one I have on.

You have to capitalize quickly on this pattern, because they're only going to stay in a frenzy a very short time. You need to have a second rod rigged up and just drop the rod and reel and fish that you've caught and then pick up a heavy, compact lure such as a spoon, Little George, or a grub and throw it. I also like a crank bait in this situation. In a tournament I've had many rods rigged up at the same time.

In 1970 I was at Toledo Bend in my very first bass tournament, and I was fishing with Joe Palermo on the first day. He said he knew I fished a lot of spoons, but why did I have five rods and five spoons? And I answered that in case we got into a big school, I wanted to be able to catch a lot of them real quick. He said he had a spoon on and

**A school of largemouths breaking the surface
over a creek channel on Lake Bixoma, Okla.**

could catch them real quick, too. We pulled up to the first point and
we caught one apiece. There wasn't much to it, because there wasn't a
big school there. At the second or third point we each caught a single.
About nine o'clock we pulled up on the edge of a river bend and threw
into about 20 feet of water right over the channel. Joe threw in first,
and right away one thumped his spoon. As he was pulling the fish up
to the boat, I saw a couple more bass following it. I made a cast and
one hit me, and as I got mine up to the boat, a couple of bass were
following it, and I told him we were into a school.

I dropped my spoon and bass in the bottom of the boat and picked
up my second rod and threw it and caught a fish. Without taking time
to unhook the bass, I picked up my third rod and threw it and caught
another one. I repeated this with the fourth and fifth rods, and I finally looked around and saw I had five rods and five fish thumping
around in the boat. One of the spoons had come out of a bass, and I
picked it up and caught a sixth one.

Joe was still there with his first bass and a pair of pliers, because
that fish had sucked in his spoon pretty good. It was halfway down his
throat, and he was trying to pull the hook out.

Here I had six bass and he had one. To make a long story short, I
didn't win that tournament, but I came in second, and I sure had
beaten my partners. One reason was I had multiple lures rigged up
and ready. I was in a school situation, and when I caught one fish, I

would get another one. We always found at least one school a day, and I'd catch a limit or close to a limit out of it. This is competitive fishing for competitive fish.

---

7 Territorial Instinct

Occasionally I catch a bass that strikes out of territorial instinct, and this is a trophy-fish situation. Bass guard their territory just the way a big bear in the woods does; when other bears come around, he chases them off.

I kept an 11-pounder for a time at Santee-Cooper in a big tank. When any bass came his way, the 11-pounder would dart out and

A lone cypress tree is a likely place to hook a really big one—but there won't be any smaller ones around; the big one owns that tree.

I saw this 8-pounder hanging around the same grassbed on Rainbow River on three different trips, but couldn't get him to hit.

chase the other fish away. We'd sneak up to the tank and have a little popping bug on the line or a little minnow on a hook, and we'd throw in the tank and catch those bass. That 11-pounder I caught about fifteen times. But the other fish would hit the bug a lot quicker; the 3- and 4-pounders would eat it up right away. The 11-pounder was smart. He'd seen a lot more lures in his lifetime. It's kind of the same way on a lake.

What does the territorial area look like?

As I stress in this book, the most important thing in bass fishing is to establish a pattern. That is, locate the depth, cover, and structure and couple it up with whatever water temperatures are productive and the water currents and wind conditions present. Then you know what to look for, and you've got plenty of places to try.

Suppose you establish a pattern, such as a point with big stickups, and you've hit the last three points with big stickups and have caught some fish on every one of them, and you come to the fourth point with big stickups and it looks even better. It has bigger stickups then the rest of them, and there's deep water close by. The wind is just right, and there's some bait there. Everything looks absolutely perfect on that spot. And yet you don't catch fish there.

I've hit places such as that fourth point, and I used to leave and run on down the lake. Then I got to thinking maybe the reason I didn't catch one was that there was a smart old trophy bass lying on that point where he had everything he needed. He'd seen bass boats and he knew all about lures, and I'd probably made too much noise. The fact is there should have been some fish there, but maybe since I didn't catch one, there were no *small* bass present.

Then I'll go back and try for that big trophy fish. Often I will start with a different lure, such as a large plastic worm instead of the 6-inch worm which catches most of your bass. I throw a 9-inch worm rigged up on heavy line with a big hook and put it right against the biggest stickup on the point and twitch it ever so slowly in that spot in hopes that the big trophy bass will be there.

___

8 Killer Instinct

This instinct has put a lot of fish in the boat for me. It also creates a lot of enjoyment. Always interesting to me is the fact that you can have a giant lure like a Musky Jitterbug or a huge propeller plug and consistently it will be the little tiny bass no longer than the plug itself that actually try to kill the big lure. That's killer instinct. The bass has

This 8-inch bass was just trying to kill that 6-inch lure, since he could never have swallowed it.

a mouth not much bigger than the plug. He can't possibly be trying to eat it; all he can be doing is trying to kill it. Quite often you throw a large plug out and small bluegills will hit it.

Something else that intrigues me is that when I'm fishing a surface plug at a distance, some of the bigger fish will suck the plug in and look like a bluegill hitting it. I don't know how many times I've been in an area working a surface plug really slow while hoping a big fish might be tricked any second, and out of killer instinct a little bluegill pops that plug. Since it might be a bass, occasionally I'll pull back so hard I've fallen down with a pair of waders on or tripped backward over a stump while anticipating a 10-pounder.

9   Ignorance

When I think of ignorant fish, I think of the bass in some of the Canadian lakes I've fished. One time I flew in a float plane to this little body of water a few hundred acres in size. The pilot cut the engine and started drifting back over where he had first touched down. I asked where we would fish, and he said to just throw out there anywhere. And he said any lure in my tackle box was just perfect. I sat there on the right float of that airplane and in the first ten casts I had ten fish on. On my second cast over to a little boulder, there was this funny sucking strike. It sounded like a toilet flushing, and it was a 2-to-3-pound smallmouth inhaling my plug.

Those bass were eager, and they really were ignorant fish. They never had seen a man or a lure before. Over the past ten years I have occasionally found small farm ponds which were unfished and had many of these eager, stupid fish. Places in Mexico are almost the same, too.

In Mexico I had the same bass strike six times in a row. I actually caught him three times. I was doing a film with Dino Economos and my wife, Mary Ann, and we were in the courtyard of Padilla City, which is now covered by Lake Guererro. I had asked Dino to film me fishing a plastic worm, and on my first cast a 2-pounder swam over and grabbed the worm, and Dino got it on film. I released the bass, and we could see him swim right back over to a little corner. It wasn't spawning season; the fish definitely wasn't spawning. I didn't think he would hit again, so Dino didn't film it, but I threw back a second

On a remote Canadian Lake that we reached by plane, we fished from a rubber raft and hooked naive smallmouths on nearly every cast.

time and the same bass grabbed the worm and I caught him again.

Dino said he didn't believe it. We were over a concrete patio and the water was only 2½ feet deep, and that was the only bass in sight. We could see the entire bottom. I released the bass again, and he went right back to the same corner. I asked Dino to film it in case he struck a third time. Sure enough, I caught that bass a third time and released him again.

Three more times that same bass struck the worm, but I didn't set the hook. I was afraid I'd kill him if I kept hooking him. I just threw back and he grabbed the worm and shook it, and I kept pulling and finally was able to ease it away from him. Each time he followed the lure all the way to the boat.

That fish would have to be classified as either mentally disturbed or else the dumbest, most ignorant, stupid fish that ever lived. I'm not saying this is not good; in fact, I would like to see a lot more of those fish, because that's my kind of fish! The problem is that in heavily fished waters, we've caught out those stupid fish. They're the first ones to hit a lure.

In hard-fished lakes, the ones that hit best are the ones that get caught, and the ones we keep are the big ones. What ends up in those lakes are small, smart fish, and a lot of them.

Dr. George Bennett, a leading biologist of the Illinois Natural History Survey, wrote a book on pond management back in the 1950s. He's recognized as one of the leading ichthyologists in the country on pond management. Bennett conducted a survey years ago on a lake

This one is not as ignorant as he was a moment ago. I release about 98 percent of the bass I catch.

which was initially stocked with 500 bass. They opened it to fishing three or four years after it was stocked. It was controlled experimental fishing; everybody who caught a fish had to fill out a report which was monitored. All who went in or out had to check with a warden, and a complete tally of how many fish had been caught was carefully made.

At the end of three years of experimenting, they decided to drain the lake to see how many fish were left. The first year they had caught several hundred fish. About half as many were caught the second year, and the third year only forty or so were caught. But when they drained the lake, they found approximately 1,400 bass! No more bass had been added to the lake, and five or six years had passed since they had initially stocked it. Many bass had reproduced, and many of them were small.

Lots of fish biologists have concluded that the initial few hundred bass which were caught were the dummies. The ones that were left to reproduce passed on to their offspring the genetic capabilities they possessed—in this case, wariness, stealth, and caution. The 1,400 which were left in the lake were basically cautious, wary fish.

Probably some fishermen will question whether ignorance is truly a behavioral reason why a bass may strike. After all, if the smartest bass in the water may strike for any of the eight other behavioral reasons I've already listed, isn't it obvious that an ignorant bass will strike for those same reasons? Sure, but the point is that a dumb one doesn't hesitate, even under conditions that make a cautious bass refuse your bait. Where the fishing pressure is heavy, of course, the ignorant ones don't last long, and a lake that's supposed to be "fished out" may hold plenty of cautious bass but very few dummies. But this doesn't mean our waters can't be overfished. On the contrary, that happens all too often.

I want to see bass fishing around for my son, Scott, to enjoy when he gets to be twenty-four years old, and that's another twenty years from now. But the way it's going—a daily limit of fifteen bass in some states, and hundreds of thousands of bass anglers in virtually every state—I wonder what the future of the sport will be. We have created more water by building 10 million acres of fine reservoirs in the past thirty years, and this has created more habitat for bass. However, in building 10 million acres of water, we have created an additional 10 million fishermen we didn't have thirty years ago. So we are overfishing our lakes.

Basically we have a good standard of living, and we don't have to live off nature. Our 10 million acres of water can't support all the fishermen if they want to eat all their bass. Let's have a comprehensive catch-and-release program. We don't need to kill these fish, particularly those eager ignorant ones and those bigger ones we all prize as trophies. I would like to see quality fishing reinstated in the average reservoir and lake in the U.S. The only way it's going to be done is to persuade the sportsmen—collectively and in clubs—to release their trophy fish.

It's hard to understand why more bass aren't released instead of killed. Maybe there's nothing wrong with a bass dinner once in a while, but I've eaten a lot of fish that taste better. Probably the most tasty fish I've eaten is a walleye. Another tasty fish is snook. I've tasted probably seventy-five species of fish, because I've lived in Brazil and have traveled in Europe and Africa, and most of these fish are tastier than bass.

Our waters contain plenty of other sources of protein which aren't being harvested. Ninety percent of the fishermen are harvesting the bass to eat, and 99 percent of the fish population is left unmolested. The latter could be utilized as a form of protein as well as delicious food. We just don't have an excuse to keep many bass.

Lures and Live Bait

PLASTIC WORMS

First of all, the plastic worm is the most versatile bass bait in the world. I would estimate that I've caught at least half of my lifetime bass on the plastic worm in various sizes, colors, and shapes. And in the major bass-fishing tournaments in the past decade, probably half of the success has been with the plastic worm. Without a doubt, it's the No. 1 lure, and there are a lot of reasons for this.

The plastic worm is the most weedless and snagless lure available. It can be fished at all depths and all speeds, and can be jigged, cast, trolled, and floated. There are so many variations in plastic-worm fishing that using the worm is a complete art and science by itself.

Some bass fishermen I know use plastic worms exclusively. Ask them what kind of bass fishing they do, and they reply, "I'm a *worm* fisherman." And that's all they take. They've sixteen rods with sixteen different types and sizes of plastic worms. Bass-fishing pro John Powell of Montgomery, Ala., estimates that he uses a plastic worm about 98 percent of the time. Plastic worms really are a big part of my bass fishing, too.

Artificial worms haven't been around all that long, at least in terms of popularity. But note the word "popularity." Larry Mayer, an avid collector of antique fishing lures, found that rubber-worm baits rigged on hooks were advertised in a Shakespeare tackle catalog dated about 1907. Obviously, however, artificial worms were far from popular between 1910 and 1950.

My first actual experience with a plastic worm came in 1957. I was still in high school and was fishing a lot of farm ponds in Maryland. I ran into an Eastern Shore fisherman named Louis Sullivan, who currently holds the record for entering the most *Sports Afield* citation-winning bass in the year; he entered forty-eight bass above 5 pounds in 1963. Sullivan had learned of plastic worms, and he ordered his first ones out of Ohio from manufacturer Nick Creme of Akron. The

Wading the grass and fishing a plastic worm is still one of my favorite pastimes on Santee-Cooper.

first worms Sullivan received were 7 or 8 inches long. On each worm was a spinner, five or six little red beads, and two weedless hooks. The whole thing was on a monafilament harness. It was a swimming-type lure, and the way to fish it was to throw it out near some cover and reel it back.

That same year I caught my first bass on a plastic worm. I was fishing a small pond with Floyd Parks, one of my school buddies, and I threw out this harnessed worm near a clump of lily pads. I was reeling it in, and I felt a little bump. I set the hook and caught a bass. Throughout 1957, Sullivan, Parks, and I caught dozens of bass, including several pretty good ones, on that harnessed worm rig.

In 1958, we'd heard just enough about DeLong worms and the Creme worms that some of the guys weren't using that spinner on the front. It wasn't that big a deal. You could take one or two weedless hooks and rig a worm behind a split shot and start crawling it a little deeper. You could throw it out in deeper water, and this was especially effective during the midday hours.

The beautiful thing about the plastic worm back then was that most bass fishermen left the lake at nine a.m. during hot weather because they were surface-plug fishermen. The plastic worm simply opened up the midday hours. Now you could fish and delve the deeper depths with a slowly moving underwater lure during hot weather and catch some good fish. That's when I really started getting into the single-hook concept of plastic worming. I still fished with light spinning tackle at that time, and this was a bad deal. But with a split shot ahead of the worm, I still caught some bigger bass, including some 5-pounders.

How we fished those worms was really ridiculous. At that time we merely wanted to keep and kill and eat everything that ever struck. We were using spinning reels with 8- and 10-pound-test lines, and we'd whip those ol' worms out there and crawl 'em along the bottom until finally something pecked at them. Then we'd open our bails and permit the bass to run with the worm just all over the place. After maybe smoking a whole cigarette or waiting a full minute, we'd close the bail and start easing in the line. The line would pull free of weeds

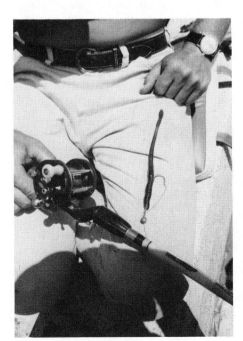

The plastic-worm rig I used till the mid-1960s: 8-inch worm, No. 4 split shot, No. 6 Aberdeen weedless hook.

or sticks, and we'd get in all the slack and then set the hook. Sure enough, those bass had swallowed it, and sometimes they'd swim clear behind the boat. We had light lines and light rods, and with the worm down in their gullets, not much of a hook set was needed. There would have been no way to release those bass; all we caught were mortally hooked. If they didn't break our lines, we caught 'em. But about half the time, those bass had gone through the lily pads or around stickups, and they broke off simply because we were letting them run forever.

This wasn't very efficient. So about a year later we started fishing more of the open-water reservoirs, such as Tridelta, Loch Raven, and Rocky Gorge. We also fished some water-supply lakes around the Washington, D.C., area and near Baltimore. We'd use a No. 4 split shot, a No. 6 weedless Aberdeen hook, and an 8-inch plastic worm in either black, natural color, or red.

Soon we learned that if we used stiffer spinning rods, we could set the hook a little better. Instead of letting them run and swallow the worm, why not set the hook quicker with a little heavier tackle and avoid gut-hooking the fish?

In 1959 Tom McNey and I set the record on bass in Loch Raven Reservoir. We had seven bass over 6 pounds in one day, and these were caught on *blue* plastic worms. Hardly anyone in the state of

Tom McNey (left) and I with 41 pounds of largemouths taken from Santee-Cooper in March 1965, all on plastic worms. The one in my left hand was my first over 10 pounds.

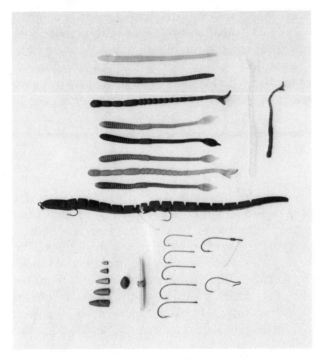

An assortment of materials for making various types of plastic-worm rigs, and a lunker rig with weedless hooks. Specific rigs are discussed in the next four sections.

Maryland had ever fished a plastic worm at that time, much less a blue one. Three years later, Tom and I really had progressed in our plastic-worm fishing. We were going out with electronic fish locators and contour maps and we were fishing deep structure which never had been fished in many of these old city lakes, and one day we caught twenty-one bass all over 4½ pounds on plastic worms.

The point is, I don't think we were all that good at bass fishing, but we were the first with truly super bait. Since I've become a professional bass fisherman, I've talked with guys who initiated plastic-worm fishing in other states. In every case I've found a small group of men who were the first to fish that lure in a given lake, and they absolutely murdered the bass just as McNey, Sullivan, and I did in Maryland during those early years.

Now those days are over with. The reason is that the easy-to-catch fish have been caught out. It goes back to the ignorance factor I have already mentioned. We were out there catching bass which never had seen a plastic worm, and they hit it without caution. They just charged into it. We also were fishing old house foundations and submerged islands—places which never really had been fished much before. They were virgin spots back then, and we caught far more bass than we can catch now from those same places.

In recent years I've gone back to Maryland and fished with McNey. We've caught a few bass, but we don't catch 10 percent as many as we did twenty years ago.

---

10 The Texas Rig

Probably the most successful bass lure currently known to fishermen is the Texas worm rig—a weighted soft plastic worm with the hook point imbedded. Until about 1964, most worms had hard bodies, and the traditional way to fish them was with a weedless hook. The hardness didn't make any difference because the hook was exposed. But by the late 1960s, worms of much softer plastic were manufactured. I don't know who gets credit for it, but some Texas fishermen were taking plain 5/0 and 6/0 Sproat hooks and imbedding the hook into the soft worm so that the point was concealed. There is no weedguard, just the plastic itself; when the hook is set, the point and barb come through the soft plastic and hook the fish. At that time, this was a popular lure in lakes around the Dallas and San Antonio area.

The first time I tried the Texas rig was at Santee-Cooper, S.C., in about 1968. I'd heard about it from a guy I fished with named Mark Workman. Mark was a tremendously tall man—he had been an All-American basketball player—and his favorite way of bass fishing was wading. He'd had special waders made and could wade in 5 feet of water, where I'd be up to my nose. Two of our big tricks at Santee in the spring were wading the blackwater ponds for spawning bass and wading around the cypress trees. Wading, as you probably know, should be a very quiet approach.

Mark brought out some plain hooks and commented that he knew I'd heard of the Texas rig. I said I'd heard of it, but down here it didn't work too well. Back then I was pouring my own worms. I'd take used plastic worms fishermen would leave in the boat and melt them down, ending up with a glob of plastic which was sort of a brown-black-greenish-red, and I'd pour it into the molds. These worms were about 9 inches long, and they were stiff. I'd use them with a big weedless hook.

Mark gave me one of his plain hooks and suggested I try the Texas rig because the boys in Texas were killing the bass with it. At that time I was fishing for trophy bass and was using 30-pound-test line with heavy 7/0 hook. The hook he gave me was a little ol' 5/0 made of lighter wire. I buried it in one of my 9-inch worms and threw over near a spawining bed, and a 7- or 8-pound bass swirled up and grabbed the worm. I set the hook, but the fish got off. I reeled in and looked at my worm; the hook never had gotten through the plastic. Then I decided to work a hole in the plastic, so I wiggled the hook around until there was a little channel through the worm.

A few casts later, that bass hit again, and this time I set the hook real hard. The water was about to come in over the top of my waders as I was sloshing around after the fish, which was going through the lily pads. I was up to my chin in water, but Mark was only to his waist, so he said he'd go after the fish. He headed toward the lilies, but when he got there the bass made a sudden lunge and straightened out my hook.

Right then I told Mark the Texas worm was foolish. Worms were too stiff and you wouldn't get the fish hooked, and anyway the hook was too light.

Obviously I hadn't perfected my worm fishing—not as I have since the early 1970s. Now there are many plastic worm manufacturers who use softer plastics and also many hook manufacturers who make good plastic-worm hooks. (Plus it makes lots of difference if you sharpen the hooks and use a good stout line and a good stout worm rod and a good hook set.) Also, now we have graphite rods. They have much more impact, so you can set the hook pretty well through that plastic.

There are some advantages to the Texas worm rig over the old weedless-hook style of worm fishing. The biggest advantage is it's more compact and streamlined. We're using cone-shaped bullet worm weights instead of split shot or the old egg sinkers. The cone-shaped weights swim their way through grass and other cover much better. Also, the hook is less exposed. There's more hook in the worm, and less body of hook exposed. With the weedless hook, you have one or two wires and the entire bend of the hook hanging out. There is more exposed metal to pick up trash.

Another advantage to the Texas rig is there's no "sprong." With the old weedguard hook, the weedguard is under tension, and quite often in the fish's mouth, the weedguard will flip up and "sprong"

All my Texas rigs have looked like
this since 1966, though line weight,
slip sinker, and hook size vary,
depending on the pattern I'm fishing.

'em. Many times this scares the fish, and it spits out the worm. This is
particularly true on light strikes or with Kentucky bass, which normally are spookier than largemouths. When I fished worms on weedless hooks, I had a lot of fish drop the rig.

Another factor is that the Texas rig is a lot cheaper to fish. Standard worm hooks are two to three cents apiece, whereas the weedless
hooks are fifteen to twenty-five cents apiece. The way we fish today,
worms are expendable. We're constantly throwing 'em into heavy
cover and constantly getting hung up. And we're breaking them off.
It's cheaper to break off a twelve-cent lure than a thirty-five-cent
lure.

The real advantage, though, with the Texas rig is the fact that it
can be snaked, crawled, and jigged across almost any bottom surface.
With plastic worms, you're constantly looking for heavy cover. To me,

worm fishing is mostly reserved for the ultra-thick cover, such as brush, stumps, and rocks. I very seldom throw plastic worms to a bare shoreline.

The Texas rig has a lot of different variations, starting with the weightless varieties and ending with ones for jigging on structure in deep water with as much as 1/2 ounce of lead ahead of the lure. They vary from 5-inch to 10-inch rigs. Some fishermen even rig with double hooks on the Texas rig. (Another advantage to the rig is that during spawning season, when bass often strike shorter, you can move the hook point farther down the worm to catch those short-strikers.)

The 6-inch dark-grape or purple worm rigged Texas-style is the most popular of all these rigs. A poll of plastic worm manufacturers revealed that of all their worms sold, nearly 40 percent are 6-inch purple or dark grape. The second choice is 6-inch black. Black is an extremely popular color during the spawning season. Third most popular size and color is the 6-inch blue worm. Blue seems to be a particularly good hot-weather color after the fish have spawned and moved to deeper water. Red and green colors also sell pretty well, as do multiple and spotted colors.

The standard way I fish the Texas worm rig is to try to find heavy cover in the form of brush. My first choice is a submerged brushpile, a tree, or some other type of wood cover. My second pick is some type of weedy cover, such as lily pads or grass, and my third favorite is boulders and rocks. One problem with the last is that worms do get caught in the crevices. Worms are not entirely snagless. When that slip weight lodges between two boulders or in rip-rap, you're going to lose a lot of worms. You'll also lose a lot of worms when you snake them through brush, because sometimes that weight catches and hangs in forks of limbs and the hook gets caught.

But worms are expendable. The average worm fisherman carries at least twenty-five different worms in the same color. He'll likely have six different colors in the 6-inch size, six different colors in the 7-inch length, and so on. In all he has 200 to 300 worms with him. At ten to twelve cents apiece, counting hook and weight, plastic worms aren't an extravagance. Probably he'll lose a dozen or so worms a day, but compare that cost to the price of the gasoline and the meals on the trip. The trip might have cost him $20, and he's lost $1.50 worth of worms.

The plastic worm is cheap and efficient, and it can be fished at all depths and during almost all seasons of the year. There are some criteria for worm fishing, particularly the Texas-style. Most important of these is water temperature. It's been my experience and that of most bass fishermen I know that very few bass are caught on plastic worms in water cooler than 55 degrees. You'll catch a few; in fact, I've caught a few when ice was forming around the edges of the lake.

Plastic worm fishing starts early in the year when the water temperature reaches 55, but better worm fishing comes when the water reaches 60 to 65 degrees. Probably the best time to fish a plastic worm is when smallmouth and largemouth bass are spawning. Water temperature then is 59 degrees for smallmouth spawning activity and 62 degrees for largemouth spawning. At this time, bass really are hitting the plastic worm because the worm is a snaky-looking creature. When it comes crawling through a spawning bed, it rouses the fish's protective instinct; and he's going to carry it out of there and try to kill it because he thinks it's after the eggs.

What size of plastic worm is right? I'm asked that virtually everywhere I talk with fishermen. I've often said the size doesn't make any difference as long as it's 6 inches, because then it'll work. But that's really an oversimplification. In tournament competition or if I'm

How to make Texas rigs in three sizes.

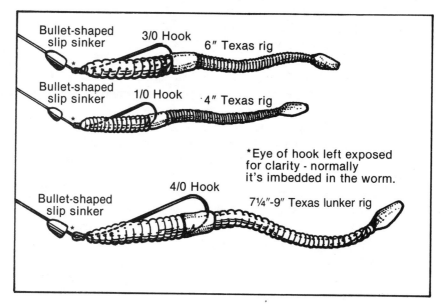

merely trying to catch a limit of bass, I prefer the 5-to-6-inch worms for catching small to medium-sized bass. I've caught a lot more bass—not the big ones, but just good keepers—on the 6-inch worm. However, if I'm after trophy fish, I go to 8, 9, and even 10 inches.

One of my favorite stories about big worms concerns a trip my wife, Mary Ann, and I made to Florida back in 1973. We were bass fishing at Lake Eloise at Cypress Gardens. At the time the 13-inch J&W Hawg Hunter worm was new on the market. It has two giant weedless hooks attached to about a 50-pound-test braided line buried inside it, and the thing looks like a tractor-tire retread. A stiff casting rod and both hands are needed to cast it. It's the most horrible-looking worm you'll ever see. However, some anglers reportedly had caught some big bass on it.

Mary Ann was after a trophy. I'd caught several big bass, including a few over 10, but she'd never got a 10-pounder, and she said her whole trip was devoted to catching a trophy bass. I agreed to try merely to catch a lot of bass, so I stayed with 6-inch worms. We fished mostly cypress trees and grass beds but also some 10-to-15-foot-deep potholes . . . all of this for five days.

She stayed with the 13-inch Hawg Hunter and in five days she caught only nine bass. Out of those nine, her smallest was 6 pounds and the largest was a little over 9 pounds. She had a 7-pound average for her nine fish. If we'd been in tournament competition, my total weight would have beaten her solidly. During those five days I averaged six to fifteen bass per day and totaled about fifty bass. But my fish were smaller. Most of them were $1\frac{1}{2}$ to $2\frac{1}{2}$ pounds, and maybe one out of ten was a 6-pounder.

So whether or not to use a large plastic worm, in my opinion, depends on whether you're after a trophy largemouth or several bass. When I'm tournament fishing, I'll start with the small, short worms in my quest for a limit. As soon as I catch that limit, I purposely go to a big worm. That was how I won the Bass Anglers Sportsman Society's New York Invitational in June 1978.

People who have never attended a tournament may not realize that these contests are basically catch-and-release events, not wasteful affairs that can reduce our bass populations. A tournament fisherman takes pains to keep his catch alive. He earns extra points for bringing in live fish and he's penalized for dead ones. When you compete in a tournament, it makes sense to try for a limit and then start culling—releasing a smaller fish from the live well each time you catch a bigger one so that the total weight increases while the number stays the same.

In the 1978 Invitational just mentioned, I caught a lot of small bass during the first round, although I had four pretty good ones in the 3-to-4-pound range. So I went to a 9-inch worm, and the first bass I caught on it weighed 5½ pounds.

I ran out of 9-inch worms, so I went to 8-inch worms. These are a lot bigger than a 6-inch worm; they have thicker bodies and weigh probably twice as much. I continued to catch some more 4-pound bass. I do think the huge worms discourage smaller bass from hitting them.

One thing about plastic worms which I think generally is over-rated is the type of tail. I have seen few instances where the swimming type of tail, such as the beaver tail, twisted tail, and minnow-action

A 10-pound, 8-ounce bass caught on a Texas rig on Lake Okeechobee in January 1971 while fishing with Jerry McKinnis and filming his TV show, *The Fishing Hole.*

tail, seemed to work better. Those occasions mostly have been when we were moving fast, such as on structure when we were working the worm fast or even trolling the worm. But 98 percent of the time you're working the worm very slow, and the worm basically is crawling through the branches and over the rocks.

I don't think the brand or shape of worm is particularly important as long as it's a good soft plastic. When I poured worms years ago I combined the worms of a dozen different manufacturers and poured them all in the same mold, and I caught bass on them just as good as with any brand-name worm. But soft plastic is one of the keys. I believe bass will hold the softer plastic longer than a harder plastic. My experience has been that hard plastic worms aren't nearly as effective.

Today you can buy both different worm weights and six basic worm-hook sizes. In *Fishing Facts* magazine, a hook chart I formulated was printed with one of my stories on plastic worm fishing. That chart basically stated that I prefer a 3/0 hook with a 6-inch plastic worm, a 4/0 for a 7-inch worm, a 5/0 for an 8-inch worm, and a 6/0 for a 9-inch worm. For worm weights, I like a $1/16$-ounce lead for 8-to-10-pound-test line. However, with light line in ultra-clear water, I might go up to a $3/8$-ounce slip sinker if I'm fishing 30 feet deep. With heavier lines, you need heavier worm weights.

I use a $1/8$-ounce weight for worm fishing at 4-to-5-foot depths. Out on structure 25 feet deep, I might use a $1/2$-ounce lead. Wind plays a big factor in choosing a suitable worm weight. If the wind's blowing ten to fifteen miles per hour, you might have to increase the weight one size. If it's blowing twenty to twenty-five miles per hour, you might have to go two sizes. If the wind is blowing thirty-five miles per hour, you ought to get the hell out of there!

One of the first tournament pros ever to use the Texas worm rig was Bill Dance of Memphis. Bill started his tournament career before I did, and this likable guy has a super track record with the worm. He even wrote a book on plastic worm fishing, called *There He Is!*

I was late getting started using the Texas rig because, as I've said, for several years I was hung up using worms on weedless hooks. The old weedless hook is fairly effective, and even today several guys still use them. One pro who does is Johnny Morris of Bass Pro Shops. This is merely an idiosyncrasy of his. I don't consider the weedless-hook worm rig as good as the Texas rig.

I sometimes use a 4-inch worm Texas-style for light-line fishing in clear water. The 4-inch rig is merely a stepping down in worm length and line size. It's good for very clear water where you can see rocks on the bottom 20 feet deep. Lakes like this usually contain good populations of smallmouth bass as well as largemouths, and smallmouths generally prefer smaller baits. Kentucky or spotted bass also likely are present.

In Alabama's Lake Martin, which I fished frequently in 1971 when I lived in Montgomery, Ala., you can get far more strikes with a 4-inch worm than you can with a 6-inch worm on Kentucky bass. The smaller worm simply is what they prefer in that lake. A typical productive worm pattern in lakes like this is large, shaded boulders. Boulders, ledges, and cliffs usually are numerous in smallmouth bass and Kentucky bass lakes where I use the 4-inch worm mostly.

Boulders 2 to 6 feet in diameter in 5 to 15 feet of water and close to deep water tend to hold good smallmouths and spotted bass. When fishing this type of pattern I usually stand up in the boat and utilize the Polaroid sunglasses to see the obstructions. I'm conscious of the sun angle and am trying to spot the shady nooks and crevices in the boulders, rocks, and cliffs. I throw the 4-inch worm 5 to 10 feet beyond these ambush points and allow it to settle, then slowly hop it into the shadows of the rocks and boulders. In this type of fishing I hold the rod a little lower than normal, at approximately a 40-degree angle, so that I'm ready for the quick strike of a smallmouth or a spotted bass. I also try to set the hook very quickly, because they're apt to drop the worm very quickly. I try to set the hook within two seconds of the strike. Spotted bass often will rattle the worm. There are two ways to set the hook on a rattling strike. Sometimes the initial set will do it, but usually when you feel the rattle, the spotted bass has the tail or lower portion of the worm loosely in his lips and he's shaking it. At times I put a little bit of pressure on the fish. The worm partly slips out of his mouth, and he thinks it's getting away and he'll grab it better. Then I let him pull down before I set the hook. Sometimes this latter trick is about the only way to catch a spot on a worm.

Also, for this method I prefer a 5-foot graphite spinning rod and a medium-sized spinning reel. I don't like the ultralight spinning reels; I like a fairly good-sized reel, because when it's loaded with 6- or 8-pound-test-line, it has a larger spool diameter and I can make a longer cast. Also, the slightly larger reels have smoother, more efficient drags. I set the drag for a pound or two less pressure than my line test. With 6-pound line, I set the drag for about 4 pounds. How the hook is set is important, and I want the drag to be able to slip. With 6-pound line, it's very, very difficult to set a worm hook, because you have to drive the hook point through the worm as well as through the fish's mouth. With the drag just below the breaking point, I pretend I'm using 20-pound line when I set the hook. Every time I overset the hook—which is constantly—the drag slips and the line doesn't break. I also use the multiple hook set—I just repeat setting the hook five to ten times as the fish is running away.

One factor which is important in worm fishing, particularly with the Texas rig, is to avoid if possible setting the hook when the bass is running directly toward you. This is especially important during the spawning season because the spawners so often have the worm only in the lips. If the fish is facing you and headed right at you, you're apt to pull the worm out of his lips when you set the hook. If he's turned the other way, the hook sort of catches him in the corner of his mouth even if he had it only in his lips.

When they run directly at me, I try to put on just a little pressure and hope they'll turn. I don't mind setting the hook when he's straight under the boat because I'm pulling straight up on him.

A lot of people ask me, "When do you set the hook with a worm?" Three or four variables determine this. For example, if I'm stickup fishing in Toledo Bend Reservoir or Ross Barnett Reservoir—some place like that with a lot of stickups—and throw in next to a shady stickup and a bass sucks it up instantly as they often do, I'm going to set the hook within a second or two if he heads toward the obstruction. I don't want him to go in there, so I'm going to set almost instantly.

But suppose I throw in by that same stickup and the bass hits and starts moving *away* from the stickup. I might wait an additional two or three seconds. I want him to move away from it, because this is to my advantage, especially if I'm using fairly light line. Again, if this is the spawning season, I'll strike back within three seconds, but if it's early summer and he's just trying to eat the worm as they often do then with the Texas rig, I'll let him go a few feet as long as he's moving away from the heavy cover.

If the water's fairly clear and I see an exceptionally big bass hit the worm or see the boil of a lunker grabbing the worm, I try to give her a little more time if she's away from the cover. I've found that some of the larger bass don't always suck the worm into their mouths when they first hit. Quite often that first tap is the fish grabbing the worm with his lips, and that second tug you feel is the worm being sucked in. I've watched this happen in my 7,000-gallon aquarium and also while diving with outdoor photographer Glenn Lau in Salt Springs and Silver Springs, Fla. When they've finally got the worm inside their mouths is the perfect time to set the hook. As a general rule when the water temperature is over 75 degrees, most bass inhale the worm on the initial strike as they hit it. When the water's cooler, such as during the spawning season, they often grab it with their lips and you've got to wait a little bit until they get it inside their mouths.

An experience I had several years ago really taught me to set the hook hard with a worm. I didn't realize a big bass has such tremendous jaw pressure until an incident in 1967. I had caught an 11-pound, 2-ounce largemouth one day at Santee-Cooper. I was guiding at Bill Jones' Landing on Santee's Diversion Canal. The shiner and herring season was over, and I put the bass in one of Bill's live-bait tanks. Of course, every time a new prospective customer came around and asked about fishing, I'd take him down to the tank and show him the 11-pounder along with some four-to-eight-pounders I had in there too. Naturally, this always whetted his enthusiasm for going fishing and hiring me as a guide. It helped his confidence.

Quickly I noticed that this 11-pounder took up a territory in the tank. He stayed in one corner and acted like he owned it. But he was shy and wouldn't eat for a long time. I'd throw in a handfull of minnows, and the smaller bass would feed on them right away. So I started holding minnows in front of the big one's face. When he'd look half interested, I'd let the minnows go and he'd suck them up as they swam by him.

Finally he grew a little bolder, and when I'd hold the minnows down in the water, he'd come up within a couple inches of them. After a couple weeks of this, he'd come up to my hand and actually suck the minnow out of my fingers. He'd simply flare his gills and open his mouth, and this created a suction which pulled the minnow 3 or 4 inches. This is much like the way they hit a plastic worm in the summertime. I've watched them, and a big one can be 4 or 5 inches away from the worm and suck it into his mouth.

Anyhow, one day my 11-pounder was just a little too hungry. He came up to the minnow, and instead of sucking it in as he'd been doing, he just crunched down on my hand. Believe it or not, the pain was excruciating! I estimated that he put at least 150 pounds of pressure per square inch on my fingers, and he almost broke them!

Instead of letting go, he held on for three or four seconds and crunched and ground his jaws on my fingers, and I couldn't pull loose. Finally he let go and swam away.

I got to thinking about that. After all, it was the first time I had ever had a trophy bass actually bite me. This led me to realize that with the tackle we use for bass, if a big fish is crunching down on a crank bait, worm, or spinnerbait with all that jaw pressure, there is no way to move the hook into any flesh. It would stay right where it was in his grasp. You'd be trying to set the hook, but actually you wouldn't be moving it at all! After a couple seconds, the fish would release the pressure and spit the whole lure out.

Quite often during those early years at Santee, I had that very thing happen. I used up to 40-pound-test line and would set the hook like a madman, but nothing would happen and the bass would spit the worm out. Some giant bass—10-pounders and bigger—did that after I'd set the hook awfully hard.

I figured the secret would be to set the hook when the fish isn't exerting that tremendous jaw pressure. So I started setting the hook with a plastic worm after two or three seconds. After that hard first set, I don't know how much jaw pressure he's exerting, so I quickly reel in all the slack and set the hook again two seconds later. I keep the pressure on, and set it a third time two seconds after that. Then after that, I keep on setting the hook every two or three seconds, and I know that at some point, he's released the jaw pressure and the hook is penetrating his mouth. When I started using the multiple hook set, immediately I started hooking a much higher percentage of my strikes with a plastic worm.

That 11-pounder which bit the hand that fed him turned out to be a blessing for me, since from that experience I learned about the great jaw pressure and developed my practice of multiple hook setting. This has helped me boat many more bass and undoubtedly has helped my tournament success. I believe lots of bass fishermen lose many trophy bass on plastic worms because they don't use the multiple hook set and therefore don't get the hook to penetrate the bass's jaws. However, I don't think 1½-pound bass exert this kind of jaw pressure. I think the smaller ones hit the worm and can be hooked usually with the initial hard hook set.

Another important thing about worm fishing—something we discovered about twenty years ago—is to have a suitable rod to set the hook. We learned that ideal rods, which today the manufacturers call

Usually with a plastic worm I set the hook quickly, before the bass drops it. But sometimes, especially in cooler water, that first tap, which I'm feeling in the first photo, just means the fish has grabbed the worm with its lips; if you strike then you won't hook it. I give the fish slack, with the rod low, for a few seconds, then set the hook hard—and more than once.

worm rods, are heavy-butted rods with a lot of backbone in the lower half of the rod. They have fairly light tips for good casting, but you're driving the hook with that butt section.

Regardless of the kind of worm rig I'm using, I like to position the rod at a 45-degree angle or higher. The main reason for this is I have far more feel of the bottom. The rod is about 90 degrees from the bass, and I have the maximum feel of the tip of the rod. The maximum sensitivity with a worm rod comes with the tip high in the air, and I'm working the worm from a 45-degree to a 90-degree or greater angle. Then the second I feel the strike or detect line movement and deter-

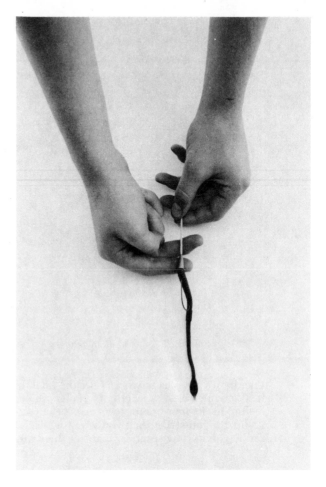

In heavy brush or cover, you're less apt to hang up if you peg the slip sinker. Just insert the point of a round toothpick and break it off flush with the sinker.

mine I have a fish, I drop the rod tip and reel up all the slack line except for the last 2 or 3 inches, and then I set the hook on a slack line. Before I set it, I'm watching that little bit of slack line to see what way he's moving. When I finally set the hook, my arms are extended and I'm pulling the reel and the butt of the rod back toward me instead of merely jerking the tip upward. I'm actually setting the hook with my arms and wrist. My arms are in close to my body, and I bring my wrists up toward my face. Instantly I start reeling as fast as can, and again I set the hook, reel fast, and repeat this procedure.

At seminars, I'm often asked how I work the worm. I fish it about three different ways. With the Texas rig, most of my fishing is done in fairly shallow water. Since the worm is a great ambush-point lure, I'm seeking out some type of cover. When I'm fishing heavy cover, I'm thinking to myself that the bass is right there by the stump or bush. So I'm either going to throw right to the obstruction or a couple feet past it. As I crawl the worm past the cover, I prefer for it to be falling straight down off of things such as off a root. About 90 percent of my strikes on a worm come as the worm is coming off of something, such as off a boulder, stump, grass, or creek channel ledge. At this time, the worm usually is sinking or falling. Very seldom does the strike occur when I'm pulling the worm up on something.

After I've crawled and jigged the worm off all the obstructions and am free of all them, if I haven't had a strike I quickly reel in, because I'm not going to fish it all the way to the boat. This is what I do especially in shallow-water situations when I'm throwing directly into cover. Then I'll throw to the next ambush point.

As I've written many times and others have written about me, I'm a line watcher. I use Stren fluorescent line, and in shallow water I identify probably 75 percent of my worm strikes by seeing the line move before I ever feel the fish. When my worm's falling straight down—and I give it slack line so it'll fall straight down rather than glide off of something at an angle—I'll detect that little twitch in the line. To make sure it's a fish, I'll put on just a little pressure, and then I can determine which way he's moving. I'm watching the line not only to detect the strike, but also to see what the bass is doing after he's struck. I do check them a lot after the initial strike, but I'm doing it only on about half a pound of pressure—just enough to know he's there.

I don't always fish the worm as I've described above; sometimes I do work it all the way back to the boat, and I do this particulary on structure. When I'm out on a big point or a submerged bar, I'm not fishing an ambush point. I'm fishing open-water structure. In this situation, I don't know exactly where the obstructions are; I merely know that there should be some objects down there. So I throw the worm out there and crawl it along fairly quickly. But when I feel something, such as a stump, I think that might be where one is hiding. Then I slow the worm down and fish it more carefully, and I do this every time I hit some piece of cover.

When I'm fishing heavy brush or cover—shallow or deep—often I peg the slip sinker to make the weight part of the worm. I take a round toothpick and jab it in the hole next to the line and break the toothpick off so it's flush with the weight. I peg the pointed end of the bullet weight, but the toothpick can be inserted in either end of the weight. After a cast or two, water will cause the toothpick end to swell up and this makes it snug.

The reason for pegging the weight is if I'm fishing heavy cover, I don't want to pull the worm up on an obstruction and get it caught in a limb. If that happens, the weight will slip down the line when you give it some slack, and you'll think the worm is sinking, when really it isn't sinking at all. Also, when you've separated the weight from the worm, you'll get hung up more. By pegging the weight, the worm becomes more snagless because it isn't separated from the sinker.

11   The Carolina Rig

One of my second choices in plastic worm fishing is entirely different from the Texas rig. It's the Carolina rig. It doesn't have a slip weight down against the hook, and about half the time it doesn't have a self-weedless hook. It features a rather heavy egg sinker with a swivel, and 18 to 30 or more inches behind the weight and swivel is the worm, which usually is floating free. The worm has either a bare exposed hook or the Texas-style imbedded hook. The latter is used if this rig is fished in brushy areas.

This rig is important because it's great for fishing deep-water structure. Quite often on deep points, structures, bars, and channels the bass are down on the bottom, but they really can see a floating

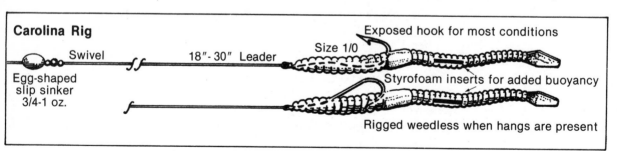

In the Carolina rig the sinker is some distance from the plastic worm, so the worm, which often contains Styrofoam or air bubbles, drifts above the bottom. The hook is usually exposed but can be imbedded as in the Texas rig for fishing in brushy areas.

**It's hard to cast a Carolina rig with bait-casting gear;
I usually use a spinning rod.**

worm better. Remember the weight—the egg sinker, which often weighs from ½ ounce to 1 ounce—is plummeting the whole rig to the bottom, but the worm is floating up. I often use a plastic worm which has been injected with a lot of air bubbles, such as the Sportsman Catch-Em-Quick Super Floater, or some of the other styles of worms that float even with the hook inside.

This floating worm is more visible to bass 6 to 8 feet away. Also, the worm has a lot better action being away from the weight. It drifts, darts, and oscillates from any currents and wave action present under the water.

When a bass grabs the worm, he feels virtually no weight or resistance. When he starts to run with it, the line slips through the hole in the weight and you need to give him some line for the first couple of seconds. This method is an especially great way to get a worm deep in a hurry. You can take a small, delicate worm which floats and get it down 30 to 50 feet in a hurry with a 3/4-ounce sinker. It's excellent in deep, rocky lakes like Bull Shoals in Arkansas, Clark Hill Reservoir on the Georgia-South Carolina border, Sidney Lanier in Georgia, and Lake Murray in South Carolina. These are all deep, relatively clear lakes, and they're perfect for the Carolina rig.

You can get the worm very deep in a few seconds. You have a lot of contact with the weight, but you need a good, sensitive rod and you need to hold it high to be able to give the fish line for a couple of seconds before you strike back at him.

In the hot summer when the water temperature is above 70 degrees, a lot of bass seek the thermocline. They get down in the depths, especially in clear water where the light penetration is pretty deep. I like to use a 1/2-ounce lead sinker with a small swivel and run it about 25 inches back. I usually use a spinning rod for this work, because this entire rig bolos when you cast it. It's sort of hard to throw and you get a lot of backlashes with a casting rod. I prefer 14-pound-test line. The leader—the monofilament which goes to the worm—can be a little bit lighter if the water's very clear. In fact, then you might want to use an 8- or 10-pound line to fool more bass. Another advantage of the lighter leader is that when you get hung up, you break your worm off but not the swivel and weight.

Hook size is extremely important. My favorite worm is the 6-inch DeLong Super Floater. It floats very well for its size, but this is true only if you use a hook no larger than a 1/0. Even a No. 1 hook works well. If you use a 2/0 or 3/0 hook, the rig won't float; the worm sinks to the bottom. If the water isn't obstructed with brush, I'll use the hook exposed most of the time. With the hook point out, I can set faster and better. I can troll or jig this rig along at a pretty good speed through quite a few stumps, boulders and rocks. It's fairly snagless because it's floating up.

---

12   The Weightless Spawning Rig

One of my super patterns in worm fishing is the weightless spawning rig. This is nothing but a plastic worm, a hook, and zero weight, rigged Texas-style with the hook embedded in the middle of the

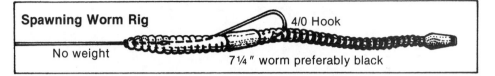

The weightless spawning rig is designed to settle slowly on the bed, provoking the bass to pick it up and get it out of there.

This is the way the hook is positioned for the regular Texas rig, with the hook eye just inside the plastic worm, but for the spawning rig the hook should be near the middle of the worm, as shown in the drawing.

worm. I use this rig strictly in the spawning season, because, as I pointed out before, spawning bass aren't hungry and don't hit out of reflex action. Instead, they're hitting out of protective instinct; they're merely trying to move that worm which is threatening their nest and get it away from the spawning bed. They'll swim with it for three to five seconds and carry it a few feet from the nest and then spit it out.

This Florida largemouth, over 10 pounds, wasn't going to let my weightless rig stay in her nest.

Keep in mind that spawning bass usually pick up a worm near the middle. You need your hook back down the worm toward the tail, and you need to set the hook pretty quickly. I don't use particularly heavy tackle, because lots of times spawning bass are in clear, shallow water without much turbulence. Therefore, you need to go to fairly light line. I like to use at least 10-pound line because it's hard to set the hook through that plastic with 6-pound line. It can be done, but it's more difficult, and you'll miss a lot more bass on 6 than you will on 10, even though you'll get more strikes on 6-pound line. Most of the spawning bass I've found are around some type of cover, such as weeds. Even in natural lakes in Minnesota and Wisconsin, the weeds and bullrushes so often found in spawning areas are enough to break a 6-pound line when a bass tangles around them. In the swamps of Lake Seminole or in Florida and in lakes in Oklahoma, where I live, bass spawn usually in the north coves around heavy brush or vegetation, and they easily can break a 6-pound line.

Another thing I do during the spawning season is continually use a new worm. I do this so that if I miss a strike, I can examine the worm and determine from the teeth marks where it was bitten. My favorite color and size of worm at this time of year is the 7- or 7¼-inch black worm. For some reason, whether you're fishing in Maine or Arizona, they seem to hit black the best when they're spawning.

Worm fishing really comes into its own when the spawning season arrives. Before that, the water is on the cold side for plastic-worm fishing, and bass don't hit worms good in cold water. But when the water reaches at least 62 degrees during the full-moon period in the spring, spawning activity begins and so does good worming. I stand up in my boat and wear Polaroid sunglasses to spot the beds and to determine the type of cover they're bedding near.

When you spot a spawning bed, cast 10 feet past it and swim the worm slowly up to it. Let the lure settle for fifteen to thirty seconds in the bed. When the bass picks up the worm, strike him within three seconds. If you wait too long, the fish is apt to drop the worm. If you catch the smaller male bass, keep casting to the bed and you might catch that trophy female. If you don't catch her, wait at least thirty minutes and then return to the area again. For particularly large bass, the period just before dusk is the best time to catch them.

For this type of fishing, I prefer a 5½-foot graphite bait-casting rod and 14-to-20-pound line. Graphite gives you a lot more sensitivity, and for almost all my worm fishing I use graphite rods. Graphite also enables me to cast a few feet farther. The line size varies with the amount of cover near the beds, but most spawning strikes are lip strikes, and the hardest spots to hook them. It's much easier to hook bass in the summertime when they're actually trying to eat the worm and have it back inside their mouths, where the flesh is softer. Extremely sharp hooks naturally are especially important.

One time before a B.A.S.S. tournament in January on the St. Johns River in Florida, my friend Paul Chamblee of Raleigh, N.C., and I practiced together during the pre-tourney warmup. We located a tremendous bunch of spawning bass, but they were shallow and the water was super clear. We had to drop down to 6-pound lines to get them to strike, but during the tournament the sun was bright, and we had trouble keeping from spooking them even with 6-pound line. This tough condition is much the same as smallmouth fishing on bright, sunny days in clear water, as Billy Westmorland often points out, and you really have to go to very light line to have any success. However, if there's a lot of cloud cover, you can step up your line size a bit.

13   The Surface-Floating Worm

The surface-floating worm sometimes is confused with the Carolina rig, but the two are entirely different. This worm really floats, and that's the difference. A lot of anglers use a weightless worm and think it's the same thing, but a weightless worm and a floating worm are two different rigs.

In South Carolina the floating worm rig has a tail planted with Styrofoam so that it lies evenly on the surface in spite of having a hook attached. I first came across this particular type of rig in Salt Springs, Fla., where the local boys were catching huge strings of bass with it. This rig is best used in the spring in weed-infested warmer waters around spawning beds. The worm floats on the surface, and gentle twitches often provoke sucking strikes and huge swirls. The floating worm is fished about the same way as you would fish a small surface plug like the Rapala.

The surface-floating worm is really for an exceptional condition. Use it only in extremely clear, weedy water. The best examples of where to use it are in an ultra-clear lake in the north or in some spring area down in Florida or in some type of very weedy bay where any slip weight would catch moss or algae.

You can make a floating worm rig by cutting strips from a Styrofoam cup and inserting them in the worm (I use a ballpoint-pen refill to make the holes and stuff in the foam). Note position of the exposed hook.

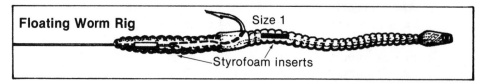

Floating Worm Rig   Size 1

Styrofoam inserts

In this type of fishing I use spinning tackle. My favorite outfit is a light-action spinning rod and open-faced reel loaded with 6- or 8-pound line. The hook usually is left exposed in most weedy areas where there aren't many surface weeds. If surface weed is there, such as lily pads or coontail moss or a stringy weed, then I rig the worm Texas-style. But when I rig it Texas-style, instead of running the hook through the fat part of the worm, I'll just barely hook it through a tiny section of the worm. It has only about $1/16$ inch of the plastic to tear

I fished this floating worm by twitching it like any surface lure, and the bass fell for it.

loose from, and the hook point is just barely in, making it weedless. When I set the hook, it's going to pop loose quickly from that small slice of plastic. In all of my light-line fishing, I hook my Texas-style rigs this way.

I like to use a fairly large plastic worm, usually one 7¼ to 7½ inches long, for this type of fishing. You can't use a very large hook because you would sink the worm. I like a No. 1 or a Style 84. A Style 84 is not really a worm hook; it's got a good open throat, and when I use it in a No. 1 or 1/0, I keep the hook exposed. It's a good, solid small hook with a lot of body that can hold a big bass.

Big spawners suck it in when it comes over the bed. You see them rise up as if for a surface plug, and then as the summer progresses in these same weedy areas, it's a good surface lure to use in the early morning and late evening or on cloudy days. It is a surface lure.

THE JIG AND EEL

To the novice fisherman, a jig and eel looks much like a weighted plastic worm, but it is an entirely different lure. The eel part is usually pork rind, though it may be plastic or some other material, and the jig hook rides up, not down. In fishing it the rod is held differently; the strike is different because the jig and eel is a cold-water lure, whereas the plastic worm is a warm-water lure. They are about the same size and are worked in basically the same areas, but the jig and eel is best as a winter and early-spring bait, while the worm is a late-spring, summer, and autumn lure.

Most of my big bass on the jig and eel—and it's a trophy-bass bait—are caught with water temperatures between 45 and 55 degrees. There is a period in the spring when the bass are what are called pre-spawning bass. They're not quite ready to move up to the shallow spawning areas, and they're lying in little creek channels and depressions just away from the spawning areas.

Incidentally, out of my some fifty bass over 10 pounds, five have hit the jig and eel. It is one of my all-time favorite trophy-bass lures, and all my big fish traditionally are caught in the pre-spawn period just before they move up on the shallow flats to spawn. A good example of what a plastic worm would do compared to a jig and eel late in the winter was an experience I had in mid-March of 1978 at Toledo Bend.

The jig and eel seems to attract the big ones; time and again I've seen it get 6-pounders where the plastic-worm fishermen are only catching small fish.

I was fishing in the American Bass Fisherman tournament, and the water temperature was about 55 degrees. I had located a drop in about 15 feet of water. It was off a shallow shoal, and the top of the shoal came up within 6 feet of the surface. I think the bass were probably on the edge of the drop and were moving up on the shoal to spawn. Some big fish were there, including some 7-to-10-pounders. I caught one over 10 in practice. My first-day partner asked me what we were going to do there. I said I was going to use the jig and eel because I'd caught some really giant fish on that lure. I told him I was using 25-pound line because of all the timber and heavy brush there, and I was using a ⅝-ounce jig with a 4-inch piece of eel on the back.

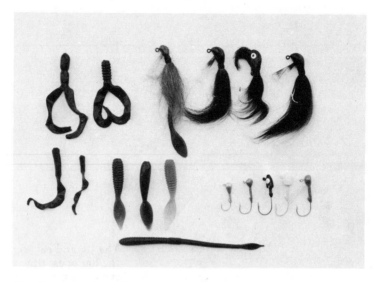

The jig and eel can be made up in a variety of forms. You can even try using a regular plastic worm for the eel part.

He said he didn't fish the jig and eel; he was a worm fisherman. He added that if I was on a bunch of big fish, he could catch as many big ones on worms. I pulled up to the dropoff and tied up to a pine tree. The wind was blowing about fifteen miles per hour and I didn't want to run my trolling motor down. I told him the fish were just out there about 30 feet away on the edge of the little drop and a big pine thicket. I advised him to fish the spot real slow and right off the bottom.

After a couple of casts, I let the jig sink all the way to the bottom, and he let his plastic worm sink. He was using a 6-inch black worm, and it looked very similar to my jig and eel. I raised the rod tip over a few limbs and then let the jig and eel drop and settle back down again, and he did the same thing. He was throwing to within a foot or two of my lure. I had the first strike. It was a largemouth in the 6-pound range, and I cranked him up through all those branches. The 25-pound line broke off a few limbs, but I finally sloshed him up to the side of the boat and netted him. Well, my partner picked up his rod and continued to fish his worm, and pretty soon he had a strike. He paused a second and lowered his rod just as he should, and then he set the hook and caught a 2-pound bass.

I commented that I'd been fishing the jig all week and hadn't caught a single small one. After a few more casts I had a strike and landed another one a little over 4 pounds. Subsequently he had a strike and caught another 2-pounder. My third bass that day weighed 7 pounds, 14 ounces, and was the largest fish in the ABF tourney. I also won the tournament, but the point is, he fished that day with the worm and caught nothing but small bass. We were throwing in the same hole and I caught nothing but big bass. I had 38 pounds of bass with an eight-fish limit. The difference was that I more than doubled his size fish. He had a limit and caught about as many as I did, and had about as many strikes as I did.

On the second day the wind blew so hard that the bass weren't on that spot good, and I caught only a few fish. The third day I had another eight-bass limit that weighed almost 30 pounds. My partner started with a plastic worm and caught a couple of small ones. Then he finally asked if I had a jig and eel he could borrow. I lent him one, and he ended up catching two big bass in a row, and he had almost as many pounds as I did.

I won with about 78 pounds of bass, and the second-place man had about 10 pounds less. I won, but not because I was catching more fish. A lot of guys were catching fish, but I really believe that the jig and eel won that tournament for me. It was enticing the big bass out of those schools.

Years ago I read about Sam Welch and fishing writer Jason Lucas and all the other big-time experts who said the jig and eel was a great bait in early spring. That was back in the 1950s, and I started throwing the jig and eel when the water temperatures were in the 50-to-60-degree range. I never have figured out why this combination is so superior then. I am a pattern fisherman, and I go with whatever pattern I can find that is working the best. I don't question the pattern. If a jig and eel is catching 6-pound bass and a plastic worm is catching 2-pounders, I can't give you a reason why. I don't know. I've never been able to figure out why. I don't know what the differences might be to the bass, but I do know the jig and eel traditionally has caught a bigger average size of bass in the colder water temperatures.

The jig and eel can be used in hot weather, but I've found that then I don't catch the lunker bass but rather the size I catch regularly on a plastic worm. Recently we've done a lot of flipping with jigs and eels. For the past two years I've used a 7½-foot flipping rod and a 5/8-ounce jig and eel. I have found with it that in the summer I catch bigger fish than I do with a plastic worm, but I think the reason is mainly that

I'm jigging the jig and eel in thick submerged bushes or other thick cover. I'm jigging it up and down repeatedly, and I think the fact it's just there in one spot so long catches the big ones.

---

14 The Cold-Water Crawl

The cold-water crawl with the jig and eel is an early-spring pattern for big largemouths. My most productive pattern is to fish it in the pre-spawning areas—the areas of the lake adjacent to where they spawn. For example, where they normally spawn in the northern coves of the lake, I'm going to fish in those same northern coves but maybe out in the center of the cove in 8 to 20 feet of water. As with the plastic worm, the depth you fish a jig and eel depends on water clarity. If the water is very clear, fish deeper, but if it's a little dingy, fish shallower. This is true particularly in the early spring when there is not much visibility in some of the dirtier reservoirs. I might fish it only 6 feet deep if the water is halfway muddy. The type of cover I find best for big largemouths is mainly heavy brush in lakes like Toledo Bend; Sam Rayburn; Eufaula, Oklahoma; and Ross Barnett in Mississippi.

These huge reservoirs of 10,000 acres or more quite often have some sections or some coves with timber, and timber is just perfect for the cold-water crawl. In other sections of the country where there isn't timber—for example, the TVA impoundments have almost no timber—the best place for a jig and eel is around stumps, particularly stumps off points. I fish the jig and eel almost always on structure, and don't fish the shoreline with it. I'm fishing points, and on TVA lakes, points often are stumpy. I also fish the edges of river channels where there is a channel with stumps on the edge, crawling the lure over heavy obstructions. In almost any southern impoundment in the spring, you'll find on some of the steeper banks some trees recently fallen into the water. They're huge trees which might be the only representative cover in the areas. In those trees the jig can be crawled through the limbs lying in the water. Again, you should fish fairly deep water or close to deepwater areas. The jig and eel is sort of a structure lure, and again the best temperature for catching huge bass on this lure is from about 45 to 55 degrees. I've caught a few on it when the water was 39 degrees—I catch very few bass on lures when the water is below 40, but I do catch a few on the jig and eel, and at these times I catch nothing on plastic worms. The jig and eel is one of the hottest cold-water lures you can find. It continues to work all through the summertime, but the huge bass don't eat it up as consistently as they do in pre-spawn conditions.

Occasionally in the pre-spring, rains create dingy or muddy water. Then I fish the jig and eel when the water is cool, such as 55 degrees, but not when it's cold. At this time I'm fishing very shallow and certainly not deep. At Santee-Cooper I fish a jig and eel around entrances to blackwater ponds. There a whole section of the lake might be muddy, but the blackwater ponds will be clear. Around the entrance to a blackwater pond is usually a little channel which extends into the pond and is 3 to 4 feet deep. I find pre-spawners in heavy bushes and cypress trees near the entrance to these ponds. The water is 60 degrees and muddy, and this is the type of area where a jig and eel generally pays off.

I have fished the jig and eel on the weed lines and the deeper structures in Minnesota lakes in June, and the lure paid off there, too. You can't fish it or other lures in early spring in states like Minnesota because of the closed season.

One thing important about fishing the jig and eel is to keep eye contact with the lure. To fish it properly you need a heavy-duty jig when the wind is blowing. I use a heavy jig—sometimes 1/2-ounce or 5/8-ounce. It should be crawled over obstructions of some sort. If you're fishing brush or other heavy cover, you need heavy line. Fluorescent line enables me to watch my line better. When you get a strike, you can anticipate a tick in your line, because fish hit the jig and eel much like a plastic worm as it's falling off a boulder or a limb.

When I'm using the plastic worm, I often let the fish run a bit, but I don't with the jig and eel. I find with the latter lure that most of my success comes with a very quick hook set, because the bait is not entirely soft like a plastic worm. The head is hard, and a bass could mouth it for five or six seconds and then spit it out.

When I'm using the cold-water crawl I hold the rod quite a bit lower than with a plastic worm. The heavy lure makes good contact with the bottom, and the lower rod position enables me to set the hook a lot quicker. I also use a stiffer rod than I use for worm fishing. I look for my object to cast to, and I throw *past* the bush, stump, tree, or dock by as much as 10 feet, and I slowly jig and crawl the lure on the

The cold-water crawl nailed this bass on Table Rock Reservoir in Missouri. The jig and eel is a good early-season rig in such clear, deep, rocky lakes.

bottom in little hops. I lift the rod up a couple of inches, and the jig is hopping off the bottom a couple of inches and is crawling, too.

Finally I start hitting the ambush point—the brush and cover—and I crawl it through the limbs. I just slowly pull up on the limbs, and when I get to the top of the limb I jig the lure. It flips off a little, and when I feel it flip off the limb, I give it slack and let it fall vertically and watch the line, because that's when the bass sucks it in. When you feel that tap and the lure is in heavy brush, you should bust him right then, and this is where the low rod positioning helps you. One of my favorite rods for the jig and eel has a saltwater handle on it. I stick the rod butt in my stomach so when I set the hook I've got leverage from that big, long handle.

Early in the season when the water temperatures are in the high 40s or 50s, the fish aren't real active. They don't fight super, and they're a little sluggish. It takes a big bass like a 6- or 7-pounder two to three seconds to get oriented. Often if you're fishing in a big tree or a bunch of heavy brush, he can hit hard and you can crank the line 6 to 7 feet out of that cover before he really gets his bearings and starts to surge and fight. Therefore, you don't have to use giant line; you probably can get by with 14- or 17-pound-test in heavy brush if you're quick about setting the hook and don't let the bass run any after he strikes.

There are some variations I use with the cold-water crawl, and these come in the mid-southern reservoirs such as Dale Hollow in Tennessee, Cumberland in Kentucky, Table Rock in Missouri, and Norfolk and Bull Shoals in Arkansas. These and other similar lakes are rocky, very deep, and usually very clear. In these situations I'm using the cold-water crawl mainly with light tackle—spinning tackle and an 1/8-ounce jig with a 2-to-3-inch pork eel. Those lakes don't have as much cover as the deep southern reservoirs have, so I'm not throwing to the brush as much as to rocks, boulders, bluffs, points, and dropoffs. The points and bluffs seem to be a popular pre-spawn area.

When I'm fishing for large spotted bass—the Kentucky bass—I catch smallmouth as well. The jig and eel is a very effective spawning lure for smallmouths whether you're fishing in Tennessee or Minnesota or Canada. I just hop and crawl the lure right through the spawning-bed area. If I can see the bed, I roll the lure over it for a moment. Again, light line, such as 8-pound-test, and spinning tackle pay off.

My favorite pork rinds for most of my jig-and-eel fishing are the Uncle Josh 2 1/2-inch baits for the small jigs and the 3- and 4-inch eels for the 1/2-ounce and 5/8-ounce jigs. At some lakes specific baits get hot. For example, at Oklahoma's Tenkiller Lake, bass just love a jig with a type of split-tail pork lizard. It's a piece of pork rind with two tails and two legs hanging off it. The bait is about an inch wide and is really a great big piece of pork. I do a lot of fishing up at Table Rock Lake, and my favorite up there is about a 3 1/2-inch split-tail eel. At Toledo Bend I use just a straight piece of eel 3 to 3 1/2 inches long.

Most of my jigs are the banana-head type. They're good in heavy brush because they tend to hang up less. For my big jigs in largemouth areas, I like the deer-hair or bucktail jigs. One of my favorite jigs, made by Championship Tackle in Louisiana, is called the Sugar Daddy. It's a 5/8-ounce jig with deer hair. My favorite jigs have black weedguards made of polyethylene material resembling ski rope. The weedguard (snag guard is really a better name) is bent back in a semi-circle and is curled up over the hook. The open hook is good. The second type of jig I use with a light spinning outfit in cold water at

Bull Shoals and places like that is the 1/8-ounce marabou with an open hook. If there's any brush around, I go to a weedless jig. In very cold water I prefer the marabou, but in dingy water I like the bushiness of the bucktail type of jig. Also in cold water I like the Bass Buster jigs in the 1/8-ounce and the 1/16-ounce sizes.

15   Timberdoodling

Timberdoodling originated in East Texas with some of the boys who fish brushy, timbered reservoirs such as Toledo Bend, Sam Rayburn, Livingston, and some of the lakes around Dallas. It's a kind of jigging technique which works very well in the early spring. You jig over the side of the boat, and you catch pre-spawning bass which haven't yet moved up to the shallow water. They are usually fairly deep—anywhere from 15 to 25 feet—and these are bass which might be called winter bass. They're down on the winter structures.

Toledo Bend and Sam Rayburn are the two lakes where I've done timberdoodling. You timberdoodle when you're in an area with trees, brush, and cover so hard to cast to that few fishermen ever throw to it. You know everybody else coming through there might throw a crank bait or possibly flip a worm near this cover, but not many fishermen can throw into the center of these trees. Yet in the very middle of the trees is where you often fish when you're timberdoodling. This type of cover is basically giant trees, such as oak trees or cedar trees 10 to 15 feet in diameter with a lot of branches. Not many anglers go up to the center of that tree, push the button on the reel, and let the lure down into the center of all those branches. But this is the technique—you're going into an almost impossible spot to fish, and you stick the rod through there as far as you can and then drop the lure right down to the bottom. You don't always go to the bottom, because sometimes the water's so deep out in the middle of these trees that the bass might be suspended at 25 feet when the depth is 30 feet. Sometimes you will catch fish just halfway down.

The kind of structure is the biggest trees, which usually are on a dropoff. The big beech trees and big oaks that are on the edge of a creek channel are probably the best places. A timbered point will pay off in addition to the creek channels.

In some lakes you can actually timberdoodle even though there's

In timberdoodling, you sneak the boat in close and jig the lure slowly up and down along the trunk.

no standing timber. For example, some small lake in Pennsylvania or New York state might have some trees which recently fell into the water. On these lying trees, you won't have quite the depth that you have on standing timber, but still the jigging technique works.

Go up to that tree and get as close as you can, and make either a short cast or stick your rod out and just push the button on your reel. If you're directly over the fish, you need a deep enough spot so you don't spook them. A depth of at least 8 feet is needed, and in cold weather you need fairly clear water. If the tree is only 5 feet deep and the water is fairly clear, there's no sense in going up to the tree and pushing the button because you're going to scare the fish. You can cast to the shallower water.

One thing I've learned about trees with a lot of thick, heavy limbs is that you want to be over the fish. If you cast to them, it's a rather bad deal because your line will be over the limbs. If you're back another 30 feet when the lure hits, you've got to get it and your line up through and over those limbs.

I jigged this 10½-pounder from Timber at Rodman Reservoir while fishing with my father-in-law, Paul Colbert.

When you pull up to one of these typical timberdoodling places and push that button, what do you do then? It's a matter of gently jigging that jig and eel. The colder the water, the slower it should be jigged. Lift the jig up no more than a foot or so in real cold weather, and sort of drop it back down with a little bit of back pressure. I don't ever let it fall completely free, but almost. When I'm jigging it around and hit a limb, I just keep bumping it. This sends out a little vibration.

I constantly watch my line when I'm jigging whether I'm using a spoon or a jig and eel. Watch for the strike, because often you don't feel it that well when you have slack line. Spoon jigging and jigging with the jig and eel are somewhat similar. I stress using 20-, 25-, or 30-pound line with a 1/2- or 5/8-ounce jig in the heavy-timber reservoirs. If you go to these big trees with anything less than 20, I think you're kidding yourself, because even a 2-pounder can mess you up. On 10-pound line, he might leap that branch and break the line.

Timberdoodling is mainly for big bass, and one reason for this is that big fish are a little bit less eager, particularly in lakes which get a lot of fishing pressure.

One of my most successful timberdoodling trips was in February of 1970 on Sam Rayburn Reservoir in Texas. Rayburn had been impounded about 1964 and was six years old then and in its prime as a big-bass producer. I'd heard of this guy named Marvin Baker. At the time he and Tommy Martin were guides on Rayburn, and they did a tremendous amount of spoon jigging and jig and eel fishing—timberdoodling. I'd heard that Marvin had recently caught ten bass in a day which totaled almost 70 pounds. The story came out in a Dallas newspaper. He did this in Rayburn during December of the previous year, and he had fished the Black Forest area of the lake.

I didn't know exactly where he was fishing, but I figured I'd go up there and try it. Well, the trouble with the Black Forest is that most of the timber out there on the river channel where I wanted to fish was standing in 45 to 50 feet of water. So I went out there and fished several of the trees. It was super-deep, and I didn't do any good. Finally I started back into the forest a little way. I wasn't quite on the river channel, but I found a little spot which came up to 26 feet. There were heavy oak trees there, and around this 26-foot hill was a lot of 34-to-40-foot water. I had found a little underwater hill near the creek channel, although the river was about 50 yards away. There were some big trees right on the creek channel, and one tree was just huge. There were limbs everywhere. I pulled up to that tree. I had 20-pound line and a big jig, and I dropped it down. The jig never quite got to the bottom. At about 20 feet it just stopped. I sort of pulled it up and it just lay there without moving. The fish which are in those trees often don't strike hard; they just roll over when they do strike. I kept pulling, and I felt the slightest little throb. I set the hook and was into a 6½-pounder.

I reeled him up and he got caught on three different limbs coming up. When he'd get hung, I'd just pull up about 4 or 5 feet of line and he'd come off and then get caught on the next limb. But I finally got him after a real effort. I probably had let him run too far. I didn't realize it was a fish until almost too late. So I rigged up again and dropped out a second time. This time I was ready and had my thumb on the spool as the jig was sinking. I watched the line and approximated how deep the lure was. Again before it reached the bottom the line stopped. I threw the reel in gear and set the hook and cranked hard; I cranked that one clear to the top without him getting wrapped up. He was a 5-pounder. That turned out to be one of the best outings of the year. I kept on catching bass by jigging the jig and eel, and ended up with ten which weighed nearly 50 pounds. On Rayburn in 1970 and 1971 I had probably ten days when I got nearly 50 pounds in a day. That's a super-big-bass day, but on that lake back then a good fisherman could have 50-pound days.

I never won a tournament timberdoodling, but have caught some of my biggest bass that way. When I'm after trophy fish, I'm going to timberdoodle on lakes like Toledo Bend and Rayburn. I might catch only one or two bass, but they're usually going to be 5-pounders or larger.

The best string of fish I ever caught in Oklahoma was on Thanksgiving Day in 1970, shortly before I married Mary Ann. I tried but failed to talk her into going to Fuqua, a 2,000-to-3,000-acre lake in southern Oklahoma, near Paul's Valley. Mary Ann's dad, Paul Colbert, said it was too cold. He and I had been to Fuqua about a month before, and we had fished spinnerbaits around what they call the Hog Pen. We had caught a couple of 4-pound bass on spinnerbaits in 5 to 6 feet of water, but it had gotten a lot colder since then. The water was fairly clear, and the entire lake is nothing but timber. I went there thinking spinnerbait because the previous trip I had caught them on spinnerbaits.

Immediately I ran up to my spinnerbait water which had paid off the month before. I tried spinnerbaits and jigged them all over the place and threw them at the big row of trees, and I never got a strike. It was about one p.m., and the sun had been on the water quite a while. But winter had struck, and it started to snow. For some reason I looked in my tackle box and saw one of Sam Welch's favorite jigs. It was one I had fished with in Maryland years before. I put it on. I was on the edge of the river channel, and there was a little open area with some submerged logs which I could see. The depth was about 8 feet, and the channel was about 15. I made a cast to the edge of the channel and was more or less just jigging it up and down. Then it stopped, and I felt a thump. I kind of halfheartedly set the hook, because this was the first strike I had had all day.

All of a sudden this big fish was on the line, thrashing around. I finally got him in, a 5-pounder. The wind was blowing, so I tied up to a tree about 15 feet from where I'd caught the fish. I made a cast again over into the channel. There was a sharp little bend, and I kept hitting limbs while jigging the jig right there in that spot. Again I felt a tap, and this time I was prepared and set the hook hard. I got that one and every bass which struck, except one.

Sam Welch must have used fairly light line, because the jig he liked had a fairly light wire hook, too light for my 20-pound line. It should have had a Sproat or a Mustad hook instead of an Aberdeen. Finally I hung a real trophy. I had caught a 7¼-pounder that day, but I got this bigger fish up, and I only can guess he was right at 9 pounds. But doggone it, right at the last moment, as I was trying to hold the fish and there were branches sticking out of the water, I turned around and reached for the net and he surged and straightened the hook out.

They finally quit hitting about two o'clock. It was snowing so hard I figured the launch ramp would be snowed over and I wouldn't be able to pull my boat out. I got home about three-thirty with ten bass that totaled 44 pounds, one of my heaviest strings from Oklahoma.

16 Night-Fishing the Jig and Eel

I've been living in Oklahoma since 1970, and I always get reports of the spring and early-summer fishing on all the local lakes. I do a fishing report from time to time on a radio station. I get reports by phone from the White River chain—Beaver Lake, Table Rock Lake, Bull Shoals Lake, and Norfolk Lake. These are four very clear reservoirs which average 60,000 to 70,000 acres apiece. The chain is one of the major sport fisheries for the central U.S.A. All the boys from St. Louis and Kansas City come down there; these lakes get tens of thousands of fishermen every week. We usually call up to see how the fish are doing. There are some big trophy bass to be caught, particularly in Table Rock, which is my favorite lake of the four.

With jig and eel there's a certain time in the spring that is great for night fishing. Some of the great strings of fish—and I'm talking about 8- and 9-pound bass and a few 10s—have been caught at night. It seems like the very best time year after year since I've been here in 1970 is to fish at night during the full-moon week of April. If you fish at this time with a jig and eel, you're gonna catch a trophy bass. This could be at any of these four lakes, out there at night. One thing I like about Table Rock—and it's something some fishermen don't like—is that they didn't clear all the brush and timber before they impounded the lake. A lot of points are timber-covered, as are almost every bluff and cove and the back of the coves. There are a lot of areas with solid timber. You'd think bass would spawn in the coves, but for some strange reason at Table Rock the very finest places to fish for big fish at night with the jig and eel are the points—the timbered points and also on the bluffs.

Biologists and skin divers have given me reports I never have substantiated. They say that on the steep rock bluffs the rock comes down 5 or 6 feet and there will be a table of rocks coming out 5 or 6 more feet. Then it will drop off again 5 or 6 feet and there will be another table of rocks like a table top. The ledges and flat rock on these bluffs are not exactly vertical. There's a lot of shady cover there, too. Divers say they quite often see bass spawning on the flat table-top rocks. One species that spawns there is the Kentucky or spotted bass, in 8 to 12 feet of water.

Table Rock is generally clear in the lower end of the lake. In the upper lake in some of the major tributary arms in the White River is dingier water, and there the bass spawn in the shallower water. Some of these bass spawn on the bluffs; you find them in the niches in the rock. Along a typical big bluff face near the White River, maybe for half a mile will be two little nooks of about 50 feet. They're still part of the bluff, and the bank is still vertical. For some reason—perhaps it's because winds blow up and down it and create currents there—the bass like to spawn in those nooks.

Fishing this particular pattern on the bluffs is a little bit different from fishing the points, because you've got to throw right up on the rock, and you've got to keep retying your line because the jig hits the rock and frays or breaks the line. Cast up against the rock and put the slightest amount of pressure on the lure, and this slightly swings the jig and eel out. You want it to fall as straight down as possible, but to feel the strike you've got to put a little bit of tension on it—at least a

Rocky bluffs and timbered points are perfect places to night-fish the jig and eel in the spring.

slight bow in your line so you can feel the strike. If you're throwing in the right spot, like in 5 to 10 feet of water, you'll hit a little ledge of rock, and at that point just barely crawl or jig the jig and eel along that rock. Pull the bait again and it barely starts to drop. Right at the edges of those ledges is where your strikes normally occur. Bass hit the jig and eel on the fall. A lot of strikes are Kentucky bass or small-mouths; they'll come toward you, so it's tough to feel the fish. Occasionally if you're not paying much attention you'll figure you're too deep and start reeling, and all of a sudden you'll feel the fish.

At night you don't have much opportunity to be a line watcher; you have to go almost entirely by the feel. I use a graphite rod and often a night light. A night light is a little light behind an opaque glass. They call it the Moon Glow light because it's a very soft light. It's not direct, and the light doesn't really spook them, and you can get right up on 'em in clear water. It does give you depth perception. The biggest problem at night when you're casting is that you can't see the trees or the rocks very well, and you overcast and have a problem. With the Moon Glow light you can make a more accurate cast.

On the timbered points the pattern is about 8 to 10 feet of water. For some reason they're not in the real depths. Evidently they're either spawning on the points or just feeding there. The Moon Glow light is very important in timber because on a dark night or even with the moon it's tough to get your depth perception fishing in the timber. For this fishing I often use 20-pound line. On the open bluffs I might go to 14. I use a lot of ¼-ounce jigs on the bluffs, but when in the heavy timber, I use the larger jigs, usually ⅜-ounce and occasionally ½-ounce. If there's any wind, I'll go to a ½-ounce jig and usually a fairly large pork eel.

There's one other exception. I was up at Bull Shoals three years ago, and they had had extremely high water for two years in a row. All the brush from the flood plain and growth in the past ten to fifteen years had grown up to what they call the summer pool level. Well, for these two years, which was back in 1976 and 1977, they raised the flood pool about 20 feet, and they kept the lake 20 feet higher. Even though the lake didn't have any timber in it, there were a lot of newly flooded small bushes and small cedar trees.

I looked for a fairly sharp cove which didn't have too much brush in the back of it and worked my boat through there. It was real thick, and there were branches with green leaves on them. But again, I was using 20-pound and 25-pound line and the light. In 1976 I learned that where I could find vines underwater, bass that particular year would be around them. The problem with that pattern is that since then they have held the lake at a different water level and the water isn't up in that flooded timber. It's lower now, and you won't find that heavy brush. Your night fishing isn't going to be in that kind of cover. I really got hung up a lot in those conditions, and it was aggravating, but while the bass were in there during the full moon in April, it sure was fun.

SPINNERBAITS

One day about noon in April of 1967 I was motoring through a large stand of thick cypress trees while looking for grass patches at Santee-Cooper, and I slipped up on what looked like a Yankee fisherman. Now I was born in Albany, N.Y., but moved out of there when only about a year old, so I never really learned the north. I moved to Maryland and finally to South Carolina. But I had lived for the past ten years in the deep south, particularly in Alabama, Florida, and South Carolina. So I had learned to wear the proper clothes for hot weather.

What a good southern fisherman should wear on a spring or summer day is a pair of faded Levi's, a white T-shirt (maybe with the sleeves cut off), and a blue or red baseball cap. Anyone who is wearing a safari hat, long-sleeved shirt, and a pair of shiny black boots has got to be a Yankee—a city slicker. On top of that, if he's tossing something as funny-looking as what this guy had on, he just has to be a real Yankee. The lure looked like an open safety pin with a spinner blade hanging off one point and some kind of jig on the other. So I approached him with the idea of having a little fun at his expense. Figuring to really impress the guy and sort of blow his mind a little, I planned my strategy. There were a couple of 7-pounders in my live well caught that morning, so I planned to ask him how he'd done and then show him my fish.

Not only did my plan backfire, but I almost fell over backward when this guy lifted a huge string of big bass. He had nearly a limit. The smallest bass on his stringer was nearly 5 pounds, and he had 'em up to 8 or 9 pounds. And all these fish, he said, he had caught on this funny-looking lure. I didn't really know what the lure was—I thought I knew but wasn't sure. The man was Billy Goff, from Columbia, S.C., who from that day on was destined to become a lifelong personal friend.

We began talking, and he surprised me with his southern drawl and a few spits of tobacco juice. He told me that in the previous year alone he'd caught more than 200 bass over 6 pounds on this amazing new lure. It was a spinnerbait. In fact, his biggest-ever bass came on that very same lure and weighed 13 pounds, 2 ounces. A friend of Goff's, Walt Rucker, who operates a live-bait farm near the town of Santee, supposedly brought the first spinnerbaits to the twin lakes. Rucker, who also became a good friend of mine, was out fishing in Texas and was given some spinnerbaits out there by local anglers.

For the record, the lure Billy Goff was using that day was a Bomber Bushwhacker, which was the first commercially made safety-pin-style spinnerbait I had ever seen advertised, but I had failed to order any. Billy's testimony about this great bait really opened my eyes, because he was catching a lot of largemouths to 10 pounds plus on a spinnerbait with a single No. 5 blade. I got to imagining what the largest bass would do to a spinnerbait if I tried a No. 8 or No. 9 blade.

Billy gave me one of his lures, and I immediately headed for home to handcraft some of my own spinnerbaits. The first one I made was really an abortion. It had a blade about 2 to 3 inches in diameter, and after several days of fruitless casting and a lot of hard cranking, I finally left it hung up on a cypress tree without a bass to its credit. My second spinnerbait had a little bit smaller blade, probably a No. 8, which was still about 1¾ inches in diameter. The first bass I caught on it was about 2 pounds, and I realized it wasn't the right setup. In desperation I put back the original No. 5 nickel blade with the green-and-black skirt Billy had given me, and I started catching bass. The first couple were over 5 pounds.

When I think back on this experience, I was a couple of years too late with spinnerbaits. I had fished a lot of Mepps Spinners and

The relatively new safety-pin-style spinnerbait is amazingly snagproof. But since you run it fast, bumping it into cover, you should check the line frequently for abrasion.

straight spinners, but I hadn't fished any snagless safety-pin-spinner-baits such as Billy was throwing. I had the opportunity at Santee, where the water is full of brush and stickups, but I was too hung up on a couple of patterns. I had caught a lot of bass on Johnson Spoons and worms, and just didn't think there was anything better. I was really that narrow-minded. Billy and his friends already had picked up hundreds of big bass which never before had seen spinnerbaits. In just a few short years hundreds of fishermen at Santee were throwing the lures, and by 1970 or 1971 the bonanza of truly eager bass was well harvested. The best fishing started in 1966 and extended through 1968.

Today in spinnerbait fishing, I never fish the lure only one way. I have developed about a dozen different patterns which all are highly productive, and in this section I'm going to mention five or six of my favorites. In no way does this mean these favorites are inclusive; I have many other patterns I use, but these six really are the ones which work best for me. The others are either variations or entirely different patterns. I'll mention weed cover later and talk about the ways to catch bass in weeds, and this will include spinnerbait fishing.

There are four or five little truths I've learned about spinnerbait fishing. The first one—and I don't care if you're from Connecticut or California—is "bump the stump." You might be bumping a spinnerbait off the rocks because there might not be a stump any where near your home lakes, but the point is the principle of bumping an object. That's my motto for fishing this wonderful chunk of metal and lead called the spinnerbait. Whether it's a boat dock, a patch of lilies, a stickup, or a stump, bump it! Head the lure past so close to the cover that the blades are interrupted in their normal rotation and momentarily flutter and pause before they quickly resume their rotation. Bass, pike, muskies, and all sorts of gamefish will slash into the lure when it looks crippled in this moment of flutter.

I'm sure a lot of readers will disagree with my statement concerning the importance of bumping the cover. Several might recall how many fish they caught ten to fifteen years ago on lures such as the Mepps Spinner, which is an open-water spinner. It's not the safety-pin design and not weedless. The Mepps has a big treble hook and is mainly for fishing at shallow depths or in open, uncluttered water. Folks caught a lot of fish on that lure and also on the ABU and the Shyster spinners, and they still do. They're good lures, but the true spinnerbait I'm describing is a weedless, snagless lure which comes bumping and deflecting through heavy brush and cover. It is so nearly snagproof that I do not throw a spinnerbait unless there's cover. I rarely throw it in open water because there are better lures for open water. I reserve my spinnerbait fishing for heavy cover.

Spinnerbaits have been around for a long time. Recently I looked at a reprint of an 1898 Sears & Roebuck catalog and saw some lures with big fluted blades. They weren't called spinnerbaits, but they had blades which rotated and probably had a flash or an appearance to a fish much like that of the modern spinnerbaits. They were similar to the Colorado spinner you'd use ahead of a live minnow. The first book I ever read on black bass fishing—I guess the first book ever published on black bass—was The Book of the Black Bass by Dr. Henshall, published in 1881, and it had several references to this type of fluted spinner blade.

The first spinnerbait I ever fished was the Mepps-type spinner, which had a straight shank. The first weedless type of spinner I used was the old Shannon Spinner, which had two wires up over the hook and spinners on the wires. The Mepps Spinners have been around for the past several years, and they're advertised as being the No. 1 spinnerbait in the world. The Mepps catches everything—not just bass—but I don't think it's the best bass spinnerbait in the world. Really, a spinner is not the spinnerbait professional bass fishermen think of, and that's the point. Probably 200 different spinners have evolved in the past century, but the true spinnerbait is the safety-pin device with the wire guard coming over the hook. It's a snag guard. Another way to describe a spinnerbait is to call it a jig with a wire attached to a metal weight, making it a safety-pin type of lure. This type of spinnerbait is fairly new; it was first developed on an experimental basis back in the 1940s, and the first one on the market is credited as being the Houser Hell-Diver, which was manufactured in St. Louis. This lure was followed shortly by the Bushwhacker. The Shannon Twin Spinner originated before 1920 and was a fairly close predecessor.

The Bomber Bushwhacker, the first spinnerbait I ever saw and used, is still around and still catches bass.

The flash point and the jig design are two major differences between a spinner and a spinnerbait. The two most common categories of the modern safety-pin spinnerbaits are the "short-arm" and the "long-arm" models. The short-arm models are being phased out somewhat today, as the trend is to the long-arm models, but the flash point of the short-arm models, such as the Tarantula by Bass Buster, is above the jig and slightly ahead of it. The spinnerbait blade flashes up in front of the jig on the shorter-armed models. The flash point of the long-arm models—my preference—is a little bit different. The blade itself rotates around the jig slightly above and behind it. The plain spinner like the Mepps has no jig; it has a flash point all along the lure, except that there's a trailer behind it.

The reason bass strike a spinnerbait is the main reason I use it, and that is that most of the strikes are not feeding strikes. They're reflex-action strikes, and about a quarter of the bass I catch in a year's time are on this same reflex action. These fish hit because I exploit their predatory nature and not because they're hungry or spawning. The crank baits and spinnerbaits are reflex-action lures, and to be most effective, they should be bumping through something. A bass seeks an ambush point. He's lying behind the bush, stump, or log, and the reflex factor is simply that the lure is so close to his territory and his

**All types of commercial spinnerbaits are available,
including one I make, but I still carry components to make
up special combinations for special situations.**

presence that it's almost going to snag him, and he hits it out of reflex. That blade flashing in his face causes him to grab it.

When you're fishing cover, go one step further and ask yourself the following questions. Which side of the stump should I throw to? Is the sun out? Is the wind blowing? What's the water temperature? Think pattern, because spinnerbaits are the strongest patterns I think I've ever seen.

Not that I know them all. In a tournament I might have the opportunity to fish with a guy from California whom I've never fished with, and he quite possibly will be fishing a spinnerbait around a type of cover or around a type of water that I've never really fished. Therefore, I'm liable to learn something new from him. I've fished in about sixty major tournaments, and don't think I've ever failed to learn a new trick at a tourney, and there are a lot of tricks to spinnerbaits.

Most large lakes, however, have about ten to twelve spinnerbait patterns through the entire course of the year. On these large lakes of 50,000 acres or more there is dingy water, clear water, all different sorts of brush and stickups, different water temperatures and weeds—the whole gambit of different cover and conditions for bass. These productive patterns seem to hold true all over the country.

Before I list the most productive ways I fish a spinnerbait, let's look at some of the basics which make for the best spinnerbait conditions. One condition found throughout the country is water between 45 and 70 degrees. In other words, the cooler waters provide the best spinnerbait fishing. There's a slight exception here, and that's in extremely muddy water often found in lakes in Oklahoma, Texas, and Kansas. These waters might have better spinnerbait fishing in the hot summer when the temperatures are 80 to 90 degrees. This is only in lakes which are exceptionally muddy. This means spinnerbaits are the most productive in the spring and fall when the water is a little cooler. When the water is really cold, like from 45 to 55 degrees, I use a smaller bait and a much slower retrieve and fish it a little bit deeper. Then I'm usually fishing a No. 1, 2, or 3 blade and a 1/4-ounce or even smaller head. I work the bait very slow and quite often bump it off the bottom almost like a plastic worm.

As the water begins to warm up and gets to 55 degrees, the fish are just about ready to spawn or are moving into the spawning beds. Then I use much larger blades—at least a No. 3, sometimes a No. 4, and quite often a No. 5—and run the lure considerably faster than when the water was 10 degrees cooler. Bass react reflexively to a fast lure. I think the reason for the cold-water slowness is their reflexes. If you run it by too fast in cold water, they don't know what is there until it's past them. The cold water dulls their reflexes and slows their metabolism. Of course, in the warmer water when the lure is a couple feet from them they're ready to nail it.

During most of the spring when it's warm and pre-spawn conditions exist, I'm looking for dingy water. It could be a cold lake in Minnesota, and there might be a little creek coming in somewhere. After some rain I might find some dingy water, and that's a good spot to fish. I might be in Kerr Reservoir in Virginia, and most of the lake is crystal clear, but I know of some tributaries in Nutbush Creek that will be dingy. And that's the secret then to catching them on the spinnerbait. In the clear reservoirs, look in the spring for runoff and little pockets of very dingy water.

But when it's really cold and muddy and the water temperature is only 45 degrees, you can't hardly catch them on spinnerbaits. It's next to impossible. This is the time to stay home.

Buzzing is a technique which many people have heard about in the past three or four years, but I think many anglers are confused about it. In one type of buzzing the lure is retrieved barely beneath the surface so there's a wake created with the spinner blades, but the blades are not jumping out of the water. This is really a warm-water pattern, and I reserve it for fairly clear water between 60 and 70 degrees and usually around the spawning season. In the hot summer, spinnerbaits can be buzzed very effectively in lakes, but only in muddy water. A very large blade should be used most of the time when you're buzzing—quite often a No. 5, 6, or 7 blade.

When the water is dingy, fish shallow; when the water is clear, fish deep. That statement applies to plastic worm fishing and spinnerbait fishing, and to all species of black bass.

Spinnerbaits are great at night, but only if the water is clear and above 50 degrees. A lot of anglers don't realize that all through the summer in clear lakes, particularly in Florida, you can take bass on spinnerbaits at night in the lily pads with water temperatures in the 90s. Black baits are exceptionally good at night, except when the water is dingy. I have never done any good at all when I'm spinnerbait fishing at night in an off-colored or muddy lake. In fact, night bass fishing is not good anywhere in muddy or dingy water.

Bright blades such as chartreuse, copper, yellow, or red are my favorites in really muddy or dingy water—during the daytime, of course. But for some strange reason, a white body and nickel blades work very well when the water is clear and from 50 to 70 degrees. This doesn't make much sense, because white is considered a fairly bright color, and a lot of fishermen would think you'd want to match clear water with a natural-colored bait. This might be true, but for some reason I can't explain, white in clear water has always been my favorite. Keep a box of extra plastic skirts and blades handy, because no matter where you're spinnerbait fishing, there's always the need to change blades and skirts. When I buy a spinnerbait I don't pay any attention to what the blade is, because I have several different sizes of blades and can change them quickly. I'm constantly changing colors of blades and skirts until I find the key combination for the day.

There are three basic retrieves I use in spinnerbait fishing. I bounce the lure in cold water; I use a medium retrieve a foot or two under the surface when the water temp is between 55 and 70; and I buzz the top in hot weather. Variations in cover and in weather conditions always alter these retrieves. For example, in the middle of the summer I might find a bunch of bass suspended in 15 to 30 feet of water off the bottom in a stand of floating timber. This might cause me to jig deep with my spinnerbait.

I have respected Bill Dance for years. When I started fishing in tournaments, he had been the most successful tournament fisherman I had ever heard of or read about. I was honored to get to room with him in 1970 at a tournament in November at Table Rock Reservoir in Missouri. The lake was a little dingy, and a lot of willow bushes and button brush were flooded. The lake also was about 5 feet higher than normal. Most of the bushes were barely under the water. In practice I tried all sorts of different baits and caught two on a jig and eel.

Stan Sloan and Carl Dyess from Tennessee had been making a spinnerbait called the Zorro Agitator (which later was renamed the Zorro Aggravator), and they had given me a new color—chartreuse. Nobody I knew had ever fished a chartreuse spinnerbait, and in 1970 there wasn't such a color in a spinnerbait. In fact, when Stan gave me that bait, I asked him what kind of a weird thing it was. He said they'd been using the color a month or so in Tennessee and were doing good with it. He gave me three of these baits, and the next day I went out there and saw so many bushes that I put on the spinnerbait. I threw past a couple of submerged bushes and sort of buzzed it with the wake coming right on top of the bush. As soon as I got on the shady side of the bush, I dropped it down there and saw this big white mouth open

up. I repeated this procedure, and 5- and 6-pound largemouths began inhaling the spinnerbait as it fell to the shady side of these green bushes.

Everybody else during practice that day was catching only a couple of bass apiece, and I couldn't hide my excitement. That day I must have caught thirty to forty bass—all good ones. I was excited when I came in that evening. Bill Dance happens to be a mastermind of worming information out of people. Dance asked me how I did, and I was tingling with anticipation. I wasn't going to tell a soul. I was just going to keep it a big secret and win the tournament.

Doggone it, and I don't know how, but he just knew that I was up to something big. He could just tell, because he had so much experience in tournament fishing. So he kept prodding me all through dinner and the rest of the night. He said he knew I'd been catching fish. Finally he grabbed my hand and looked at my thumb, and he says, "Uh-huh! A lot of scratches on your thumb! That's a lot of teeth marks. You've been handling a lot of fish today." He had broken my barrier.

"Yeah, boy, I sure did!" I replied. "I caught thirty good bass and had just a super day."

Dance admitted he wasn't catching but a couple a day, and he hadn't caught any big fish at all. I told him he wouldn't believe it, but I had murdered the bass in shallow water. The next day he said he didn't want to find out any secret information from me and that he was sure I'd win the tournament, but that day something had happened to his boat. It wouldn't quite run right (although to this day I don't know whether or not he purposely caused it not to run right).

He asked me what I was going to do, and one thing led to another, and we ended up fishing together the second practice day. He showed me some good jig-and-eel water and we caught a couple of bass, but about three p.m. I went back into some dingy water and put on this chartreuse spinnerbait and caught a 4-pounder on my first cast. Bill asked me what I was using, and I showed him it was a spinnerbait. He said he'd never seen that color or that spinnerbait with two blades.

He had some other baits that looked fairly similar, and he tried different sizes of blades and colors of skirts, but they didn't work. They didn't act like my chartreuse Agitator did. Finally I lent him one, but told him I just had to have it back. We went ahead and caught four or five more bass in there that day.

On the last day of the warmup, he asked me where I was going to

This 2-pounder jumped my spinnerbait when I buzzed it through a submerged stump field. I was using a large, fluorescent red blade.

fish when the tournament started. I said down by the dam and in Indian Creek, and I told him I wasn't going to fish up the lake at all. He said then he'd fish up the lake. That wasn't such a bad idea, because Bill knew the muddier water was up the lake. Well, that afternoon there was a small one-day tournament on the lake. It was one of those deals where if anyone wanted to fish at a cost of $25 per head, they could get together with several locals and have a jackpot tournament. Bill suggested we go watch the weigh-in, see what they were catching, talk to some of the guys, and maybe learn something.

I was walking down there with Bill, and we saw this little old guy all dressed up for this real cold day. The old fellow had black hair and was wearing a big hat and snowmobile suit. He was walking up the hill with a nice string of bass. I asked Bill if he knew the guy, and Bill said that's not a guy . . . that's a woman, and her name is Mary Ann Colbert. I said that doesn't look like any woman to me. He said that

was a woman who catches a lot of fish and fishes a lot of tournaments with her dad, Paul Colbert. Then I commented that she had a bunch of fish. He commented that I wasn't married and she wasn't married and she was about my age and she was a good fisherman and I ought to meet her.

I told Bill I sure wished he'd introduce me to her, and he did. He said, "Mary Ann, I'd like to have you meet Roland Martin." Mary Ann had this big string of bass, and she wasn't concerned about anything but weighing them in. She said, "Oh, hi! I'll see you later." Then she walked away. I said, "Well, damn, Bill, she didn't want to talk to me." He said, "Hell, Roland, she's more interested in weighing in those fish right now."

Well, the woman I had thought was a little old guy dropped out of sight and out of mind, and that night Bill and I and Trip Hadad and a few other guys went over to Kimberlin City to dinner at the Holiday Inn. When we sat down, across the room I saw this woman again . . . this Mary Ann Colbert. I mentioned her, and Trip said he knew her, and he asked me if I'd ever met her. I said I'd met her that day, but she kind of blew by me like she didn't want to talk to me. Trip said she was more relaxed now and we should go talk to her and her dad. Trip introduced us formally for the first time, and we sat down and had a drink and finally dinner. We got to talking fishing, and finally Paul Colbert told Trip he'd ride back with him. Mary Ann and I were left alone. We had a couple more drinks and danced a little bit, and about two a.m. I went back to Bill's room, and she went to her dad's place.

About three hours later, Dance awakened me and said it was time to get up because the tournament started in an hour and a half. I was sleepy after the big night. Well, I went down near the dam and caught ten good keepers and finished the day in second place. And wouldn't you know . . . Bill Dance was leading. He had 2 or 3 pounds more than I did, and we were about 10 pounds ahead of anybody else. We both had caught over 20 pounds. That night I went over to the Holiday Inn, and there was Mary Ann with her dad again. We had a few drinks and decided to run on up to Springfield, Mo., that night. We went to several places with live bands and had a big time. We got back about three a.m.

Dance woke me up about an hour later and said it was time to go fishing. Fishing somehow wasn't really on my mind that day, but I did manage to take the lead. Dance slipped to second place and was about

4 pounds behind me. That night Mary Ann and I went out as planned. We partied, drank, danced, and had a wonderful time until four-thirty in the morning.

After I'd had thirty minutes of sleep, Dance woke me up for the final day of the tournament. By this time I had begun thinking pretty seriously about a future with Mary Ann. I had been thinking she was quite a gal, and had only secondary thoughts about the tournament. I fished despite another hangover—my third in three mornings—and Dance beat me by 7 ounces. I came in second. I had one fish that was right at the 12-inch mark (the minimum size limit back then for Bass Anglers Sportsman Society tournaments), and rather than take a chance at the time I thought I'd weigh in the others and still win the tournament. I didn't think Dance would beat me, because somebody had told me he had only 15 pounds, but really he had more.

If I had weighed in that bass and Ray Scott had not checked it, I would have won. But if he had checked it and determined that it was a fraction short, he would have penalized me and I would have fallen to third place.

Mary Ann and I steady-dated after that for several months, and we got married the next year. That chartreuse Zorro Agitator was quite a spinnerbait. Dance caught all his bass on the one I gave him. He won the tournament, I came in second, and he introduced me to the woman I married. So, to me, spinnerbaits have a special significance.

---

17   Slow-Rolling the Stickups

Stickups are one of my most productive patterns, and one reason is that most new lakes have stickups. I try to travel the country and fish as many of the new, productive lakes as I can—lakes which are five or six years old. I'm talking about hundreds and hundreds of different reservoirs in the south, the midwest, and even in the north. If you hit them after five to seven years, you'll find there are still a lot of stickups. This is secondary growth. After the timber was cleared, a lot of stickups grew during the first couple of years before the impoundment finally filled up. Quite often these stickups hold a lot of bass, and the spinnerbait is one of the fastest ways to catch 'em. You cover a lot of water making thousands of casts. Look for stickups along the shorelines.

This sounds really crazy, but a good, solid pattern is slow-rolling the stickups. What I do is throw past the stickup and then bump the stickup with the spinnerbait. As soon as it comes over the top of it, I drop it down with just a little bit of tension to the shady side of the stickup and just roll it over the limbs. Most of the time this gets their attention—the fact that it's bumping the stickups and limbs. As it rolls down to them in the shadows, that's when they hit it. Bass have no eyelids, so most of the time they seek deep water in most reservoirs. But because of the heavy stickups that provide a lot of cover, even in the summertime the fish will be in 2 to 4 feet of water and often hiding beneath the dense, shadiest part of the stickup. Particularly in a new lake where there are simply a lot of bass, these fish are right in the shade. You've got to drop the lure right on top of them. And the strike is a reflex action. The lure's coming right into their territory—right into the space they're occupying. It doesn't work to cast by the stickup and retrieve it past the bass; you have to really bump through the limbs and drop it on top of the fish. That's the kind of retrieve which pays off.

All my deeper-water spinnerbait fishing is done with a single blade, because I can feel the blade rotate—particularly a No. 4 or 5 blade—if I'm using a good sensitive line like Stren. I put just enough back pressure on that spinnerbait with a No. 4 or 5 blade to feel the little thump, thump, thump as it's sinking. If you use two blades, you won't feel that thump because the two blades counteract each other. Anytime I'm dropping a spinnerbait deep, such as with the slow-roll stickup technique, I'm fishing the single blade on a long wire. I like the long arm for the weedless effect, and also the long wire gives me a flash point well back by the jig, so when they attack the jig or the flash point, they've got the hook.

There are a couple of patterns which are very important about slow-rolling. A bass can position himself in the shade of even a 1-inch-diameter stickup. It's not much cover, but he can angle himself so that the inch of shade falls over both his eyes. It's all the shade the fish needs on a hot summer day. Some of the best structure to look for during the feeding season in summer is the deepwater points on the main lake. During the hotter weather, the more extreme or more exposed points are best. Again, in the spring or pre-spawn season, the highly protected coves are usually best. Water temperatures which work best for this are in the 55-degree range. The water is fairly clear, and they start hitting spinnerbaits. If the water is a little dingier, they start hitting best in the 60-degree range. I continually monitor the water temperature; I leave a surface temp gauge turned on all day, and I also have a hand thermometer that I check at least five or six times during the day just to see if my surface temp gauge is working properly. I'm looking for the sections with the warmest water—usually the north pockets—in the spring, and in the summer it's usually the other way around. Then I'm looking for cooler water. The coves are usually warmer than the main lake. The optimum temperature is 72 degrees. When bass are at 72 degrees, they're at the maximum peak period of their feeding. They're going to leave 80-degree water to go to 72, and they're going to leave 65-degree water to go to 72, so you get 'em both ways.

One factor about spinnerbait fishing is the sun, and the reason stickups are so good is that sunny days concentrate the bass. They might have been roaming around in shallow water which has only one stickup every 50 feet, but when the sun comes out strong, they're going to go to areas with shade. With cloud cover, bass are going to spread out all over; you might catch a lot of fish then, but you're not going to catch them particularly in the stickups.

Wind also is an important factor. Bass cannot swim backward, and they're going to face the wind. Regardless if it's a stump, a rock, or a stickup, a bass will be in the shade facing the wind, because the wind creates a slight current. It's important to remember they're going to be facing the wind as well as being in that shade. To get the typical reflex strike, throw into the wind and retrieve downwind downsun, and as soon as you reach the stickup, he's going to be right behind it in the shade facing the current. Drop the bait right on top of the fish as close as you can to where you think his eyes are.

I like to play a little game by conjuring up an image of at least an 8-pound bass. Thinking big is fun, and it really is effective. Be optimistic and look at that stickup; there might be a hundred of 'em, but look at the one you're going to throw to and conjure up an image of a truly big fish—something you want to catch. It really instills confidence and keeps your enthusiasm going. Much of the enjoyment and pleasure of fishing is nothing more than to anticipate what's going to happen on the very next cast. Figure all the factors and drop that spinnerbait right on his eyeball and you'll catch him. He might not be 8 pounds; in reality he's probably 2, but the point is you've figured out where he is and had fun doing this anticipation bit with that fish.

What I use for most stickups is a 1/4-ounce bait. I don't want it to drop very fast, and it makes a softer splash than a heavier spinnerbait would make. I'm throwing past the stickup, but when I come over the top of it and let the bait roll through the limbs, the ¼-ounce spinner bounces through there pretty good. I usually use all kinds of tails. I might use a plastic minnow body, a skirt, a worm trailer, or a piece of pork rind. There are all kinds of possible different combinations and variations you can experiment with. I have usually at least a No. 4 blade and sometimes a No. 5. Nickel and gold are my standard colors, but in very muddy water I might go to red, chartreuse, or bright orange.

I always throw either crosswind or slightly upwind with heavy tackle. The strike is nothing more than a tick when it's dropping through there; it's just a small tick, and in hot weather sometimes you don't even feel the tick. They sometimes overtake it, and all you see is the line moving to the right or left or toward you. And at other times in hot weather you'll feel the strike. The shady side is the key to stickup fishing, but I use Stren fluorescent line, and I can see what's going on even if the water's dingy. I watch for any side movement,

Most newer lakes have stickups, and getting right in there where you can drop a spinnerbait on the fish is one good way to work such a pattern.

because sometimes half the fish which hit you will hardly feel. You'll just see that line start to move maybe 3 to 6 inches to the side. If that happens just the slightest bit, the lure might be falling down a limb, but go ahead and set the hook anyhow. You'll get hung up a few times, but it'll be worth the effort. If the bass grabs the spinnerbait for more than four or five seconds and chews on it much, he's going to spit it out unless you set the hook quickly. By keeping a little back pressure on the lure you can tell what's happening.

You need heavy tackle unless you're in ultra-clear water which is fairly open except for a few isolated stickups. For the latter you can get by with light tackle and can throw 6-, 8-, or 10-pound line as long as you drop the spinnerbait on the close side of the stickup and there are no other stickups between you and the lure. In a lake like Santee-Cooper (which actually is two lakes—Marion and Moultrie) or Lake Seminole or some weedy lake in Texas, there are likely ten more stickups between you and where you dropped the bait, and you might not see any of them. In waters like this I favor at least 17-pound line. Sometimes under these conditions I've gone to 20-pound or 25-pound line with a 5½-foot stiff casting rod.

I do almost 99 percent of my heavy spinnerbait fishing with heavy casting tackle. I usually have my drag adjusted pretty tight in this kind of cover, because the object is to pull 'em upward and get 'em up to the top of the water if you're fishing 4 or 5 feet deep. I might have 30 feet of line out, so I can have a tight drag and yet the line will stretch. When I get one on top and he starts jumping or splashing, that's good because he's now away from the deep limbs and won't snag the line. As soon as I get him right up to the boat, I loosen the drag. I constantly back my drag off a little bit on a real hot fish, because it's been only seconds since he was hooked, and he's lively and fighting every which direction. If you try to horse him into the boat, this is where you're apt to lose your fish. When you have a hot green bass, even though there might be stickups underneath the boat, you've almost invariably got to back off on your drag and give him some line if he's over 5 pounds. Don't stop him at the boat, because it's too much of a shock even with 20-pound line. A 5-pound bass can break 20-pound line if you try to horse him into the boat within three or four seconds after he struck. Play him around the boat a little bit and keep him on top, but give him enough line if he wants to run. Let him run on top, and generally he'll tire after 10 to 15 seconds. Slide him into the net. If you want to play with him, play with him when he's in the boat.

18 Prodding the Weedlines

One of my favorite patterns is prodding the weedlines. These aren't weeds that you see; they're weedlines which often are out of sight.

Back in 1971 when I was doing promotional work for Lowrance Electronics, Carl Lowrance told me to go out to Virginia because we wanted to sell a bunch of locators out there and it's a good section of the country. Mary Ann and I went to Smith Mountain Lake in Central Virginia. We got there on Sunday, and we met Bob Mayes, who was a Lowrance representative at the time and is a good fisherman from Roanoke. He had a trip lined up for us at Smith Mountain, and Roanoke newspaper outdoor writer Bill Cochran, and Tom Sutton, who is a draftsman and makes lake maps throughout the southeast, went along too. The five of us went out in two different boats. We caught about ten bass, including a 4-pounder, that day.

Sutton, Mayes, and I went back there early Monday morning, and we had a time limit. We had a store promotion that night, and a local TV station had called and said that if I could meet them at the store at noon, they would interview me and have the interview on the evening sports.

We got started fishing at eight a.m., and an idea hit me. I suggested we try a "nothing bank" and explained that sometimes in tournaments I pick the crummiest, worst-looking spot I can find, with my thinking being that every other fisherman thinks the same way and consequently the place never gets fished. There was a crummy-looking spot across from the boat ramp. It was adjacent to a farmer's field, sloping grass with nothing but solid grass coming into the water.

We went over there and worked back into a pocket and never got a strike. I started the big engine and looked at the locator. It showed a big line of weeds almost to the surface, although the water was about 5 feet deep. I shut the motor off and we drifted out to where the solid weeds quit and the water was 6 to 7 feet deep with a bare clay bottom on out. I threw back over the boat wake with a chartreuse Zorro spinnerbait and let it tick along the grass until I didn't feel anything, and I let it drop down. A good bass of about 3½ pounds stopped it. We were about 50 yards off the bank, and I grabbed a marker buoy and threw it to the edge of the weedline. I circled around with the trolling motor and located the edge of the weeds again and threw out another marker.

Bob Mayes caught the next bass—about a 6-pounder—by throwing his spinnerbait right on top of the weeds and pulling it to the edge and then letting it settle to the bottom. Then he pumped the bait upward. The bass were right on the lip of the weeds about 3 feet deep, and they weren't difficult to catch. With the aid of the locator, we found a 100-to-150-yard stretch of weeds. They were the only weeds on this nothing bank and probably the only ones within five miles of where we were. We were right across from the ramp, and we hadn't burned a half gallon of gas.

We started nailing the bass. Sutton caught a couple around 5 pounds, and Bob caught his biggest bass ever in Virginia—an 8¼-

I got this 3½-pounder by prodding the weedlines. Sometimes, as here, I use a grub-type tail instead of a plastic or rubber skirt on the spinnerbait.

pounder. I caught a few in the 5-to-7-pound range. We kept seventeen largemouths and put them in the live well. We hurried back to Roanoke and got there just in time for the television interview. They filmed our fish. We weighed the biggest ten and they totaled 55 pounds.

The film ran on the sports show following the six-o'clock news, and we had the biggest ten in a 40-gallon tub full of ice and water. Most of the bass had died, but a few still had their gills moving. Shortly after the news, we started hearing tires screeching in the parking lot, and a couple of red-faced fishermen rushed in and started questioning us. We convinced the first fifty people who came in the store that we actually had caught those bass that morning and what they had seen on TV was an interview conducted as soon as we got back to town.

There was a gross of Zorro spinnerbaits in the store, and they were all sold by seven-thirty p.m. They had about twenty-five fish locators, and we sold them and took orders for eleven more by the time the evening was over. Sutton sold several of his maps on Smith Mountain, and he marked all the areas we'd fished.

Every year I go to probably thirty different store promotions, but never have I seen a more enthusiastic crowd than those 500 to 600 people who came in the store that evening following the TV interview. Smith Mountain is not known for its big largemouths, and 5-to-8-pounders make news in Roanoke.

I had merely found a good shallow weedline, and we had worked the edge.

I grew up in Maryland near a few lakes with weeds, but this was before I fished spinnerbaits. During the past ten years, I've fished a lot in Minnesota, Michigan, Wisconsin, and all through the northern-tier states. In many of the natural lakes there, you'll find a lot of weedlines. With Al Lindner one time in Wisconsin, we hit a lake in late April, and the bass were on the weedlines. Toledo Bend has a lot of weeds, but often the weeds aren't visible, and early in the spring to find bass in the pre-spawn season you have to rely on your "underwater eyes"—a fish locator. Santee has some deep weedlines, and they're hard to see in the early spring before they really start to grow up good. Some sections of the upper lake in the Jack's Creek area have deep underwater weeds. Right on the weedline is the first area where the bass move into from deep water, and they hold on this structure until it's really warm enough for them to go in to spawn. The most productive depth depends on water clarity. In real clear waters of the north, the weed lines might be 15 feet deep. At Minnetonka in Minnesota in the spring we caught a lot of bass on both spinnerbaits and plastic worms in Jason Lucas' favorite lake, so it was a memorable experience for me.

If you go to a shallow, dingy lake such as Lake Seminole in Georgia, the weedlines might grow out to 6 feet deep. At Toledo Bend you're apt to find the weedlines growing no more than 7 feet deep. The type of lure I use here is a 3/8-ounce spinnerbait. It's kind of an intermediate depth, and since I'm working the edge of the weeds, I'm not concerned with the shallow water, only 2 to 3 feet deep. I really want to fish that part right on the edge, dropping the bait down. Some TVA lakes, mainly Pickwick and Guntersville, have a lot of milfoil, and

A bass caught in shallow water over a weedline can have lots of energy—always a thrill.

milfoil is common in lakes even in Texas and Oklahoma. But in the spring when the water temperature is still cold, it's recessed and is not growing right to the top. These milfoil weedlines are extremely productive with 3/8-ounce spinnerbaits.

The long-wire spinnerbait is needed to keep the lure from getting snagged up. Often in the weeds you can put on a trailer hook. This works good because you don't have much to hang up. If the trailer snatches some of the milfoil or elodea, snatch the bait just as hard as you can and often you will break the weed off the trailer hook. But you need at least 14-pound line. Actually, 17-pound is excellent for this because it doesn't stretch much.

The kind of structure I fish is adjacent to the spawning coves during pre-spawn conditions in the spring when the water is a little dingy. The irony of it is that most lakes with weeds normally are very clear. Many clear lakes aren't good spinnerbait lakes, but in the early spring before it really gets warm, a lot of rain and wind might give the water more color. The weeds have not grown up and they're still deep. Then you can get by with heavier lines. Figure the weedlines as a ledge, and if the sun is shining, it's forming a shadow on the ledge.

In the spring I like to find small, irregular features in the weedline; it isn't always straight and might have a little point or pocket. If the wind is blowing in, the bass are facing that wind, and they'll be on the current side of the grass. If there's a pocket, the pocket has two points—one on each side of the weedline. The point facing the wind usually is the best pocket. Pockets and points produce fish particularly when the wind blows.

The technique of retrieving the spinnerbait is important, but determining just how far out the weedline is is something you need to do before you even fish. Start zigzagging the weedline with your boat running if you're looking for a weedline in 7 to 10 or more feet of water. You might be able to approximate how far out it is from what you can see, but marker buoys and your electronic locator are the best way. I take four markers and try to cover 50 to 60 yards at a time. When I line all my markers up, I now have a reference point, and then I idle along the edge of those markers with the big motor or the trolling motor. Sometimes I can see the irregular parts of it, such as a point I didn't know was there.

For weedlines in 1 to 4 feet of water in the shallower lakes, you need to drift over them or perhaps use your trolling motor. Once you've got a couple of markers out or at least some reference where you can throw, the technique is to parallel-cast into the wind on the shady side and try to tick the weedline as I mentioned doing at Smith Mountain. When you quit feeling the tick, drop the spinnerbait and watch your line and keep a slight bit of back pressure on the lure. It's just as you do in stickup fishing. The strikes are not vicious, particularly from pre-spawners; they'll just stop it. Some of the biggest bass in the lake are on the edges of the grass line.

Florida is a perfect place for spinnerbait fishing in the spring. When the water's 55 degrees, you can catch a 12-pound or 13-pound largemouth in Florida in the eel-grass areas of Lake George, all through Rodman Reservoir and in Lake Kissimmee. The possibilities here are fantastic. There are not only exposed weeds, but some waters have underwater weeds. Lake Jackson has a lot of clear water, and a lot of weeds are 10 to 11 feet deep before they form the weedline. Weedlines are the key to some trophy bass just before they spawn, and this is true from California to Connecticut. Any weeds will do.

---

19   Ticking the Logs

When I think of the lying-log pattern, I immediately think of Jeff Green, a former guide at Toledo Bend. He now lives in central Texas; he used to be from Tulsa. When I'd go down there for tournaments in the early 1970s, I'd look up Jeff and ask him what the fish were doing. He'd invariably tell me it didn't make any difference where I fished in the early spring, the pattern to look for was a log lying out in the water. It could be in 2 feet or 20 feet, but it offered shade, and he'd say just cast a spinnerbait out there and run it down the shady side of that log.

Since Jeff told me about that pattern, I've tried it, and it really does work. Another good friend of mine from Oklahoma is Jimmy Houston, and lying logs are one of his favorite patterns. Jimmy's one of the finest spinnerbait fishermen in the country. He designed the Red Man spinnerbait, and he won the B.A.S.S. tournament at Santee-Cooper in 1976 by fishing stickups and lying logs—always the shady sides. He and Jeff Green used to fish a lot together in Oklahoma.

Fishing the shady sides of lying logs sounds easy, but there's more to it than meets the eye. Lots of fishermen don't consider boat position, and this is critical. You need to cast your spinnerbait within 2 or

3 inches of the log and retrieve it from 1 to 4 inches deep along the entire length of the log. You simply must have perfect boat position to fish the entire length of a 60-foot log. Remember, too, with the reflex strike you get with a spinnerbait, the first cast is the most important cast. When you see a log, don't just cast at it, because if the lure doesn't come right past the bass, he doesn't get a chance to hit it out of reflex action. Then he's 'alerted; he's heard that spinnerbait go by; he's going to be leery and hard to catch. The average fisherman who comes up to a log—and it's apt to be lying in most any direction—simply throws at the log and bounces his bait over it. That's not the way to fish a lying log. That first cast has to be right down the log. If it takes you 20 seconds to get lined up properly on the log, then it does. But don't make that first cast until you're positioned right.

Bass get beneath these lying logs because they're some of the only horizontal cover they have. Logs frequently lodge against the shoreline, and as they stick out in the lake, the opposite end might be in over 10 or 15 feet of water. Along such a log bass can travel from a foot of water next to the bank to 15 feet of water in the shade as they search for baitfish. The logs offer horizontal movement to the fish, and this horizontal movement is not found in standing trees. The little bit of shade behind the standing timber is only in that one spot, and the same applies to a stickup. But with a lying log they might have from 40 to 60 feet of running room, and with all this latitude, a lying log in timber is better than the timber itself. A lying log on a regular shoreline with no timber is better than a lying log in timber. The more isolated the log, the better its potential.

Jimmy Houston placed high in a tournament at Ross Barnett Reservoir in Mississippi, and he did this by running to every lying log on the west side of the lake and fishing only the shady sides. That west side of Barnett must have only twenty to thirty lying logs, but he'd run from log to log, and most of those logs had one bass apiece beneath them. Lying logs are not school-bass situations, but it's a fast pattern where you can run up to the log, drop your trolling motor, get into position, and make one to three casts and leave and look for the next log. This is pattern fishing supreme!

The larger logs are better because they obviously provide more shade. Logs are enhanced if they're near a point, a creek channel, or any deep water. The best lying-log pattern usually is in the spring when the water tends to be a little dingy and on the cool side, such as in the 50s. But if the lake's very muddy, spinnerbaits are productive in

80-to-90-degree water temperatures, and lying logs are apt to pay off good then, too. A light spinnerbait with a fairly small blade is good for lying logs because the bait moves fairly slowly, and also a heavier spinnerbait, such as a 3/8-ounce with a No. 4 to 6 blade, is good because the resistance slows it down and permits it to travel 2 to 4 inches deep.

Most of the time with the lying-log pattern, you can watch your lure and never lose eye contact with it, because it's traveling barely beneath the surface. Always use a trailer hook, because there are virtually no limbs to hang on, and if you make an accurate cast, you'll seldom get hung up. Sunny days are good on the lying logs because the sun concentrates the fish. On cloudy, overcast days they don't need to go beneath the logs for shade.

A maze of logs lying in many different directions is not good for this type of pattern because the bass could be beneath any of the logs and that first cast likely will spook them. The spinnerbait is good for fishing single logs at a time. The best logs almost always are lodged

A lying log is a great pattern in early spring. The tricky part is positioning your boat so that you retrieve your bait along the entire length of the shady side of the log.

A log extending out from the shoreline is especially good because it gives bass cover from shallow to deep water.

into timber or against the shoreline. Free-floating logs out in the lake do not pay off well. The logs need to be stationary, just as floating hyacinths do. I catch bass on hyacinths which are stationary but not on the ones drifting free in the lake.

Even in a lake which has been cleared of timber, a lying-log situation can develop because of high water in the spring. The high water might move logs off the shore. Not too long ago I was fishing for smallmouths on Rainy Lake across into Canada from Minnesota, and I was amazed at the logs in the lake. Masses of cut timber headed for paper mills are floated down the lake. I guess that in periods of rough water, these logs had drifted away from the logging operation. In the backs of a lot of pockets were logs. Some of them had sunk, but others were floating and sticking out along the rocky shoreline, and small-mouths would smack spinnerbaits and crank baits when the lures came past them. The fish were beneath the logs.

Most all lakes have fallen trees, and the pattern for fishing them is similar to the lying-log pattern. Position your boat so that the branches and forks in the limbs point toward you. Cast toward the base of the tree and retrieve toward the end of it. If the branches and forks are pointing toward you you'll have less risk of getting the lure snagged up. If there are a lot of branches and forks on the tree, you might be better off to remove the trailer hook on your spinnerbait to reduce hanging up. If there are several big limbs coming out from the tree, you need to make repeated casts to each of the limb areas. Also, you might need to move your boat around to the other side of the tree to get good shots at limbs on that side. Take it easy and slow. I use 17-to-25-pound line for this fishing, reserving the heavier line for dingy water. Particularly in fallen trees you have to get the fish to the top of the water and keep him on top to prevent him from tangling in the deeper limbs.

---

20   Bumping the Stumps

Regardless of where you are, today you're probably within a two-hour drive at the most from some decent bass fishing. The U.S. has 15 million acres of good bass water in reservoirs, natural lakes, and farm ponds. The natural lakes don't have many stumps, but many farm ponds, impoundments, and flowages have plenty. A plain simple truth in bass fishing is that you can catch a bass on a stump with a spinnerbait.

In the big southern impoundments, such as the TVA and the Army Corps of Engineers lakes, there are millions of stumps, particularly on the edges of the river channels. Bass will lie on these edges, but more specifically they lie on the stumps. At Pickwick Lake in Tennessee, they night-fish with spinnerbaits and catch smallmouths around stumps in 3 to 5 feet of water. At Santee-Cooper, they fish spinnerbaits in the stumps in the Pinopolis and Russellville areas. At Sidney Lanier, a deep, clear lake at the outskirts of metropolitan Atlanta, points might have two, three, or five stumps, but that's where the bass are in early spring. A knowledgeable bass fisherman who knows where the stumps are and can see stumps with Polaroid sunglasses really catches bass on spinnerbaits in the dingy waters in the spring and in the windswept waters in the fall when the current caused by the wind moves shad into these stumpy banks.

Bumping the stump is an excellent way to catch a bass. This is strictly a reflex-action strike. The fish is lying right next to the stump; it's his only cover and shade and protection perhaps within a 100-foot area. He's so close to the stump that his body likely is in contact with the lower section where the roots start to spread out. That stump is probably 18 inches to 3 feet high, and it gives him just enough depth to have shade.

That's the time to play the old game again and conjure up an 8-pounder image and picture him in the shade. Throw past the stump,

Manmade lakes are apt to include not only visible stickups but thousands of underwater stumps—a fine pattern for spinnerbaits.

In very shallow water such as this, a spinnerbait with a double blade is good because of the extra flash.

make a wake with the spinnerbait, and when it gets to the stump, drop it and bump the stump and fall right on the bass. It really works!

At Santee I had a lot of experience with spinnerbaits in the stumps in the fall months when the water level was lower. In the spring the twin lakes were high, and there would be so much good shallow cover, such as button bushes, weeds, and lily pads, that I fished this cover and didn't mess much with the stumps. But when the lakes were pulled 3 feet in the fall and the best remaining cover in the 171,000 acres of water were stumps, that's where I put my spinnerbaits to good use.

The trick is first knowing exactly where the stumps are. You can fan-cast stumpy areas and bump the stump and catch 'em that way, but the best way is to spot the stump and keep visual contact with it. Most of the time when I fish I'm standing up. I seldom sit down, particularly in tournaments. This high location plus keeping the sun at my back when I'm looking for underwater cover helps me find the stumps. If you're looking in the water and the sun's back over your shoulder, you can see a little deeper and you can spot the stumps a little better.

You don't always have to bump the stump. You can buzz the spinnerbait over it as long as you get really close to the bass. You'll get the same kind of reflex strike. I like to make contact with the stump, but don't always drop the bait down. Sometimes I bump the stump and keep running my bait, and they grab it. The long-arm spinnerbait is good for this kind of fishing, and I like a ¼-ounce bait because heavier ones get lodged more easily in the cracks at the top of the stump. You don't have to use extra-heavy line; I usually use 14 or 17.

Especially with autumn fishing, it really pays to study the wind. Often in southern reservoirs shad are blown into bays. In the fall, shad populations reach their peak, as many of them are winter-killed. Part of the fall pattern is to learn the direction of the prevailing winds. Study them for the previous week. If the wind's been blowing out of the south, it's been pushing a lot of shad slowly to the north coves. Then find north coves which have stumps, and fish them. If there's any deepwater structure, such as a good point with ten to fifteen stumps on it, imagine how many schools of shad are moved through there. It's a perfect ambush point for not only one bass, but a big school of them. Where the wind's blowing and pushing water in a shallow lake in the fall is the only condition I've seen fish break the surface to any extent.

I'm not talking about a big school of bass, but maybe two or three running two or three shad. This doesn't seem like much, but an alert fisherman will watch for this. At this time of the year the shad are 2 to 4 inches long and are mostly threadfin shad with a few gizzard shad mixed in. Anytime you see a couple of shad skipping on the top or a good boil on the surface, throw your spinnerbait at least 6 feet past the spot. Don't drop your lure on the boil, because you'll scare the bass, but throw it past where he was and run it 4 to 6 inches deep right through the spot. If he doesn't strike, let the bait fall to the bottom and bounce it a few times. Intermittent twitches and pauses have about the same effect as bumping the stump, because you're interrupting the rotation of the blade, and this gives the bass following it all the more reason to nail it right then.

A crank bait is good in deep stumps. If you're on a point in a fairly clear lake and you can see stumps 4 to 6 feet deep, this is a good place to throw a crank bait. A spinnerbait, however, is much more shallow-running and snagless.

I won two major tournaments at Watts Bar Lake in Tennessee on spinnerbaits. One of the tourneys was in the spring, and I was fishing stumps and duck blinds in the upper end of the lake. The water wasn't more than 2½ feet deep, and I was buzzing the lure. I would move along for 100 yards and not see anything, but occasionally spot a dark stump. The water was very dingy, and the dark spots usually turned out to be stumps. I did the same basic thing as at Santee; I'd go into shallow bays and look for the dark spots. Then I'd drag the bait up to the stump and try to bump it. I moved the bait faster in the fall when the water was warmer and slower in the spring when it was cooler. In the fall when the water isn't quite as dingy, you can make a wake with the bait right under the surface. This is particularly good if the bass are busting shad, because the wake makes the bait look like a minnow skittering along on top.

A buzzing situation like that is a good time to use a tandem-bladed spinnerbait, but when I'm dropping the bait I like the single blade so I can feel it better. In 2 to 3 feet of water with stumps, a double blade is good because it has extra flash and might look more like a shad.

Stumps in deep water are excellent, but the problem is in finding them. They're extremely difficult to find. Some contour maps show you where the trees used to be and where the fields once were. If you can find where the trees used to be, you can expect to find the stumps.

On Kentucky Lake and Lake Barkley in Kentucky and Tennessee, a pattern exists which is similar in many man-made farm ponds. Shallow bays will have small creek channels which are only 3 or 4 feet deeper, but there'll be three to five times more stumps and trees along those creek channels than anywhere else. It's the same in man-made farm ponds, especially where a creek was dammed up to impound the water. The creek channel might be only 5 feet wide, but that's where the majority of the stumps will be. Since these creek channels often twist and turn, it really helps to watch your locator. You can, with the aid of the locator, stay directly over the creek channel and fan-cast around and feel the stumps and work your way all along the creek. On Lake Barkley, this is the best way to execute this pattern. When you find the stumps on the edge of the creek channel, you've done a double deal; you've got the structure, cover, deepwater—the whole ball game.

I'm frequently asked by beginners and novices how to get a spinnerbait to run right. A combination of things make a spinnerbait run right. The wire with the spinners on it—the arm—needs to be directly over the wire leading to the jig head, and the angle of the wire is important. Generally if the wire leading to the jig head comes off at a 30-degree angle and then makes another 45-degree angle to the wire attached to the spinner, this latter angle balances it out. The line pull is now above the jig, and the torque of the blade and weight of the jig are counteracted. It's a triangle situation with the line pull in the middle, the torque of the blade (or blades) pulling on top, and the weight of the jig on the bottom. This way the bait will run true and will not roll over or run with the blades off to the side.

Houston, Ricky Green, and Jerry Rhyne are three of the best spinnerbait fishermen I know, and Cliff Craft is another excellent spinnerbait man. I'm not as good with the spinnerbait as those guys are and I seldom rely on it as much as they do, but I do know their tricks. I fish it on six to eight different patterns in almost every tournament. In 1976 Jerry Rhyne qualified for his first BASS Masters Classic, and he said he used spinnerbaits to catch 90 percent of his bass. That's really relying heavily on a spinnerbait.

One advantage to spinnerbait fishing is that the pattern is usually fast, especially in the case of stumps. In a shallow bay at a lake such as

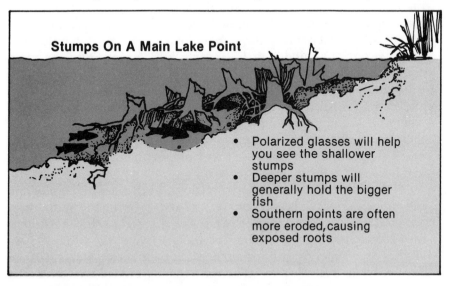

Stumps On A Main Lake Point

- Polarized glasses will help you see the shallower stumps
- Deeper stumps will generally hold the bigger fish
- Southern points are often more eroded, causing exposed roots

Lake points are as important in stump-bumping as in other patterns. However, a spinnerbait may not get you down to the deeper stumps; you'll need a crank bait.

Santee-Cooper, there might be as many as 3,000 stumps in the cove. There all you need to do is flip your trolling-motor switch on high and get as many casts to as many stumps as you can. Stand up high, stay alert, and make a bunch of casts. The cast has to be accurate, because the first cast almost always is the one that gets him. Throw 6 feet past the stump, bump the stump, and *hold on!* With a good, sharp hook and a good stiff rod, you'll get 'em.

Speaking of sharp hooks—and now's as good a time as any to mention this subject—it's super important to have extra-sharp hooks. I use a Weber stone about 3 inches long and an inch wide. It costs about 75 cents. I sharpen each single hook about twenty seconds and put a needle point on it. Another thing I do is angle the point of the hook out just a few degrees. This increases the hook size about one size.

A spinnerbait is a deadly night bait for smallmouths, Kentucky bass, and largemouths in several deep, clear TVA and Corps of Engineers lakes in Tennessee and Alabama. This fishing's still a bump-the-stump deal. In lakes such as Pickwick, Guntersville, Wilson, Center Hill, Watts Bar, Dale Hollow, and several others, guys like Stan Sloan, who manufactured the Zorro Aggravator, bump the stumps on the edge of the river channel. Smallmouths from 6 to even 9 pounds come up out of that river channel and get in the stumps lining the channels. Those channels have solid rows of stumps for miles and miles. Where they find a little feeder creek coming in to the main creek or a little bar that splits or drops off deep, guys like Sloan and Bill Dance and a whole bunch of those Tennessee boys get out there and bump the stumps at night with their spinnerbaits. They know where the stumps are, and with a single blade and a slow retrieve, they feel the lure hit the stumps. At night, of course, they don't get much of a view of their line and they can't see the strike; they have to feel it.

They often use sort of a yo-yo retrieve. They throw out to where they think the stump is and keep raising and lowering the bait almost as you'd fish a worm. When they feel the spinnerbait hit the stump, they keep twitching it a little faster and get it over the stump. These stumps aren't merely stumps alone; with their root systems, they're like pedestals, because the dirt beneath them is eroded away and each stump has ten to fifteen roots which make contact with the bottom. Smallmouths often are in the maze of roots, and they really bust that spinnerbait as it falls down on 'em.

One night back in 1974 I was fishing Pickwick Lake, right on the exact spot of the intersection of Mississippi, Tennessee, and Alabama, with Bill Dance, and he said to remember one thing about small-mouths: When you feel the spinnerbait bump over a stump and then you feel a little teeny tick, set the hook. I kept my rod sort of low and was really concentrating on this little tick. I threw over this stump in 6 feet of water, and there wasn't a tick. Something hit my bait on the run and seemingly at twenty miles per hour. I was using 17-pound line, and the drag zoomed and about 30 feet of line went out. A super-acrobatic smallmouth blew through the surface and went airborne. That fish jumped and thrashed four or five more times. I landed him finally, and he weighed 4½ pounds. We caught several other nice ones that night, but all of 'em really crashed the spinnerbaits rather than ticking them. Looking back, I sort of think Bill was kidding me about waiting for a tick.

21 Crashing the Willows

Every bass fisherman who has fished any length of time thinks back to fifteen or twenty years ago when the fishing was really easy. Then he thinks that back then if he'd just had the sophisticated boats, rods and reels, fish locators, surface temp gauges, lures, and all the other stuff we have now, he really would have caught a heckuva lot more bass. I'm reminded of this when I think of crashing the willows with a spinnerbait. But twenty years ago when I was still a teenager, I certainly didn't look for difficult water to fish; in fact, I didn't look much for it even ten years ago when I was guiding for Bill Jones, a former camp operator on the Diversion Canal at Santee-Cooper.

Years ago I looked for nice open water where I could use my diving plugs and surface plugs and occasionally some plastic worms. Twenty years ago I didn't have a free-spool casting reel, I didn't use a spin-nerbait. But back then (as well as now) there were a lot of bass hidden way back underneath the willows, heavy timber, and trees. We didn't go after them; we really didn't have the tackle or the lures to go after them (in this case, a snagless spinnerbait); and, too, there were so many more "easy fish" to catch, and those easier ones were what we fished for.

Within the past two decades it seems that just about all of the easy fish have been caught. Everybody's pounded the daylights out of all the nice open areas, and not many of the bass that stayed in those open areas are around any more.

The great majority of the bass which are left are descendants of those in the heavy cover. Those bass we never bothered years ago in that heavy cover survived the onslaught of heavy fishing pressure, and their offspring are more wary, more seclusive, less accessible.

Less accessible bass certainly are the ones you'll be fishing for when you try crashing the willows. Almost any lake, whether it's Santee or a flooded lake in the upper Mississippi River drainage area or a lake in Ohio, has some willow trees. If you're good at being real sneaky, put on your Polaroid glasses and peep way back into the depths of a partly submerged willow tree. You're apt to see a largemouth 20 to 30 feet back in those branches.

Doug Odom, a friend of mine who moved to Orangeburg, S.C., from Florida in the early 1970s and started fishing Santee-Cooper, developed the system of crashing the willows, and it's a very effective way to fish. What Doug does is use a giant long-armed spinnerbait—a ⅝-ounce or a 1-ounce size—and he makes a very hard, beeline, bulletlike cast right into the willows. About half the time his bait hits a heavy limb and stops, but the other half the time it blasts through the leaves, branches, and twigs and gets to the center of the tree. Once he gets it all the way back there, he simply jigs the spinnerbait up and down. The bass are in there, and it's just a matter of angering them a little bit, and jigging a lure makes them angry.

Odom catches a lot of big bass—5-to-7-pounders—at Santee by crashing the willows in this manner. In fact, during the second **BASS** tournament at Santee (1976), Odom crashed the willows and nearly won. He finished second.

My first experience at crashing the willows came a year or two before that, but I didn't do this quite the way Doug Odom does. I was at Kerr (Buggs Island) Reservoir on the Virginia-North Carolina line, and I had seen some bass way in behind some partly submerged willows. With two types of lures—plastic worms and spinnerbaits—I'd get fairly close to willows which were up to 20 feet tall, and when I'd spot a bass, I'd make a very high, arching cast to the top of the tree. I'd shake the lure and keep shaking it until I got it free and down into the water.

This system had its advantages, but the biggest disadvantage was that once I finally hooked the bass, I couldn't get him out without cranking up the motor and crashing back there. I was parachuting the bait through the limbs and juggling it and lowering it down to the water. I now use the technique Doug Odom came up with. I use a heavier bait and make a hard, direct cast through the limbs to get to the center of the bush.

One condition needed in willow crashing is some deep water. You need to find a willow tree that hangs over deeper water. Two feet of water isn't good enough, although some spawning bass get beneath willow trees in water that shallow. Mainly it's a hot-summer pattern when water temperatures are in the 70s to 80s and the very shady places hold a few big bass which are virtually inaccessible. You also need to look for water which has a little bit of color or dinge. In super-clear water they'll spook somewhat when you crash your bait into the willows.

In most every large reservoir, willow trees often grow along the riverbanks in the upper end at the headwaters. For some reason in very hot weather the bass prefer a little current when they can find it. They like to lie in the shade of the willows or logs or stumps and let

Willows seem to flourish along the riverbanks in the upper end of most impoundments—and with a spinnerbait you can get right in them.

This 2½-pounder was just fanning in the willows till my spinnerbait came jigging by. Look for willows in fairly deep and somewhat dingy water.

the current drift to them. They're in a good ambush point. Santee is typical of this type of reservoir, and in Oklahoma there are Grand Lake and Hudson and others. These impoundments fluctuate very little; any lake with generally the same water level throughout the year with less than 3 feet of fluctuation often has these willows. The older the lake, the better the chance of there being willows, because the willow trees are secondary growth. After the lake is impounded, the willows start growing.

When I'm crashing the willows, I want the water to be 4 to 10 feet deep, and I jig the spinnerbait 2 to 3 feet deep. The best willows usually are found on large points. At the upper end of the lake might be a little shoal or an island. With the current, this is an isolated structure usually with a dropoff, and this is the kind of area which bass—even schools of bass—use. The advantage of using 20- pound and 25-pound line is that small willow branches are very brittle, and when you hang on these branches, you can jerk and snap the lure right off the branch with no trouble. Another thing I do is when I see a particularly long limb sticking out, I purposely cast over the limb so I can jig the spinnerbait. This jigging technique is what entices the larger bass. The little ones hit right away, but often the 4-to-7-pounders hit only after you've jigged the lure ten to fifteen times.

22 Pumping the Timber

Deepwater spinnerbait fishing is something I very seldom used to do before being paired with a good ol' Georgia boy named Cliff Craft in the B.A.S.S. tournament at Toledo Bend in 1976. I wasn't very familiar with the pattern one might call "pumping the timber" with a spinnerbait until I fished with this young pro who lives near Lake Lanier. Cliff is quite a spinnerbait fisherman, and Lanier is a deep lake, and he likes to fish deep with the spinner.

I'd gone out in practice at Toledo Bend with a good friend, Paul Chamblee from Raleigh, N.C. Paul's a regular fishing partner of that Columbia, S.C., fisherman Billy Goff, who, as I've mentioned, first showed me what I'd been missing at Santee-Cooper by not using the spinnerbait. Anyway, Paul and I fished that warmup period when it was cloudy and the bass were real active and eager. We'd thrown a lot of small red crank baits and a few jigs, and we'd caught some really nice bass. One day we caught sixteen from 4 pounds on up. We figured we really had found the best spot in the whole 190,000 acres of Toledo Bend. We were fishing the upper end of the lake along some ridges and timbered areas. We weren't worried, and we just knew we'd take the first two places in the tournament.

Well, I got paired with Craft in the first round, and he had several spinnerbaits tied on his rods, and he mentioned he'd been catching bass 10 to 15 feet deep with the spinners. We got out to my jig-and-eel hole and I told him the bass were 10 to 15 feet deep but they weren't hitting spinnerbaits—they were hitting the jigs and eels. My first cast through the hole produced a bass slightly over 5 pounds. Then I threw back and caught another 5-pounder. Cliff believed me and said he was going to try the jig too, if that's what they were hitting.

We threw jigs, and even threw some worms, but after those two bass the action slowed down. That's all we caught, and finally after about half an hour on that spot, Cliff said he'd fished too many spinnerbaits deep in this kind of heavy timber not to believe the bass in this spot wouldn't hit 'em. He tied on a white spinnerbait with a

½-ounce head and a No. 4 nickel blade, and he cast out there to where we'd been fishing the jigs and eels. He let the spinnerbait sink to the bottom, and then he just pumped it up about a foot or so and let it sink back down as if he were fishing a worm.

On his first cast, he was holding the rod high, and as the bait was fluttering down, he said, "Oh! There's a strike!"

He didn't set the hook instantly; he just lowered his rod and reeled in the slack and about three seconds later he set the hook and caught a 6-pounder. I asked him about not setting the hook when he felt the fish. He said that in deep water they'll hold the bait a few seconds and he just reels down so he'll get a good hook set. He was using a standard spinnerbait with no plastic or pork trailer! I couldn't half believe what I saw!

I missed a couple of bass on the jig and eel, and I figured I'd stay with it. But Cliff repeated his procedure. He said he had a strike, and then he reeled down and set the hook and got another one. He started catching 4-to-6-pounders. Every five to ten minutes he'd nail a big bass, and I wasn't getting any strikes.

The area we were fishing was a flooded forest with limbs everywhere in the timber. Cliff simply pulled his spinnerbait up into the limbs and shook it through them. When he got it 3 or 4 feet off the bottom, he'd let it flutter back down. Many of his strikes came near the bigger trees. As his lure fell, he watched his line and would detect a little twitch. Then he'd reel down and set the hook two to three

Pumping the timber requires a ½-ounce head with a long wire and No. 4 or No. 5 blade. The spinnerbait is used pretty much like a jig.

seconds later. He had eleven strikes and put ten of 'em in the boat and those ten totaled 44 pounds. I ended up with only five fish weighing 19 pounds. Cliff led the tournament after the first day. I finally put on a spinnerbait, and on my first strike I set the hook too quickly and missed him. Then on another fish I set too hard and broke my line.

The second day Cliff tried some different water, and he caught only a couple of fish, but they were 5-to-6-pounders. In the meantime Paul Chamblee had been fishing spinnerbaits early in the shallower pockets and shallower ridges, and later in the day he worked out deeper with his red crank baits (he was using a Mud Bug). Paul finished second in the tournament, and Cliff Craft was third as the result of having a good third round. Cliff also caught the largest bass. Spinnerbaits helped account for second and third places in that tournament, and it was the pumping technique which really worked for Chamblee and Craft. I just didn't catch on to it.

Paul and Cliff were both using spinnerbaits with 1/2-ounce heads. They were using the long-wire models with the wire coming all the way back to the hook. This made the bait very snagless, and both of them were using No. 4 and No. 5 blades. Paul was using a white blade, and Cliff used a nickel blade. Neither was using a trailer hook, because it was so brushy you couldn't get a trailer hook through the limbs and timber without hanging up. They were using single blades because they wanted to feel the thump as the bait settled. Paul was fishing a little shallower than Cliff, but he also was pumping the timber. Paul was setting the hook a little faster than Cliff was, and he missed a few fish.

This was early spring, and the water temperatures were in the low to middle 50s. It was a pre-spawn condition, and the pre-spawners were in schools and were slow and lethargic. When the water's cloudy and warming up fast, these fish will come up a little shallower and will hit crank baits better. But when it's bright and sunny, they'll lie under the brush and they're quite hard to catch. You really have to aggravate them. That's exactly what the spinnerbait was doing when it fluttered down on 'em. I think they were hitting it somewhat out or reflex action and out of anger.

The jig and eel is a good bait for some of this type of fishing, but I think they strike it more out of hunger when they're more active. At times the spinnerbait with it's slow, fluttering action in heavy timber will outproduce virtually any other bait.

The south has twenty-five to thirty good timbered reservoirs

While pumping seems to work best in big timber, don't be afraid to try the smaller trees.

where this pumping technique will catch a lot of bass. These reservoirs range from Table Rock in Missouri to Santee-Cooper in the southeast, Seminole in Georgia and Toledo Bend and Rayburn in the southwest. This type of bassing is best in pre-spawn conditions when the water is 50 to 60 degrees, and the basic depths are 5 to 15 feet. Almost all water clarities pay off, but in a very clear lake such as Table Rock, the bass will be a little deeper—maybe 20 feet down. In the dingier lakes, they might be only 5 feet deep.

I prefer the ½-ounce and ⅝-ounce spinnerbaits for pumping the timber. When you're fishing deeper, such as in Table Rock, the slightly heavier spinnerbait flutters down a little faster and gets to the bottom of the cedar trees better. Table Rock has a lot of cedar trees 15 to 25 feet deep, and you almost can jig the spinnerbait in some of these trees and catch bass. With this pattern, wind doesn't seem to make any difference, but the sun puts them a little deeper. I like a stiff-action casting rod—almost a worm type of rod—and look for heavy matted timber and throw well past the big trees. I cast and leave the button pushed on my reel until the lure settles to the bottom. I also use 20-pound line.

When the bait's on the bottom, the retrieve is similar to deepwater worm fishing. Pull up the bait until you hit a few limbs. If there aren't any limbs, pump it up a foot or so and let it flutter back to the bottom. Hold a little bit of back pressure on the lure so you can feel the strike. In deep water, 90 percent of the strikes occur as the bait is falling. This is true with plastic worms, spoons, and grubs as well as with spinnerbaits. If there's a lot of heavy brush, your spinnerbait actually has to ride up 5 or 6 feet to clear a lot of those limbs when you're retrieving it. The bait will get hung temporarily in the limbs, and you have to lower it a foot or so and sort of jerk it a little to get it to roll over the limb. Occasionally you'll get hung up and lose your bait. Also, you need to be a line watcher for this fishing.

I've never been one to let a bass run with a spinnerbait, but Cliff Craft says when they strike in cool water, he likes to let them take it and get the slack out of his line and lower his rod to get a good hook set. Cliff pumps the spinnerbait in Lake Lanier where there's very little timber. He just calls it pumping the structure. He's fishing rocks, boulders, and structure. This same basic pumping technique could be applied to pumping weedlines and rock shoals in northern lakes during this pre-spawn period—provided, of course, that the state fishing season is open.

TOPWATER PLUGS AND BUZZ BAITS

The late James Heddon, who founded the Heddon Tackle Company, is credited with manufacturing the first commercially sold plug. As the old story goes, Heddon was sitting on the bank of a creek near his Dowagiac, Mich., home town and was whittling a piece of wood while awaiting his fishing companion on down the stream. He flipped the wood idly into the water and happened to see a bass come up and knock hell out of it. This experience induced him to go home and carve a piece of wood and fasten hooks to it. His first wooden plugs were shaped to resemble small frogs, and he carved them for himself and his fishing buddies.

Clyde A. Harbin, an outstanding fishing-lure collector in Memphis, Tenn., has one of Heddon's original frogs. Harbin fished the first B.A.S.S. tournament. But Heddon's first lure on the market was called the Dowagiac Expert, and it was a surface floater.

I vividly remember my first topwater strike from a bass. I was only twelve and was working a little torpedo-shaped topwater plug along the shore in Lanier Lake in central Maryland. A small bass, about 1½ pounds, boiled at the plug. He didn't really get it the first time, and I jerked the plug clean out of the water and up into the trees behind me. The boil looked so big I just knew that I had a 5- or 6-pounder to hit out there. When I threw back on the second cast, he sucked it in, and this time I caught him. I also remember my second; after I set the hook he started jumping wildly.

One thing about a surface strike is the fish is already on the top, and often right away he starts jumping. The visual contact and excitement of watching the lure combines with the anticipation of the strike, the strike itself, and the subsequent jumps of the fish to make topwater fishing one of the most exciting forms of fishing I know of. Unfortunately, surface bait fishing has not been the most successful way of catching heavy strings of bass. Of the approximately one hundred bass-fishing tournaments I'm familiar with, only three or four ever were won with surface baits. Shorty Evans of Houston, Mo., won an old Project: Sports Incorporated (PSI) tournament about 1972 at Sam Rayburn. He was using a chrome-finished Heddon Chugger. Charlie Campbell of Forsythe, Mo., won the B.A.S.S. Chapter tournament at Table Rock in 1974 on the Zara Spook top-water plug. He caught 55½ pounds. And another guy whose name I've forgotten won a $50,000 PSI tournament in 1971 on Rayburn with a Burke popper-type plug. That was in hot summer, and the guy was twitching the plug in heavy timber. In the BASS Masters Classic in 1972 at Percy Priest Reservoir in Tennessee, Stan Sloan caught a 5½-pounder on a Jitterbug on a rainy, overcast day, and that took big-bass honors in the tournament.

One of the premier topwater-plug fisherman in the country has to be Ed Totenbier of Natchitoches, La. Ed's now in his fifties, and he's traveled all over the country. He's owned fish camps in Florida, and fished perhaps a hundred different major reservoirs in the country. His whole bag is challenging a bass with a topwater plug. Sure, he knows there are many times he can't catch them on surface baits, and then he'll go to worms and other lures in cold weather, but when he

This tacklebox has an accumulation of old and new baits. I've never stopped to count them.

finds any sort of decent topwater-plugging water, he's going to challenge them on the surface. Ed's told me many times that outside of a tournament, he wouldn't trade catching a limit of bass on an underwater lure for catching one on a surface bait. He gets that much excitement and enjoyment out of fishing a topwater plug.

Totenbier does a lot of special things to his topwater plugs. For one thing, he likes to build his own plugs and modify others. He'll take a regular Nip-I-Dee-Dee (a South Bend propeller-type surface plug) and remove the propellers and carve the body of the bait to make it more streamlined. Then he bends the propellers so they'll rotate faster and puts them back on the plug. He paints a lot of his plugs wild colors, but he's one of the first to agree that the color of topwater plugs

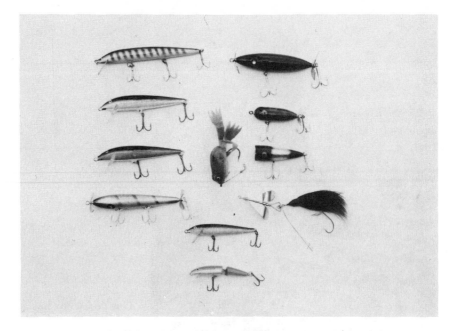

My favorites: stick-type plugs with and without props, jointed plug, popper, weedless frog, and a Floyd's Buzzer.

doesn't make a tremendous amount of difference. He just likes to come up with unique lures.

One time at a tournament at Lake Millwood in Arkansas, Totenbier gave me a yellow cut-down Nip-I-Dee-Dee. I had been practicing with him, and he guaranteed me I'd catch a limit on that plug he gave me if I used it. I went up to the headwaters of the lake on the first day of the tournament, and sure enough I caught a fifteen-bass limit that day. I can't ever remember a more exciting day of tournament fishing. But the next two days I caught bigger bass on crank baits in heavy timber, and those bigger ones enabled me to win the tournament. But I had far more fun and excitement twitching that ol' customized yellow Nip-I-Dee-Dee and luring the bass to hit on those creek channels. I'd let that plug lie there for five or six seconds and see a boil come up around it. A lot of the fun was in knowing the next time I slightly twitched that plug, the water was going to explode.

Two friends of mine I used to fish with when I was in South Carolina in the army at Ft. Jackson and later when I guided at Santee were Odell and Betty Haire from Charlotte, N.C. Both had caught a lot of big bass, including several over 10 pounds and one apiece over 11 pounds in the late 1960s. By 1970 they weren't tired of catching bass, but they needed a sort of shot in the arm to boost their interest and enthusiasm. I happened to mention to Odell that in all my seven years at Santee, I'd caught twenty-four bass over 10 pounds, but only one of them was on a topwater plug. It got Odell to thinking, and he and Betty set out in 1970 to catch bass over 10 pounds on surface baits.

That same year Odell was down in the Russelville Flats, a 10,000-acre area of the lower lake (Lake Moultrie), and he was working the

When a bass hits a topwater lure you can usually depend on jumps and surface acrobatics.

Jon Petree, who filmed my early TV series, lands a Florida largemouth that took a topwater plug next to a cypress tree.

button bushes about 2 feet deep with a plug I helped design and develop—Capt. Jim Strader's Diamond Rattler. The large prop plug is about 4 inches long, and Odell was using a blue one. He was churning it along slow in the shade of these bushes, and an 11¼-pounder grabbed his plug. It turned out to weigh exactly what his biggest bass ever had been, and that other one had been caught on a plastic worm. He and Betty have caught several bass over 10, but to this day he says that one which hit his Diamond Rattler was the most exciting fish he ever had strike.

In Florida I caught two other bass over 10 pounds on top water. But catching a 10-pounder on a surface lure is very difficult. Conditions have to be ideal, and this happens maybe only 10 to 20 percent of the time during the entire year. You need a calm or nearly calm surface, warm temperatures, and possibly some cloud cover, as well as big bass willing to strike on the surface. There are a lot of prerequisites to topwater fishing that don't often happen.

I've caught bass up to 13 pounds on live bait, but strangely enough the biggest one I ever took on a lure struck on the surface. That was the 12¼-pounder I caught in Rodman Pool in Florida in 1973. The

Conditions have to be right for topwater fishing. One requirement is fairly quiet water, as here.

plug—a hand-carved balsawood bait made by Mike Estep of Oak Ridge, Tenn.—is not really a surface bait, but this big bass struck it on the top. It was a weird chain of events. I was out with my father-in-law, Paul Colbert, during practice for the Florida Invitational B.A.S.S. tournament on the St. Johns River. I made a long cast to a leaning log in the middle of Rodman, and I had the most peculiar line tangle in my reel that I've ever seen. The line was all twisted up. Paul said it was a backlash, but I've never seen a backlash like that. I was sitting there picking out this tangle and the Estep plug was floating in the ripples. It was lying right against the log, and when I finally got my line untangled and was reeling in the slack, the least little bit of pressure on that plug moved it away from the log. It was moving on top when this huge fish just exploded on it. Luckily he hit it so well that he sucked it completely inside his mouth, and when I got my line tight and was able to get a good hook set, he was there. I had a heavy rod with 20-pound line, and the fish started jumping. I never before or since have seen a bass that big jump and clear the water that many times. The fish was in the air about eight times, each time trying to throw the plug.

Several lures fit the category of topwater lures. I'm going to discuss the floating-diving lures like the Rapalas, the Chugger types, and the propeller types like the Diamond Rattler, and also another type of topwater lures called buzz baits or buzzer baits. (These latter really are spinnerbaits rather than plugs which float, but they're retrieved fast and the spinner chugs the water and keeps the lure on top.)

Another type of topwater fishing that's productive is spoon fishing in heavy grass. The spoon is run on top of the water, and again you have visual contact with the lure. Even a plastic worm can be used as a surface bait on top of lily pads and weeds. Just snaking anything on the surface is what I'm calling topwater fishing.

One of the truths about topwater fishing is that it works good only from spawning season on. In other words, it's not a good pre-spawn pattern unless the water temperature is at least 55 degrees. It begins a little at 55 and gets better at 60. Once they start spawning, they're in the shallow flats, and that's when they really start hitting topwater plugs good. The best temperature seems to be after they spawn. They come off the beds and are fairly hungry, and if there are any bass still shallow and hanging around the shallow bays, they'll hit a surface plug good in the 70-degree zone. At about 75 degrees you get your hardest, most vicious surface strikes and probably the most strikes. You can continue to catch bass on top in the summer all the way up to the 80-degree water temperature when the weather is really sultry and hot, but usually at that time of year a lot of the bass seek heavier, deeper structure. During the July and August dog days, right at dawn and right at dusk are good times to use little prop plugs, and one of my best topwater tricks is working a Musky Jitterbug at night in weedy lakes from Florida to Minnesota.

---

23 Rapala Types for Spawners

There is an interesting history behind the Rapala Plug since it initially was introduced in this country in 1959. (Many anglers call it the "Ra-PAL-uh," but if you want to pronounce it as the inventor, Laurie Rapala, pronounces his last name, say "RAP-ul-uh.") For the past four years I've worked with the Normark Corporation, which imports and distributes the Rapala, and so I know Ray Ostrom and Ron Weber. They're the two guys who discovered the plug over in Finland and

My first Rapala-caught 10½-pounder came from a small pond in the Ocalla National Forest.

brought it to the U.S. to check it and test it out. They and their friends caught so many fish on it that they finally got the U.S. distributorship on it. They tell some exciting stories about the first year it came on the market.

No balsawood types of minnows were on the U.S. market back then, and the old floating/shallow-running plugs of that era were like the Heddon floating River Runt in that they floated at rest and wiggled slowly on the retrieve. The Flatfish and the Lazy Ike were similar. But this small, thin swimming balsa minnow was great for twitching on the top. It had a lifelike, quick little wobble underwater and would pop back to the top real quick on slack line. The high flotation caused an exciting wiggle which bass and other sportfish had never seen before.

Ray Ostrom said that in several of the natural lakes in the Minneapolis area, guys used the Rapala and started catching bass immediately and caught fifty to a hundred in a day. These were taken on the initial dozen or so Rapalas Ray and Ron brought back to this country. There was such a demand for the plugs that Ray and Ron, who had a small tackle shop, started renting out the baits for fifteen to twenty dollars per day. Whoever rented a Rapala had to put up a deposit, and if the guy lost the lure, he forfeited his deposit. This was also done in Florida with the first Rapalas in that state.

Finally in 1959 Ostrom and Weber acquired the distributorship for Rapalas in this country. The plugs cost two to three dollars apiece, but because of the demand and quite often in the tackle shop itself, the plugs were marked up to four, five, and six dollars. The Rapala for a long time was an "under-the-counter" bait. You had to ask for one, because you wouldn't see it on the shelf. Many tackle-store operators reserved Rapalas for themselves and their friends.

One thing that added greatly to the demand for Rapalas was a feature story in Life magazine about 1960 on Laurie Rapala and his lure. Billy Westmorland, a pro and friend of mine from Celina, Tenn., remembers well when the Rapala craze hit Dale Hollow Reservoir, his home lake. He was guiding back then, about 1960, and boat-dock operators wanting newspaper publicity on the fishing out of their docks supplied him with one Rapala at a time. Westmorland says his customers wanted to buy the lures but couldn't because there just weren't any for sale.

The fishing-tackle industry credited the Rapala's introduction into American waters for bringing back the "hard bait" market, which had sagged in the late 1950s after the plastic-worm craze struck.

Ostrom and Weber tell me that to get shipments of Rapalas in from Finland takes almost a year because of the procedure involved. They first have to negotiate the price and figure in the current exchange rate. Then they have to contract for X number of plugs. Then the Rapalas are slowly built by hand. Each one is hand-carved and hand-tested, and it is a very laborious process. After months and months have passed, the plugs are ready for shipment. Then comes the delay in exporting the baits. They have to go through customs, and then they're held in U.S. ports until they're finally cleared and counted and finally distributed up to Normark. From there the baits are shipped to the distributors and then to the tackle shops.

At first, Normark was a small company, and they didn't have enough front money to order a million Rapalas. They had to pay cash for a year in advance, and it was hard for the small company to come up with from $200,000 to $500,000 against sales which would occur the next year. This is why for the first couple of years there was a continual shortage. Normark just couldn't get the financing to order enough plugs.

This shortage of Rapalas really helped create a demand for American-made plugs which are similar to the plug from Finland. The original Rapala was more in demand than the American baits, but the fact that it was so unavailable led to millions of dollars in sales for other companies. Two of the early American long minnow-type baits on the market were the Rebel Minnow (made by Plastics Research and Development at Ft. Smith, Ark.) and Jim Bagley's Bang-O-Lure

A No. 11 Rapala took this 6-pound bass from an Oklahoma strip pit.

(manufactured by the Bagley Bait Co. at Winter Haven, Fla.). The Rebel and the Bang-O-Lure got hot not only because they caught fish, but because fishermen had to settle for them when they couldn't get Rapalas. Bagley was able to carve out Bang-O-Lures quickly and sell and distribute them in a month or so. With plastic injection molding, Rebel was able to mass-produce their lures in a hurry, too.

My first experience with the Rapala was on the Eastern Shore of Maryland on the Chicamacominco River in 1961. I was fishing with Lynn Torbett. Lynn, who died a few years ago, was a casting expert. He machined his own casting reels. He'd take his Pflueger Supreme reels and lap the gears with toothpaste to get them to run faster and smoother, and he even drilled holes in the reel handles to make them lighter. He used very light parabolic rods and light lines, 8-to-12-pound-test. His bag was long-distance casting accuracy, and he was probably the finest caster I've ever met. Torbett machined out a Pflueger Supreme for me several years ago, and we could take a No. 11 Rapala, which weighs only 1/4 ounce, and throw it with a casting rod. You can't do this today with even our modern casting gear, even with a lightweight Ambassador reel, though you can throw a No. 13 Rapala fairly well. Lots of bait casters today use the No. 13 Magnum Rapala, which is 5 1/2 inches long and fatter than the regular model, or the No. 18, which is about 7 inches long.

The small No. 11s were relegated mainly to spinning and spin-casting tackle, and this is another reason the Rapala became so popular. In the late 1950s, American fishermen were being swept up with the spinning-tackle craze. The little 1/5-ounce and 1/4-ounce Rapalas were just perfect for novice and veteran fishermen alike with their spinning or pushbutton (spin-casting) outfits, and the lures were universally used. Virtually everybody could catch bass, trout, northern pike, or some type of gamefish on these little floating-diving-swimming plugs from Finland.

My first bass over 10 pounds in Florida ironically was caught on a No. 11 Rapala out of a small lake in the Ocala National Forest in 1976. That fish weighed 10 1/2 pounds. I had a four-wheel-drive Suburban, and we found a 200-acre lake with no launching facilities. With that Suburban, we launched my bass boat. I'd taken light spinning tackle—8-pound line and a 6 1/2-foot rod—and started twitching Rapalas along the north shore where there were some spawning areas. That's how I caught that bass.

The biggest bass I ever heard of on a Rapala was an 18-pounder

In the clear, shallow areas where bass typically spawn, casts must be long; light spinning tackle will get the Rapala out much easier than will baitcasting gear.

caught from Wall Lake, about twenty miles out of Palatka. Larry Mayer did a newspaper story on Lonnie Petty, the man who caught the monster. Petty, who used to operate a country bar near his Putnam Hall, Fla., residence, was fishing with a No. 11 Rapala, Zebco pushbutton reel, and 8-pound line back in January of 1964 when he caught that fish. Petty said the bass headed out to deep water and the line got caught on one springy strand of bullrush, and the rush kept giving and caused the fish to tire out. I hope I'm that fortunate if I ever hook one that big on 8-pound line—or even on 30-pound line, for that matter.

The pattern which produced that 10½-pounder for me on the Rapala is a dandy one involving spawning bass. A spawning bass hits quite often, and this is particularly true with surface plugs. He's not hungry; he hits the plugs out of protective reasons, ane he's trying to kill the bait. The best day I ever had with a surface bait at Santee was with a large propeller-type plug, the Diamond Rattler. The bass were rolling on the bait that day and were hitting it with their mouths closed. I finally changed the hooks and put real sharp trebles on the bait and actually foul-hooked the four largest ones I landed that day—two 9s and two 8s. One of them was hooked in the tail, two were hooked in the side, and one was hooked on the side of the gill plate. These fish weren't trying to eat the bait, although they were striking it hard.

The same thing happens when you fish a Rapala or a plug similar to it for spawners. When the plug is thrown right over the bed, it intimidates the bass. It's barely twitching for seconds right over the bed, and finally the bass comes up and sort of rolls on it to push it away. Maybe half the time he's eating the plug, but quite often his mouth isn't even open. A Rapala has three fine-wire Aberdeen treble hooks, which are extremely sharp. If the angler's quick on his reflexes when the bass rolls on the plug, lots of times he can drive the hooks into the area of the mouth. He might hook the fish on the side of its jaw, its face, or even on the side of its body and still land it.

The pattern for fishing the Rapala for spawners means going out and finding the spawning areas first. A good fish thermometer will work. When you find a spawning bed, go slow with your trolling motor or get out and wade. If you find several bass in a little pocket, you really need to work slowly and cautiously. Fish the Rapala early in the morning or late in the evening or during cloudy weather. The technique is to throw 2 to 3 feet past the spawning bed. When you're in shallow water and are looking toward the bed, it often appears to be a little closer to you than it actually is. This is because of the reflection angle of the water. When I'm casting to the bed, I purposely throw a couple of feet past the actual outline of the bed.

This type of fishing needs to be done on a completely calm day. Wind messes up this pattern because it drifts the plug away, and if the bass is there on the bed, he doesn't have to be concerned with the lure because it drifts away by itself. But if it's completely calm, the plug hits a foot or so from his bed and lies there motionless. Keep sufficient slack line in the water and don't put any pressure on the lure, because any tension would cause it to move. Let the plug lie there for ten to even thirty seconds. The bass really gets nervous at this point, and usually it's the small male bass that gets the most nervous. He's normally more aggressive than the female, and he'll often be the first to rise up and slap at the bait.

After ten to thirty seconds, give it that first small twitch. Don't even make the bait go beneath the surface. Finally after about three twitches, make it dart under for the first time. If he didn't hit it during those twitches, he's apt to be looking at it. Now the bait is probably a few feet from the bed. Run it 2 or 3 feet beneath the water and let it float back up to the top. Then run it down for 2 or 3 more feet and let it float up to the top again. Usually if a bass is following it that first couple times it dives, he often will nail it when it floats up that second time. At this time the plug is still halfway between you and the bed, so you can reel it back in. Occasionally you'll be reeling it in a foot or so beneath the surface, and you'll come over another bass or another spawner you didn't see, and you might get that one to hit. This swimming action back to the boat accounts for 10 to 15 percent of my strikes with this pattern, even though these can be considered somewhat accidental.

This is one reason the Rapala and similar plugs are more effective than the old surface plug which floats all the time. With the strictly floating plug, when you've fished the ambush point (in this case, the spawning area), you finally reel in the plug and it skits along the top, and you get very few strikes on a regular surface plug during that last part of the retrieve. With the Rapala, you get those bonus strikes on the last part of the retrieve.

Sometimes the topwater twitching technique doesn't work. After a couple of casts where I've worked the lure in those small twitches and didn't get the fish to hit, I might try a faster retrieve. I know the fish is there, and I'm trying to provoke him. I cast repeatedly and run the lure faster right over the bed. Sometimes after six to ten casts, each time swimming the lure over the bed, the bass blows his cool and hits out of anger in addition to his protective instinct. I don't really give up on a spawning bass.

As I've explained previously, the male not only is more aggressive and less cautious than the female, but he spends three weeks guarding the nest, so chances are you'll catch a lot more males. Sometimes you'll still see a big female bass, but she won't strike. After I catch the male, I release him and usually return later, because with topwater fishing, the first cast is probably the most important cast. If the female doesn't hit after eight or nine casts, I figure she's a real trophy and I'll return and try again for her later. I like to go back about thirty minutes later. Bass don't have a long memory; when they spook, they normally get over their wariness in fifteen to twenty minutes. In thirty minutes I sneak back there and try to make that first long cast perfect.

Generally you need light spinning tackle for the long cast, because most of the spawning waters are in clear, shallow areas. If there's any wind blowing, you probably won't be able to cast properly. A small Rapala floats in the wind. On that first cast, give the lure another ten-to-thirty-second pause and then the series of slight twitches. This is most effective for a big female, and after you've caught the male, she usually hits on that very first cast when you return.

Another thing about spawning bass is that you definitely need to be ready for a tiny strike. For some reason—I've never been able to figure out why—lots of times when a big female hits a topwater plug of any description, she sucks the bait in so delicately that it looks like a bluegill has barely pulled the plug under. What she does is flare her gills and create a suction or vacuum which pulls the plug under and into her mouth with no wake, boil, or swirl on the surface. The plug sort of just disappears, and that's exactly what happened when I got that 10½-pounder on the Rapala.

---

24 Prop Plugs for Feeders

When I was a kid, I fished Heddon's Tiny Torpedo for smallmouths in the Potomac River, but I had never caught any lunker bass on a propeller-type surface plug. My first serious experience with these prop plugs was in 1967, when I met Jim Strader out of Florida. Jim had come to Santee-Cooper for me to guide him. He had heard about my success with Santee's big largemouths, and he had designed a new plug, the Diamond Rattler. The plug is a cigar-shaped propeller plug about 4 inches long, and it has little glass diamond-like eyes with two very sharp English-type treble hooks with round-ground points like the old Mepps Spinner hooks of several years ago.

When Jim met me that morning, he said he was promoting a new bait which he really wanted to fish at Santee. He wanted me to fish the plug, too, and he was confident we'd catch a lot of bass on 'em. I reminded him the time was July, the water was 85 to 88 degrees, and the weather was clear, and that we'd catch ten times more bass on worms than on his propellered topwater plug.

Billy Goff and I had a theory called "big bass, high noon." We'd go to the heavy stickups and thick cypress trees and catch bass on plastic worms on the hottest days of summer at high noon. Writers like Earl Shelsby, who was with a Baltimore newspaper back then, had done stories on us catching big bass in the middle of the day. But the whole thing had been with plastic worms, and none of us really had ever tried surface plugs then. The bass were in about 5 feet of water which was fairly clear, and they were way down in the shade beneath those heavy branches.

Anyhow, Jim Strader said he still thought he could catch a few bass on his Diamond Rattler. He had a blue one, and he said blue was the best color. We started out first thing in the morning and went to some grass beds and lily pads. Sure enough, he caught a couple, including a 6-pounder, on his new plug. I explained—sort of dismissed it—that he'd caught those bass because the sun hadn't gotten up yet on the water. Jim was working the plug pretty fast, and one thing about hot weather is that you often can work a surface plug quick over a lot of weeds, whereas in the early spring you have to slow it down. Bass have high metabolism rates when the water's warmer, and they'll hit a plug pretty fast.

About nine o'clock the bass quit hitting in the shallow water, and I told him that for us to catch any really trophy bass, we'd have to go to the heavy, deep willows and fish about 5 feet deep in the center of the lake and the center of the bays. He still was confident he could catch a few of 'em on his topwater plug, but I thought his optimism was completely ridiculous. No bass would come out of 5 or 6 feet of water to hit a dumb ol' topwater plug in the middle of the day. About an hour later we were fishing in these heavy willows, and Jim gets a strike. The bass was about 8 pounds, and he smashed the plug pretty hard. The fish was already on the top, and with 20-pound line and a fairly stiff rod, Strader rolled him right on out past the last couple of limbs and into open water. The bass jumped five or six times. I really was amazed at a topwater strike like that in clear weather in hot July.

Of course, I'd been worm fishing, and I thought the bass I'd been catching were on the bottom, but I figured out that many of the fish weren't always on the bottom. Some were probably only a couple of feet deep in the shade of the bigger limbs. Jim, who is a very accurate caster, was putting his plug right in next to the logs and limbs.

Next we came to some cypress trees, and again he could cast his heavy plug beneath the overhanging limbs to the shady side of the trees right next to the trunk. That's what I was doing with plastic worms. You needed to have your lure right against the trunk on the shady side beneath the limbs. There was almost no wind, and his Diamond Rattler lay there for fifteen to twenty seconds, and the very first time he twitched it, a 6-pounder blew all over it. I couldn't say much at this point; I knew the bass were in the shade, but the fact they were hitting topwater plugs really freaked me out! I had caught several bass on surface baits in the spring around the shallow weeds and the spawning areas, but certainly not in the middle of the summer. We were fishing deepcover, 5 and 6 feet of water, in the middle of the lake, and he was catching big bass.

Finally about noon I told him I just had to try one of those plugs. I caught one almost 8 pounds, and we ended the day with four big bass. I had caught a few on the worms, but the largest bass were the ones

I spotted this one chasing shad— an ideal situation to try a prop plug; he tried to take my Devils Horse away from me.

we got on topwater plugs. We took some fine photos of those big bass, and Jim Strader subsequently used some of the pictures in his advertising.

I've been throwing topwater plugs for a long time, and I recognize their limitations, but a propeller plug for feeding bass is a superstrong pattern. You need fairly clear water, and the pattern usually works from 2 feet to 6 feet deep. If the water's clear enough, they'll hit a surface plug in 6 feet of water. This is a very old pattern which old-timers used in the summertime. They'd go out on the water at the crack of dawn and be back in by the time the rest of the people were getting up around the resort, and they'd get three or four big bass on a good morning. All a lot of 'em used back twenty-five years ago were prop plugs like the South Bend Nip-I-Dee-Dee, the Heddon S.O.S. or the Wounded Spook, and the Creek Chub Injured Minnow. Those were big ol' fat plugs with propellers on both ends, and they were heavy enough to cast good with 25-pound braided nylon line and the level-wind casting reels of that era.

The best and probably the major feeding time of the whole day is the first two hours of the morning. That's when the old guys went out—when it was just light enough to see, and somewhere about eight or eight-thirty a.m., the sun got on the water and the activity quit. Many times you'll not see any fish breaking on the lakes. Part of the pattern is the fact that no matter what I'm fishing, if I see any surface activity, I know the prop plugs will catch those fish. These are feeders in that area actually feeding. A prop plug excites them and makes a lot of noise. It draws fish from a long distance away. Those short twitches which make the propellers churn the water are really effective on feeding fish.

I basically look for shallow points, shallow brush, or shallow weedbeds during the first two hours of dawn. I move the prop plug fairly quickly. Throw it out and let it sit four or five seconds, give it a short twitch, and then repeat this procedure. With the ambush points, I use a different system. I throw to a single tree, bush, or stump, and once I twitch the plug 4 or 5 feet past the ambush point, I don't think he'll hit if he hasn't done so already, and I retrieve the lure back quickly and throw to another ambush point. Along shallow weedlines or shallow points I retrieve the lure all along the area, because the bass could be anywhere along the point or weeds.

One spring I was in Tyler, Texas, for a store promotion. It was May, and the bass had finished spawning. We went up to Lake Pales-

This is a good spot for early-morning feeders. If you see any surface activity, you can almost always get a bass to hit a prop bait.

tine, which is a timbered reservoir characteristic of many of the Corps of Engineers lakes in Texas. Texas has 179 major reservoirs with a total of over 2 million acres of water. The guide took me into a big cove where he said the bass had spawned a week or two before, but now the water was 75 degrees. I had my 18-foot Ranger bass boat. He said we needed to get in behind a bunch of logs, and right away the boat got hung up in the logs. I made a few casts with a spinnerbait and a worm and caught a couple of small ones, but way back in there where we couldn't reach with the boat, I saw some bass chasing shad. We didn't have any waders, but I suggested we jump out of the boat anyhow and go wading back into there. So we did that. I had some plastic worms in my pocket and also a Devils Horse wrapped up in a piece of paper. (The Devils Horse is one of the modern favorites in the propeller-plug family, and it's been that for probably twenty years.)

A lot of logs were lying under the surface. I tied on the Devils Horse and threw it back where the shad were jumping. I was twitching it along in little short spurts when about a 4-pounder blew over it. I wasn't ready for him and I didn't have heavy enough line, and the bass dived down in the heavy brush and hung the plug on the log. That's the problem with logs and brush fishing when you're not using heavy line. Much of the lure usually is on the outside of the fish's mouth, and when he goes beneath the brush, the plug gets snagged on something. This is true with a crank bait as well as a surface bait.

The bass was hung on the log and was thrashing around, and he put so much pressure on the hooks that he straightened them out and got off. That's what usually happens with a good-sized bass when he gets hung up like that. I got my plug back and bent back the hooks and proceeded to catch another one of almost 5 pounds. This was early in the morning, and for the next two hours those bass continued to feed. I went back to town for the store promotion with my limit, and they weighed a little more than 30 pounds. We had a pair of 6-pounders and some 4- and 5-pounders. My companion said he had a small pond which he'd like to put those bass in, so we put them in my giant live well in the boat and that afternoon took them out to his pond and released them. They all survived, and they're in his small pond to be caught again another day.

Topwater patterns really can pay off if you observe the conditions and particularly if you see any fish breaking early in the morning. Put on a good prop plug and cover some water and work it fast, and you're liable to hit some of the most explosive fishing you've ever had. It might not last long—maybe only twenty or thirty minutes—but it certainly might be memorable.

---

25 Drifting a Surface Bait

This is an obscure pattern, but at times it has put several extra bass in my live well. It's really a super trick which I doubt if a lot of fishermen have thought about. I ran across it a few years ago on Oklahoma's Grand Lake, which is almost like a mountain lake in that it has no timber and is very clear. The water at the time was high, and the lake has a lot of willow bushes and hundreds of boat docks around the shoreline in the different coves. I had heard the bass were hitting

This one strikes my surface bait
with fury and dives for cover.
You can get them in such a state
of mind by repeatedly drifting
and twitching the lure over them.

topwater plugs pretty good early in the morning. This particular
morning I'd gone to some points and had caught two or three bass on
swimming lures and a couple on a Devils Horse. About ten a.m. I quit
plug fishing.

I saw a guy I know who is a tackle salesman for Okiebug Tackle in
Tulsa. He was in a cove near Horse Creek, and there were a lot of big
willow bushes hanging in the water. I eased up to them and noticed
the wind was blowing in there, but I didn't think much about it. I
happened to look up and saw this guy set the hook and battle about a
5-pounder. I went over to him and looked in his live well, and he had
three real nice bass. He said he'd been catching them on the surface
for the past two hours. I commented that it had gotten bright and
sunny since about eight o'clock.

He said that didn't matter because he was drifting his topwater
lures. I asked him what he meant, and he used the big willow tree
where he'd caught the 5-pounder I saw him get as an example. He said

he had thrown his plug, a Bang-O-Lure, to the upwind side of the willow and about as close as he could get to it. There was a five-mile-per-hour breeze, and he kept stripping out line and letting the plug drift 6 to 10 feet back up underneath the willows. You never could have cast back that far where he was getting his lure. Finally when his lure got just as far back under the willows as it would go, he would twitch it a couple of times. The bass which were lying there in the shade would explode on the plug.

Since then I've fished this pattern effectively, not only beneath willows but also up under boat docks as well. You sure can get your bait back into places you can't throw to. This pattern worked well for me once in a tournament on Kerr (Buggs Island) Reservoir in Virginia back in 1973. I used Rapalas and Devils Horses and let the gentle breeze blow them back under the willows.

This pattern is by far at its best in the summer, with the advantage being that in hot weather the bass seek very heavy shade in the middle of the day. From ten a.m. on through the heat of the day, the bass are up under this heavy cover. It could be a boat dock or a leaning tree in addition to willows. You don't want a real strong wind—just a gentle breeze. Fairly clear water is needed, but the depth isn't particularly important because the bass are suspended. The depth might be from a foot to 25 feet in the case of a big old willow tree leaning over the edge of the river channel. But the bass will be suspended up beneath the branches, and they'll really hit a topwater plug if the water's clear and the weather's hot.

A lot of patience is required to do this type of fishing. It takes from ten to twenty seconds for the plug to drift slowly up beneath the object. You have to keep paying out line off your reel to keep it drifting back, and you need to watch closely because many times the strikes aren't hard. They just suck it in when it gets back over 'em. Another problem is that a lot of bluegills often are concentrated beneath the willow trees and boat docks, too. They'll pop the plug, and if you set the hook real hard on them, you've blown the cast.

I've done this same thing beneath the cypress trees at Santee-Cooper. I'd use a prop plug and let it drift back against the trunk of the tree, and as soon as it got to the trunk I'd give it a quick twitch. Then I'd let it drift back to the base of the tree and twitch it again. Sometimes I'd do this five to ten times at the base of the same tree, and finally he'd bust it. This would be an anger strike. After you've repeated this drifting and twitching process several times in the same spot, a big bass gets infuriated, and he strikes with a lot of fury and vengeance. Some of the most exciting surface strikes I've ever had have come after these repeated drifts and twitches back beneath over-hanging cover.

26   Buzzing the Cover

How'd you like to win $25,000 with a lure? That's what Rick Clunn did in the 1977 BASS Masters Classic on Florida's West Lake Toho-pekaliga. He was "buzzing." And how would you like to win $15,000 the same way? That's what I did in the B.A.S.S. tournament that same year on West Point Lake on the Georgia-Alabama line. I too was "buzzing," and I won the tournament by catching some of my biggest bass on the buzzer.

Buzzers have been around for probably more than fifty years. There are all sorts of spinner-type baits which really are surface lures, but for some strange reason they were out of vogue for ten to fifteen years before about 1974. During that period hardly anyone fished a spinnerbait-type lure with a propeller.

Three or four years ago I was at Kerr Reservoir in Virginia for a B.A.S.S. tournament, and Loyd McEntire of Indianapolis had this brand-new bait. It was a Floyd's Buzzer made by Pat Floyd of India-napolis. I knew Loyd from several previous tournaments, and when he showed me the bait, I asked him what the heck it was. He said it was a buzzer, and he explained that you just throw it by a bush or a stump in a shady spot, crank it back real fast right on top of the water, and keep buzzing it right back to the boat. Loyd noted that a lot of bass were simply exploding on the plug now that the water was clear and warm. He said you get super-strong strikes on it in the late spring and summer, and I told him he had to be kidding. I said the fish are hitting worms, not a topwater bait that's running ten miles an hour.

The thought just seemed completely opposite from what I thought summertime bass should do. My thinking was that in the summer you should fish for them slowly and cautiously with the least noise possi-ble and use something deep like a plastic worm.

Loyd McEntire insisted that the biggest bass he'd been catching in practice for the tournament had been on that crazy buzzer. He was

This Lake Livingston 8-pounder hit the treble-hook trailer on my buzzer. The trailer is practical only in open water, of course.

throwing it past the bush and buzzing it until it bumped into the limbs and passed in the shade of the bush, and as soon as it got a foot or so away from the bush, here would come a 4-to-6-pounder just madder than a tomcat blowing at the bait. I told him I'd try it and that I didn't have one.

Johnny Morris from Bass Pro Shops in Springfield, Mo., and Loyd and I all kind of worked together for this particular tournament. Johnny had a couple of Floyd's Buzzers, and we were going down to Nutbush Creek the day before the tournament. The weather was hazy and a little overcast. I ran my trolling motor on high and started throwing this crazy lure at the submerged willow bushes, and man, those bass started blowing at the bait! The only problem I had was that out of something like twenty strikes, I caught only two or three bass. They were big ones, but many of those bass were knocking the bait away. The lure has a big weedless hook on it.

I told Loyd about my experiences that night and how I'd caught only two or three of the nearly twenty strikes. He asked me if I'd used a "trailer." I said a *what?* He said the bass were striking short and that I needed a second hook attached to the weedless hook. He said even a treble hook might work.

The tournament started, on a bright sunny day, and I knew where those bass were. I went back to that area and started throwing a plastic worm. They ate the worm up! I ended up second in the tournament, but I didn't use the buzzer much. Loyd led the tournament the first day, but the weather conditions changed and the wind blew, messing up his buzzer fishing, and he didn't do much more good.

I really got excited about the buzzer later. I was on Lake Eufaula in Oklahoma with Ray Ostrom and Ron Weber of Normark Company, and I pulled out this lure they'd not seen before. By this time I was using trailer hooks on it. I started throwing it to submerged willows, and my first strike was about a 5-pounder which blew up on the bait and missed it, but the treble hook I was using for a trailer caught him in the cheek. I caught the second bass about the same way, and out of about ten strikes that day, I caught eight bass. I lost only two bass because I had a 5/0 trailer hook behind the main hook and then a treble hook on the trailer hook.

The only disadvantage with the buzzer when you run all those trailer hooks on it is that it then has to be used as an open-water bait. You have to find a spot which has isolated trees or stumps or bushes where you can throw past them in open water as you're buzzing by the spot.

This past year the culmination of my efforts with the buzzer really paid off. I have gone to using treble hooks for trailers almost exclusively on the buzzers. At that tournament I won on West Point Lake, I found some small coves which looked good for the first two to three hours of the day. A lot of others in the tournament were using a buzzer bait called the Lunker Lure. It's a larger-type bait, although now they make a smaller Lunker Lure. The large one makes more noise than Floyd's Buzzer. I was going right behind guys like Roger Moore and others who were using the Lunker Lure. They were catching some

Notice the commotion that buzzer makes. Buzzing is basically a hot-weather pattern—I like the water temperature about 85 degrees!

bass, but with the quieter bait I was using, I was able to catch bass right behind them. Basil Bacon from Rolla, Mo., also was using the Lunker Lure.

Another advantage I had was using the treble hook for a trailer. In fact, one day I even put a treble hook *behind* a treble hook. Roger and Basil were getting strikes and catching several fish, but my extra hooks enabled me to hook a few more bass than they were. I caught three to five bass each morning back in those shallow pockets, and they were the biggest ones each day. The rest of the day I fished worms and crank baits and was able to win the tournament fairly easily.

In the approximately twenty states where I've tried it, I've found buzzing works best in the hot weather. This sounds incredible, but the best water temperature I've ever found for this type of fishing is 85 degrees! On three different lakes I've gone out in the scorching heat of summer, in July and August when it's super-hot, and caught some of the best strings of bass I've ever taken on the surface. I'm talking about 7- and 7½-pounders out of Oklahoma and Texas waters, and they hit right up during the heat of the day in August in the very shady places by willows, stumps, and stickups. They hit both Lunker Lures and Floyd's Buzzers.

For buzzing, you need some fairly clear water. It can be slightly dingy. You just can't catch lunker bass this way when the water's muddy. If it's slightly dingy, I fish shallower cover. In clear water, I can catch 'em over deeper water. At Bull Shoals and Table Rock—clear water—I've had bass blow on the buzzers over 20 to 30 feet of water, but they're coming out from old submerged timber and cedar trees to hit the lures. But in shallower, dingier lakes, you can catch 'em only 2 to 3 feet deep.

I like to fish buzzers on most any kind of point early in the morning. A slight wind can be blowing. Other good places are the creek channels in the back of the coves. In many of the shallower reservoirs, there are a lot of flat coves, and in the summer there are stickups and stumps 3 to 4 feet deep along these creek channels. You're out in the middle of the cove and toward the back of it, and you're apt to find bass feeding along the edge of the channel where the water's only 2 or 3 feet deep and the center of the channel is 5 to 10 feet deep. The bass will be around stumps, brush, and stickups along the edges of the channels, and those places are excellent for buzzing.

Stay in the deeper water, throw the buzzer to the shallower areas, and come right past or over the stump or stickup and back into deeper water. As the lure comes off that dropoff, that's usually when the strike occurs. One thing about Floyd's Buzzer is that it torques out to the right. In other words, when you throw it, it keeps running to the right because of the way the blade spins. It might run 2 feet to the right on a medium cast. I often use this factor to my advantage. I'll see an overhanging willow and will throw past it to the left. As I retrieve the lure, I hold my line low underneath there and the bait moves to the right and passes beneath the limbs or overhanging branches. If I had thrown to the right, the bait would have tended to pull out away from the bush.

I've taken a few of Floyd's Buzzers and bent the blades the opposite way to make the lure run to the left. That particular lure I'll have rigged up on a rod on the *left* side of my boat, and the normal lure which runs to the right will be on a rod on the *right* side. When I come up to a bush, I determine which side I need to throw to and choose the appropriate lure which runs in toward the bush instead of out away from it. During the middle of the day, a good shady bush is an excellent place for the buzzer.

You never want to throw to a bush—always throw *past* the ambush point where you think the fish is. Throw past it at least 6 feet and point your rod at the fish. If you hold your rod high, you won't get a good hook set. You need to strike and set the hook hard. I use fairly heavy line—14-pound in clear water like at Arbuckle in Oklahoma and Table Rock and Bull Shoals, and in the heavier cover in lakes like Toledo Bend I'll use 17 or 20. In Florida I use 25 and I've been tempted to go to 30. With the heavy line you're able to slosh big bass out of heavy cover. They really jump and fight hard right on top when the water temperature is 75 to 85 degrees or more.

Buzzer strikes, of course, are visual strikes, and I've never seen a more explosive strike. The average strike on a buzzer is harder than the average strike on any other topwater lure.

One advantage to buzzer fishing over all other types of surface-bait fishing is that you're covering more water. You're making retrieves at four to five miles per hour, and you're hitting hundreds and hundreds of ambush points. You can run your trolling motor fast and go down a couple of miles of bank in just an hour or so. And you're catching the hot, eager bass, particularly early in the morning in any kind of shallow cover. You have just a few bass every 100 yards or so which are actively feeding, and by covering tremendous amounts of water quickly with the buzzer, you're going to catch some feeders during those initial two hours of the morning and again in the middle of the day when they're beneath the cover. You can cover so many, many places for bass to hide because you're making a cast every fifteen to twenty seconds. You're making saturation casts and really covering the water.

SWIMMING PLUGS

Swimming plugs are pretty much like floating plugs except that they don't float—which puts them in a class of their own. Of course, they've been around since the turn of the century. My first serious bass fishing came with sinking plugs in the late 1950s. That was when I met Lynn Torbett, whom I mentioned earlier as having introduced me to the Rapala. My first meeting with Lynn was over on the Eastern Shore of Maryland when I was using topwater plugs—Plunkers and Jitterbugs and baits like those—around the lily pads. This guy came by me in an aluminum boat, and he had a heckuva string of bass. He'd caught 'em on sinking River Runts. He was about fifteen years older than I was, and while I was fishing out of a rubber raft, he had a

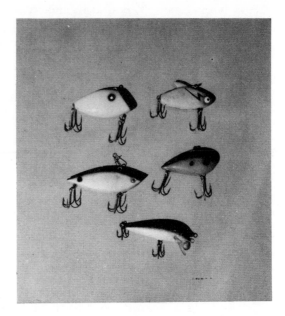

A few of the swimming plugs I use. Although crank baits are popular now, I still depend frequently on Cordell Spots and Countdown Rapalas.

trolling motor and a small outboard on his aluminum boat; he was really set up for serious bass fishing. He was using bait-casting tackle, whereas all I had was spinning tackle, and as I said before, I have never seen a more accurate caster. His whole trick was to go around Eastern Shore tide streams and make extremely accurate casts right into the bank or next to a cypress stump. He'd drop that sinking River Runt down a couple of feet and then retrieve it a couple of feet and let it bump the knees of those cypress trees. He'd retrieve it out to deeper water and pause it again, and then he'd slowly crank it back. His retrieve was part of his success, but his accurate casting was the most important part of it. I was much impressed.

I got to talking with Lynn. We lived about fifteen miles apart. He invited me to go with him the next week. All I brought was some spinning tackle, and even though he wasn't trying to beat me, he really put it on me. I was throwing a River Runt like the one he was using, but he explained that I simply wasn't accurate enough and that I couldn't be accurate throwing a fairly heavy plug on 6-to-8-pound line. I was overshooting my targets. Spinning tackle is accurate, but not with heavy plugs on light lines. He had some extra casting tackle, and he showed me how to cast with it, including how to hold the reel

A bass looks over my swimming plug. When I let it drop a few feet he'll probably grab it.

handles up, how to adjust the spool pressure, and how to thumb it.

Lynn Torbett and I struck it off real good, and we started making regular trips over there in 1959. I probably learned more about swimming plugs from him than I could have learned any other way. His favorite lures were the 9100 series of Heddon's sinking River Runt in a shad finish. They were 1/2-ounce baits, and they sank at a moderate rate. Since then, many fishermen have gotten away from swimming plugs and gone to crank baits. But I still use them. I use Cordell Spots on points, and I also use Countdown Rapalas.

27 Burning the Spot

Two of the most popular lures for this pattern are the Cordell Spot and the Heddon Sonic. I like the small 1/3-ounce Sonic in a yellow finish, and I use the 1/2-ounce Spot. These are similar plugs in that they're sinking and also are fast vibrators. I throw them with both spinning and casting tackle, but with high-speed reels.

Burning the Spot is a water-covering technique, and it's hard work—long casts and quick retrieves of the heavy swimming plug, hour after hour. But it's rewarding.

This is mainly a springtime pattern to use when the water is 50 to 60 degrees and the bass first come up on the dingy clay banks and points. You can burn these plugs down these crummy-looking flat banks and catch a lot of bass. Guys like James Thomas of Birmingham, Ala., and Junior Collis of Decatur, Ga., do especially well in spring tournaments with this pattern. In lakes like Gaston in North Carolina, all Thomas does is throw a small yellow Sonic on these flat-looking banks. Junior uses spinning tackle and about 12-pound line, and he fishes the dingier waters of Lake Lanier, Hartwell, and Clark Hill with a 1/2-ounce Spot. He looks for clay banks, puts his trolling motor on high, and makes a cast every 15 to 20 feet, and his trolling motor's running three to four miles an hour. He fishes all day like that, and sometimes he catches thirty to fifty bass a day.

There's really not much skill involved in "burning the Spot," but there's a lot of thought and hard work involved. First, it's like using a crank bait, but you're making more casts and retrieving a bit faster than you would with a crank bait. If you burn one of these baits all day long, you'll cover more water than with any other method of fishing I've ever seen. There's no other method where your lure travels through more feet of water than when you're burning the Spot. You need to be in excellent physical condition to do this. A lot of fishermen aren't able to make these long casts and fast retrieves all day long for eight to ten hours. These lures have a lot of lead in them, and they cast a long way, and this is good because you're fishing flat water and you need to cover a lot of it. You're not fishing dropoffs, and you're not really fishing targets all that much. You'll occasionally see a stump or a stick coming out of the water, and you'll want to throw near that, but these lures aren't like crank baits; they won't bounce over obstructions or through heavy cover. You don't want to try to bump the stump as you would do with a crank bait or a spinnerbait, because the Sonic or Spot will get hung up.

This type of fishing usually is for pre-spawners when the water is about 55 degrees. The banks usually are sloping, and you should stay a cast-length out from the bank in water less than 10 feet deep. Good places to fish this way are in the backs of major creek channels where the channel itself is pretty silted over and is no longer very defined. The last mile of that creek might be a massive flat and often has a few stumps around. Junior Collis will stop half a mile from the end of the cove and with his trolling will work around the sides of the cove. Again, he'll get out on the main lake and find clay points without much definition or deep water nearby, and he fires that Spot up to the bank and hums it all the way back.

When you're humming that Spot, it has a very definite throb, and this throb is one of the most important parts in working the lure. You really need to identify the feel of the throb, because you seldom identify the feel of the strike. What often happens is in that 55-degree water, the bass hears the plug or feels the vibrations from it, or both, and he is apt to follow it and hit it from behind. Probably 75 percent of the time when you get a strike, the only thing you detect is the stopping of the plug's vibrations. When the bass hits, the plug quits vibrating. With the small Sonic when the wind's blowing, at times the only thing I notice is my line moving off to the side. I'm using a graphite rod and am really watching, but this line movement is the only indication of the strike. Sometimes the fish moves toward you, and you don't see the line move. But if you're paying close attention, you'll quit feeling the vibration. I like graphite rods for this fishing because you can feel the throb better. Graphite is more sensitive. Set the hook at even the slightest interruption in the throb. It also pays to watch your line, and set the hook when the line makes the slightest deviation in the arc it's making as you're retrieving the bait while your trolling motor is moving the boat.

A lot of fishermen miss a lot of bass when they're burning the Spot. A big reason for this is that they don't sharpen their hooks enough. Super-sharp hooks are especially important in this type of fishing.

There's another situation which arises that is almost the reverse. In Louisiana there's a bait made which is called the Rattletrap. The manufacturers advertise that with the Rattletrap, you'll get the most jarring, vicious, startling strike you've ever experienced with a crank bait. It's a good late-spring and early-summer bait on the flats in lakes such as Toledo Bend where there's timber and stickups and where you're fishing for suspended bass around the trees and in deeper stump fields and creek channels. The Rattletrap looks like the Spot. It weighs about the same and burns through the water with about the same vibrations.

But for some strange reason—and I figure it's just a quirk of the bass—when the water temperature's 65 to 70 degrees, instead of hitting it from behind, the bass sort of angle in from the side and really smash it. The strikes are very vicious and hard, and the bait is moving fast anyhow. Mary Ann and I agree with the advertising on the lure box. We fished the Rattletrap at Percy Priest in Tennessee, and we had super-vicious strikes. We fished it again at Toledo Bend in the spring before her Bass'n Gals tournament, and the bass really nailed it. They just stopped it cold!

The same basic principles apply to the Sonic, the Spot, and the Rattletrap. All three are high-speed, underwater-swimming, fast-vibrating lures. They're not crank baits because they don't float, and the way to fish 'em is not so much at ambush points as with crank baits and spinnerbaits, but rather along shallow banks and flats and the ends of coves. These are useful tournament lures because during practice or even in the actual competition, if you want to know if there are fish in a certain area, you can find out in a relatively short

The best banks are sloping. Fire that Spot up to the bank and hum it all the way back—again and again as you move along the shoreline.

time with them. If you spent one hour burning the Spot in a big flat, you would have made over 200 casts, and you'd get some indication if there were any bass there.

One other consideration is that when you burn these plugs, you probably catch bass which are feeding and hungry more than any others. It's not particularly a reflex-action bait because you're not primarily throwing at ambush points. You're mainly catching bass which are roaming and feeding. That's why they chase down these fast-swimming baits. Early morning and late evening are prime times to look for feeding fish, and then you want to cover a lot of water. You might also check the Solunar Tables and fish these lures during a major period. When you find them feeding good on a flat or a point, you can limit out in an hour with these vibrators.

28 Counting Down

A totally different pattern exists with a slow-sinking plug such as the Countdown Rapala or that slow-sinking River Runt which the late Lynn Torbett used. Counting down is a relatively new pattern in my repertoire. It's not something I've been doing long. They have

When they hit a Countdown Rapala, they'll knock the bow out of your line and you'll feel the strike.

made a Countdown Rapala for years, and it looks just like the floating models, but it's an entirely different lure for entirely different uses.

The Countdown is a lead-filled Rapala which sinks fairly fast and swims and wobbles along. It also has a good wobble while it's sinking. Don't throw it into 2 or 3 feet of water as you do with the floating models, but instead fish it on relatively shallow structure, such as on a rocky point. One of the best places to fish it is in the shade of a weedline. One of my favorite places to fish it is on a point. I try to estimate in my mind how deep the water is by judging from the slope of the point out of the water. Doing this takes a bit of mental geometry. If I think the fish should be about 10 feet deep, and from the slope of the point I judge that I'll find 10-foot water 100 yards out, that's where I'll start fishing the Countdown.

On my first cast, I'm counting to myself . . . one . . . two . . . three . . . as the plug is sinking. (This is why the name "Countdown"; you can actually count it down to the desired depth.) If it hits the bottom on a count of ten and takes about ten seconds to sink, I'll figure the water is close to 10 feet deep. I also might check my locator to see exactly how deep it is. I don't want the lure to run 10 feet deep because it would get hung on everything on the bottom. On the next cast—if I can get that first one in without hanging up—I'll count it down to eight or nine and start my retrieve with the plug about a foot or two off the bottom. You have good depth control with this plug.

This is a technique I learned as a teenager years ago from Jason Lucas, my favorite fishing writer back then, in his book *Lucas on Bass*. He didn't use a depthfinder, and he didn't care much for plastic worms, but he made some amazing discoveries in fishing. The most important thing he ever wrote about, I think, was counting down a sinking lure. I count down every sinking lure I use, whether it's a Countdown Rapala, plastic worm, grub, jig and eel, or whatever. Every single cast I make with a worm (other than a floating worm), I'm counting as it sinks. I even do this in stickups; stickups are in different depths of water. If I'm catching bass on plastic worms 3½ feet deep in stickups, and I throw to a 5-foot-deep stickup and don't get a strike and then I throw to a stickup 2 feet deep and don't get a strike, this makes me aware that nearly all the bass—if not all of 'em—in the area I'm fishing are hitting at 3½ feet deep. When you're throwing 40 feet away from you, lots of times you don't know if there's a ditch or depression there or if the bottom's flat or there's a hump in that spot. But you can learn what's out there by counting. I count *every time* I make a cast with any lure that sinks.

One thing about a Countdown Rapala is that it'll hang up on everything it bumps. You can't bump anything with this plug and not get it hung up. And other than wasting time trying to get your lure free and blowing that cast and that shallow spot, keep in mind that Countdown Rapalas aren't exactly as inexpensive as plastic worms! A Countdown Rapala is an open-water lure, but it can be used in areas with cover as long as you count it down properly and get your depth control worked out. Another thing to keep in mind about depth control is that when you make a long cast with a sinking plug, you're pulling the lure at a horizontal angle during the first part of your retrieve and it swims at that depth pretty good. But as you keep retrieving, you're building up line on your reel and you're pulling at a sharper upward angle on your lure. For example, if you make a 50-foot cast and count the plug down to about 6 feet, it might be running right at that depth for the first 10 or so feet. But if you're turning your reel handle two revolutions per second, by the time you get the plug back to 20 feet from you, you've got a bigger line buildup on your reel

If the bass are 15 feet deep on a little point like this, you can't reach them with a crank bait, but a Countdown will find them. You have to count carefully and learn the proper retrieve speed—for one thing, the expensive lures hang up very easily.

and you're moving the bait faster when you crank your reel handle two revolutions per second, and you're also pulling the bait upward and shallower instead of horizontally. So to keep that 5-to-6-foot depth, the closer you get to the boat, the slower you need to retrieve. It's not easy to keep this consistent depth control; doing so takes quite a bit of practice. Lots of little tricks like this you can learn, but don't be disappointed if you don't master them overnight. I certainly didn't, and neither did Bill Dance, Homer Circle, Tom Mann, Rick Clunn, or any of the experts I know.

One way to learn to maintain this consistent depth control is to use your locator and find a big flat where the bottom is almost as level as your living-room floor. If the water's, say, 9 feet deep everywhere out there, make a long cast and count the lure to the bottom. If it took you nine counts, the next time cast out long again and count to eight. When you get the lure about halfway back to you, let it free-fall to the bottom. If you were retrieving it 8 feet deep, it should reach the bottom on a one-count. If it hit the lake floor on a three-count, you were bringing it in only 6 feet deep at the moment you let it fall. This is a good way to practice and learn depth control. Remember, too, the size of your line affects the speed at which the lure will sink. A Countdown Rapala will sink slower with a 14-pound-test line than it will with 8-pound-test. Different reels affect this, too, because they have different speeds. By practicing and working out the system, you can learn to maintain an almost totally horizontal retrieve. It's all a matter of timing, and once you get it down pat, you can get this lure to run at any depth you want it to run.

Some fishermen stick their rods straight down in the water almost to the handle and maintain depth control that way. It works, but I don't like to do this because I'm all out of position for the strike. I prefer to work out the system and occasionally check by letting the lure free-fall halfway through the retrieve, as described above.

This counting down is very popular at Watts Bar, Dale Hollow, and Percy Priest in Tennessee. The boys up there take No. 7 Countdown Rapalas and run 'em on 6- or 8-pound line with spinning tackle. Most of the lakes up there are gravelly, with a few stickups and stumps and chunky rocks. They like to fish particularly on points with the wind blowing in, because that little No. 7 Countdown closely resembles a small threadfin shad. They throw it across the point and count it down to whatever depth they want it to run, and they retrieve it at a slow speed.

You really need to run the Countdown slower than you would a crank bait such as a Bomber or a Fat Rap. The difference between a Countdown and a conventional crank bait coming across the same point, even if they're similar in size and color, is that you have to run the crank bait much faster to get a desired depth. There are times when bass won't hit a fast-moving lure, but they'll hit the slow-swimming bait. I do like to use crank baits, but there are times when the fish might be deeper than the crank bait will go. If the bass are down 15 feet, there's not a small crank bait in your tackle box that will reach them. Even if you have a crank bait that will run 11 feet deep, you can't get it down there immediately, and it might be moving too fast for the fish.

But you can fish a Countdown deep and bring it slowly across a point. Most of the strikes are discernible; you don't have much difficulty with this factor because you're usually fishing the bait slow and the plug does not wobble with a violent action as a crank bait does. You're not putting much pressure on your lure. The line isn't slack, but it does have a slight bow in it. When they hit it, they usually knock the bow out, and you feel the strike. The hooks are extremely sharp, and you don't miss many fish with it. Often you're fishing it slow and in clear water, and they zero in on it and engulf it. Sometimes they take the small Countdowns way down in their throats, and you need a pair of needlenose pliers to extract the hooks.

---

29 Casting the Breaks

A lot of people live in certain sections of the country and bass-fish all their lives in those areas without ever seeing a school of bass breaking on the surface. The pattern for schooling bass seems to include the presence of a shad population. I've done a lot of fishing in Minnesota, Wisconsin, and Canada, and I've never seen bass breaking in those waters, though maybe they do. In general in those northern lakes without shad, bass feed on bluegills, which aren't surface-breaking fish like shad, and they feed on the bottom on crawfish. Therefore they're not chasing schools of food which are on the top.

In nearly all of the big southern reservoirs, thousands upon thousands of schools of shad drift along right near the surface. That's where these shad live, feeding on algae and plankton near the surface. A school of shad might consist of 1,000 to 20,000 fish—all an inch or two long. When they drift over an ambush point or maybe over a single bass, that fish will tear into the shad if he's hungry. Immediately the shad start scattering and skipping all over the surface. This can and does get to be a frenzy situation which triggers other bass to join in, and then you've got schools of bass attacking schools of shad, and they're all up on the surface. Twenty to thirty bass might be breaking simultaneously, and schools of striped bass and white bass also do this.

Schooling activity usually occurs during the summer and starts during the full-moon periods usually in June but occasionally in May. It probably gets the best in September and October and lasts right on into late autumn until the water temperature drops below 55 degrees.

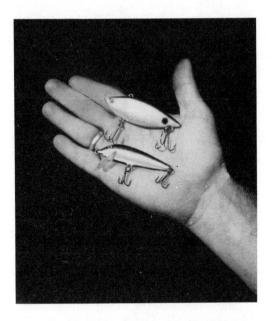

The ½-ounce Cordell Spot and the No. 7 silver Countdown Rapala are my favorites for casting to surface-breaking schoolers.

Generally the water temperature is at a minimum of 55 degrees for much surface schooling to take place. I have seen good schooling activity take place in the winter on Toledo Bend, but it's a definite exception as well as being an unusual lake in that it has thousands of schools of suspended bass in its 190,000 acres.

How do you catch 'em when they're schooling on top? You "cast the breaks," and this is very exciting and thrilling. First, you have to wait for the conditions to get right. You wait for the full-moon period in June and the right weather conditions. Good schooling activity on the surface might take place only two or three days during the entire month. Ultraviolet filtration from the sun is needed; in other words, it takes a little bit of overcast weather. Right after a front passes through, shad and bass go deeper because the sun shines through so brightly and brings a high penetration of ultraviolet light. There's no haze in the air to filter out ultraviolet rays.

High cirrus clouds make for excellent surface-schooling activity because they provide plenty of filtration and cut the ultraviolet rays to half what they would be immediately after a front. Then the shad come up closer to the surface, and the bass move up accordingly. Couple this with a calm day and a full moon, and these conditions really put the bass to moving. With a full moon, calm weather, haze, and water temperatures pretty warm, the conditions are right for the bass to get, as the old-timers say, in the "breaks" or "jumps." The old guys in Tennessee and the mountains of North Carolina call the sport "fishin' the jumps." Even on the hottest day of the summer with the water temperature 90 degrees, they're apt to school on top like mad if conditions are right.

Not many bass fisherman are set up correctly for schooling bass. Most of them get out early in the morning and tie on a plastic worm on one rod and a surface plug on a second rod and a crank bait on a third rod, and then they go to a point first and then to a spot across the lake. The only thing I do different here is have a fifth rod rigged. (I'll have a spinnerbait on the fourth rod.) It's for the breaks. It's not stored in the rod locker; instead it's the most accessible rod I've got, lying out alone and ready for me to grab and cast with instantly. I'll grab that rod anytime I see a fish break, particularly a school of fish. This is true whether or not I'm in a tournament. When I'm running down the lake, I always watch for any surface-breaking fish.

A school of bass I found by accident enabled me to win the B.A.S.S. tournament at Ross Barnett Reservoir in Mississippi back in 1971. It was a fluke deal, but if I hadn't fished 'em, I wouldn't have won. I'd been catching bass in the lily pads, but by the third and last day of the tournament, I'd run out of fish. I took off that morning and ran 40 miles an hour down the lake without knowing what to do. Suddenly about 400 yards ahead of my boat, I saw two or three fish break. It was a hazy, calm day, and when I reached the spot, I threw out a marker buoy right where their ripples were. I started casting, and wham! wham! wham! I sat there and caught a limit of bass in a few minutes. I was able to make the most of the opportunity because I was ready. I had a marker buoy ready and a rod all set up, and I was watching for fish. Jim Bracken was with me, and when I stopped, I caught three bass before Jim ever got his lure tied on.

One thing you must remember about schooling bass is that they usually break for only two to maybe five or six seconds at a time. Therefore, you need to get to 'em in a hurry. Lots of people criticize high-speed bass boats, but such boats have caught fish for me when a slower boat wouldn't have. Several times I've been fishing along a timberline, and a quarter of a mile away I've seen the bass break. Theoretically by running 60 miles an hour, I could be there in fifteen seconds, but it takes a little longer. I can put my rods down, jerk the trolling motor up, put my life vest on, crank the motor, and get there in 30 to 40 seconds. When I stop, I'm casting, and there's a good chance that in those 30 to 40 seconds, the fish haven't gone very far. They might not be on the surface, but they're still right close by.

How do you "cast the breaks"? Normally in the summer when I'm expecting to see breaking bass, I'll have either of two lures tied on my rod for schoolers. My first choice is a No. 7 silver Countdown Rapala, and my second choice is a ½-ounce Cordell Spot in a shad finish. These plugs look very similar in size and color to a threadfin shad. When I come up to a school of bass on the surface, if some of them are still swirling on the surface, I simply throw into the swirls and reel the plug through them. At these times there is no counting it down because the bass are right on the top. If they've gone down and a big school of bass is there, you'll see them on your locator. When I shut down the big engine, I like to drift right over where the swirls were and find out how deep they've gone. Then I can throw out and count down to the depth the school went to. As soon as I see blips on the dial, I know what depth they are, and I cut the steering wheel to the side. This stops the boat's forward movement. Then I throw back behind me to where I saw the fish light up the screen. With either the Countdown Rapala or the Spot, I count it down to the depth they were.

If the fish went down 20 feet deep, I count the Spot down to about fifteen, because it sinks faster than a foot a second with 14-pound line. Then I start a medium retrieve. With the Countdown, I'd throw out and count a little longer and retrieve a little slower. The Spot enables you to make a longer cast and cover more water, but they often hit the Countdown Rapala better, and sometimes it's the only one of the two they'll hit. But again, I can throw the Spot farther and can cover more water with it; I've found it too has its advantages. I use both lures.

CRANK BAITS

In the 1940s, '50s, and until the late '60s, plugs such as the Bomber, Waterdog, Hellbender, Deep-R-Doodle, and Go-Deeper River Runts were classified as deep-diving baits. To today's modern breed of bassmen, these plugs which float at rest and dive at medium speeds to deep water are called crank baits. Crank baits are not supposed to require a great amount of intelligence and skill. Lots of fishermen think they're "dummy" baits which anyone can use to catch fish on, and that all you do is throw it out and retrieve it back. But there's a whole lot more to crank-bait fishing than that. I figure I spend at least 25 percent of my bass-fishing time using crank baits, and estimate I catch at least 25 percent of my bass on these plugs. In tournament competition I catch at least a third of my bass on crank baits. I rely on them heavily in tournaments and have won four with them. Therefore I've tried hard to improve my skills with crank baits, and these small improvements are what I'll discuss in this section.

The Go-Deeper River Runts of the late 1930s were among the main forerunners of our modern crank baits. They were designed to be thrown out and retrieved back in (or else trolled; trolling will be covered in a later section). The Deep-R-Doodles were fairly popular in the late 1940s. In fact, in December of 1949, a retired army captain, Paul Flanagan, caught the South Carolina state record largemouth—a 16-pound, 2-ouncer—at Santee-Cooper on a Deep-R-Doodle. But there wasn't any great popularity in deep-diving baits until the Bomber lure was created in Texas. In the late 1940s, the war had ended, and a lot of servicemen were back home and going fishing, and the Bomber really caught on. It was by far the most popular of the early crank

A collection of crank baits. They float at rest, but the lip makes them dive to 10 feet or even more on the retrieve.

baits, and it was again what the tackle industry calls an "idiot bait," meaning that *anybody* can catch fish on it.

About this same time, many of the TVA and the Army Corps of Engineers lakes were coming on strong. A lot of the reservoirs were new or else only three to five years old, and the bass fishing in them was fantastic. These waters had a lot of timber, brush, and stumps, and the old sinking lures like the sinking River Runts got snagged up. Also, fishermen couldn't cover enough water with those plugs to suit them. These impoundments were huge, and the guys wanted to cover a lot of water.

With its long lip, the Bomber had the advantage of being almost a snagless lure. Up to this time there weren't many underwater lures which could be retrieved through any type of heavy cover, such as stumps, stickups, and brush, without getting them hung up. The Bomber was one of the first fairly snagless deep-diving lures. Whereas many of the other early crank baits have either been discontinued or else have faded into oblivion, the Bomber is still going strong and remains one of the nation's top crank baits today. Its large metal lip deflects off the logs, stumps, and limbs usually without hanging up. When it does get hung up, the fact that it's a floating lure enables you to bob and twitch it around, and often it floats free of the snag. Another advantage is that if you hang it up and break your line, quite often it comes floating to the top again if it was lodged in a crevice. So fishermen didn't lose as many Bombers as they did the conventional sinking types of plugs.

My first experience with crank baits came in the late 1950s after they built several reservoirs in Maryland. I fished a lot back then with Tom McNey, and we got onto a plug which might be the deepest-running crank bait ever manufactured: the Waterdog, made by the Bomber Bait Company. It has a very large lip and a longer body. We used the largest of the three sizes, which is about 5 inches long, and we'd make long casts with 15-pound line and spinning tackle and crank it down to 14 or 15 feet on a straight retrieve. We tested the depth it went by getting out on a point which had a big rock 14 feet deep. This was at Liberty Lake, and we could bump that rock on the cast. I don't know of another crank bait on the market that will get down to 14 feet on a regular cast.

Liberty was a clear lake and was only four or five years old at the time, and it had a lot of mature bass which had grown to 5, 6, and 7 pounds. They'd never seen a plug like that Waterdog, and not many people went to the trouble to get permits to fish the lake. Tom and I fished a lot of structure. We cast those Waterdogs to points, rock piles, old house foundations, underwater islands, bridges, and anything we could find that was from 10 to 15 feet deep. We did this in the spring. In the summer we fished plastic worms on a little deeper structure, but when the water was 55 to 60 degrees we cranked those Waterdogs, and we caught a 6-pound, 5-ounce smallmouth and a 6-pound, 4-ounce smallmouth, and I caught a 6-pound, 2-ounce smallmouth. I also had a 7½-pound largemouth, and Tommy had a 7¼-pound largemouth. We had a total of nine bass that day over 5 pounds, and we caught all of 'em on Waterdogs. This was in Maryland, and those bass approached state-record-sized bass.

When you look at the history of what crank baits have done on the TVA lakes in Tennessee and think of the strings of big smallmouths guys like Billy Burns from Lexington, Ky., caught on Bombers at Dale Hollow, it's amazing. Billy Burns, who's now seventy-five years old and still going fishing, used to catch 7-to-8-pound smallmouths on that Bomber. He used to put together some strings of smallmouths which weighed over 50 and even over 60 pounds in a day with the Bomber. Look also at the tournament record, and you'll find that the biggest ten-bass limit was caught on a crank bait. Larry Hill of Winston-Salem caught those ten, which totaled 60 pounds, 6 ounces, in an hour and five minutes back in February of 1973 at the Florida Invitational B.A.S.S. tournament on the St. Johns River. Larry was using an original Big-O, the handcarved balsawood plug which Fred Young of Oak Ridge, Tenn., designed, and he caught those bass in Rodman Reservoir.

One of my most memorable experiences with crank baits happened in a B.A.S.S. tournament at Lake Seminole in May of 1973. I was in ninth place going into the final round, and I wasn't doing any good that day. By one p.m. I knew I didn't have much of a chance to win it, as I had only two or three more hours to fish. But if I could just find a school of big bass and catch them, I might pull it off. I figured the best and quickest way to catch several big ones was with a big crank bait. I put on a Magnum Hellbender, which dives to 11 or 12 feet, and decided to crank some choice spots on the edges of the Spring Creek channel. The first place I stopped at was a worm hole where I'd caught some big bass up to 8 pounds in previous years. On my first cast I caught a 10¼-pounder, which was the big bass for the tournament. Then I caught an 8-pounder and a 7-pounder. My fourth bass was a 6-pounder. In about twenty minutes I caught over 30 pounds of bass and won the tournament as well as big-bass honors.

It was a lucky deal, and I probably won't ever do anything like that again. But Larry Hill did it and so did Billy Burns, and I know about ten other fishermen who've hit 'em like that with crank baits. Why do fishermen catch big bass, and several of 'em, in short periods of time with crank baits? Well, let's look at some of the criteria involved, and then we'll examine some of the best crank-bait patterns. Water temperature is probably the main factor in crank-bait success. A crank bait is an excellent pre-spawn lure. Before they go on the beds, a lot of big female bass move up adjacent to the spawning waters. They get on points and ledges of creek channels and in shallow timbered and brushy areas. They move to areas where the water is slightly warmer than other parts of the lake. If most of the lake is 50 degrees and you find some 55-degree water, check it out closely. I've done better with big largemouths on crank baits in the spring when the water's 55 degrees than I've done at any other temperature. Slightly dingy water

If you know the right color of lure, the right retrieve, and the right cover to fish, you've got a good chance with a crank bait.

is better than clear water. Clear lakes with a lot of weeds and lily pads aren't good crank-bait lakes, in my opinion.

Generally a good crank-bait lake is a TVA lake where the water is slightly turbid and the wind blows in on the shores in certain sections and perhaps creates a mudline. Dingy water in a lake like this is ideal for crank-bait fishing in the spring when the water is 55 degrees or higher. The converse to this is that occasionally there will be good crank-bait fishing in a clear lake at lower water temperatures. I've been able to catch bass better on crank baits in crystal-clear water at 45 degrees than at 75 degrees. But if you've got very muddy water at 45 degrees, you'll not catch *anything.* In cold, muddy water, bass aren't able to see, and they don't have the lateral-line sensitivity to follow things around; they're virtually without any senses in these conditions.

Crank baits have worked best for me on big bass in the spring when the water is at about 55 degrees.

If you're on a good pattern and know the color of the lure to use and the right retrieve and the right cover to fish, you can cover more water with a crank bait than with a worm or even a spinnerbait. Crank baits are high-saturation lures, and if the bass are feeding for, say, only twenty minutes in the morning, you can make more casts and show the bait to more fish in that twenty minutes with a crank bait. This is one of its big advantages. The only other type of lure which would cover as much water would be a Sonic or a Spot or some fast swimming plug like that.

Nearly all of the tackle I use for bigger crank baits is heavy casting tackle, including No. 6-action Fenwick rods, high-speed free-spool reels, and 14-to-20-pound line. When they're hitting crank baits, I'm usually hooking them good, and I don't lose many except on very small crank baits. The small crank baits such as the Deep-Wee-R, the little Scooper, and the small Fat Rap have small No. 4 treble hooks, and with these I'm usually using 10- or 12-pound line because I'm working clearer water and catching smaller bass. For some reason you can't put the pressure on those fish with lighter line, and I end up losing more than I lose on the bigger lures and heavier lines. When you're running the bigger lures fairly fast, you halfway hook the fish that strike just with the speed of the retrieve alone. I hardly miss a bass when I'm running the 1/2-to-5/8-ounce Hellbenders, Big-Os, Fat Raps, Bombers, or Estep plugs on 20-pound line. The hooks are bigger No. 1 or 2 trebles, and I have 'em sharp and am running the plugs pretty fast.

30 Cranking The Creek Channels

This is a pattern I reserve for early spring. In many of the shad lakes in the flatlands—reservoirs like Toledo Bend, Sam Rayburn, and Santee-Cooper—there are creek channels back through big flats. When you get back in the cove, it might be big, half a mile wide, but the water is pretty shallow. The entire flat might be only 4 to 8 feet deep, but the creek channel is another 5 to 10 feet deeper. Most of the time I crank the creek channel, which is a little bit dingy in the back of a major cove.

Big female bass come back in the creeks in early spring. Just before they spawn they lie up on top of the creek ledge, and the depth

Big females come back in the creeks in early spring before they spawn and lie up on top of the creek ledges.

ranges from 3 to about 8 feet. I work my boat down the center of the creek. In timbered reservoirs it's a little easier to stay in the creek channel, because you can look at the trees and tell where the channel is. In an open reservoir the creek channel ledges are lined with stumps, and it's more difficult to follow the creek. In the latter you need to put out buoys to mark the channel. There are apt to be just as many fish in an open cove as in a timbered cove, but it is easier to fish in a timbered cove.

One February I was fishing Sam Rayburn with Jim Walker. February isn't considered a top bass month for Rayburn, but an extreme warming trend was in progress when we got there. The water was pretty dingy, and nobody had been catching any bass anywhere. The shallow water had really warmed up, and I told Jim I thought there might be some bass working in the creek channels and we might get them to hit crank baits. We went to the back end of Ash Bayou and found 55-degree water instead of the 45-degree water in the main lake. It was just a perfect temperature for crank baits. There were a lot of old oak trees on the edge of a small creek channel we went into. The channel was hard to follow because it was less than 10 feet wide and it twisted and turned.

Jim and I went down the center of the creek as best we could and cast to the sides of the trees. Because the big females were looking for the warmest water they could find, they were on the *sunny* side of the trees. They were only 3 feet deep in about 5 feet of water, and sometimes we'd see the swirl of a fish after the plug. The trick was to bump the edge of the tree, and that often produced strikes. I caught mine on an old brown Bomber, that had been in my box for years. Jim and I had ten bass over 5 pounds that day. We had some smaller ones, too. Later that day we talked to several guides and other fishermen who had spent the day mostly on the main lake. They caught some bass, but nobody had big ones like ours. What I think happened is we found the best available water temperature for those big pre-spawners, and that's why they were there. That pattern lasted all week, and that also is one of the first patterns to develop in the early spring. Jim Walker died as a young man. He was my age, but a couple of years ago he had a heart attack which was fatal.

Since most lakes are not timbered, most creek channels are in open water in the coves. The way I approach this fishing is to run back into the cove until I hit a bottom depth of about 8 feet. This is about as deep as I can crank a crank bait effectively. I put out a marker buoy there. If I have a contour map of the lake, I'll look on it for a major bend in the creek I'm on. A creek bend usually has a better dropoff, and the structure aspects of fishing creek channels are important. Chances are, this major bend is undercut, and any stumps which might have been there probably have exposed roots which stick out over the water. This is a good suspending place for bass, and the severity of the dropoff often indicates that the bend will hold bigger bass and more of 'em. I keep working back toward the end of the cove to shallower water until I get shallow enough that I can see the stumps. With Polaroid glasses, they'll appear as dark spots in the water. This is as shallow as I'll fish with a crank bait, although occasionally the bass will be shallower. If they're in a foot of water, this isn't a crank-bait depth, and in that case I'll probably go to a spinnerbait or a plastic worm or something else.

Often in the summer I turn the trolling motor on high and go up the creek channel, casting at every tree.

Five-foot depths on the bends of the creek channel are usually very good places to fish. Sometimes you need to mark these spots with a marker buoy or two. It's important to stay in the deeper water in the creek and throw the crank bait on the flats. I like to throw it 10 feet past the edge of the creekbank and make it bump bottom. With luck, the plug will hit a stump. This is the key to this fishing, as often the stumps are right on the edge of the channel. Even if before the lake was impounded the area you're fishing was a farmer's field, the farmer probably left the trees on the edge of the creek through his land. Look at any farm and you'll almost never see the trees cleared along a creek which runs through the land.

While you want to bump those stumps, you don't want to get hung up, so you need to use a crank bait with a big lip which will deflect off the stump. Sometimes I cut the lead hook off the front set of treble hooks on the plug, but I prefer not to do this. I'd rather use heavier line if I'm getting hung up a lot and try to rip the lure loose. With 25-pound line I usually can rip the lure free by half straightening the hooks out. The Bomber is an excellent lure for this because it's relatively snagless. The deep-diving Bagley B baits also are good. I helped design the Fat Rap series, and the No. 7 size is good for this creek-channel pattern. The No. 7 has a large lip and bounces off stumps real well. Almost any crank bait with a large, extended lip is relatively snagless.

I mentioned this pattern relating to pre-spawn fish, but there's another time cranking the creek channels pays dividends. In Oklahoma there are some 800,000 acres of reservoirs, including timbered reservoirs like Kerr in southern Oklahoma and 102,000-acre Eufaula. These are super crank-bait waters, but for some reason Oklahoma's often so muddy, cold, and windy in the spring that you don't often have good creek-channel fishing in the spring. Some of Oklahoma's best crank-bait fishing occurs during the hot summer, because it might be the only time of the year when the water clears up. The bass are there the whole time, but they really start feeding good only when the water starts clearing up, even though the water temperature might be 80 degrees.

Pre-spawn bass will often hold on brushy ledges of a creek channel, usually at 5 to 10 feet in clear water or 3 to 6 feet in dingy water.

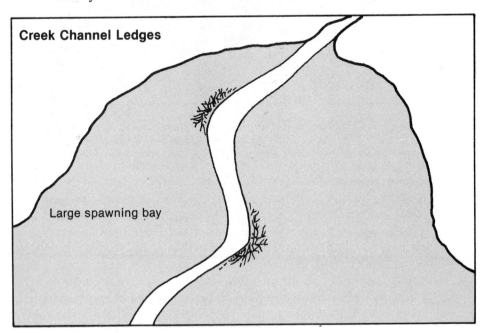

Creek Channel Ledges

Large spawning bay

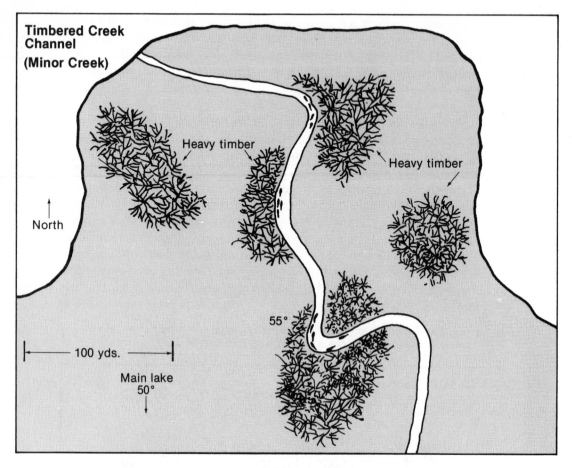

Minor creek channels in flat or gradually tapered coves located on the north side of the lake can hold concentrations of pre-spawners. The timber can be either permanently submerged or just temporarily flooded.

We pretty much fish exclusively on the creek channel edges during the entire summer. Probably 90 percent of our summer fishing is done there on Kerr, Eufaula, and Lake Oolagah. These are large lakes with a lot of timber, dingy water, and shallow creek channels. I fish these channel edges with crank baits, spinnerbaits, and worms, but when I really think they're feeding and I want to cover a lot of water, I use a crank bait. I can find the bass with it better, too. Often in the summer I turn my trolling motor on high and go up a creek channel and cast at every tree. In the summer they're usually in the shade of the trees. I throw to the shady side and bump the tree and retrieve back. I make one cast per tree and keep on going up the channel.

Bass in the summer often are concentrated, just as pre-spawn fish get bunched up. You're apt to find an area where every tree has a bass. Maybe all thirty trees around one bend have a bass. You might not get all of 'em to strike, but they're apt to be there just the same. You're likely to get several strikes and maybe catch five or six of 'em, and they easily could be 5-pound or better fish. We usually get several 5-pounders on crank baits in the summer in Oklahoma, and I've heard of 40- and 50-pound strings getting caught on crank baits. My experience has been I don't catch 'em all on crank baits. When I catch two or three on crank baits, I've located the school. Then I might go to a worm or a flipping jig and pull up to those trees and flip a jig or a worm in there on the shady side, or I'll slow-roll a spinnerbait through that same spot. Changing lures sometimes helps, but the bait certainly is a fast way to find 'em.

---

31 Bump More Stumps

If we were to add up all the stumps in all the lakes, rivers, and ponds in this country, we might come up with something like 8.2 billion trillion stumps. And there probably is no stump in less than 10 feet of water in any southern reservoir which hasn't at some time or other had at least one bass on it.

When I speak of bumping the stumps, I'm thinking mainly about the stumps on the points and on the creek channels. Sometimes I find stumps on an underwater ridge or a submerged island on a shallow lake. On the exposed areas—the points and shoals—wave action usually causes erosion, and the dirt, sand, or gravel bases of these stumps are washed away. Then instead of being merely a stump flush with the bottom, it is almost suspended, with roots coming out in all directions, looking like an octopus. The more the stump is eroded, the better the ambush point it makes for bass. It becomes a dynamite spot for a bass in spring, summer, and fall.

To fish these eroded stumps, I have to prepare for heavy fishing, because I know I'm going to get hung up. Since I'm usually fishing dingy water, I'm using a large crank bait with a big lip to bounce off the wood and very heavy line. The big line is not necessarily for the

Large stumps usually have eroded bases, leaving them almost suspended on their roots—great bass cover.

size of the bass, but because I'm getting hung up a lot and I want to be able to pull the plug loose as many times as possible. With 12- or 14-pound line, I'd lose a lot of lures, but you can rip most of 'em loose with 20- or 25-pound mono. Another reason for the heavy line is it prevents the plug from going as deep as it would travel on lighter line. I might be fishing a point and want to hit only the tops of the stumps and not run too deep. With 12-pound line, the crank bait would go considerably deeper, and when it hung up, I might not be able to reach it with my rod tip to poke it loose. It's human nature to get exasperated when you start hanging up a lot, and you tend to pull too hard. If you're using lighter line, you'll break off some plugs. And lots of these crank baits today cost four and five bucks apiece.

When I think of bumping the stumps with a crank bait, I think back to the B.A.S.S. tournament at Ross Barnett Reservoir in Mississippi in 1973. The craze in crank-bait fishing which was spawned by Fred Young's hand-carved balsawood Big-O was getting into full swing. I'd located some bass in front of Pine Island, which is in the midsection of the lake, and they were on the south bank. The wind was blowing hard from the north. I had only one bait they'd hit—a hand-carved balsa plug made by Mike Estep of Oak Ridge, Tenn. It had a black back and chartreuse sides. Since it was the only thing they were hitting, I decided to run it on 25-pound line so I wouldn't lose it. I got back into 7 or 8 feet of water to throw up on those 2-to-4-foot flats with stumps along the edge of the drops.

My game plan was going good except that during the first day of the tournament, the wind blew thirty miles an hour! When I got to my area, the wind was whitecapping the water across that bar. Four or five others had found those same bass. Tom Mann had found 'em, and Bobby Murray knew the bass were there, and so did Billy Westmorland. A lot of us had planned to go fish that area, but the wind was nearly impossible to deal with. I was determined to fish it anyhow. I threw my anchor out and tried to hold the boat that way. This didn't work, so I ended up running my big engine in reverse and running the bilge pump to pump out the water which was sloshing in over the stern. I also ran my trolling motor as fast as it would go against the wind. Fishing that place was almost impossible, and I was continually getting hung up. I didn't want to run up to the ridge where the shallow water was, so I had to pull the plug loose and hope like heck

Mr. Bass has been watching that crank bait wiggle, and he pounces on it.

my line wouldn't break. Two or three times my line did break, but my plug floated up and was out there bobbing in the waves. I'd wait for it to drift away from those bass, and then I'd circle around in the rough water and go net my plug.

I fished for three days in that rough water and ended up catching a little over 72 pounds of bass to win the tournament, simply because I got out there and stuck it out. I had only that one lure they were hitting. The last morning I caught nine bass which were good ones. One of 'em was over 6 and another was over 5. About one o'clock that afternoon I was trying for my tenth bass, and I hung the plug up and broke the line and it didn't float up. I had several other similar plugs, and I tried them, but they didn't work. I even had some other Estep plugs almost the same size and color, but they didn't produce either. Finally I managed to catch one more bass, which made my limit. But the point is I had the secret lure the fish wanted.

Bumping the stumps with a crank bait is saturation fishing; you just keep fan-casting around until you bump something. You might want to make three or four casts to the same stump, because lots of times they won't hit on the first couple of casts and you have to anger them a little. But often they strike out of reflex action on the first cast. Sometimes on my crank baits I use in the stumps, I replace heavier hooks with lighter wire hooks. I don't want to use hooks which won't straighten out partly when I pull the bait off a stump with 20- or 25-pound line. I have had bass hit when the plug pulls loose from the stump. It zings off and I start the retrieve, and that bass has been watching it wiggling there on the stump and all of a sudden it shoots off the stump and then wobbles away, and he pounces on it.

32 Ripping the Rip-Rap

I never used to think much about rip-rap fishing. It never made much sense to me why there should be bass on rip-rap, which is just a jumble of stones protecting a shoreline. But back in the late 1960s at Santee-Cooper, a bunch of guys would come down there from North Carolina and troll in front of the dam. The water where they trolled was 30 to 40 feet deep. They trolled that rip-rap in front of the spillway, and they caught big coolers full of bass. This would be in March when I was wading in the blackwater ponds off the main lake.

Run parallel with the rip-rap and throw ahead of the boat so that the crank bait returns at an angle.

I couldn't understand why those bass would be 30 to 40 feet deep at that time of year, but I figured out they weren't really trolling down that deep. What they were doing was trolling shallow right up next to the rip-rap. They were going slow, using Bombers and other long-lipped crank baits, and were actually trolling 4 and 5 feet deep. They held their rods out toward the rip-rap so their plugs would be bouncing over the shallow rocks. When I finally figured out what they were doing, I got to wondering how I could do if I cast the rip-rap.

I went up there and tried casting. Sure enough, the water was 40 feet deep out off the rip-rap, and I was out in the middle of the lake. I picked a bright, sunny day during the pre-spawn season when the water was 50 to 55 degrees, and I started catching big bass right off

Ray Ostrom of Normark caught his first 9-pounder on Santee-Cooper rip-rap. He used a prototype Fat Rap in 44-degree water.

the start on crank baits. Then I got to thinking how much rip-rap there was at Santee. The lower lake has 38 miles of it, counting the East Dike and the West Dike and the dam down there, and in the upper lake there's the 301 bridge. The two lakes have about 100 miles of rip-rap. I tried several other rip-rap areas, and I caught bass all along the areas. Some of them were 7- and 8-pounders. I threw mainly Bombers and Hellbenders—plugs which don't get hung up too bad.

There was a lot more to rip-rap fishing, I found out, and I learned this when I started fishing with Forrest Wood, Bobby Murray, and Bill Dance. By 1970, when I started fishing the tournaments, these guys had perfected rip-rap fishing pretty good. Their spring pattern back then often consisted of going and finding a bridge with some rip-rap. Some guys still spend the entire tournament day fishing one bridge and working back and forth. Back in 1969 Bobby Murray won the fall team tournament on Lake Eufaula, Ala., fishing rip-rap along the Chewalla bridge when the water temperature was about 50 degrees. He had the high string on the winning team, which featured Forrest Wood, Dance, and Bob Ponds. There are times in the year when the water is 50 to 60 degrees that the bass suspend right along the rip-rap. At Santee I think the rocks had a lot of crawfish along 'em. The rip-rap had the only rocks around, and the bass would be there every spring and every fall. Tommy Salisbury and I and a few others got to experimenting in the fall, and when the water got a little cool and slightly dingy, we'd nail 'em on the rip-rap.

My rip-rap fishing improved after I talked with Forrest, Bobby Murray, and Dance. I learned how to get better boat positioning and where to cast and how to retrieve. There's a lot more to it than merely throwing to the rip-rap. In fact, you don't throw *to* the rip-rap; that's the biggest mistake you can make. The way to fish it is with proper boat control. Get *parallel* with the rip-rap and run your trolling motor along the rip-rap. I like to keep my trolling motor in 8 to 10 feet of water. Most rip-raps have about a 40-degree angle or grade. I guess different construction crews around the country have worked up about the same angle, and there's not much difference in the angles. Instead of throwing to the rip-rap, which I'm about 30 feet away from, I throw ahead of the boat down the rip-rap and almost to it. I try to drop the plug in 2 to 3 feet of water, and for the first 5 to 10 feet of the retrieve, the lure is coming out at an angle and is really digging into the bottom and bouncing off rocks. As it bumps its way deeper, it gets down 6, 7, and 8 feet. That's about as deep as I am, and with a plug such as a Hellbender, I'm hitting rocks and bottom during the entire retrieve. By keeping the proper angle on my cast, I have my lure hugging the bottom on the entire cast.

One little trick I like to try in rip-rap fishing is the old pause trick. About halfway to the boat, I stop the lure and let it float up a couple of feet, then I start it again and run it a few more feet and stop and pause it again. Those stops and pauses really work well at times. A guy I know from Mississippi, Jim McKay, fishes Bagley crank baits almost exclusively, and he fishes about every crank-bait pattern there's ever been. Probably his biggest suit in crank-bait fishing is the pause he gives the plug. He does this change-up trick with all his crank baits, and he's maintained that the colder the water, usually the more pauses you need, because the bass are more lethargic and will follow something halfway, and when it stops in colder water, they have a greater tendency to strike. In warmer water, you can run crank baits faster and really burn 'em along, and they'll likely hit it best that way. Every second or third cast in the colder water, I'll try different pauses and retrieves and speeds. I certainly have experienced many times when they hit only when I paused the bait and they wouldn't hit without the pause. This is especially when the water's fairly cold and I'm using a smaller crank bait. These strikes on the pause seldom are violent strikes; I've been watching my line float up when I'm pausing the lure and see the line just stop, and sure enough he's on there.

33   Throwing into a Crowd

When I speak of throwing into a crowd, I mean throwing into a whole bunch of bass. Lots of times I'll be fishing a variety of lures when I run into this situation. I've gotten strikes on other lures, and when I'm bringing that bass up to the boat and the water's at least reasonably clear, I'll see another fish following the one I've got on or my partner has on. Then I'll pick up a crank bait and throw in there.

One time when this happened, I really capitalized on this little trick. I was fishing with Pete Churchwell of Tulsa, who at the time worked for Lowrance Electronics, and we were using worms at Grand Lake. I needed to catch a couple of big bass for some publicity photos for Lowrance. We'd fished all day and hadn't had any luck at all with big fish. Pete made a long cast to a willow bush leaning over the water, and he had a strike and set the hook. His rod bowed over, and the fish took some drag and boiled at the top. When it boiled, I saw a second boil right by it. When his bass came past the boat, I thought I saw another bass with it. He said, "Get the net!" and I said, "Wait a minute—another big bass is following your fish." I had a crank bait on another rod I hadn't been throwing, and I picked it up and threw out right next to his fish, which was about a 5½-pounder. I cranked the plug down about 3 feet and paused it for a second, and *wham!* Another big bass had hit my plug, and we managed to get both of 'em.

**Jack Wingate and I do our best
to control the crowd
on Lake Seminole, Ga.**

Pete started to rig up another worm, and I said there was a school of 'em there, and the fastest way to catch 'em would be with a crank bait. I threw out and caught a second bass and then a third one. Pete got a crank bait tied on, and we were making double casts. As soon as one of us got one on, the other guy would throw right in near the hooked fish, and he'd get one. The ten to fifteen bass that were there would be chasing after the bass which was hooked. We sat there and caught ten bass, and seven of them were 5 pounds and over. This happened in about ten minutes.

The average fisherman would have made a mistake here. He would have caught the first one near the willow bush on the worm, and then he would have put it in the live well after looking it over leisurely and guessing how much it weighed. He probably would have taken his De-Liar out of his tacklebox and weighed the bass, and likely measured its length, too. Maybe his wife or buddy in the boat would have dug out the camera and taken a picture right then. Then he would have rerigged his worm and three or four minutes later he would be ready to make another cast. He might have even moved on down the bank to another willow bush. By this time, those bass would have lost their frenzy and would have calmed back to normal. Quite possibly he wouldn't have gotten another strike.

The point is to keep in mind the possibility of a school of fish, and sometimes it really pays off to have a crank bait ready for such an occasion. When my partner hooks a fish, if I have even the slightest idea there's another bass or several more right there, I pick up a crank bait and throw in there. That's the quickest way to find out. Throwing into a crowd really means throwing into a school of bass. When bass

I like to keep a rod rigged with a crank bait handy, so if I suspect the one I or my partner has just hooked has some excited friends, I'm all ready to take advantage.

get worked up and are super-excited, you don't want to give them any time to cool off, and with a crank bait, you can keep them excited by making several quick casts and whipping the plug through them. Even if they're not hitting every cast, you're creating more excitement that you would by throwing a plastic worm repeatedly to that spot. Even if you catch a fish on a plastic worm, it certainly doesn't hurt anything to throw back to that spot two or three times with a crank bait. Sometimes this will add four or five bass to your stringer in a hurry. Even if you're worm fishing, have a crank ready on another rod for such situations.

34 Running the Points

Back in the early 1970s, I drew Ricky Green for a partner in an old Project: Sports Incorporated tournament at Lake Ouachita in Arkansas. He's a fine pro who is noted as a spinnerbait fisherman. He's a super caster and a good crank-bait fisherman as well. We flipped a coin to decide whose boat we would take, and I won, so we went in my boat. He asked what patterns I wanted to fish, and I said I had five or six points, and he said he had five or six more. We compared notes and discovered we were on the same pattern. We were doing about the same thing with similar lures in similar depths of water and in about the same areas.

I pointed out that if we were finding bass on these ten or twelve points, there were another hundred spots on the lake that were identical to those, and I suggested we hit as many of those points as we could after we fished the ones we'd tried. He agreed, and we worked out a game plan where we'd alternate running the boat. For one point he'd run the boat and I'd be up front, and then we'd switch around. We'd come in fast straight at the point, and 100 feet from it we'd shut off the big engine. The bass we'd found in practice were in 6 to 8 feet of water out off the points, and we were keying in to what we figured would be 6 to 8 feet of water. The forward momentum of the boat would carry us on in, and about 40 feet away from the point, we'd turn the steering wheel to broadside the boat. The guy up front got the first cast, but we'd both fire long casts across the point, and we'd crank our crank baits down. The pattern was to crank all the way down until we hit the bottom and then we'd pause and let the bait

Some points have hidden structure, such as a dropoff, patch of stumps, or boulders. A locator helps you figure out the best route for your crank bait.

float up about a foot and then we'd crank it back down to the bottom and pause it again. Somewhere between the time it hit the bottom and floated up a foot or so, the bass would nail it.

The fishing wasn't red-hot that day, and we didn't catch 'em on every point, but on every three or four points, one of us would catch a bass. We'd make three casts apiece on the point and then hit the starter and take off like the proverbial bat for the next point. We never even took time to unzip our life vests, and we didn't waste any time. Usually we didn't even put the trolling motor down. We added up the points we fished, and the tally ran to seventy-five points that day. On two or three points we caught three or four bass per point. I caught twenty-two bass that day, and Ricky had twenty-three. We were within a bass of each other, and our weights were almost identical. We each weighed in ten bass which totaled slightly over 20 pounds. Right near the end of the day I had caught about a 5-pounder and ended up with a pound or so more than he had.

This was in May right during the spawning season, and some bass were spawning whereas others either had finished nesting or hadn't started spawning yet. Not all the bass spawn at the same time. The points were excellent places because of all three of these conditions being present, and Ouachita is well known for its point fishing. The water had been a little dingy, and there was a little bit of wind and overcast weather. One of the major considerations for point fishing, I think, is the wind, and what I like to find are points with the wind blowing in—not any super amount of wind, but a ten-to-fifteen-mile-per-hour breeze. I don't want it whitecapping, although I have caught 'em on points when it was whitecapping.

When you're fishing a point, those initial three or four casts usually are the most important. They need to be well placed. First I try to establish just how deep the bass are on the points. I keep marker buoys handy and throw them to the shallow and the deeper parts of the point, and I'll try all different depths on that point. Finally when I get a strike, before I even get the fish in, I reach down and throw a marker out to where I think the fish hit. After I catch one, I'll cast back five or six times to that same spot. Even if I don't catch one, I still want to establish the exact depth and the structure that's there. Some points have hidden structure and cover you might not be aware of, such as a dropoff, a patch of stumps, or a big boulder or two. I get out on the point and use a locator and probe around to find exactly what's there. I want to find out if the bottom is rock, gravel, or mud, and sometimes poke around with my rod tip or a push pole to find out these things. Knowing what's there could be an extremely important part of the pattern. For example, on a gravel bottom, it could be they were in there feeding on crawfish. On a mud bottom, they might be feeding on shad. If they were feeding on crawfish, I'd want to use a crawfish-colored crank bait; if they were hitting shad, I'd want to use a shad color.

Running the points is a matter of efficiency. It's one of the reasons I run a big, fast boat. It's not that I merely want to go sixty miles an hour down the lake. If points are the pattern, then I want to be able to fish seventy-five of 'em in a day, if that's what it takes. If I think the bass might be on the points, then I'll check it out. This is one of the fastest patterns to check out that I know of. In one hour of running points, I can hit perhaps ten points—one every six or seven minutes. I'll try different types of points, including some which the wind is blowing in on, some which are rocky, some with gravel and some with mud bottoms. I'm trying to establish a pattern, and when I find a bass or two on a point, there's usually a definite pattern. It might be a

This 7-pounder took my Fat Rap on a Lake Tenkiller point.

rocky point, whereas the others I tried weren't rocky, and the bass also are apt to be at a certain depth on a certain type of dropoff. Ricky Green and I were looking for a certain depth on a certain kind of bank, and by near the end of the day when we pulled in on a point, we could pretty well tell if we were or weren't going to catch a bass. We had hit so many points that day that we really knew the pattern.

In general, the windswept points have been the most successful for me. I have seen times when I didn't catch 'em on points where the wind was blowing away from the point, but I could go across the lake to points where the wind was blowing in to the point and catch 'em there. The wind needs to be at least pushing the water in front of the point.

One thing I've noticed when scuba diving is that I can be still underwater on a point and stuff will come drifting by in front of my face mask. There might be a one mile-per-hour current moving suspended particles along. The wind will be blowing, and it pushes and circulates the water. I don't know whether bass simply are inclined to feed better in the wind or if the baitfish look like they're distressed and more vulnerable then, but I've always done better with crank baits on overcast, windy days than on bright, calm days. Bright, calm days are usually the worst there are for crank baits.

---

35 Working the Weedlines

Working the weedlines with a crank bait really takes some skill. It's not simply a toss-and-retrieve type of fishing. I'm talking of weeds such as coontail moss, elodea, water cabbage, moss, and other aquatic vegetation which is only partly visible if at all visible. Often the weeds cranked are completely invisible, and the only way I know they're there is by using the locator.

When your crank bait runs into a bunch of weeds, they're a total nemesis. You can't crank into a bunch of coontail moss or milfoil without getting your crank bait trashed up, and with a glob of vegetation hanging on it, you're not going to get anything to hit it. An extremely sensitive feel is needed here. When I crank down and hit the vegetation for the first time, I stop cranking instantly. Maybe the plug will float free. If it's still caught, I give it a hard yank and sometimes it will tear free, and then I let it float up again to clear the weeds before I start cranking it. Sometimes you'll get a strike as it's floating up. Again, if you feel a tick when you start cranking, then let it float up again, but the problem here is sometimes the ticks are light strikes. You've blown the opportunity to catch that bass if the tick was a light strike and you let the plug float up.

In most instances I'm not really cranking over the top of the weeds. I'm throwing to the weed edge where it quits growing and drops off to a bare bottom. That's the dropoff and the structure for the bass. Parallel casting is how I usually work the weedline, but this is difficult because you don't always know where the weedline might bend. If I cast and don't feel any grass, I throw nearer to where I think the grass line might be, and I keep doing this until I tick the moss. I'm

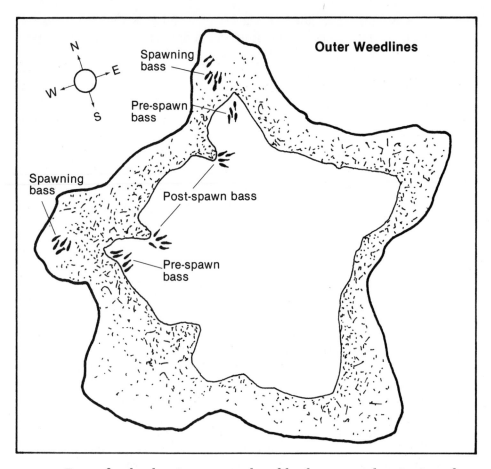

Spawning bass

Pre-spawn bass

Post-spawn bass

Spawning bass

Pre-spawn bass

Outer Weedlines

N
E
W
S

Except for the close-in spawners, bass like the coves and projections along the outer weedline. You have to probe with your lure to locate these irregularities.

very carefully feeling for the weeds so I'll know where the line is. A graphite rod is helpful for this fishing, although at other times when I'm throwing crank baits, I don't normally use a graphite rod because I get hung up so much. But in moss and weeds you don't get hung up that often and it's good to have the extra sensitivity of graphite.

One thing very important about cranking the weedlines is to keep in mind that this is structure. And the *irregularities* of structure are what pay off. Therefore, a straight weedline is not nearly as good as a broken weedline. Where that weedline changes, for example where there's a nook or a little point, is usually where most of the bass are. If you're really watching closely, you might come to a spot on the weed-line where a 100-foot nook goes back, and in the back of that nook is where you're apt to find a concentration of bass. A little point of grass which strikes out 20 feet farther than the other grass also is apt to be where the bass are. It takes careful observation to detect those kinds of places. If suddenly you bump into some grass, then you know the grass extends out on a little point, and you might have to use marker buoys to figure out where the grass point extends out to. Two places they'll usually be on a grass line are at the end of a grass point and in back of a nook.

Sometimes you'll find a grass line which runs straight and then maybe 20 feet on out in the lake there'll be another small rise again and another patch of grass along it. Those are really hard to find because you're casting the grass line and you don't know that little grassy island is out there isolated. Again it relates back to structure in that some of the best structure is *isolated* structure. Sometimes about the only way to find these isolated spots is by running and watching your depthfinder and being observant. It doesn't help here to look at a contour map, because it won't tell you where the weeds actually grow.

In working the weedlines, you don't need to use the deepest-running crank bait in your tacklebox. Often the bass are suspended along the weed edges, and they might be only 4 to 6 feet deep. Shallower crank baits often are excellent. If you find a big moss bed or grass patch all 5 feet deep, it wouldn't hurt to stay out in deeper water and throw in on top of the moss or weeds and retrieve out to the edge. They will be on top of the moss or weeds in the flats, but the bigger concentrations will be on the edges of the vegetation.

This is a clear-water pattern. You're not going to find deep moss or deep vegetation in a muddy lake. The best time to fish this clear water is when there are low light conditions, and again if the water is clear, the cooler water temperatures pay off better. A light wind or breeze will help somewhat because it breaks up the light penetration into the water. There is much more light penetration from the sun down through slick water. That added light helps them detect your line and see the lure too well. With some riffles or chop on the surface, they don't get that good a look at the lure as it comes past. In ultra-clear water a very fast retrieve sometimes works best because they don't see the bait as well and it can fool them.

In clear, weedy waters, the best crank-bait colors seem to be the chromes, shads, and the other light colors. But in a muddy lake where you're cranking stumps or creek channels, the best colors are the crawfish colors, reds and chartreuse colors—the bright colors. In very clear water is one occasion when you can benefit from using light lines. At times then I use spinning tackle with 8- or 10-pound line. This will enable you to get your crank bait considerably deeper. Also, that lighter line will pay off better in super-clear water.

Weedline crank-bait fishing is an entirely different type of crank-bait fishing. When you're cranking the weedlines, you really need to pay close attention and keep thinking structure.

JIGGING LURES

Jigs are "jigged"—fished with an up-and-down action. True jigs are weighted so the hook rides up and are often dressed with hair or other materials. However, spoons, plastic worms, and tailspin lures also qualify as jigs when they're fished that way, so I'll discuss them in this section too.

36 Tweaking the Grub

The grub lure has been around in saltwater fishing for a long time—probably twenty-five years or more. They used the old Salty Dog grub for seatrout and channel bass off the coast. It's been a standard. Never had it been used much in freshwater bass fishing until late 1970 or early 1971. This type of lure has a jig head with the hook protruding upward through a soft or semi-soft molded plastic body. Usually the body mimics a grub but it can be an imitation of some other live and tasty morsel.

The guys most responsible for the freshwater application of the grub were the Murray brothers—Bobby and Billy—from hot Springs, Ark. Bobby Murray used the grub in the spring of 1972 when he won the B.A.S.S. tournament at Ouachita. I came in second; he beat me by a pound.

After the tournament was over, he gave me a couple of grubs and told me how to use 'em. I'd heard rumors about grubs, but I wasn't crazy about light spinning tackle and I wasn't too excited about them. Finally a month later I was back in Oklahoma and I went up to Grand Lake. It's similar to Ouachita in that it's clear and has a lot of rock shoals and very little cover. It has a lot of spotted bass and large-mouths and a variety of panfish and other gamefish. I put the grub on and started jigging around some of the bluffs. My first fish was a white bass, and then a crappie, and finally I started catching some Kentuckies. I was fishing the grub much as I would work a regular jig. I was just swimming it along rather than "tweaking" it.

Eventually I learned how to "tweak" or jig it properly as a structure lure. A guy named Jack Perry was doing an article for *Field & Stream,* and I took him fishing and told him I had a brand-new bass lure which just had been developed and wasn't really on the market yet. I also told him how I'd been catching a lot of fish on it. That day we caught 300 pounds of assorted fish. We had only seven bass, and they ranged up to 5 pounds, but what was so amazing is we had

Three basic styles of grub. These are very effective deep-water lures for jigging on structure.

thirty-seven drum, and these ran to more than 5 pounds. I caught a 29-pound buffalo (it's similar to a carp) and had a couple of 2-pound channel catfish as well as some crappies and white bass. All of them were caught on the grub.

I don't know of any other lure in my tackle box I've experimented with and caught so many different species of fish on as the grub. Through the years I've caught just about as many other species of fish on the grub as bass. The grub is a very effective deep-water lure for jigging on structure.

That summer on Grand Lake, through experimenting I came up with a way to tweak the grub. How I do this is either make a short cast or merely open my bail and let the lure go to the bottom and then jig it. Instead of simply pulling the lure up off the bottom as I would a worm or a jig and eel, I actually bounce it off the bottom. I use a 5½- or 6-foot stiff graphite rod and 6- or 8-pound line. I want the grub to jump violently off the bottom much as a crawfish does. A grub is the size, color, and shape of a crawfish. A crawfish jumps off the bottom and then falls back down, moving in little short motions or spurts. This must be what the grub imitates.

But by tweaking it, you have one other advantage, and this is that lots of times bass will soft-mouth a lure as it's sinking back down. You're keeping the slightest amount of back pressure on the lure and you're watching your line closely, so you'd think you'd feel the strike, but lots of times you don't! The strike almost always comes as the lure is sinking. By tweaking it—ripping it upward—you set the hook in bass which hit it undetected, ones you didn't know were there. You're setting the hook blindly without even knowing there's a fish around. This tweaking also enhances the action of the grub; I get more strikes when I tweak it off a foot or two and then let it flutter back down. I keep a slight bit of back pressure on it and watch the line as it sinks, and again, as with all jigging lures, 98 percent of the strikes occur on the fall.

My biggest day with the grub came that autumn when I qualified for the Project: Sports Tournament of Champions. It was held on Lake Amistad on the Texas-Mexico border. Bobby Murray and I were the only two grub fishermen there. I went way up the lake on the Mexican side and found an old vertical ledge in a cove. On the top of the ledge was 10 to 15 feet of water, but it dropped straight down into 100 feet of water, and there were mesquite bushes on the edge of it. Rather than casting, I just dropped the grub down through the bushes to the

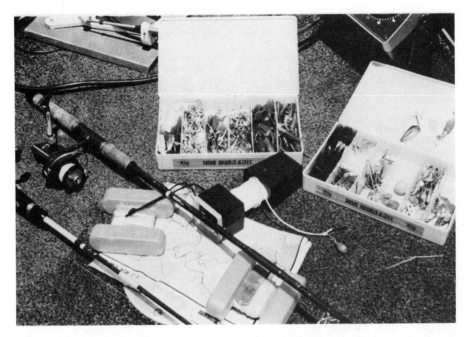

Here's everything you need for tweaking: grubs, jig heads, temperature gauge, topo map, locator, floats, and a light spinning rig.

top of the ledge. The advantage here of jigging it vertically is that if you jig it directly straight down, it frequently dislodges itself if it hits a bush or any other cover. If you jig it around carefully through the cover, you probably won't lose more than a few a day, and grubs are cheap. If you're vertical, you actually can tweak pretty heavy brush and cover.

My partner that first day asked me what I was going to do and I told him I was going to grub the ledge. He said he sure as heck didn't know what that was, and he added that he was going to use plastic worms. I put out two marker buoys about 20 feet apart and fished right between them where the ledge was. All I did was open the bail on my spinning reel, and the grub dropped to the top of the ledge. I was watching my locator, and in addition to the mesquite, I thought I saw a school of fish. As it turned out, I pulled up right on top of a school of largemouths, and the first eleven times I opened my bail and let the grub sink, I caught ten largemouths and missed one. My partner had made a long cast off the ledge, and instantly I hooked one and asked him to get the net. He put his rod down and netted my first bass.

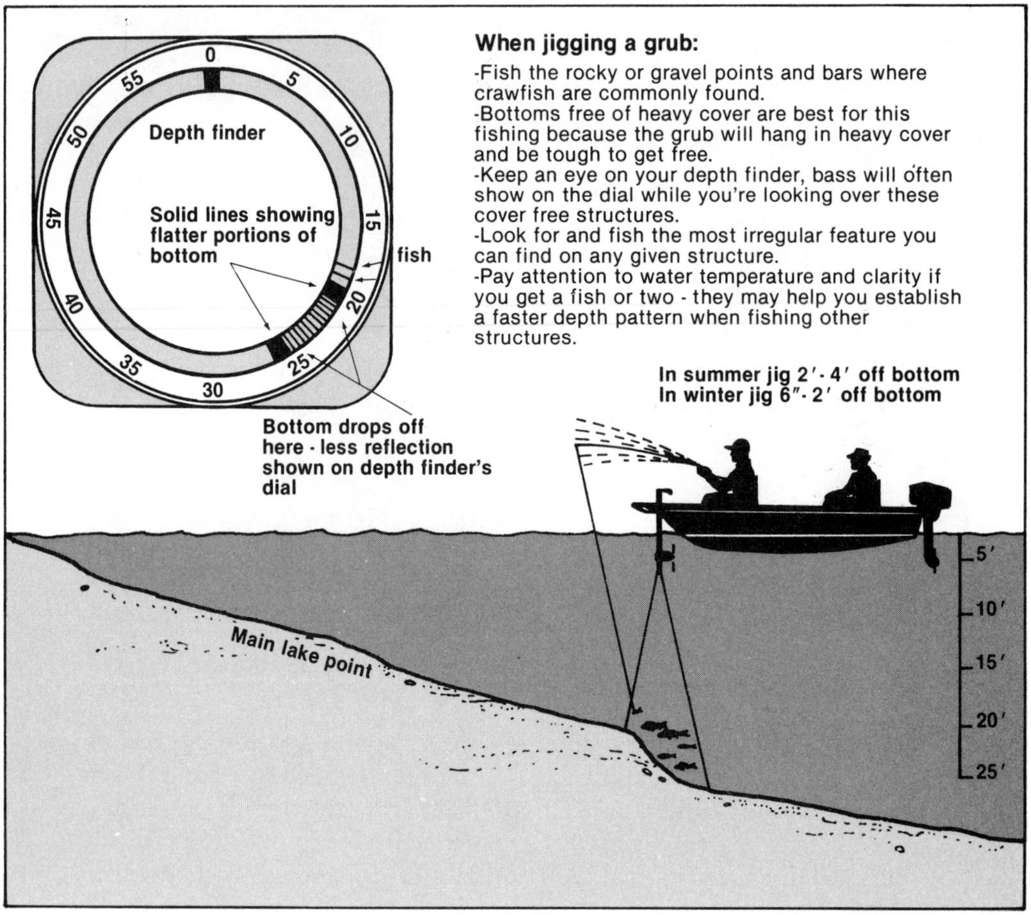

Depth finder

Solid lines showing flatter portions of bottom

fish

0
5
10
15
20
25
30
35
40
45
50
55

Bottom drops off here - less reflection shown on depth finder's dial

When jigging a grub:

-Fish the rocky or gravel points and bars where crawfish are commonly found.
-Bottoms free of heavy cover are best for this fishing because the grub will hang in heavy cover and be tough to get free.
-Keep an eye on your depth finder, bass will often show on the dial while you're looking over these cover free structures.
-Look for and fish the most irregular feature you can find on any given structure.
-Pay attention to water temperature and clarity if you get a fish or two - they may help you establish a faster depth pattern when fishing other structures.

In summer jig 2'- 4' off bottom
In winter jig 6"- 2' off bottom

Main lake point

5'
10'
15'
20'
25'

You really need a depth finder to pinpoint the structure for a vertical method like jigging. I often use two, one on the transom and the other on the bow, to give me a kind of stereo effect when I'm scouting structure.

Then I dropped back down and he picked up his rod and I was yelling for the net again. He put his rod back down and netted the second one. I finally had five or six bass in the boat which he had netted, and he still hadn't retrieved his first cast. After that, he says, "Now, wait a *minute!* You net your own damn fish and let me fish awhile."

I had a limit in the boat, and those bass totaled 23 or 24 pounds. Finally he asked me if I had a grub that he could borrow. I said I did, but really I was planning to leave the spot immediately. He said he didn't have his limit yet, and I reminded him this was the Tournament of Champions and that I'd found this spot and I couldn't afford to let him sit there and catch the bass I'd found. He got a little upset, and I said I'd make a deal with him. I'd give him a grub and show him how to use it and let him catch one or two bass on that spot, but then we were going to leave that hole. He went along with that idea and dropped his grub down there and followed my instructions, but he didn't react quick enough to his first couple of strikes and missed them. I'd seen his line move, and he didn't notice it or feel anything. Finally he caught two, and I said, "Okay. We're gone!"

Well, the next day, it was exactly the same deal on that spot. I caught my ten and left again. On the third and last day of the tournament it was real windy and I couldn't get on the ledge and couldn't anchor because I didn't have a long enough rope. All I could do was make a few wild casts, and I managed to catch a couple of bass in those 3-foot waves. I had to go back into a cove and tie up to some trees and fish plastic worms, but I did manage to win the tournament by 5 or 6 pounds. Tweaking the grub enabled me to win.

Lots of fishermen ask me when to use the grub. I consider it a summer structure type of lure. I usually fish it in water over 10 feet deep and down to 40 feet deep, and normally I fish it on points and ledges and in creek channels. I generally reserve a grub for more open areas, whereas I reserve the other jigging lures (the heavy spoons, tailspin lures such as the Little George, and plastic worms) for heavy cover. The grub is a clear-water lure, whereas the spoons and worms sometimes don't pay off as well in crystal-clear water. On a lake like Mead in Nevada or Powell in Utah, I'd likely fish the grub because the spoon might be too gaudy and flashy. An advantage to the grub is that you can fish it with as light as 4-pound line, although I prefer 6- and 8-pound. With light lines you should use a jig head with a sharp Aberdeen hook. This makes for easy penetration when you set the hook.

I mainly fish the grub in the structure months—June through

October—when the water temperature is 70 degrees or higher. It's more of a summer and fall lure than a springtime lure, but I have seen it work right around spawning season on deeper points adjacent to the spawning areas in clear lakes like Bull Shoals. An advantage of the grub over the plain jig is that the grub is a much faster lure. The grub is a school-bass lure, especially with Kentucky bass. I think it's the most effective lure ever devised for a school of medium-sized Kentucky or spotted bass. Spots eat many crawfish, and the grub is a very quick way to check if they're there. You can drop a grub down into a school of spots, and you might catch only one or two before you spook 'em, but I've never gotten over a school of them and dropped the grub down and jigged it without catching at least one of 'em. If I don't get a strike, I'm convinced the Kentuckies are not there, and I don't even think about using another lure in that place. In a school of Kentuckies, there's always at least one aggressive fish. Spotted bass are smart fish, and maybe I'll find 'em with the grub and catch one or two, and they'll sort of spook off. Then is when I might take a small bear-hair or deer-hair jig and pump it slowly through there and catch more. Or I might tie on a 3- or 4-inch plastic worm and crawl it along through that area, and I might even try to catch a couple by jigging a spoon.

Today there are several different sizes of grubs on the market. I use a medium size about 3 inches long most of the time, and I usually use it on a 1/4-ounce jig head. Sometimes I go to a slightly smaller head—about 1/5-ounce—and if the wind's strong, I might go to a 3/8-ounce. A grub head is different from a regular jig head in that the grub head has a tiny spur on it. When you run the grub on the hook, you continue with it up on the lead, and that spur helps hold it in place. With just a plain jig head, the grub will slide back down the hook and bunch up at the bend, or it will twist on the hook. When I rig the 3-inch grub, I always have the tail flat rather than up and down. (One of my favorite grubs is the little Vibortail, which has a little fin near the tail and looks like a minnow. There's only one way for it to be attached.) On the Bagley and Mann grubs, the tails are flat and should be run on the hook so that when they're sinking or being jigged, the tails are flat with the surface of the water. This gives it a better flutter and makes it sink slower.

I don't know if the grub is as good for smallmouths as the hair jig and pork rind, but I'm convinced the grub is a better Kentucky bass lure, and it's also an excellent lure for largemouths in clear lakes and particularly on rocky points. I like to fish it on rock ledges and rocky, gravelly points without much cover. It's a very fast way to learn if there's a school of fish present.

---

37   Jigging with Spoons, Worms, and Tailspins

About the time I started guiding at Santee-Cooper in 1963, a guy about my age from Summerville, S.C., named Tommy Salisbury became serious about his bass fishing. We got acquainted and really hit it off, and for nearly fifteen years now we've been very good friends. Tommy had fished three or four bass tournaments, and he asked me when I was going to enter a tournament. I told him that when I entered one, I really was going to be *prepared!* Well, I decided to go to Toledo Bend with him for a Bass Anglers Sportsman Society tournament in January of 1970. It was my first tournament, and I especially wanted to do well.

Tommy and I sent off and got a bunch of topographical maps, and we really did our homework long before we left South Carolina and drove to Texas. We marked creek channels and high spots and everything that looked good on the topo maps, and we went out there ten days early. We got out there about three o'clock one morning, and there was ice on the trailer steps at Pendleton Bridge Marina. It was really cold. Tommy had his boat and I had mine, and the best day either one of us had was three bass the first three days we were there. We fished mostly jigs and eels. And we'd heard about jigging those Texas spoons, so we jigged them in the creek channels.

We ran into Billy and Bobby Murray, and they were catching bass, and they showed us how they were jigging their spoons. Toledo Bend was only three years old then, and the trees had all the branches on 'em. The Murrays were pulling their boat through the branches and dropping their jigging lures right down alongside the tree trunks, and they were catching bass. We started doing what they were doing, and we started catching some fish.

The weather started warming up, and about three days before the tournament it got up to 80 degrees. Tommy and I agreed to meet one day about lunchtime at the Texas Bluff area. Tommy was headed there, and he came across a cove and smelled some fish. He thought maybe they were bass, so he suggested we go back there. The cove was

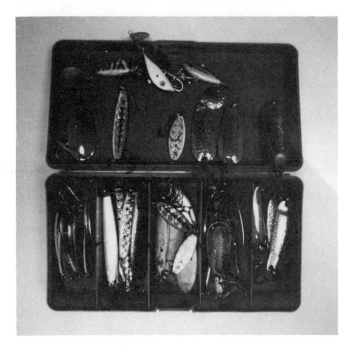

My jigging box includes a variety of spoons— hammered, smooth, painted, fat, slim—as well as some lures of the Little George type.

almost solid trees in 60 feet of water. I had a spinnerbait on and started throwing it, and every little alley I could get the bait through, we'd see ten to twenty bass coming out of the trees after it. And the water was 50 to 60 feet deep below them! We finally measured the water temperature, and for the first three feet, the water was 55 to 58 degrees. Below that it dropped about 10 degrees. Those bass were up near the surface sunning themselves. That afternoon we caught about seventy-five bass. The next day we split up, and each of us looked for similar coves where the water was slick. Where we found slick water, we could run the spinnerbaits and catch 'em close to the top.

The morning of the first round of the tournament, we got out on the water with the rest of the boats. It was just getting daylight, and we saw this big, black cloud coming. It was what the Texans call a blue norther. The wind blew, and it rained and stormed, and man, did it turn cold! This all hit within five minutes after Ray Scott shot the gun. Tommy fished with Glenn Carver, who now owns Mr. Twister lures, and they jigged spoons about 20 feet deep in Slaughter Creek, and Tommy was in eighteenth or nineteenth place after the first day. I'd drawn Joe Palermo. (I told earlier about having five rods rigged up with five spoons and catching six bass in a row while he was catching one and trying to get the hooks out of it.) I culled bass—releasing the smaller ones—after about nine a.m., and I soon got into the top twenty-five.

There were two different jigging patterns on Toledo Bend during that tournament. There were school bass suspended 20 feet deep over 50 feet of water on the river channel. These were mostly 1¼-to-1½-pounders, and they were what I caught the first day. The second day I drew J. B. Warren from Arkansas. He and Jack Price had found five or six super holes full of big bass in the creek channels. J.B. was confident about his chances of winning because he and Price had all these big bass located. The first day he'd caught only five or six, but they were in the 4-pound range. He took me into a creek. He was fishing a jig and eel, but I'd been fishing spoons for a couple of weeks, and I knew they were hitting spoons. He caught the first one, about a 4-pounder, on the jig and eel.

I told him I was going to try a spoon. The water temperature was about 50 degrees, because another cold front had hit, and the way to fish the spoon was to raise it up about 2 feet off the bottom in this heavy tree-and-brush cover and almost lower it down by keeping slight back pressure on the lure as it fell. These were cold-water bass, and cold-water bass don't strike hard; they just sort of stop the lure. I use fluorescent line and watch for the slightest twitch when I'm fishing this way in cold water. If the bait doesn't sink back all the way, usually it's a fish and you need to set the hook. That day they were halfway hitting at the spoon and missing it, and the lure would fall on their backs. I'd feel the hesitation and set the hook, and two or three of the bass I caught with J.B. were foul-hooked in the side of their gills. The bass I caught were mostly 3-to-5-pounders, and I weighed in 39 pounds that second day. It put me way up in the standings with one day left. J.B. had a slow day, and that evening he told me he didn't stand a chance to win, but I did, and he said he wanted me to go back to that creek channel he knew about and stay there and win the tournament on that hole. I told him I didn't want to do that and that I wanted to honor his hot spot.

The third day I didn't go to J.B.'s hot spot. I went to another creek with my partner, Jim Saxton from Texas, and we jigged spoons around different high spots. I caught 26 pounds and finished second. But the odd part about it was that when I came back to the weigh-in, J. B. Warren asked me if I'd gone back to that creek he and I had

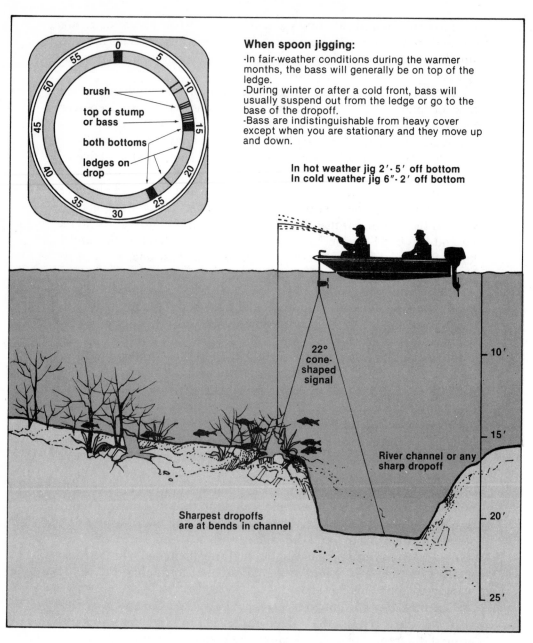

When spoon jigging:

-In fair-weather conditions during the warmer months, the bass will generally be on top of the ledge.

-During winter or after a cold front, bass will usually suspend out from the ledge or go to the base of the dropoff.

-Bass are indistinguishable from heavy cover except when you are stationary and they move up and down.

In hot weather jig 2'- 5' off bottom
In cold weather jig 6"- 2' off bottom

brush

top of stump or bass

both bottoms

ledges on drop

22° cone-shaped signal

River channel or any sharp dropoff

Sharpest dropoffs are at bends in channel

10'

15'

20'

25'

Once you've located structure like this, you can fish it very effectively with a spoon; unlike a grub, a spoon will usually come free when hung up.

fished, and I told him I hadn't. Well, as it turned out, he hadn't gone back there either! It was the hottest place on the lake, and neither of us had fished it! I figured he should fish it, and he figured I should fish it. *Nobody* fished it!

Here again, I count down the spoon as I do my other underwater lures, and this is important. Lots of times when you're drifting and jigging, you'll find a little mound or a dropoff much easier and quicker if you're counting the spoon down. In the winter and cold water, I don't lift the spoon more than 2 feet off the bottom, but in the summer you can jig it much faster and lift it higher.

The biggest tournament I ever won with a jigging spoon was at Santee-Cooper in the 1975 South Carolina Invitational B.A.S.S. event. I fished the lower lake (Moultrie) and jigged with a Hopkins Spoon. The water temperature was 75 degrees during the first week of June when the event was held, and there was a lot of wind. The bass were active, and I lifted the spoon much higher, and they hit much harder. I was using a large popping type of rod, and I'd lift the spoon 4 to 8 feet off the bottom. With a 6-foot rod, you can lift a spoon 15 feet off the bottom when you put the rod tip almost to the water and then bring it back over your head and finally your shoulder. We learned this jigging the spoons for striped bass at Santee, and we found the rockfish like a much higher lift and much more violent jigging motion.

Jigging fish are structure fish whether they're stripers or black bass. In the summer a good jigging spot could be a submerged hill, a point, or the edge of a creek channel. But in the winter, creek channels generally pay off better. Bass generally like high spots in the summer and creek channels in the winter. I prefer jigging heavy spoons rather than casting lures because jigging is more direct. The only time I cast is when I'm looking for fish, but I miss a lot of fish casting because I don't have the direct control of the lure. The best way to catch 'em is to get vertical and drop the lure right down on the fish and jig it on the structure. I don't fish the spoon shallower than 15 feet because deep-structure fish are 15 feet or deeper. Most of the deep-structure lakes where you can catch bass good by jigging spoons are clear-water lakes, and particularly in the summer those bass on structure are at a minimum of 15 feet deep and often 20 to 30 feet deep. I have caught 'em deeper. I came in second in the B.A.S.S. tournament at Sam Rayburn in 1971, and the best string I caught there, about 30 pounds, was by jigging a spoon 46 feet deep. Those were the deepest bass I've ever caught in a tournament.

Sometimes the bigger standing timber is good for spoon jigging. The fish will suspend near the timber and are apt to hit anytime during the spoon's fall.

I get asked by fishermen when I use the spoon and when I vertical-jig the plastic worm. The spoon is for both warm and cold water, whereas the worm is strictly a hot-weather bait. In the summer the bass on deep structure will be at the thermocline levels in water 60 to 80 degrees, and this is a good time to jig the worm. Jigging a spoon really gets 'em excited. But I do a lot of changing up. I might be jigging a spoon and catch two or three bass and then they quit hitting the spoon. Then I drop a worm or a grub down there, and often I'll catch more after changing lures. I have seen times when they would hit the worm and not the spoon, but usually when you run into a school of bass, you catch a couple right quick on whatever you're using. The spoon is simply the fastest way to find them. Nothing sinks as fast as a spoon. When I jig a worm, I use 6-to-8-inch worms rigged regular Texas-style, but I usually use a 3/8- or 1/2-ounce lead.

Four of the popular jigging spoons on the market today are the Hopkins, Bomber Slab, Salty Dog by Bagley, and Mann-O-Lure. One thing about these heavy spoons with their heavy treble hooks is that you might jig one of 'em all day without losing it. When it hangs in heavy cover, you can keep jiggling it and the weight of it often will cause it to knock loose. You might not believe it, but you can jig the same cover all day with a single-hook Johnson Spoon (the Silver Minnow), and even though it has a weedguard, you're apt to lose ten of 'em in a day! The weight of the Silver Minnow is not compacted, and it won't shake loose like a heavy metal-bodied jigging spoon.

My standard tackle for spoon jigging includes a heavy worm or flipping rod and at least 20-pound line. I often use 25-pound, and like Stren Fluorescent line because I can watch it and detect light strikes.

No section on jigging spoons would be complete without mentioning Blake Honeycutt from Hickory, N.C. The Hopkins Spoon was around for many years in saltwater fishing before it ever caught on with freshwater anglers. And Blake was one of the pioneers of adapting the Hopkins to freshwater bassing. He's a master at jigging the spoons, and he also holds the all-time B.A.S.S. tournament record for the most pounds caught in a three-day tournament. Back in July of 1969 he caught 138 pounds, 6 ounces—thirty-four bass—to win the tournament at Lake Eufaula in Alabama. There was a fifteen-bass daily limit for that tournament. Blake also was one of the first to master structure fishing. He used to fish with Buck Perry, also from Hickory, who is known as the grandfather of structure fishing.

Honeycutt says that at times you can take a Hopkins Spoon and try to hold it a foot or so off the bottom real still and not move it, and bass will come up to it and knock the heck out of it. He believes the water current is causing the spoon to move back and forth just a little bit when it's suspended off the bottom. This might be, but I believe, too, that from using the spoon, a little bit of line twist develops, and when you're holding it still like that, the line straightens out and causes the spoon to turn a little bit, and this is what attracts the bass.

We got onto using the jigging spoons early at Santee-Cooper, as far back as 1963, but back then we used them exclusively for stripers. The first bass I ever caught on one was one time when I was fishing with

My Lowrance Chart Recorder helped point out this fish lying on the dropoff.

another guide, Bob George. He's an expert rockfish guide, and we were out fishing for fun for stripers, and I caught about a 4-pound largemouth off Pinopolis Point in the lower lake. Then I started trying the jigging spoon in shallower water where the largemouths stayed. Most of the stripers we caught jigging were out in 40 to 50 feet of water. On the 20-to-25-foot-deep bars, I started catching some large-mouths on the spoons.

Jigging spoons will catch the big largemouths which are down deep, but the reason I don't think they catch more big bass is that a lot of the 7-to-10-pounders are in shallower cover rather than down 20 to 30 feet deep. At Santee during the seven years I fished regularly there, I caught twenty-four bass over 10 pounds, but only two of them ever came off deep structure. However, the jigging spoons are super for catching bass from 2 to 4 or 5 pounds, and that size I'm sure after when I'm in a tournament.

The most popular of a few tailspin lures on the market is the Little George. Tom Mann, the manufacturer, named it after the Alabama governor, George Wallace, and Tom says Wallace got quite a kick out of the name. It has an oval-shaped lead body and a spinner which revolves on a wire behind the body. The spinner revolves as the lure sinks as well as when it's pulled upward. Tom's sold probably a zillion of 'em, and one of the reasons is it's not like a Hula Popper that you can fish for fourteen years without losing it. Having one Little George is like having one potato chip; it's not enough. You're going to leave some Little Georges hanging on stumps and lodged between rock crevices in deep water.

I like the Little George more for casting than for vertical jigging. If I'm fishing a bar, shoal, or dropoff, I make casts with it. These tailspinners can be vertical-jigged, and they're great lures, but they don't get to the bottom as fast as the spoons do.

WEEDLESS LURES

A Texas-rigged plastic worm is a weedless lure, and so is a safety-pin-style spinnerbait, because in both cases the hook is pretty much kept out of trouble. But in this section I'm talking about weedless lures in the narrow sense—lures that have the hook point protected by some special device, usually a springy wire weedguard.

38 Grazing the Grass

This pattern brings back some very fond memories of the late 1960s when I was at Santee-Cooper. I did some experimenting by taking a black Johnson Spoon (the Silver Minnow) and attaching a 4- or 5-inch tail section of a black plastic worm. The first good bass catch I made on it was in the spring of 1967 in the lower lake near the mouth of the Diversion Canal. Two weeks later I was guiding a Mr. Smith, and I was telling him all about catching several 8- and 9-pounders on the black Johnson Spoon with the worm trailer.

Sometimes when you're grazing the grass you need waders; bringing in the boat would spook the fish.

I rigged one up for him, and he threw out by this grass bed, and he hooked a 6½-pounder which really ate up his spoon. He fought the fish to the boat and I netted him, but he didn't say a word. I'm all excited and telling him about this brand-new technique and how great it is. I'll never forget what he then said.

"Son," he said slowly, "I'm seventy-six years old, and the Johnson Spoon was my father's favorite bait."

I was catching those bass in May of 1967, and by May the next year, I'd figured out something most of us didn't realize. We thought that after April, Santee's bass were through spawning. We didn't realize that during May and even early June, we could look around and actually find a few spawners. In May of 1968 about the middle of the month my customers and I caught two or three bass from 8 to 10 pounds per day, and this lasted for a week. We got them on the black Johnson Spoons, around the full moon. The full moon in June also produced well in the grass. At that time, however, the grass beds were dying, and the next year there'd be only two-thirds as much grass as the year before. From one standpoint this was good, because it tended to concentrate the bass more.

Finally by May 1969 I'd gone to big, heavy popping rods, 30-pound line, and hooks that I'd bent out on the spoons to make them a little bigger. I also switched to Bagley's Hardhead plastic worms, which were a harder plastic. And I'd figured out to throw into the wind so the grass I was pulling the spoon over was bent toward me and the lure would slide over it better. When fishing clear water, you often want the sun at your back because your visibility is then good, and fish don't like to look into the sun. But when you're grazing the grass, you won't see much anyway and the fish are more likely to see your shadow than to see you. So I also learned to throw into the sun as much as I could in order to keep my shadow down.

That year was a super year, and in that month of May was when I set all my personal bass records at Santee. My customers and I caught forty-two bass over 8 pounds that month. On May 14, I caught ten largemouths which totaled 87 pounds, and they all were caught on that 1/2-ounce No. 2 Johnson Spoon with the black worm trailer. Five days later I caught ten on the spoon that totaled 79 pounds, and three of them were each over 10 pounds. Both days were cloudy days.

A couple of things Tommy Salisbury and I discovered about our "grazing the grass" pattern with the Johnson Spoons was, first of all, unless it was a cloudy day, we had to catch our bass before nine o'clock in the morning or at dusk when the sun got off the water. Between nine a.m. and dusk, the pattern was dead if the weather was clear. We had one good hole, and we got to wondering if those bass would hit at night. I was guiding two college students one day, and I talked them into getting up at three a.m. and going to that hole. We fished for an hour and a half without a strike. We waded all along those grass beds and threw everywhere, and finally the sun started showing through the trees.

I saw a boil and threw over there and caught a 1 1/2-pound white bass on the Johnson Spoon, my first and last white bass ever caught on the spoon. I told the guys we'd messed up and that there weren't going to be any bass coming in there. Finally it was full daylight, and just before the sun broke completely over the trees I caught a 2-pounder. When the first rays of the sun finally hit the grass bed, a herring about 10 inches long went skipping across the surface, and I threw in there and caught an 8 1/2-pounder. One of the college boys caught one about 8 pounds. Then we got a 7-pounder. This continued until about nine o'clock, and then they quit. But in an hour and a half we caught a bunch, and our ten biggest weighed 70 pounds. And we'd fished there for an hour and a half before we got the first strike.

The best fishing always came during the first couple weeks of May when the green grass grew up and laid a mantle on the surface. Before that we caught some bass on the Johnson Spoons around the brown grass. I run my spoons on the surface or just an inch or two under, but Tommy Salisbury likes to skip his spoon across the top and use it strictly as a topwater lure.

Tiny Lund, the racecar driver who owned a fish camp on the lower lake, used to fish for bass only with a black Johnson Spoon and a worm behind it as I did.

Despite the fact that a Johnson Spoon has a single hook and a weedguard, I don't lose many bass on it. When I first started fishing it, I was using a 6-foot rod and an Ambassadeur and 20-pound line, and I lost several fish. The 20-pound line is marginal; 25 and 30 is better. That's what I want. The other problem is that with that heavy spoon, you have a tendency to make a long cast. When I was on a big grass bed, I'd find myself making 100-foot casts, and when they hit way out there, I couldn't get the hook set good enough on 'em. To set the hook properly, I went to a popping rod and a casting rod with a big salt-water handle. I wanted something I could hold in my stomach for leverage.

Probably the most important aspect of grass-bed fishing is to *point the rod at the spoon.* If you hold the rod high, then you don't have any way to strike back good. Also the low rod position enables you to work the spoon better.

This pattern works very well in Florida. A Johnson Spoon probably catches more bass over 8 pounds in Lake Okeechobee today than anything other than a live shiner. In fact, it probably catches more than the shiners, because shiners aren't all that popular down there. It's a great springtime lure for spawning bass, and down there January and February are big spawning months. The spoon also works good in Wisconsin and Minnesota in the lily pads and weeds, and in Canada for northern pike as well as bass. I like the black spoon for a dark day and the gold one for a sunny day.

Even in Oklahoma and Texas, you don't think of having grass beds in lakes like the grass and milfoil in North Carolina's Currituck Sound, for example. But the Lone Star State and the Sooner country

Point the rod right at the spoon, so you'll be in position to strike hard. This is particularly important when you're making long casts with the heavy spoon.

has grass called pond weed. It grows usually in 2 to 4 feet of water, sometimes a little deeper, and it has oblong leaves about 1½ inches long. Snaking the spoon right on top of the grass really pays off, and the heavier the grass, the slower you can work it. Work it slow in that heavy cover, because there's so much stuff for them to get through to hit the spoon.

I've experimented with all sorts of trailer hooks on the Johnson Spoon, but none of 'em performs well. You're fishing so much heavy vegetation that a trailer hook just doesn't work good. I advise you to forget about even trying a trailer hook.

Some guys thread their plastic worm on the weedguard of the

Sometimes I rig the Johnson Silver Minnow with a rubber skirt rather than a plastic worm.

Johnson Spoon and then run it up to the bend of the hook. This gives the lure a different action, but I don't rig it this way very often. I guess it's just that I've seen so many bass from 8 to over 11 pounds blow up on it the way I rig it that I've never seen any reason to change. My biggest on the spoon weighed 11 pounds, 3 ounces.

Some guys really like the Weed Wing Spoon which Johnny O'Neill designed. It's a very fast spoon, and it's great in hot weather, but one thing I've found out is that when the water's in the 50s to low 60s in the spring, the big bass don't move real fast for the spoon, and a slower retrieve catches lots more of 'em. The hotter the water, the faster they move for a spoon. Another good spoon on the market is the Timber King, which Charles Spence of Memphis, Tenn., manufactures. It's similar to the old Rex Spoon made years ago by the old Weetzel Bait Company in Cincinnati.

Tommy Salisbury and I thought our grazing-the-grass pattern was strictly a springtime deal, but we later found it would work to some degree in June, July, and even August. We caught some bass then in the grass.

One thing to remember is that in different lakes in different regions, the aquatic vegetation changes. At Santee we fished Johnson grass. Lake Kissimmee in Florida has the same type of grass, but in Okeechobee, it's pepper grass. At Currituck Sound, which is probably the finest Johnson Spoon water on the continent, it's Eurasian milfoil. Toledo Bend has milfoil and some pond weed. And if you fish the Johnson Spoon in your uncle's farm pond in Illinois, you might be fishing lily pads. Regardless of the type of vegetation, the spoon approach still works, even if you're using it in reeds.

Think *big* bass when you're grazing the grass.

---

39   Gunk Fishing

Marty Friedman from New York City first used the word "gunk" to mean masses of half-dead and half-alive vegetation on the surface. I'd been fishing all this crud for a decade, but I didn't know what to call this pattern. The vegetation is floating and is scummy and blows around and piles up. Some of it is duckwort, which has very tiny leaves. The stuff is all within 3 to 4 inches of the surface, and it's an excellent place for bass to hide and be shaded from the sun.

At Thousand Islands in New York in the summer of 1978, Marty showed me some real innovations in gunk fishing. This was after the New York Invitational BASS Tournament, and we made a TV film together for my show. I'd won that tournament with the worm on structure. We had practiced together one day, and he showed me this pattern. It was my secondary pattern, but I never had to go to it during the tourney.

The pattern was that back in the spawning coves, these bays were shallow, only 2 to 4 feet deep. The bass were in there to spawn, and the water was very clear. Once the sun got on the water, they'd be looking for shade, and they found it under the gunk. I'd always used the Johnson Spoon for this type of fishing, but Marty showed me another lure which was equally effective. He was using the old Rex Spoon, and the way he rigged it up was impressive. This spoon and the Timber King are a little wider and stay on the top easier, and they have a removable hook which is attached with a screw, and a rubber skirt is secured between the hook shank and the body of the spoon.

Marty put a black skirt on a silver ½-ounce Rex Spoon, and he

Some fishermen can't believe that bass would get under all this gunk—but they do, and they'll come up through it after a spoon-and-trailer combination.

attached a chartreuse Phenom worm with a curly tail to the hook as a trailer. He dragged the lure across the gunk, and about half of the strikes occurred then. The way he set the hook was important. He waited momentarily after the strike until the fish actually pulled on the line. Often they'd bust at it and miss the lure entirely. When I'd get a strike, I'd set the hook, and I missed several bass, but when he'd get a strike, he'd keep reeling until he felt the fish. The other half of the strikes came when you reached the edge of the gunk. That's where the curly tail on the worm came into prominence; when you reached the edge of the gunk, you simply let the lure sink straight down. There was a lot of wiggle and flash, and the Rex Spoon sinks slower than the Johnson Spoon. You'd let it sink, and you'd watch your line, and it would jump when you got a strike. The water was clear, and sometimes the lure hadn't sunk 6 inches when you saw the flash of the bass as he grabbed it.

Marty definitely had perfected this type of fishing which I'd been doing for years. He perfected the lure and the pause before he set the hook, which he did only after he felt the fish.

The Timber King Spoon won Bobby Murray $25,000 back in October 1978 at the BASS Masters Classic at Ross Barnett in Mississippi. Bobby painted the spoon black with a marker, and he used a trailer hook and put a No. 4 Hildebrandt Spinner ahead of the spoon. Bobby and some guys had got to experimenting during the B.A.S.S. tournament back in January on the St. Johns River in Florida. They were trying for spawning bass in Lake George, and the wind was real bad. Their lures were getting blown around, and they were using spoons and buzz baits. He and David Owens from Arkansas had heard guys were catching bass on Hildebrandt Snagless Sally lures, so they got the idea to put the spinner ahead of their spoon.

They learned that even if it's windy, your line stays tight because the blade digs into the water. It's very similar to a regular spinnerbait. David Owens led the tourney the first day, and he was using a Johnson Spoon. Bobby and I communicate a lot at tournaments, and he showed me his spoon the first day of the tournament. I had some of those spinners with me, and I put them on the front of a Johnson Spoon and a Timber King Spoon. I caught a few bass on the spoons rigged this way, but I just didn't catch enough. The bass were striking short, and I lost a limit each day. They'd knock the spoon from one lily pad to the next one, and I couldn't hook 'em. It was exasperating. All I could say would be use a trailer hook, but I used a trailer hook and it still didn't help. Lots of fishermen in the Classic said they hooked a small percentage of what they had strike, and Bobby lost fish, too. I don't know what we could have done, but I'm sure there must be some way to do it.

I certainly don't claim to know all the answers. When I chose the title for this book, I was aware that there are at least 101 other ways to catch 'em. Lots of these other ways I'm still working on and am trying to perfect, and I'm sure lots of other bass fishermen are trying to perfect ways they've come up with. One thing great about this sport is that you never quit learning new things, and you can keep learning better ways to do old things.

One thing I'd like to learn is how to hook every single bass that strikes. It certainly would have helped me if I'd known how during the 1978 Classic.

40 Frogging the Pads

There are four or five weedless plastic frogs on the market, and they include the SnagProof Frog, the Bill Plummer Superfrog, the Joe Sabol Frog, a frog made by Burke, and a couple of local ones made in the deep south. The two I use the most are the Bill Plummer Superfrog and the SnagProof Frog. The SnagProof has double hooks, whereas the others have single hooks.

Frog fishing is an art in itself; to fish it right takes a lot of self-control. The secret is to *pause* the instant a bass slurps in the frog and give the fish time to get the lure completely inside his mouth. Make a good cast into the pads and use a stop-and-go retrieve and twitch, burble, and slide the frog across the vegetation. Strikes come either when the frog is sitting there quietly or when it's being pulled with short twitches. Again, when the bass strikes, *let him take the frog!* This doesn't make much sense to a lot of anglers, but if you set the hook instantly when you see the strike, you'll miss an awful lot of strikes.

The trick is to almost pretend you're fishing a plastic worm, because the frog is a soft plastic bait, too, and when a bass grabs it, he'll likely try to eat it much the same as he usually would try to devour a plastic worm. When he strikes, he might have the frog only in his lips, but he'll mouth it and get it securely inside his mouth.

When the bass hits the frog, give him completely slack line and pause for two to three seconds. As he turns and dives down into the pads, he'll sort of gulp the bait again, and then is the time to set the hook. When he's moving away from you and you set the hook, you have a far greater chance of setting the hook at least into the side of his jaw than you had when he might have been facing you. Also, two to three seconds later, chances are the frog is completely inside his mouth. However, you can't wait too long, and you can't let the fish feel any pressure. When he hits and is whirling around, if he feels any

Strikes can come either when the frog is sitting quietly or when you're pulling it in short twitches.

pressure, he'll likely spit the frog out. And if you let him run more than three seconds, he's moved off 6 feet and likely is around a dozen lily-pad stems. It's a matter of timing. You don't want him to get the line around a bunch of pad stems because then you'd never get the hook set sufficiently. You merely want him to get turned good and started down before you set the hook.

Heavy tackle is needed for frog fishing the same as it is for gunk fishing. Six-foot popping rods or light-action muskie rods are my favorites, with at least 20-pound line. When you're going over heavy gunk or heavy pads, they don't see your line, and you often have a problem pulling those bass out. The lightest rod you should use is a worm rod. With a popping rod, you can stick the butt in your stomach and have both hands above the reel much the same as with a boat rod, and you can put a lot of pressure on the bass and pull him a lot harder and stronger than you can from the wrist strength you put on a regular bait-casting rod. I've had bass in the 10-pound range hit in the gunk and the pads, and when I set the hook properly I could hold them on top because the gunk and pads were so thick. As he's splash-

You need hefty tackle for frogging; you've got to control the fish and keep it from wrapping your line in the weeds and lily pads.

ing and thrashing around on top, a big bass can't get into the water good and get his fins to digging in. I've been able to slide and pull him across the top of the pads, and this is a super way to battle him.

If he's already down in the pads or the gunk, I battle him differently. I'll give him line if he's down in the vegetation. All you'd do is break your line if you pulled him too hard. If you try to stop him cold in one spot, he'll turn and wrap around pad stems. Give him enough line to move off on any big surges he makes under those pads, and get your boat to him immediately. Then when you get to him, your line won't be around a bunch of stems. As you get up over him, you can keep pulling your line up, and it'll be cutting through the tops of the pads. Herein lies an advantage to a single-hook lure: if the bass has it completely inside his mouth, there are no hooks on the outside to hang on the vegetation as he powers through it.

Frogging the pads is primarily a hot-summer pattern. You think of frogs being out in the spring, but I've never done especially well with the frog before hot weather arrived. One thing about hot weather is that it causes a certain amount of bass to seek the oxygen and shade from heavy weeds, and often there'll be cooler water beneath the shade of lily pads. Evidently the pads reflect the sun enough so that they don't retain a lot of heat. I've frequently waded in lily pads, and I've noticed the water around them is cooler than the water out in the open away from the pads.

An advantage of the frog over the spoon is that the spoon has to be fished fairly fast. If the fish are really active, they'll hit the spoon fast. But you can fish the frog very slowly. It floats, and if they prefer a very slow-moving lure, the frog will pay off better. When you hit a small open pocket in the pads, stop the frog right in that spot and let it sit there. That's when a wary bass which isn't particularly hungry and is not actively feeding often will come up out of curiosity and watch that frog. Then when you twitch it, he'll often suck it in gently. Remember to let him turn and move off for two or three seconds, and then bust him!

LIVE BAIT

41 Drifting and Trolling Shiners

I used to look down on live-bait fishing at one time in my career. Back then I didn't realize its potential or what a fine way it is to catch trophy fish. My first experience with big river shiners—and I'm talking about the 10-to-12-inch wild shiners which weigh up to a pound— was in Florida with a guy named Chuck Mooney. He's formerly from Ohio and is a guide down in central Florida, and he's caught some 200 bass over 10 pounds, with his biggest 16¼ pounds. I met him during a Bass Anglers Sportsman Society tournament in 1970, and aside from any tourney fishing he does, he's strictly a shiner fisherman. All his really giant bass are caught on these large shiners.

My first bass over 10 pounds on a shiner was caught at Watermelon Pond in Florida in 1970 in August while fishing with Chuck.

A lively shiner can get you an explosive surface strike—the most electrifying moment for a bass fisherman.

This was back when Watermelon Pond was a full 7,000 acres. Now it's only about 3,000 acres. Back then it was probably the best lunker hole in Florida. What we did essentially was anchor out in the center near small potholes 10 to 15 feet deep. We also drifted across some potholes with a float and a shiner on about 6 feet of line. We'd get only a couple of fish a day, but very seldom would we ever get a bass under 6 pounds. Normally what we caught would be from 7 to 10 pounds or a little bigger.

I was all keyed up. I'd been fishing at Cape Hatteras and was using a surf rod and had 40-pound line on the reel and my drag set real tight. I got a strike, and he really pulled that float down, and Chuck said to let him take it for a while. When I hit him, I struck back so hard that I sloshed the bass right up to the top. I had to pull him through some lily pads with stems as thick as my thumb. That fish weighed 10½ pounds, and he probably would have wrapped up and broken 20-pound-test line. But my 40-pound cut through the lily pads and I finally landed him.

One thing about shiners I found out is that you just can't buy those big river shiners anywhere for the kind of bass fishing Chuck talks about. Basically you have to go out and catch your own shiners. A few guides and commercial outfits go out and trap them. When you can buy them, they normally cost from four to six dollars per dozen. A 12-inch shiner is probably a five-year-old fish, and in a pond it would take so long to raise them that size that it wouldn't be profitable. Of course, you can buy lots of 3-inch shiners, and that's what lots of fishermen use.

About half the fun of shiner fishing is catching your bait. First you have to go out and put the bread out and bait up the spot. You also can use oatmeal or meal cake or something like that to attract the shiners. In most of the Florida lakes shiners are found around coontail moss and underwater grass out from lily pads in the backs of bays and coves. After you put the shiner bait out, you have to wait anywhere from a couple of hours until even the next day, and then you come sneaking back and anchor real quietly on the spot. You catch them with a hook and line, and they're hard to catch. I like to use a 12-to-16-foot cane pole with 8- or 10-pound line and about a No. 12 trout hook with a small shank and an itsy bitsy split shot a couple of inches above the hook. Normally you fish from 3 to 10 feet deep for shiners, and I use a tiny float which is very sensitive to the slightest nibble. I use either a very tiny piece of wadded-up bread or biscuit dough about the size of a medium-sized garden pea. Some guys even use tiny gobs of peanut butter. Fish right over your chum spot, and watch your float real close. Even though these shiners are ½ pound or bigger, they'll suck in that bread or dough much the same as a carp would do. Lots of times the float will just quiver a couple of times, and they'll steal your bait easily. Shiners fight, jump, and thrash around about like a trout. They just go crazy, and they're a lot of sport to catch.

You need a big live well to put three or four dozen shiners in. I usually use a bass-boat live well with a pump which circulates lake water to keep them fresh and alive. Don't put your hands on the shiners any more than you have to, because their scales will fall off and

A close look at a shiner and some of the results of fishing them.

you'll kill 'em. If you can, swing the shiner into your live well and flip him off the hook without touching him. You have to be careful when you open the lid on your live well because shiners will jump clear out of your boat. You need a real lively shiner if you want to catch a super-big trophy bass.

When you've got several dozen shiners and you're ready to go bass fishing, you need to rig up your heavy tackle. What I mean by heavy tackle is line that's at least 20-pound-test, and really 20-pound is rather light. I prefer 25-to-40-pound. In creek channels and deeper areas of the lake, you probably can fish deeper with lighter line if there's not too much trash. But quite often when you're trolling or drifting the weed edges, which are the shallower edges where the lily pads start, you really need to use heavier line because the bass are hunkered up in heavy cover. When they hit and go back into that grass you can set the hook and still pull 'em out of places like that with 40-pound line.

The trick is to put a giant live shiner on about an 8/0 hook. I like to use *two* hooks when I can, such as a 5/0 or 6/0 hook in the front and maybe an 8/0 hook in the tail. Sometimes in open water where there are no weeds I use a treble hook in the shiner's anal fin and run a 40-pound leader up to my front hook and then extend the leader up to the float. Even if I'm drifting, I like to use the float to see when I'm getting a strike. The float helps tell you where the shiner is, such as a couple of feet out from a weed edge. The float really is your reference point concerning which direction the shiner is moving.

If your shiner is real lively, he gets scared and nervous when a bass comes toward him. The shiner starts quivering, and the float twitches and jumps. Lots of times the shiner comes to the top just before the bass grabs him, and the shiner actually jumps out of the water three or four times. A really big bass often misses the shiner on two or three surges before he catches him, and this adds to your excitement and anticipation. The shiner keeps jumping and the bass keeps charging, and after three to five big swirls the bass gets him and the float goes under. If you've got a treble hook on and you're in a lot of cover, I set the hook quickly, as with a plastic worm. I just drop the rod tip and reel up the slack and bust him hard to try to move him out of the cover. When he first hits the shiner, he might get it crossways in his mouth and both hooks could be hanging on the outside. If it's open water and I can let him run for ten seconds, I'll do that. After he moves off 5 or 6 feet he'll usually stop and turn the shiner in his mouth and engulf it. Then you've got twice as good a chance of hooking the fish. There's a lot of visual contact in shiner fishing when you're using a lively shiner and you get that explosive strike on the surface and the bobber goes under.

When you set the hook, one thing a big Florida bass likes to do is jump right away. He usually doesn't run to deep water when he's around the weedlines. In Florida when you hook one which tries to jump but doesn't clear the water, a standard rule of thumb is that you've got one on over 10 pounds. I have seen 12-pound and even 14-pound bass clear the water, but that's an exception. Huge fish usually slosh around on the top, with the shiner in their mouths.

I think most of the trophy-bass hunters in America prefer to fish shiners in central Florida over any other place in the United States. For some reason southern Florida doesn't seem to have the strain of really big bass. They catch fewer bass over 10 pounds from Orlando on south than they do from Orlando on north. The biggest trophy bass come from Orlando to Jacksonville between Lake Kissimmee and Lake Jackson at Tallahassee. This seems to be the area where the genetically largest bass are. I've caught my biggest ones in the smaller lakes. In Lake George I've never caught many giant bass, but all around Lake George in the Ocala National Forest there are some 200 smaller lakes from an acre in size up to about 7,000 acres. I prefer those 500-to-1,000-acre lakes where I can get my bass boat in and out. I winch my way in and out of those lakes. One main reason I prefer those smaller lakes is they don't get the fishing pressure many other lakes get.

One of my favorite tricks when I can afford it is to fly a day over these lakes, and I'll especially look for one which doesn't look as if it's had any travel. The road to it looks overgrown and there's no trash around the shoreline, and it doesn't look as if anyone's been in there for quite a while. On the average I spend two weeks a year fishing for trophy bass. I fish with my wife, one of my cameramen, and possibly with one of the trophy-bass guides such as Dennis Rahn. In the average two weeks we land three to six bass over 10 pounds. Even though I've caught a couple a day, you don't catch them every day. A good average is one every two or three days.

The time of year which seems the most productive with shiners in those smaller lakes is the colder winter months when the water temperature's in the 50s. From 50 to 60 degrees seems to be the ideal water temperature. The good fishing starts as early as December, but

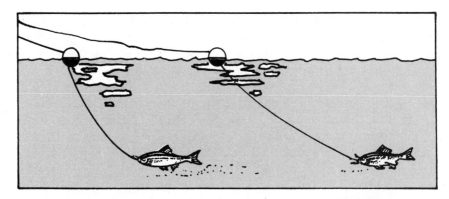

For open water I like to use two treble hooks—a 5/0 or 6/0 in the front and an 8/0 in the tail. When fishing around or through cover, a single weedless hook is better.

January usually is a better month. February is an excellent month, and March usually is the best month. I'd say February and March are the two months when trophy-bass fishing with shiners is best. Generally the biggest ones you catch are pre-spawners. Of course, in some of the bays and warmer springs they'll spawn in January and February, but the majority of the central-Florida bass spawn in March. Just before they spawn and the water's 50 to 55 degrees the big female bass aren't taking artificial lures well at all.

Many fishermen know that until the water gets over 60 degrees, Florida bass don't hit plastic worms good. They hit surface lures some, and they'll hit crank baits some, but Florida bass basically like to hit lures in hot weather. I don't like to use artificial lures in Florida except during the summer months.

Trolling shiners is generally the same as drifting them, except in some lakes with structure such as Rodman Reservoir and Lake Eloise near Cypress Gardens. In these latter the structure might be trenches or potholes, and in them I like to take marker buoys and put them on the dropoffs where the depth drops from 10 to maybe 20 feet. With three or four markers I'll outline that hole, channel, or point. Then with my trolling motor I'll fish a shiner real deep. I don't need to use a float for this type of fishing because I'm in open water with very few obstructions to get hung on. Sometimes I mark my line 40 feet from the hook with a black felt-tip marker. Then I let about 70 feet of line out and use a small weight to slowly bump that shiner along the dropoffs as I circle the structures. When something shakes my bait and I can tell something heavy is pulling on my shiner, I open my bail (on a spinning reel) or push the button (on a free-spool bait-casting reel) and let the bass take out line. Then I reverse the trolling motor and run toward where I think the fish is and reel in slack. When I hit that 40-foot mark I put on my line, I'm at the right striking distance; feel I can set the hook better 40 feet away than if I was 90 feet away. If I'm in open water I'll let the bass take the shiner in deeper, maybe for twenty seconds before I set the hook. If the water's real clear, I'll use lighter line, such as 17- or 20-pound-test.

One time I troll is if it's a calm day when I'm not getting much minnow action. When you hook a shiner through the lips and troll him, he'll live a lot longer, because he's getting lots of oxygen. The problem with a single-hook system like that is you really have to let the bass swallow the bait. But you can do that by going back to your 40-foot mark on your line and getting all the slack out.

One of my favorite hooks for big shiners is the Kahle hook, which is made in Minnesota. Throughout Florida, where they do a lot of shiner fishing, you can find Kahle hooks in most any tackle shop. The Kahle is a real big offset hook with a huge bend in it. Even though the shiner's head takes up part of the bend, there's still enough throat left in the bend to set the hook point properly. Some of the biggest bass I've ever caught were taken while trolling shiners rather than just drifting them along the weed edges.

I usually use a muskie rod—a Fenwick 5½- or 6-footer—which is big and stout and has a straight handle with a saltwater reel seat. It has power; you'll never break a muskie rod on a bass. The rod also has a long butt which you can stick into your stomach to get a better hook set. Some worm rods such as Fenwick's and Lou Childre's are No. 6 actions. Based on a number system, a shiner rod would have to be a No. 10. It has to be about twice as stiff as the heaviest, stiffest worm rods. You not only have to drive a very large-diameter hook through a bass' mouth, but you also just cannot afford to miss a single strike when you're shiner fishing. You might get only one or two strikes all day, and you have to have it all together—complete efficiency.

Every year when we go to Florida in February, we try to do a film on shiner fishing. For the past four years I've fished with Dennis Rahn, and for four years in a row we've caught a bass over 10 pounds on film. This is quite an accomplishment considering we had only a few days. We've had two over 12 on film. One day I was fishing with my wife, Mary Ann, and it was raining and we couldn't film. Dennis said we'd try the old Ocklawaha River because lots of times in real cold weather some big fish move up into the warmer waters of the Ocklawaha. It's fed by Silver Springs and has a little bit warmer water following major cold fronts, and fish migrate up that river at these times. We looked for the sharpest, deepest bends in the river, and in some of those the water is 40 feet deep.

We had anchored out in the river, with the sharp, deep dropoff bend about 30 feet away. We were fishing in a circle around the bend, and there were a lot of logs and trees jutting out into the water. We had saltwater rods and reels with 40-pound line and double trailer hooks, because there are so many trees and logs there that the second a fish hits, you have to set the hook. If you get one, he'll be over 10 pounds, but if you let him go three seconds he'll be underneath a log and you'll lose him. Actually you let the shiner swim up real close to the log so that he's just about 4 inches from the log. The bait's right up on top, and you have to keep him from going beneath the log. You let the shiner swim back into crevices and holes in the cover, and then you pull him back out. He keeps cruising up and down the bank and makes a 100-foot circle while staying up against the bank.

Finally after a few minutes a great big bass hit Mary Ann's shiner right by this big log. She set the hook just right and caught a 10½-pounder. It was her first 10-pounder in her life. A tornado warning was out, and the wind was howling about forty miles per hour, but we were fairly well protected by the big trees around the shore. Well, one hit me, and I waited too long before setting the hook, and he got under the log on me and wrapped up my line and I finally had to break him off. I rerigged and threw my shiner in again and about that time this big limb came crashing down out of the tree and fell on my line. At the same time I had a bass taking my shiner, and I set the hook with the big limb over my line. I reeled this bass, which was about 10 pounds, up into the limb and he got all tangled up in it and I ended up losing him too.

Mary Ann threw out a shiner away from the cover out in the middle of the river. The shiner was the biggest one we had in the live box, and this tremendous bass crashed it about three times. I could see the bass and I guessed it at 12 pounds. Well, she set the hook and rolled it up on top and finally got it into the net. It weighed almost 12½ pounds. She had two big ones and I hadn't caught anything.

A little later she had a shiner out and a bass about 9½ pounds crashed her shiner by a log, but by this time it was raining hard and

My wife, Mary Ann, used shiners
to catch these "little fellows"—
9¹/₂, 10¹/₂, and 12¹/₂ pounds!

she was cold and miserable. Anyway, she caught the 9¹/₂ and that one
gave her *three* big ones, and I've still not caught my first one. It was
about noon and I took her back to the motor home, and she told me to
go back out and fish because I was still after a trophy; she was going
to get warm and take a nap.

I went back out and did some trolling and did manage to catch two
bass. One was almost 10 and the other was about 9 pounds. We ended
up with five fish that day, and the five of 'em weighed almost 50
pounds.

The most exciting shiner fishing I ever saw was back in the early
1970s when they first impounded Rodman Reservoir. There weren't

any boat docks on Rodman and not many people were fishing it. There were many trees in the water, and probably this discouraged people. It was a navigational hazard to fish it unless you ran your boat slowly and were extra-careful. It also was hard to get into. You had to go through the locks if you came from Welaka, and there were just a few little ramps along the Ocala Forest. For the first five or six years thousands of bass grew big in this 14,000-acre lake, and they were pretty much unmolested.

Back about 1973 or 1974 I started fishing Rodman, and I saw right away that it was the best big-bass hole in Florida. Rodman was better than Jackson was when it was hot, and also better than Watermelon Pond was when it was hot. From 1972 through 1974 it was *the* best lake in the country for bass over 10 pounds. I was doing a film in 1974 with Glenn Lau for Lowrance Electronics. There was a lot of underwater camera work involved, and we'd been out filming all day. Dennis Rahn was on the lake that day and had caught a 12-pounder. I knew the bass were biting, and I'd brought along thirteen shiners in hopes I'd have a little time to fish that day. It was sundown when we finished our film work, and Glenn commented that I hadn't had a chance to fish that day. I told Glenn to go on in and that I had thirteen shiners along and planned to fish until dark and then I'd meet him at his house.

Glenn leisurely went back to the boat dock, and on his way home he stopped to get gas. I had only thirty or forty minutes to fish before black dark. I think he also stopped to get a sandwich at a convenience store. Anyhow, when he was turning into his driveway I had caught up with him and was right behind him.

What I'd done in those forty-five minutes or so was pull up to a spot near the canal they'd dug through Rodman. I put down my anchor and put out four rods with shiners, and almost instantly all four bobbers went under. I landed three of those four fish. One of 'em was about 10, another was about 9, and the third one was about 7. The fourth bass broke my line. The next time I baited up with two rods and threw them out, and I got strikes on them. In just 20 minutes I used up my thirteen shiners and ended up with ten bass.

Glenn asked me if I'd gotten a strike, and I said that as a matter of fact I had. I said I'd gotten a limit, and he didn't believe me. He said I hadn't been out there long enough to have gotten a limit. I had 'em on a rope, and Glenn was saving a lot of bass at that time for underwater work on the movie *Bigmouth* and films for The Fisherman series we

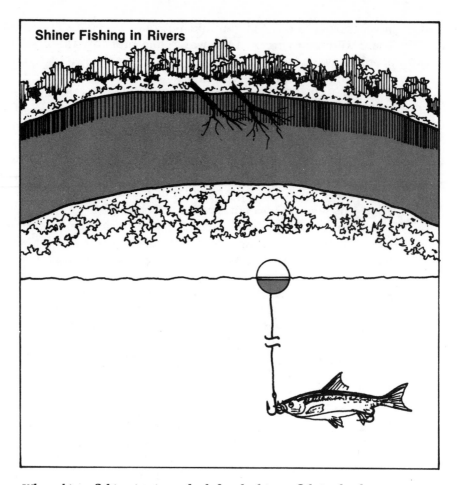

Shiner Fishing in Rivers

When shiner fishing in rivers, look for the bigger fish in the deeper water around the outside bends or turns, especially where there are fallen trees, brush piles, or other debris. The double treble hook is appropriate for fishing next to this cover.

did with Homer Circle, and he needed big bass to put in his big aquarium. I'd kept 'em alive in my live well, and we put the rope full of 'em on his big scales and they weighed 73 pounds.

That was the fastest action I've ever seen. Back then at Rodman there were actually schools of these big bass, and I'd gotten into one. They often roamed the middle of the lake, and when you caught one, five or six or eight bass would follow the one you'd hooked right up to the boat. Quite often you could just anchor at that point and cast all around and doggone near catch your limit right from that one spot. There's still a lot of big bass in Rodman, but it's nothing like it was back in 1974. At the hole I had where I'd caught those ten, in a month's time I caught a total of sixty bass 6 pounds and over. I really didn't catch all that many bass over 10 pounds from that hole; I probably averaged one every two or three days.

On one of my best days at Rodman I had an 11¾, an 11¼, a 10½, and a 10¼. I also had two bass right at 9 pounds.

But my best day was with Glen Lau's eleven-year-old son, Davie. We fished one day in April of 1975 when I was finishing up some film work. When I took Davie with me, Glenn told me not to spoil him by letting him catch too many fish because he'd think bass fishing was too easy. But I really did spoil him. I let him set the hook, and he caught an 11¾-pounder that day as well as a 10½ and a 10¼. Imagine that! An eleven-year-old with *three* over 10 in one day! I also caught a 10-pounder, and we weighed our top eight bass and they hit 68 pounds.

---

42 Running Shiners

"Running" the shiners is a completely different pattern from drifting or still-fishing with shiners. When you run shiners, you're seeking out heavy cover and remaining stationary while the shiner does the moving. You let him go beneath the cover. The hyacinth beds in Florida are where running shiners really pays off. Some of the central-Florida lakes in particular have huge shelves of hyacinths which stick out from the bank. Typical lakes with these masses of hyacinths are any lakes along the St. Johns River system. Probably half the lakes in the Ocala National Forest—and these are public lakes—all have big patches of hyacinths.

The wind blows the hyacinths around, and they move from day to day. When you find hyacinths which have blown against a good edge with deep water beneath them, let your boat drift up to the edge or anchor about 10 feet out. Put a single hook near the tail of the shiner above the anal (bottom) fin of the baitfish and don't use any weight. The weight of the hook holds him upright. Cast him to the edge of the hyacinths, and by pulling him backward a little bit, you get him to run away from you. Cast him softly, because you want to keep him as lively as possible. Keep fiddling with him and give him slack so that he runs away from you and goes beneath the hyacinths. The bass almost always lie in the shade beneath the hyacinths, and sometimes they're 10 to 20 feet back beneath the hyacinths.

If the shiner is running high in the water, he'll get wrapped in the hyacinths, so you need to keep him running as low as possible. The roots of the hyacinths hang down about 2 feet, and if you keep him running low, he'll get back beneath them without hanging up. Maybe out of a dozen shiners, only three or four will make good runs beneath the hyacinths. Many of them will circle out to open water, and others will run beneath the hyacinths a few feet and see a bass and then they'll head out toward open water. They're not dumb; they don't want to become lunch for the largemouth.

When you get a shiner back there 15 or 20 feet, he might wrap up slightly around the hair roots of the hyacinths. Just let him sit there. When a bass hits him, he blows the shiner upward. Lots of times you'll see the hyacinths rise up in a huge bulge. That's the bass boiling up and engulfing the shiner.

Quite often it's hard to tell if you've got a bass on or if the shiner is doing the moving. It takes some practice to tell the difference. When you pull back, if you all of a sudden feel a surge on your line, you've got a bass on. But often when a bass hits, you'll see the line jump and take off at a fairly steady rate. The shiner moves along in short twitches or spurts.

Even though the shiner is way back beneath the hyacinths, when a bass hits, I like to let him run 10 to 20 seconds before I set the hook. Before you set the hook, the best thing to do is get as far forward in the boat as you can and try to get all of your slack line reeled in. Stretch out forward toward where you think the bass is, reel in the line fast until it's tight, and then set the hook with a big sweeping motion with the long rod. Then back up three or four steps and set the hook again, and back up some more and set again. Finally after all that hook setting, you've straightened your line out and you've got the bass hooked.

For this type of fishing I like to use extremely heavy line; I prefer 40-pound-test. The bass that hits way back in the hyacinths still is apt to get wrapped up and tangled in all the vegetation. Getting him out of there is not very glamorous, but he's apt to be a trophy fish.

Occasionally you can run shiners in lily pads, but in the lilies, the

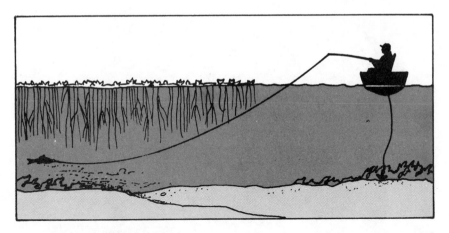

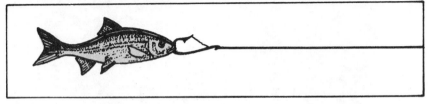

A large, lively golden shiner which is allowed to swim unweighted beneath a blanket of floating vegetation will often bring out a trophy bass. A single weedless hook will help avoid hangups.

shiner is going to get hung up a lot worse. Pull up to the edge of the pads and let the shiner out and let him run up into them. Quite often you don't ever get the shiner back, because he will wrap up in them. When you pull him back, you tear him off the hook. When you run shiners, you use a lot of shiners. Sometimes I'll use six to eight dozen in a day. You're constantly losing your bait because it gets wrapped up in vegetation. You also get a lot of strikes which pull the bait off the hook. Chain pickerel or "jackfish" are bad about doing this or killing your shiners.

When I'm running shiners, I frequently use the smaller shiners instead of the larger ones. I like the 6-to-7-inch shiners because they run good. The 12-inch ones have power, but they don't have as much stamina as the smaller ones. A good, lively 7-inch shiner will do more swimming around and will last longer than a big one.

My father-in-law, Paul Colbert, thinks there's no greater fishing in the world than running shiners. He'd rather anchor 10 feet out from a

My father-in-law, Paul Colbert, thinks there's no greater fishing than running shiners in under the hyacinths.

hyacinth patch and sit there and run shiners back in under the hyacinths all day than do any other kind of fishing. Every winter when he and his wife, Mary, accompany Mary Ann and me on our annual migration to Florida, Paul makes sure we've got Dennis Rahn booked up for a few days of guide work so we can run shiners and catch some big ones.

One of the best places in the world to run shiners has been a big hyacinth patch Dennis found three years ago in Rodman Pool. He and his customers caught more than 1,600 bass of all sizes from that two-acre area back in 1976. He's taken Paul and me in there, and at times the action was so fast that we'd all three have bass on at the same time. Sometimes when the bass are super-active, they chase the shiners out from beneath the hyacinths, and we've seen them run the shiners right up close to the boat and blow and swirl and grab them right in front of our eyes a few feet away.

One time J. D. Skinner of Birmingham, Ala., and I were in the Welaka, Fla., area waiting for the start of the three official practice days for a B.A.S.S. tournament on the St. Johns River. The St. Johns, and any water connected to it, was off limits to all the tournament fishermen before the practice round, so I suggested to J.D. that he and I fish a little lake not connected to the river system. I had fished a 200-acre lake called Silver Lake and suggested we go over there and fish shiners and try to catch a trophy bass. J.D. was all for this, so I got four dozen shiners and we took his bass boat and my four-wheel-drive vehicle.

We'd caught a 7-pounder drifting, but not much else was happening. Finally we found a patch of dead hyacinths, which were about the only ones in the lake. We anchored about 15 feet away and started running shiners. I had three or four strikes and caught a 4-pounder, but J.D. hadn't had a strike. Then I pulled a shiner out to the edge of the hyacinth patch, and a huge bass rolled up and crashed my bait. I gave him a few seconds and then set the hook real hard, but I didn't get him hooked. J.D. started reeling in and said real excitedly, "Boy, I'm going to catch him!"

"You want to bet?" I asked as I reached into the shiner box and grabbed one and got it on my hook as fast as I could and threw back. There was a big race to see who could get in there first, and my bait hit half a second before his did. Instantly that bass grabbed him. I won't recount what J.D. said. I let the bass run for twenty seconds before driving the hook home. That bass weighed 12 pounds, 13 ounces. When I rolled him up to the boat, I yelled for J.D. to net him. We didn't know how big he was, but when the bass came sloshing up out of the water, it scared J.D. so bad that he froze. I was yelling, "Net him! Net him!" and finally he overcame the shock and did.

---

43 Bullhead Minnows for Spawners

In 1959 a college buddy of mine, Floyd Park, and I made our first trip to Florida. We didn't have much money, so we pooled what we had for the guide fees—we had a veteran Florida guide from the Welaka area named Joe Schmidt. We slept in the car at night to cut expenses. Joe had located a bunch of spawning bass around Silver Glen Springs on Lake George. This and Salt Springs and Juniper Springs are the major springs which feed Lake George, and the water coming up out of the ground in these springs ranges from 72 to 76 degrees year round. It was February, and the main lake had water from 52 to 55 degrees.

Joe said he had about 200 bedding bass located at the mouth of Silver Glenn, and it was supposed to rain, so not many people would be fishing. He said we'd be able to kill 'em on bullheads. He said we'd be using spinning tackle with 10- or 12-pound line and weedless hooks, and when we spotted a trophy bass on the bed, we'd throw in and catch her. This all sounded pretty farfetched to me, especially since I didn't know what a bullhead minnow was.

Joe would stand up in the boat and with the aid of Polaroid glasses find the beds. He used a push pole for extra quietness, and he'd spot the fish. Then he'd say we didn't want that particular one because it was only 5 or 6 pounds. When he spotted the first big one, he asked whose turn it was, and we looked at each other. We flipped a coin and I won the first shot. He anchored the boat about 20 feet from the bed and put the bullhead on my line, and before the cast, he explained that the water caused an optical illusion making the bed look closer than it actually was. He said we needed to throw 5 to 6 feet past where we thought the bed was. He cast the first bullhead right in the bed. He handed me the rod and told me to close the bail and to set the hook as soon as my line moved. He said not to worry about the first strike because about 98 percent of the time it would be the small male bass striking.

About thirty seconds passed, and my line moved and instantly Joe yelled, "Set the hook!" I did and caught the little male bass—a 2-pounder. He said to release him, and I did, and then I baited up and threw back. Thirty seconds later my line twitched, and I set the hook, expecting the big fish. I caught the same little male I'd caught two minutes before. It had a hook in his mouth. Joe reassured us they would hit again like that, so I released him again, wondering how many times this was going to repeat itself. I threw back in the bed again, and I was standing up looking but I didn't see anything. Joe was standing beside me, and he said, "There she is! I see her coming!" I kept looking and still couldn't see anything. "She's right there by it!" Joe said. "I think she's going down for it!" Then my line moved, and he yelled, "Set the hook!" I did and rolled in an 8-pound, 14-ounce bass. It was my first big Florida bass.

Then it was Floyd's turn, and he boated one almost as big. We went on and fished two days for only the big bass on the beds. We ended up with thirty bass, and the smallest was 6¹/₂ and the biggest was 10¹/₂. This was probably the biggest string of bass I've ever assembled at one time. Our ten biggest came close to 90 pounds.

The bullhead used for bedding bass in Florida is a Caledonia minnow which lives in the tidal estuaries of the eastern and north-central part of Florida. He ranges from 1¹/₂ to about 4 inches long; the best size to use is about 2¹/₂ inches long and about as big around as your index finger. They run big seines on sandbars at night and catch these minnows. They don't cost much. A dozen run around a dollar. They're very hardy; when you're wading and fishing, you can put four or five of them in a small plastic bag with half a cup of water and they'll stay alive for an hour or so if you change the water at intervals.

After you spot the bed, you have to make a very accurate cast so that the bullhead ends up right in the bed. If you can't hit the bed accurately, you can wade over or pole your boat over to the bed and drop the minnow right down in the middle of it. Then back off 30 or 40 feet and wait awhile for the bass to come back. You've got a lively minnow which darts all around the bed. You have to keep the bait deep on the bottom, so you need to use a ¹/₄-ounce sinker 4 or 5 inches ahead of the minnow. You need to set the hook instantly, because all the bass is trying to do is move that bullhead out of the nest. The fish is not trying to eat it. The male or female will move it a few feet and spit it out.

Most of the bed fishing I do is in fairly clear to very clear water

An 8-pound-plus bass blows out of Lake Okeechobee cover after hitting a bullhead minnow.

such as in Lake George, Lake Jackson, Lake Kerr, and other central-Florida lakes. Most of the good spawning areas are out in fairly open water. In Lake George, there's eel grass on flats in 2 to 4 feet of water, and there's not heavy cover for the bass to get wrapped up in. Therefore, a 15-pound line is about all you need even for the bigger bass. It will cut right through the eel grass. A 1/0 or 2/0 hook is ideal for using the bullheads, and keep the hooks really sharp. Another trick is to keep the sun over your shoulder. This gives you better visibility, and you'll see the bass before she sees you. Fish don't like to look into the sun. If you fished toward the sun, the bass likely would see you first and also your visibility wouldn't be nearly as good. Run your trolling motor at a very slow speed to keep from spooking the fish. If it's too windy, weedy, or shallow for a trolling motor, a push pole is the old standby, and it's what Florida guides have been using for decades.

When I started guiding at Santee, I couldn't get the bullhead minnows, but I was able to get spring lizards and crawfish. I used the same principle as in bullhead fishing. If I had a customer who wanted strictly a trophy bass, I'd find the bed with the fish. I carried forty Styrofoam floats, each with 2 feet of line and a sinker on the end of the line, and I'd spot bass of from 5 to 12 pounds and mark each bed with a float. Then I'd wade, because I found that wading was by far the best approach. Santee had so many bushes back then that if you hooked a bedding bass from a boat, she'd go around the bushes and you couldn't get to her. But by wading I could tear off after her and get her, and I almost never broke line on a fish.

One time I located three bedding bass each over 10 pounds at Santee. I was fishing with the magazine writer George Reiger. I told him how we'd catch them and explained that he'd catch the small male bass first. Well, the first bed we came to, he threw in the spring lizard, and almost immediately the line started moving. I told him it was the male and to go ahead and set the hook. He did, but it was the big female which had hit first. She was huge, and when she wallowed up out of the water, George froze up. She got around a stump, and I guess I hadn't explained the whole program to him, because when I told him to go after her, he didn't know to give her some slack line and wade toward her. She broke his 20-pound line.

But the effort wasn't a total failure. George was doing an article for *Popular Mechanics*, and the art director of the magazine was with us. I put him on the second fish, and he caught the small male first and then hooked the big female, but the hook came out of her mouth. I got the third and smallest—a 10¼-pounder—after catching two males first on the bed. They used a photo in the magazine showing me catching that bass.

I have used the example of fishing bullhead minnows on the beds, but really this pattern applies to any live bait for bed fishing whether you're after spawning bass in Connecticut or California. If you can't find bullhead minnows, spring lizards (a southern term for salamanders), or crawfish, a good fourth choice is a big gob of live nightcrawlers. Nightcrawlers are not as good as the others, but they do work and they're fairly available most anywhere.

This bed fishing probably is the most efficient way to catch a trophy bass. Several bass fishermen don't consider this sporting—they

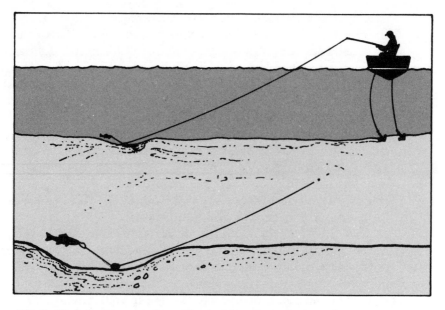

The bullhead minnow is hated by bedding bass, since it feeds on their eggs. You can fish the minnow about 12 inches behind a slip sinker with a 3/0 weedless hook, and smack in the middle of the bed.

think of it as a meat technique—and in some states the fishing season is closed during the spawning season. There's a big difference between keeping every bass you catch on the beds and turning a lot of them loose. Some readers might think I'm promoting fishing for bedding bass. Whether you think it's a good practice or a bad one, you still might like to know how it's done. I'm not encouraging you to do a lot of this type of fishing. We do need to conserve our bass whether they're caught spawning or not spawning. No matter how, when, or where I catch bass, I always release 95 percent of them unharmed. I'm fishing for the sport of catching them. If I hook one too deep or we keep one out of the water too long while taking pictures of it and the fish dies, then I bring it in and fillet it.

Another thing to consider is that many bass fishermen simply do not realize they're catching spawning bass. There's a period during the spring when bass are spawning that dozens of fishermen using plastic worms catch numerous limits of bass. Almost everybody out fishing really catches 'em then, even the bank fishermen. Many of them don't know it, but they're catching spawning bass. Many midwestern lakes have dingy water and fishermen can't see the spawning beds, and when that plastic worm comes through the bed, the bass is going to grab it the same as he would a bullhead minnow or a salamander.

Bed fishermen get criticized, but the guys fishing the banks and catching spawners don't. I'd say at least 60 percent of the bass over 5 pounds which are caught in those 2-to-3-foot depths in the spring are spawning bass. In most of the clear reservoirs in the south, bass seldom get near the banks in water that is shallow during the daytime unless they're spawning.

When you catch and release a bedding bass immediately where you caught her, she'll swim right back to the bed. No fewer than ten times have I or friends or clients at Santee hooked a bass on the bed and broken the line, and then come back to that spot the same day or the next day and caught the very same fish. She'd have the first hook in her mouth.

44   A Gob of Worms

Live worms I use two different ways. In the north country they're super for smallmouths. One of the best ways to catch a big smallmouth is with a live nightcrawler. In the south I don't cast with the nightcrawler as I do up north, but I use him or a big gob of red worms.

It's a well-known fact that bass will eat worms just as other fish do. In clear northern lakes with established weedlines out in 10 to 15 feet of water, smallmouths and big largemouths really hit nightcrawlers rigged similarly to a plastic worm and fished like the plastic imitation along the weed lines. I fish the nightcrawlers with an exposed hook rather than a weedless.

This past August when my crew and I were making a walleye film at Port Clinton, Ohio, on Lake Erie, one of the charterboat captains, Dan Galbincea, had a party out after walleyes, but they got into a bunch of smallmouths which really gobbled up their spinner-and-worm rigs about 20 feet deep. (Galbincea is better known as "Erie Dearie Dan"; he makes a weighted spinner to use ahead of the hook and live worm and calls his lure the Erie Dearie.) But a plain nightcrawler without the spinner will annihilate smallmouths.

The best way to fish a nightcrawler for northern smallmouths and

Here's one that fell for the old gob-of-worms trick.

largemouths is with spinning tackle and 6-pound line. You're fishing open areas at the outer edges of the weeds. Don't use much weight. A single split shot a foot or so above the hook is plenty, and use a small hook, such as a No. 6. I hook the worm in the head and thread it on and bring the hook point out of the worm.

When I've used worms for bedding bass in the south, I've taken five or six big red worms and bunched them up on the hook—either a plain or weedless hook—so that ten or twelve worm ends are dangling loose and wiggling. They won't let that worm gob lie on the bed very long.

45 Crawdads for Kentuckies

I think of catching Kentucky or spotted bass on crawfish because crawdads are a favorite food for this bass species, but the craws also are well liked by smallmouths and largemouths. I remember growing up in Maryland and how in the summer the lakes and streams along the Eastern Shore got hot and the bass grew inactive and went deep.

But a great exception was the Potomac River, which produced all summer because the rapids aerated the water and helped keep the bass more active. In the summer the bass could be found around the white water where the river surged over the rapids. On bright days when they wouldn't hit surface baits and were in the deeper holes, we caught 'em on crawfish. Mostly we got smallmouths; occasionally we'd get a largemouth and rarely a Kentucky. Sometimes a big catfish came along and really stretched our string, and I even caught a couple of carp on the crawfish.

Where crawfish are native to the water, they're a preferred food for several species of fish. Later we fished Loch Raven and Liberty reservoirs in central Maryland, and during September we caught both largemouths and smallmouths there on crawfish. We regularly caught 5-to-5½-pound smallmouths in September in Loch Raven. There were a few long shallow points with elodea growing out to about 14 feet deep. (I was in college at the time, and learned the vegetation was elodea because I brought some to my botany professor and he identified it.) The bass moved up from deeper water to the base of that elodea in September, and we'd fish the crawdads right on the bottom at the outside edge of the grass. That pattern paid off right at dawn and again at dusk. During the day we frequently found the bass on the deeper dropoffs at 25 feet.

Most everywhere, I'll find crawfish in the bass' stomachs. I've noticed this in the Thousand Islands area of New York, and in the spring at Toledo Bend every bass you clean is stuffed with crawfish. Judging from the success with crank baits, which simulate crawfish, I would estimate that at times in the early spring at least 50 percent of a bass' diet is crawfish. This seems true in almost all of the major bass lakes I've ever fished. Pre-spawn bass eat a tremendous number of crawfish. In ponds, lakes, and rivers where you don't even see crawfish, you'll know they're present when you clean some bass and cut open their stomachs.

Lots of times when I've had bass in my live well, they've regurgitated, and crawfish shells get crammed in the aeration pumps. I've seen this even at lakes where locals say there aren't any crawfish. I think when bass eat crawfish, they carry the indigestible parts such as the claws in their stomachs for a while and then spit them up. Crawfish have to be extremely important in the diets of many a bass.

Another reason I think of crawdads for Kentucky bass involves the White River chain of lakes in northern Missouri and southern Arkansas. On this chain are Norfork, Beaver, Bull Shoals, and Table Rock reservoirs. These are prime bass waters. In September they're super-clear and the bass spend the day down on the thermocline about 35 feet deep. Other than at night, one of the best ways to catch them is with live crawfish. Take a bucket of crawdads and go fish the points at the thermocline level. You're apt to limit out almost any day at this time of year with the crawfish. Since most of the points drop off steep, the best way to fish them is to pull right up on the bank on the point, tie your boat to a rock or tree, and cast straight out off the point. Usually you can throw out deep enough to get the bait down to 35 feet deep. Watch your locator when you're running in on these points so you'll know the depths.

The way I rig a crawfish for Kentuckies is using 6-pound line and a spinning rod and a No. 6 Eagle Claw Style 84 hook. You can hook the craw through the shell behind his head or in his tail. If you hook him too deep in the tail, this damages his muscles and he doesn't swim good. I prefer to hook them in the top shell, because they swim better that way. They always swim backward. I also prefer a softshell craw-fish to a hardshell one. Some fishermen use a small plain jig head and hook them in the tail and walk them across the bottom. A small split shot sinks the bait quicker if you're not using a jig head, but if you don't mind waiting for the craw to sink, forget the weight. A 2-to-2½-inch crawfish is a good size for all bass.

The hardest thing to do is find the softshell craws. Crawfish molt four or five times during the summer, and if you bait a trap with old meat and put it out in a stream or pond, a percentage of the ones you catch will have lost their hard shells. Bass won't spit out a softshell, but they sometimes spit out the hardshell ones.

Out in San Diego watershed lakes they stocked the Florida bass and have 'em up to more than 20 pounds already. I fished Otay and El Capitan reservoirs, and I noticed lots of crawfish shells around the banks. Locals say the crawfish crawl out of the water to molt. Many of the most successful big-bass fishermen in the San Diego and Southern California areas use crawfish. They crawl big softshell crawfish real slow across the bottom.

A very close friend and business associate of mine, Glen Lau, who is in the film-production business, used to be a guide on Lake Erie. His big bag was catching smallmouths at Erie, and probably 90 percent of the thousands and thousands of smallmouths he and his guide parties caught through the years were on crawfish. He'd catch 'em on lures

A long point with some vegetation provides a haven for the bass to lie in wait for your crawdad.

when they were spawning, and other ways, too, but Erie has many rock piles and deep ledges out off the islands in 10 to 20 feet of water, and crawfish paid off best in the deeper water. Erie smallmouth anglers use softshell crawfish, but they call 'em softshell crabs.

46   Leeching Smallmouths

I'd never heard of catching a bass on a leech until I got to talking with Spence Petros of *Fishing Facts* magazine. He'd run a few articles in the magazine about guys catching smallmouths on leeches. I was wanting to do some filming three years ago in Minnesota, and I called Al Lindner. Al said he had a good buddy, Grant Hughes, up on Lake Vermilion who had a lodge called Muskego Point. Al told me Grant caught a world of 5- and 6-pound smallmouths all summer long.

I reminded Al that I'd fished for smallmouths a long time and pointed out that *nobody* catches a world of 5- and 6-pound small-mouths just all summer long, especially during August. Al countered by saying August was the best month and that Grant Hughes just murders 'em then and catches dozens of 'em over 5 pounds in August. I said *nobody*. . . . Al wouldn't argue. He just said call Grant.

Well, I called Grant at Cook, Minn., which is on the banks of Lake Vermilion and about a hundred miles south of the Canadian border. Vermilion has about 50,000 acres, and for years it's been known for walleye and northern pike fishing, and I'd never heard anybody talk about how good Vermilion's smallmouth fishing was. Grant tells me on the phone he's about the only one up there who fishes for small-mouths. He said that during the seven or eight years he had been there, he'd fished for smallmouths about every day during the season but there weren't more than three or four other guys on the entire 50,000-acre lake who fished strictly for smallmouths. He said walleye and northern pike fishermen caught smallmouths but almost by acci-dent because the lake had so many of 'em.

Grant also pointed out that during the previous twenty to thirty years, Vermilion's smallmouths had been virtually unmolested, and if a guy knew structure and how to fish a *leech*, he could catch nearly a limit of 5-pound smallmouths every day! Within three hours I was all packed up and was driving my Chevy Suburban about seventy-five miles an hour headed north.

This was the third week of August, and Grant had some walleyes and some northerns located. When I first saw the lake, I wasn't very impressed with it. There were a lot of cottages on the shoreline. Grant stretched out a contour map of the lake, and it showed a bunch of rockpiles way out in the lake, which is not a deep lake. Every couple of miles was a major rock shoal which stuck up 5 to 10 feet off the sand bottom.

I didn't know how to fish a leech, and I was a bit reluctant to even pick one up. I thought they'd bite and suck blood, but I watched Grant stick his hand down in a bucket of 'em and pull out about twenty which were clinging all over his hand. He simply picked 'em off one by one and went ahead and baited up. These leeches, when curled up, are only about an inch long and 1/2 inch wide. When they're stretched out, they are from 2 to 3 inches long. Grant used 4-pound line and a tiny Size 8 or 10 Style 84 hook, and about 6 inches above the hook he put on a tiny split shot. Leeches have both a tail sucker and a mouth

This leech-caught 5½-pounder helped Grant Hughes make a believer out of me.

sucker. Grant ran the hook through the mouth sucker and back again through it and then through the body. His hook was exposed. He almost vertical-jigs the bait. He fishes the rockpiles, and if you make a long cast to them, your split shot and bait frequently get caught in the rock crevices, and then you spend more time tying on hooks than fishing. You need to use a front locator on your boat and get right over the fish, then open the bail on your reel and drop the leech to the bottom. Then with your trolling motor work very carefully all around that rockpile. Our pattern depth during the week we were there was about 20 feet deep. Jig the leech up 3 or 4 feet and drop it back to the bottom. When you get hung up, you're directly over the bait and all you have to do is twitch your rod tip a little and you usually get loose.

Don't set the hook the instant a smallmouth hits the leech. Open your bail and let him run with it for four to five seconds. With 4- or

These five smallmouths, weighing 24 pounds, fell for leeches and became the stars of a TV segment I made with my friends Tommy Salisbury of South Carolina and Mike Viersba of Minnesota at Lac LaCroix in Canada.

6-pound line—and I prefer the 6-pound—you don't set the hook hard when you close the bail. Just set it firm and keep a tight line. The smallmouth exerts a slow, steady pressure, and with a big one you won't feel any tail movement. The bigger the fish, the steadier the pressure he exerts.

Grant Hughes made a believer out of me real quick. The first bass he stuck was about 5 pounds. He had found some schools of 2-to-3-pound smallmouths, but he didn't want to fish for them. He had some lunker holes—some rockpiles which produced strictly 4- and 5-pounders. We'd catch only one or two big ones on a spot like that, but during our first full day of leeching, we caught ten smallmouths over 4 pounds, and three were over 5. My biggest weighed 5½.

Leeches made my day on a trip this past spring with Tommy Salisbury, my old buddy from South Carolina, and Mike Vierzba of the Stearns Company. We went to Lac LaCroix in Canada with my film crew, and for the first few days we caught several 1-to-3-pound smallmouths, but we weren't getting the big ones. They were spawning, and we located five or six beds, but all we could catch were the small males. The big females—some we saw were 5 to 6 pounds—would follow our plugs and sometimes roll up at them, but they wouldn't strike.

Bill Zupp, who operates the camp where we stayed on the lake, said he just had received a shipment of leeches from the U.S. I got to wondering if they'd work on those bedding females. We took some leeches with us, and we got the cameras all ready and I threw a leech on a bed. We saw this big smallmouth moving off, and my line moved off, too. I set the hook, and she boiled up on the surface and gave me a real battle. We were yelling, and the cameras were going, and everybody was excited. I finally worked the fish up to the boat, and 3 feet away from the boat, she tore off the hook.

We went on and did some more filming, but I got to thinking about that one bass being on the bed and how she might hit again. So we went back to that spot again. I made two casts in there without a strike, and the camera was on when I threw in a third time. My line started moving off, and I set the hook into that same big bass. We got the cast, the strike, and six or seven jumps from this big bass all on film, and I landed her. She weighed 5 pounds, 9 ounces. That bass on the bed hit twice within an hour. For the previous two days, we'd thrown at that fish with lures and hadn't got her to hit. But the leech did the trick.

There are times, such as during the spawning season and also during hot weather when the smallmouths are on structure, that lures just don't produce well. But at these times if you drop a leech in there, you're likely to get your line stretched!

I'm convinced leeches would work on smallmouths even in places where they don't use leeches. I told Billy Westmorland about my experience with this live bait and asked him if they ever used 'em at Dale Hollow Reservoir where he lives in Tennessee. He said he didn't know of anyone who ever used leeches for smallmouths. The largest smallmouths in the world probably are in Dale Hollow, and I'm curious about how effective leeches might be for them.

Technique Patterns

TROLLING

Unfortunately, trolling has a bad name. Many bass fishermen consider it nonsporting, and virtually no bass tournament permits it. Yet it's a great sporting way to catch bass, and also it's a great technique. I don't know if tournament organizations disallow it because it's too effective or because it's considered not as sporting. I've never been able to figure out why.

I think figuring out bass patterns and their depths and catching them are all challenges whether you're trolling or fishing in shallow gunk. It's all a great sport. Bass exhibit a lot of different patterns, and one of 'em is that they can be caught on a fast-moving lure out on structure in deep water. Trolling enables anglers to fish open structure quickly, and frequently this structure is not fished any other way. In impoundments with monstrous flats which run for miles, bass often roam in schools or stay stationary on stumps. The average caster who throws crank baits will find the bass too deep many times to get his plug down to on even long casts.

The troller often is fishing for unfished bass—fish which other structure fishermen aren't aware of. When trolling on structure and making the turns with my boat, my lure is coming through water on turns that I consider unproductive, but yet at times I'll catch a bass there. It might be a flat with no dropoff where I made that turn—a place I'd never normally fish—but yet a bass hits there. Therefore, trolling opens up new areas of the lake which are not being exploited or utilized. Shorelines are beat thoroughly, and well-known structure spots are fished hard, but at the most these hard-fished areas represent only 5 to 10 percent of the entire lake. The remaining 90 percent can be trolled effectively and at times very productively by fishermen without a lot of expensive equipment. Basically all you need are a boat and motor, a depthfinder, a contour map, and some good deep-running lures.

Trolling is a leisurely type of sport in which everyone in the family

I got this string by trolling. The technique gives you command over the huge percentage of the lake that otherwise never gets fished.

can enjoy the fishing. A three-year-old, such as my son, Scott, can hold a rod and reel in a fish, too. Trollers don't have to be expert hook setters because the bass virtually hook themselves. Operating the boat in trolling does require some skill. It's really the captain's game. The speed he's running, the type of structure he's going over, the depths, and the type of lures are important. These little specialties can get very complicated, but for the average fisherman in the boat, this technique is an easy, relaxed way, and sometimes it will be the most productive way.

47   Spoonplugging: Perry's Style

Speed trolling is a unique concept employed by Buck Perry from Hickory, N.C., with a heavy metal lure he invented called the Spoonplug. He uses a stiff rod and frequently trolls much faster than that lure or any other can be retrieved by casting. He's after reflex-action strikes.

Summertime trolling with a Buck Perry's Spoonplug on structure is likely to force some reflex-action strikes.

Where speed trolling really pays off is in summer structure-fishing situations with bass concentrated on the edge of a creek channel or a bar or any irregular feature. Then they often can be caught very quickly, and some of them are apt to be huge fish. What Buck Perry's method involves is covering a lot of water quickly. He makes passes over the structure at a couple of different depths. If a thermocline is present, he knows the preferred water temperature for the bass. If the water is clear, he trolls deeper. A great structure fisherman like Buck is in to all the scientific aspects, and he can go out and cover probably ten times more water in a day than I can by casting—and I'm a fast fisherman, even on structure. At least his lure will have traveled through ten times as many feet of water as mine by the end of the day. Through reflex action he's getting those eager fish.

When I'm out fishing for fun and not in competition, I use Buck Perry's theories to the degree that I'll troll to find them if they're slow hitting and a little hard to find. It's the fastest way to cover a lake, so I'll often troll a Spoonplug at three to seven miles per hour, particularly during the hot summer. As soon as I catch one I'll throw out a marker buoy and probably make one more pass through there. If I've found a school, then I'll cast a worm or jig a spoon in that spot. Locating bass is the prime reason I troll. Buck's Spoonplugs come in eight or nine sizes which run different depths.

Perry maintains that all bass basically live in deep water and are structure fish. I disagree somewhat with that opinion. You'll note that in this book, most of the ways I describe of catching bass are in shallow water. Sure, bass go out in deep water, but a lot of them live beneath lily pads and boat docks all year. The only difference in our thinking here is he says they're all structure fish, and I say a lot of bass live in other places.

Buck Perry coined the phrase "structure fishing," and he's called the grandfather of structure fishing. Trolling his style is an exact art.

48 Troll That Worm

One thing we've been allowed to do in tournaments is troll a plastic worm behind a trolling motor. Blake Honeycutt, from Hickory, N.C., who is an old fishing companion of Buck Perry's, won the 1969 B.A.S.S. tournament at Eufaula in Alabama with a record catch. He caught 138 pounds, 6 ounces with a fifteen-bass daily limit, and he trolled an 8-inch worm with two lead weights ahead of it in 17 to 22 feet of water. He used the extra weight to be able to cover a little more water quicker. His thought, and my thought, too, is that when a worm is trolled, it's never off the bottom; when you're trolling creek channels, eventually you can find the fish. If you're casting, you'll miss little gaps. Trolling covers the water more efficiently. All the structure is covered, and of course you can get more speed than by regular casting.

An added advantage comes during the hot summer in that you can get reflex strikes when the worm is moving faster. Normally you don't get reflex strikes with a worm.

In 1970, after talking with Blake, I put worm trolling to good use. I

After I've located a school by trolling a worm along a ledge, I throw out a marker buoy and cast to it with a worm.

found a little ledge with a nook which ran back a few feet along an island at Santee-Cooper. Every time I'd fast-troll a worm across it, I'd get a strike. But when I stopped and cast back into that nook, I'd usually catch only one bass and wouldn't get any more strikes. But when I'd resume trolling, I'd get a strike every pass.

It's illegal in tournaments, but when you're fun-fishing you're not limited to using one rod at a time. You can troll worms on two or three rods at once. When I've drifted and trolled worms with Grady Holton, a guide from Jasper, Texas, at Sam Rayburn, Grady always fished two rods and I fished two rods. The two of us were fishing four worms on structure. That way you can try different sizes and colors of worms at the same time.

During the practice for the 1975 B.A.S.S. tourney at Santee, I went to the lower lake (Moultrie) and did some worm trolling and found a school of bass. I was able to win that event with a combination of structure tactics. I'd troll a ledge to find the school and then throw out a marker buoy, pull up to it, and make another cast with the worm. The first day I caught two bass in a row, and I noticed a bunch of

This one took a trolled worm. I like a fairly heavy sinker to bump the bottom, and a floating worm to stay about a foot off the bottom.

marks on my locator. I'd drawn that school of bass up under my boat. Two or three were following my second fish to the boat. Instantly I grabbed my spoon rod and dropped a ½-ounce Nebco Spoon down to the bottom in 15 feet of water and jigged it a couple of times, and one hit it. I put sixteen straight bass into the boat with that spoon.

Worm trolling is a great way to locate bass. Often when you locate them you can catch them faster after that by casting to them, but sometimes the only way they'll hit the worm solid is if it's trolled.

I troll two types of worm rigs. One of them is the Carolina rig. With the floating worm and the leader, swivel, and big egg sinker, the weight is bumping along the bottom and the worm is drifting up about a foot. This makes for better visibility for the fish. I troll this rig more often. The second rig is simply a standard worm rig, but I put more weight on it because I want to keep good bottom contact and feel for stumps and dropoffs. I use a ⅜- or ½-ounce weight, and if there's any wind, I'll use an ounce. When you're worm trolling, you're in a position to get hung up frequently, so I like a fairly stout line, such as 14-pound or 17-pound. I also like a fairly stiff rod.

49   Bombering for Bass

When I was at Santee, the old-timers caught a lot more bass on the Bomber than any other lure they trolled. When I moved to Montgomery, Ala., and fished Lake Martin and areas on the Alabama River, the old-timers who trolled caught their bass on Bombers. In the early stages of my career when I lived in Maryland, guys did lots of trolling with Bombers and caught lots of fish on them.

Today, in Oklahoma, where there are plenty of striped bass and white bass in addition to largemouths, Bomber trollers add a little different twist. They add a three-way swivel with a little jig. White bass and rockfish often hit the jig, whereas the largemouths and spotted bass frequently strike the Bomber.

The Bomber really has been a universal standard plug among the trollers in many southern and western lakes for years and years. Billy Westmorland says when he was growing up on Dale Hollow Reservoir, the old-timers trolled Bombers in deep water and caught 6- and 7-pound smallmouths.

There are good reasons why the Bomber has been *the* lure among the trolling fraternity. It's fairly snagless; it has a good lip, good hooks, solid construction; it trolls well; and it's easy to tune by bending the little line-tie clevis right or left.

Although the Bomber is the traditional lure, any crank bait will work for trolling. Getting the bait to the right depth is important. By trolling with a long line, you can get a 600 Series Bomber down as deep as 25 feet. The big Hellbenders and big Waterdogs will get down this deep, but not many others will do so unless you use wire or lead-core line.

Bombering for bass is not much different from the Buck Perry style of Spoonplugging. The Bomber is a bit more snagless, and when you do get hung up and break it off, many times it will float up. Also, since it floats you can get right over it and wiggle and twitch it around when it's hung up, and lots of times it pops loose. When a Spoonplug gets hung up, it often stays hung and you lose it. Incidentally, when you troll a man-made reservoir, it will have stumps and rocks, and having a plug knocker along is essential. It's nothing more than a heavy lead weight, usually with some chain on it. You attach your line to a clip and get directly over the plug and let the plug knocker line

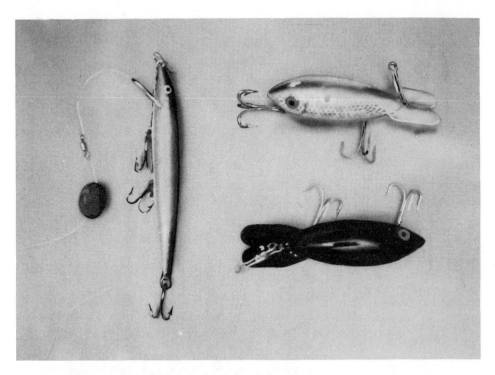

Bombers in silver and crawdad are my favorites, and another twist is to rig a floating Rapala with a swivel and barrel sinker to hold it a foot or so off the bottom.

down. The chains usually get hooked up on the hooks, and with the heavy line on the knocker, you can retrieve the bait. For less than thirty-five cents, you can make a plug knocker with a heavy swiveled barrel weight and a snap. Simply snap the weight to your line when you're directly over the lure and let the weight down to the lure. Lift up and down, and usually your bait will be knocked loose by the weight.

A short, stiff rod is ideal for trolling, and rod holders on your boat come in handy. While speed trolling is effective in hot weather, trolling slow is apt to pay off better at times, especially in the spring and fall during cool weather. Good trollers frequently change their trolling speeds and give their lures a series of erratic jerks to entice bass to strike.

Another twist in trolling involves rigging a minnow type of floating lure such as a Rapala 18 to 24 inches ahead of a swivel and a

A bombered bass. You can make the lure more attractive to the fish by varying your trolling speed and giving erratic jerks to entice strikes.

barrel sinker such as you'd use with the Carolina worm rig. The lure moves along a foot to 18 inches off the bottom. Sometimes this technique really pays off. One time we made a walleye film using this method in Minnesota, and we caught some bass by accident.

I'm sometimes asked how far back behind the boat you should troll. When I'm Bombering for bass, I'll make a medium cast about 75 feet out behind the boat. Then I know how far back the plug is. Unless you have your line marked or use a level-wind reel and mark the revolutions the handle makes, you won't know how much line you have out if you push the button and let the line out. I usually make this cast and troll at that distance, about 75 feet out. With 20-pound line, a 600 Series Bomber will get down 17 to 20 feet deep. Usually when I'm watching my locator and come up on a shallow ridge, I hold my rod up and reel in 15 to 20 feet of line. This raises the plug 5 to 6 feet off the bottom and will help you clear a shallow hump. When the water falls off deeper, I'll push the button and let out 10 to 15 feet of line, and this allows the plug to work back deeper.

I don't see any need to troll 200 to 300 feet behind the boat. It takes you more time to get your lure unhung when you've got that much line out, and also you're unable to follow the contour as well. You might be trolling out on a point which makes a turn, and with too much line out your lure never gets near the point when you make that turn. I like to make a loop turn rather than cut the corners sharply. If you cut a corner sharply, your lure doesn't get as close to the point as it should.

SPAWNING

As I mentioned in discussing using bullhead minnows for spawning bass, there is a lot of controversy over whether sportsmen should fish for spawning bass. I enjoy catching bass at all times of the year whether they're spawning or feeding. I don't keep many bass, and of the entire number of bass I weighed in during the ten or so tournaments I fished last year, I brought in one dead bass. The others were released to be caught again another day. In the spring during the pre-spawn and spawning seasons, most of the tournaments have a 90 to 95 percent release rate. Tournament fishermen do not kill many bass during the spawning season. In fact, Ray Scott and the Bass Anglers Sportsman Society try to avoid scheduling a tournament right during what will likely be the biggest spawn. They try to schedule on either side of it.

I don't think states should close fishing during the spawning season, but I think they should regulate it more. I think the creel limit could be reduced to one bass per day at this time. In some states which have a closed season, you're not allowed to fish. In Minnesota when the bass season's closed, if you throw in a bass lure, they'll arrest you. I don't agree with their rule. I think you should be allowed to fish even if you're not allowed to keep any. Why not be allowed to catch them and release them? This would be good sportfishing with no harm to the resource.

I normally fish for spawning bass about seven months out of the year, because they're the most fun to catch. They're in shallow water

Spawning bass are usually in shallow water and are easy to spot and fun to catch. This does no harm as long as you release them.

almost always, they display anger, they hit topwater plugs, they hit spinnerbaits in muddy water, and they hit everything. I usually start my season off right after Christmas with a trip to Florida's Lake Okeechobee. On the full moon in December or January, there'll be a spawn on Okeechobee. I have seen it as early as December 20.

The traditional spawning time in central Florida from Lake Kissimmee to Palatka is the full moon of February. On Lake Seminole in southern Georgia the big spawn comes on the March full moon. Late March and April are good spawning months in the Carolinas, Virginia, and Tennessee. On March 28 for four consecutive years at Santee-Cooper I caught a 10-pound spawning bass. All the states from North Carolina through Oklahoma have good spawns in April. May is a prime month in states farther north, such as Maryland. In the northern-tier states such as Michigan, Minnesota, and New York, June is the big month. In some of the bass lakes in Canada north of Montreal, such as around Lake MacGregor, I've found spawners in July.

For this progressive spawn in the northern hemisphere, I use three distinct patterns, and they're dynamite!

50   Weightless Worming

By far the most effective lure pattern for catching spawning bass is weightless worming—fishing a plastic worm without weight over the spawning bed. Plastic worms are not good cold-water baits, as I've discussed before, but the first time the worm really takes on significance in the year is right on the spawn. For some reason I cannot explain, a black worm seems to work the best for spawners. Since spawners are around a lot of cover, I like to throw a fairly large worm. This tends to deviate from normal worm fishing in that most tournament fishermen agree that you'll catch a lot more bass on 5-to-6-inch worms. However, during the spawning season, even the small males savagely hit 7-to-8-inch worms.

Worm fishing during the spawn is entirely different. The hook is put in a different position, the worm color and size are different, and you use different tackle and a different retrieve. The fairly large worm gives you added casting weight. (If you do use any lead weight, use only a tiny BB split shot.) Since the worm is large, I use a large 5/0 or 6/0 Mustad hook. When bass are spawning, they're not hungry and they're not hitting out of reflex action, but rather out of protective instinct. They're guarding their nests, and all they're trying to do is attack or kill the worm and move it away from the nest. When they grab it, they'll swim away from the nest 4 or 5 feet and spit it out. Those who like to wait a long time after they feel a bass pick up the worm frequently find out in the spring that they no longer have a fish on. Some figure the strike was from a bluegill.

I like to use a new plastic worm which is poured and has a smooth surface. When you get a strike and later examine that smooth surface, you'll always see the fish's teeth marks. Even the smallest amount of jaw pressure from the fish will put tiny pinlike marks in the worm. By checking closely you can see where he picked it up, and my experience has been that about half the time a spawning bass picks up the worm in the middle. If you rig the worm Texas-style, you'll miss him when he picks it up in the middle. When you strike back, he doesn't have the hook. Many fishermen who position the hook near the head of the worm discover that at spawning time when they set back on a strike their worm gets bitten right behind the bend of the hook. It's because spawning bass seldom get the worm completely inside their mouths

The male bass usually hits first, but a big female like this one is probably there to back him up, so don't just release the male and take off.

that they're so hard to hook. This is why I run my hook down to the middle of the worm and then hook it Texas-style.

Some pros use a 4-inch worm for spawning bass and say they do better with it, and this also makes sense because the fish is more apt to get the whole worm in his mouth. I prefer the big worm because it casts better on bait-casting tackle, which I like to use. With an extra-sharp hook and heavier line, I'm able to drive the hook through the fish's lips, which are very tough. Spawning bass, being in shallow water, jump immediately when they're hooked, and if they're not hooked good, they'll shake off. With the hook in the middle of the worm, I can hook at least 75 percent.

There are two phases to fishing for trophy bass on the beds. First, with Polaroid glasses, you need to sneak along and try to spot an area where they're spawning and look for movement. When you get your first strike, 90 percent of the time it's the male bass. You need to catch him first. He'll jump instantly, and you need to use the multiple hook set I described in the section on the Texas rig for plastic worms. After you catch and release the male, which almost always will be under 3 pounds, anchor your boat right there.

Now begins the second phase—it's time to try for the big female. Throw 5 to 10 feet past the bed and make slow retrieves by swimming the worm a couple feet at a time and let it sink to the bottom. When you get to where you think the bed is, stop the worm for ten seconds. Then move it an inch and allow it to sit five more seconds. Then move it a couple inches. When you think the worm is out of the bed, swim it a couple more feet and let it sink again. Repeat this procedure five or six more casts. The female is much more cautious, and you need to annoy her.

The first bass I ever caught over 10 pounds was at Santee-Cooper in 1963. I saw her on a bed, and I threw in and caught the male. I made repeated casts and couldn't get the female to hit. I went back to that spot at noon and saw her again, and I caught the male again. She never would hit. At dusk I sneaked back and on my first cast, a giant

A good spot for weightless worming—back in a shallow cove where the bass like to establish their beds.

swirl erupted. I waited too long and by the time I set the hook, she'd already dropped the worm. I made about ten more casts and it was almost dark when I finally felt a little tap and saw my line ease off a little. I set the hook and caught a 10¾-pounder. I'd made approximately seventy-five casts to that bed during the day before I caught her on that black 7½-inch Creme worm with no weight.

51 Spotting Their Beds

This is a technique in itself. When I get into a potential spawning area, I trim up the big engine, because the water's usually too shallow to run. When someone's with me, I let them run very slow while I stand up in the bow and look for any kind of fish movement. Often there will be carp and gar in addition to bass in those shallow areas. When you're running the motor, you seldom see the fish, but when you're looking down, you see the bed. When you see a couple of beds, you know you've found a spawning area. There might be forty more beds around.

Then I shut off the main engine and either put down the trolling motor or take a push pole and get the sun at my back. This latter is critical. If you're moving toward the sun, the reflection off the water will prevent you from seeing as well, and also the bass will see you easier because they're looking downsun. When moving with the sun at your back, you're moving toward them from their blind side and you have better visibility than they have, and you'll often spot them before they spot you. One advantage of the push pole over the trolling motor is that if you spot a bass, you can stop the boat quickly and quietly with the pole. Trying to stop quickly by reversing the trolling motor is a little noisier.

When I am moving along with the trolling motor, I usually take a 20-pound anchor and hang it over the stern, and I run the rope up the center of the boat and secure it on a cleat up front. When I see a bass 50 or 60 feet away, I shut off the trolling motor and drop the anchor. I can get stopped far enough away without scaring the fish. Also, as soon as I spot the fish, I duck down low just as if I'd seen a big greenhead mallard and didn't want to scare him. Also, when you're working downsun, you need to be wearing dark clothing. You don't want a white shirt or a white hat or a shiny watchband which will reflect into

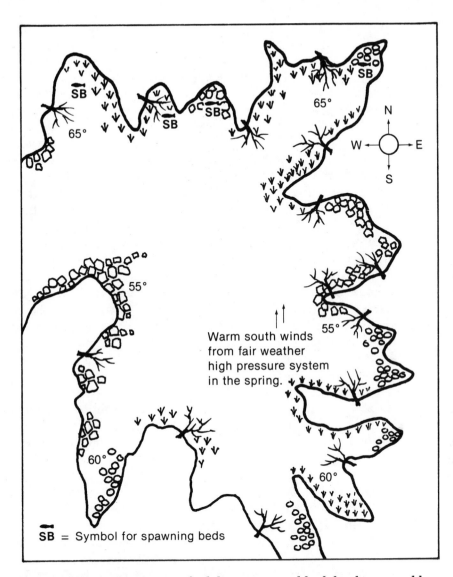

SB = Symbol for spawning beds

The shallow northern coves of a lake are warmed both by the sun and by south winds piling up the warmer surface water, and that's where the early spawners will be.

the water. Be extra quiet, too, because spawning bass are really spooky.

Sometimes when you spot a big bass, you scare her. About the time you see her, she sees you and she moves off. I take little pieces of Styrofoam and tie about 3 feet of monofilament to each one and attach little slip weights to the ends of the line. I have a whole pile of these little floats and weights rigged up in the front of the boat, and when I'm easing along and see the whoosh of a giant bass taking off, I flip out one of these markers. I try to position it where it won't interfere with my casts. I'll pick a pattern, such as throwing each marker about 10 feet to the east of the nest. When I come back later, I might have twenty of these markers out with each one 10 feet to the east of the bed. I use a compass to determine the direction. Since the shorelines move in and out, the simple directions right and left won't have any significance.

I've been very successful with this system at Okeechobee and Lake George in Florida and Lake Seminole in Georgia. When I guided at Santee, I regularly put out forty markers a day during the bedding season. My guide parties and I came back to the markers and waded when we fished the beds. The high position in the boat enables you to spot the beds much better, but wading enables you to be lower and make a much quieter approach. We'd wait thirty minutes to an hour before returning to the beds, and catch a good number of the females.

As I mentioned in the segment on fishing bullhead minnows for spawners, water refracts the image to a degree. The image you see of the bass on the nest is really not exactly where you see it. The fish is a little farther away than he appears to be. If you see a bed in the distance and cast right to where you think it is, you'll fall short by a foot or two. I throw 10 feet past where the bed appears to be, and when I'm retrieving, I stop the lure or bait 2 or 3 feet past what I see, and then the bait drops right into the bed.

Probably the best way to learn this is to get out in a clear lake and pick out a rock in shallow water. Back off 40 or 50 feet and throw a plastic worm 10 feet past the rock and retrieve it back to where you think the rock is. Then drop the worm and move over there in your boat and see where your worm is. You'll be surprised the first ten times you try this at how far off you are. You might be 4 feet on either side of it. Being accurate in dropping a bait directly in the bed takes a lot of experience and practice.

Polaroid glasses are a must in spotting the beds. One thing you look for on a sand bottom is a bright spot. The bottom will have a certain amount of sediment, and a freshly cleared bed usually will be a bright spot. When he makes the nest, the male fans away the sediment and dirt.

---

52   Muddy-Water Spinnerbaiting

In some areas, particularly many parts of states such as Oklahoma, the water is muddy at spawning time. For some reason, when it's very muddy, the spinnerbait is the king spawning bait. Spawning bass normally will hit the worm anywhere, but the spinnerbait gives you the advantage of being able to cover a lot more water in a day. If you're in an area with a lot of brush, cover, and muddy water, you can work a spinnerbait through a lot of water. Even though they'll hit the worm, it's much slower to use.

Since muddy-water spawners are very, very shallow, such as a foot to 18 inches deep, you need a light spinnerbait with a fairly large blade. The large blade slows the bait down. The larger the blade, the slower it runs, and the lighter the body weight, the shallower it runs. I prefer a No. 5 or 6 gold blade if the water's muddy, but if it's super-muddy I like a red or bright-orange blade. I use copper if the water is semi-muddy. I'll take a 1/4-ounce head and with a knife shave off quite a bit of the lead to lighten the lure. The torque of that big blade on a little spinnerbait would roll the bait in the water, but since you're running it slow, it doesn't roll. Hold your rod high and this allows it to run slower, and the blade almost creates a wake.

Since the timbered reservoirs in Kansas, Oklahoma, and Texas are flood-control lakes, by spawning time there is almost automatically high water which gets up in the grass and bushes. Often even in reservoirs without the timber you're fishing in flooded fields. Since you don't spot many fish in muddy water, you need to look for movement more than anything else. I try to avoid the wind and find a calm cove so I can detect fish movement. Spawning bass are always moving around. You'll see carp moving, too, but throw to them anyway.

One of the best strings of bass I ever caught was when I thought I was throwing to carp, and they turned out to be half carp and half

This muddy-water spawner hit a slow, shallow-running spinnerbait.

bass. Mary Ann and I caught ten bass totaling 45 pounds at Oolegah Reservoir in Oklahoma by throwing to where we saw a lot of carp working. We threw spinnerbaits and caught 4-, 5-, and 6-pound spawning largemouths. They were right up where the carp were rolling. Usually carp spawn at the same water temperatures and in the same areas bass spawn in. You can tell the movements of carp from bass because when you spook them, carp take off straight as an arrow, but bass move out for 10 feet or so and then make an arc and slow down. Bass end up about 10 feet from their beds after they make that loop. Then they ease back to the bed.

Spawning bass are notorious for hitting a spinnerbait with their mouths closed. All they're trying to do is bump it out of the way. I almost always use a trailer hook, and if the area is a little bit open, I sometimes put a treble hook on the regular trailer hook. You can use the short-arm spinnerbait for spawners because you're running it so shallow and are coming over the logs and submerged bushes. Two good short-arm models on the market are the Scorpion by Bass Buster and the Red Man which Jimmy Houston designed and sold to Norman. You can go to a No. 3 or 4 blade if you shave the head down to about $1/8$ ounce. You definitely don't want a fast-moving spinnerbait, however.

Sometimes if the water's a little deeper and I think I know exactly where the bed is, I'll buzz the spinnerbait right over the bed and at the last instant drop it right on her. If it falls right on her, out of instinct she's apt to inhale it.

When you're wading for spawning bass, you want to avoid stepping in a nest and messing up the eggs. The bed is usually 2 to 6 inches deeper than the regular bottom. Balance your weight on your rear foot, and slide the foot you're going to step with as if you're trying to find your way in the dark in a motel room. Slide your foot and plant it and then shift your weight to it. Also, this helps keep you from tripping over stumps and logs. If you feel the edge of a depression, that's likely the bed, so then you can wade around without disturbing it.

FLYRODDING

One of my biggest challenges each year comes when I'm doing a couple of flyrod popping-bug segments for my TV show, *Fishing with Roland Martin*. This flyrod bass fishing is probably the most satisfying to me of any work I do in the year. At times I regret that in tournament competition and so much of the other fishing I do I'm interested usually only in catching a bunch of bass and several big ones. I and others tend to overlook the pure sporting type of fishing which the flyrod offers. The sportsman who is involved in flyrod fishing for bass is the truest form of bass fisherman I've ever met. They're the finest sportsmen. They seldom keep their fish, and they're usually after the aesthetic qualities, the quiet presentation, the strike, the enjoyment of nature, and the challenge of man against fish. When you hook a bass on a flyrod, all you have between you and the fish is the hook, line, and rod; you don't have the mechanical aid of a spinning or bait-casting reel. You don't play the fish with the reel; you battle with him with your hands. The line and leader you're using are much more delicate, and the art of flycasting is precisely that—a delicate art.

I really wish I could spend an entire summer using a flyrod. This is the epitome of bass fishing. And in addition to all these aesthetic qualities, a flyrod is at times a highly efficient way of catching bass.

Once I was at North Carolina's Currituck Sound doing a film on flyrod popping-bug fishing in the milfoil patches. Four casting enthusiasts were with me. One of them liked surface plugs such as the Devils Horse. Two of the guys liked plastic-worm fishing, and another one enjoyed using weedless spoons. All of these methods are effective for bass in Currituck's milfoil. The sun came out one day and it was calm, and I told them I thought a popping bug worked quietly through the pockets in the milfoil would take some bass.

I waded out in front of my campsite and caught a limit of bass—eight—100 yards out from about 200 motor homes. I was throwing a small popping bug into the open holes and letting it sit and then twitching it. The bass literally exploded all over it. In addition to those eight, I had another eight good strikes. This was all in a morning's fishing.

For many years there's been quite a discussion among flyrod bassing fans concerning what tackle to use. Since the development of graphite rods I think it's been unanimous among the truly great flyfishermen such as Lefty Kreh and Leon Chandler that the No. 8 and 9 weights of graphite rods are perfect for flyrod bass fishing. I use Fenwick graphite flyrods in those two weights. These are 8½-foot popping-bug rods, and I use Scientific Angler's bass-bug-taper floating line. The line is tapered for the first 10 feet, and then there's about 15 feet of very fat No. 9 line, and the remaining line for backing tapers back down. I use a single-action reel and prefer it over the automatic fly reel. I strip the line with my hand and let it lie in coils in the water if I'm wading. When bass bugging out of my boat, I put a piece of tarp or plastic over my trolling motor, depthfinder, and anything else which could snag the line. I keep the tarp or plastic clean, because dirt and grime on the line will cause it to sink.

Another friend of mine, Ben Hardesty of the Shakespeare Corporation, who is an expert flycaster, developed a system of wrapping the loose flyline around two of his fingers. He sort of coils it on two fingers

The challenge of flyrodding isn't over when you've got a fish on; you need skill to control the fish without the mechanical aids of spinning and bait-casting tackle.

of his left hand and when he makes another cast, the line peels off his fingers. His technique prevents the line from getting caught on objects in the bottom of the boat.

I also tie my own tapered leaders. This isn't hard to do if you know two knots. One of them is the nail knot, which connects the heavy butt section of the leader to your flyline. This knot can be learned readily from any book on knots for fishermen, such as Lefty Kreh and Mark Sosin's book or Vic Dunaway's book. I start with a 50-pound section 2 feet long and tie it to the flyline tip. To the 50-pound mono I tie 2 feet of 30-pound. To the 30 I add 2 feet of 20- or 17-pound, and to that I tie 2 to 3 feet of 8-, 10-, or 12-pound. The entire leader is 8 to 9 feet long. I tie the mono together with a blood knot, which also can be learned from the knot books. The clearer the water, the longer the leader you need. I have gone to leaders as long as 12 feet, but usually a leader about the length of your rod is sufficient. The longer the leader, the more difficult it is to cast. If you're a novice with a flyrod, you might start off with a 7- or 8-foot leader, and when you learn to handle that size well, you can go to a longer one.

An experienced flycaster can get by with a level line and an 8-foot level leader. Tapered lines are much more expensive than level lines. A good rule of thumb is to use at least the size of line recommended on the rod label, and one size larger often works a little better. A poorly balanced flyrod-and-line combination is next to impossible for even an expert to cast well, so getting the right weight line for the rod is extremely important. Keeping the line clean and dressed is also important for good casting. Dirty lines begin to sink, and this also makes for terrible casting, because a line which sinks is hard to pick up off the water.

A good bass-bug rod has a slow action and definitely not a fast, whippy action. It's similar to a salmon flyrod. If you have a fiberglass flyrod, you might get oversized guides put on it. The larger guides make for easier casting.

Looks like trout fishing—and it certainly has many of the same esthetic and sporting qualities, though the tackle is heavier and the fishing patterns are sometimes quite different.

The better single-action fly reels, such as the Pflueger Medalist, have an adjustable drag. For bass fishing, a regular flyline is long enough so that you don't need any backing. Even though experts are able to cast 70 to 90 feet, the fact remains that most bass caught on bugs are taken on casts of 40 to 50 feet. If you are fishing in lakes with striped bass as well as black bass, you might catch a few stripers on your bugs.

When you choose popping bugs, be sure to select ones with the hook well back from the cork body. If the hook point is too close to the cork, this makes hooking the bass much more difficult. Also, don't select bugs which dig into the water very deep, because these are hard to pick up from the surface when you're casting. You can catch a lot of bass on a medium to large bug, but most of the extra-large sizes are difficult to cast because they're wind-resistant. One of my favorite series of popping bugs are the Peck's Poppers. They were designed many years ago in Chattanooga, Tenn., by the late E. H. Peckinpaugh. The Peckinpaugh Company was sold a few years ago, and the last I heard the Peck's poppers were being made in Baton Rouge, La. One of my favorite sizes, tied on a No. 2 hook, is a medium-sized bug.

---

53   Deer Hair for the Quiet Approach

Deer-hair bugs are very popular with smallmouth fishermen, particularly the old-timers such as the late John Alden Knight. When I go to good lakes in Minnesota and Canada, such as Lac LaCroix, in June, a dynamite pattern for me is the deer-hair bug for the quiet approach. Most of this fishing is for smallmouths, although deer-hair bugs work equally well for largemouths. I probably have no greater fun than catching smallmouths in those northern waters on a flyrod and deer-hair bug. I use a small bug because a big deer-hair bug is hard to cast. It's compact and doesn't have hair legs, which are too wind-resistant. It's tied on a No. 2 hook and looks like a miniature mouse with its small leather tail. Another one I like has a little tuft of hair coming back by the hook. This hair makes it almost weedless.

When these bugs are dry, they land softly on the water. For some reason smallmouths in those clear northern lakes like a quiet bug. They probably see it coming through the air, and they don't like the

Here are a few of my deer-hair favorites for northern smallmouths.

noisy splat of cork or plastic-headed bugs; I've found I can catch more on the deer-hair bugs. These smallmouths are seldom in shallow water except around spawning time, and then they're cautious, wary fish. Early in the morning and late in the evening and on a cloudy day they've got their eyes tuned to the surface. When they're spawning, this could be the best flyrod bass bugging you'll ever find.

I'm looking for spawners, and again I'm looking in the northern coves in the lake. In these coves I look for large individual boulders and small submerged grass patches. These are key areas. I throw the bug in there and let it sit motionless for a long time. With Polaroid glasses, often I can see the smallmouth rise up to within a foot of the bug and sit there and watch it. If you twitch it too hard, you'll spook him. But when you twitch it gently, he usually charges right into it. Smallmouths usually rush the bug rather than suck it in as large-mouths normally do. Occasionally when they're really active, they'll shoot up into the air and come down on the bug and take it on the way down. These are the most exciting strikes you'll ever get. In fact, I've

Ron Weber of Normark does some early-morning flyrodding for smallmouths on the Minnesota-Canada border.

been trying for five seasons to get this aerial-bombardment type of strike on film because it's just so dramatic.

Deer-hair bugs don't make nearly the popping sound on the water that a regular popping bug makes. They're quiet and resemble a moth on the surface. They're designed to be worked slowly and quietly. With the weedless type of deer-hair bug I mentioned, you can pull it and skitter it along over the grass and catch bass that way.

Some of the greatest smallmouth fishing I've ever enjoyed was a couple of summers ago with Spence Petros at Lac LaCroix on the Canada-Minnesota border. We found a shallow bar out on the main lake, and the bass were on this structure. We'd caught bass around the edge of that bar on crank baits during the day, but that evening the fish moved up on the bar and started chasing minnows on the surface. I suggested we try a bug, and we got into a school of 4-to-5-pounders. Spence caught a 5½-pounder—his biggest ever—on a bug, and I landed a 5-pounder. We caught approximately forty bass in a couple of hours until it was pitch black, and our top ten averaged 4 pounds apiece. Five or six times we each had good ones on. Those were the most smallmouths over 4 pounds I've ever caught in any two-hour period, and we got them on flyrods and bugs.

Nothing is any stronger in fresh water, and nothing tests flyrod tackle any better, than a big northern smallmouth bass. Four-pound smallmouths on flyrods and bugs are the ultimate.

54 Poppers: Attention Getters

Popping bugs are one of my favorite patterns for catching large-mouths. While the Peck's Popper with a No. 2 hook and a concave mouth has been my old standby, this past year I found an excellent bug made in Norfork, Va. It looks like the Peck's bug, but it has epoxy rather than paint and it's the strongest, finest bug I've ever seen. I bounced it off numerous cypress trees along the North River near Currituck Sound, N.C., and I caught twenty to thirty bass per day on it, and yet it still looks brand new. Most popping bugs are fragile; the paint gets knocked off the head and the hook works loose from the cork. But this bug is super-strong.

One advantage with a popping bug is that even with 6- or 8-pound leader, when you set the hook with that limber rod you hardly ever lose a bass. The bug hook is light wire and sharp, and I sharpen them even more. Once you hook a fish, you very seldom lose it. Lots of times a largemouth will inhale that bug and you'll hook him in his tongue area. This is really a super place to hook one. About the only way you'll lose a bass on a bug is if he breaks your leader. When he jumps, he doesn't get the leverage from the light bug to throw the hook that he does if you hook him on a $5/8$-ounce topwater plug.

All you have to do is nurse him along. Hold your rod high in the air and put some pressure on him—not too much—by holding the line. In lakes with lots of cover, they easily can dive into the brush or pads and break your leader. This is a problem at Okeechobee and Kissim-mee and on the east shore of Lake George in Florida. But in an open lake like Lac LaCroix, you never have to worry about even a 5-pounder wrapping up and breaking your leader.

It's an advantage to have a flyrod and popping bug rigged up in your boat when you're out fishing for fun. If the bass simply aren't

**A collection of poppers that will
work well for a flyrodder when
bass is the game.**

hitting much and the action is slow, you can tie on a tiny popper with
a Size 8 or 10 hook and probably catch some nice bluegills. This can
make the day when the bass don't cooperate. Bluegills will knock a
bass bug, but they very seldom get the hook; you need a smaller bug
with a smaller hook to catch them. In Oklahoma and some states
there's a species of panfish called the green sunfish. They have bigger
mouths than bluegills, and you can hook them on small to medium-
sized bass bugs. I've frequently caught them on my bass bugs. They're
fun, too, because they really blast into a bug.

Many old-timers insist that bass bugs are among the most effective lures you can throw in the summer when the sun's up bright and
the bass are in weeds and pads, because the bugs offer a much quieter
approach. Something I experimented with at Currituck turned out to
work good, and that was making my bugs weedless. I took some 60-
pound steel leader and pushed a 2-inch length of it through the eye of
the bug and then right into the cork head so that it came out the top of
the head. Then with needlenose pliers I bent the wire and made a
weedguard. I could drag the bug over the milfoil without the hook
snagging. I missed a few more strikes because of the weedguard, but
not enough to offset the advantage of the weedguard.

Thinking of popping bugs and Currituck Sound reminds me of a
funny incident I experienced there seven or eight years ago. I was
fishing with a variety of lures, and saw a flyrodder wading near an
island. Every few minutes I'd see him hook a bass which would jump

Spence Petros and I caught this string on poppers on an August morning.

and thrash around. He was stringing them, and with the North Carolina daily limit being eight bass, he was already culling fish. I could
tell he had a bunch of 'em 3 pounds and better. I'd been fishing all
morning and had caught some bass, too, but mine weren't running as
large as his fish. Finally I eased up to him and asked him how he was
doing. He said casually he'd caught a few, and I tried to be real non-
chalant and said I'd caught a few, too. I didn't want to make it obvious I really wanted to know what he was on to. I mentioned that I'd
seen him catch a couple of nice ones, and he held up his stringer
which had eight all over 3 pounds. His biggest was about 5½. His fish
made my mouth water, and he was catching and releasing them right
and left.

I really was trying to figure out his pattern, and he sensed this. He
was an older gentleman, and finally he says, "Well, I'll tell you what,
son. It really doesn't make much difference what color or size these
bugs are as long as they're these one-inch bugs in a frog color with
green feathers."

I've found out since then at Currituck that he's right. That frog
color with greenish-yellow feathers in that certain size he was talking

about is far the best bug in that water. I'll catch three bass on that size and color to one on something else.

I have noticed too that in certain lakes, a certain-sized popper in a certain color will be far superior. I can't find any rule of thumb to this, such as saying in clear water use a light-colored bug. I do know it pays to go into a tackle shop around a good popping-bug lake and ask what their best-selling popper is. The color and size makes a lot of difference in some areas.

55 Streamers for Aristocracy

Two friends of mine—Lefty Kreh and Charlie Most—are excellent streamer fishermen, and they like smallmouth rivers along the East Coast, such as the Potomac, Susquehanna, and Shenandoah. Lefty is one of the premier flyrod fishermen in the world, and Charlie, who also is good with a flyrod, is an information officer with the U.S. Fish and Wildlife Service in Washington, D.C. Lefty fishes a lot with a Muddler Minnow, which is a type of streamer fly. Charlie grew up in Montana and fished trout waters, so when he moved east he adapted his trout methods to smallmouth bass and he has been quite successful at it.

Charlie uses Muddler Minnow types and salmon-fly types tied up on a No. 2 hook, and his fly is about 2½ inches long. He rigs up the way you'd rig up with a popping bug, but his manner of retrieve is typical of any good streamer-fly fisherman. He makes a long, accurate cast and works his fly in little 2-to-3-inch jerks. He does this by tugging on the line with his left thumb and index finger. Lefty Kreh does this same thing, and both of them point the rod almost toward the fish. They'd hold the rod just high enough so there is a slight loop in the line, and they watch the loop. When they get a strike, the loop twitches as your monofilament does when a bass sucks in a plastic worm. Those twitches are their only indication of the strike.

The Muddler Minnow darts along when it's twitched properly like a little stonefly larvae or a hellgrammite or a small minnow. These are foods smallmouths love. In addition to the shade and cover along a river, you have to consider the current and how to cast to it. With popping bugs, deer-hair bugs, or streamer flies, never cast downstream. Use the same precept for river smallmouths which stream trout fishermen employ. Always either cast sidecurrent or upcurrent—with upcurrent meaning upstream.

Two approaches to river fishing which Kreh and Most use which are interesting are fishing directly in front of and fishing directly behind boulders in the river. They wade up within casting distances to submerged boulders and fish both sides. A boulder has a cushion of water in front of it and a small eddy directly behind it. Smallmouths might be positioned in either spot so they can dart out and grab something which happens by. I've tried their technique, and first I make a cast about 5 feet in front of the boulder. This keeps the flyline from spooking the fish when it hits the water. The current drifts the streamer fly down. When the flyline floats up near the boulder, you start twitching the fly by making short strips with the line in your left hand (if you cast righthanded). Strikes come as the streamer starts darting away when it gets near the boulder.

Most of those which get in front of the boulders are active feeders, and they're most likely to be there early in the morning and late in the

Streamers make the transition from trout to bass easy for the flyrodder; they're fished very much the same way.

My cameraman, Bob Swanson, zooms in on some streamer action. When he's got enough footage for my TV series he sometimes lands a few himself.

evening. If they're resting and cooling it during the midday hours, they're apt to be in the eddies behind the boulders. This often takes a straight upstream cast, because on a cross-stream cast, the line often gets swept too fast by the current. Get below the boulder and cast straight upstream to the slack water. Then you can work the streamer at the right speed down through the eddy without spooking fish.

Streamer flies are most practical in water from 6 inches to about 4 feet deep. When you get deeper than 6 feet, they're impractical even with sinking flylines. The flies tend to sink slowly, and when your line's down that deep it's hard to pick up and cast. Like the deer-hair bug, the streamer fly offers a very quiet approach.

Streamer flies work good in lakes and ponds for bass, too, especially when they're fished fairly shallow. Another way you can detect the strike is to watch the spot where your leader connects to your line. When you see the knot or flyline eyelet twitch ever so slightly—even just an inch—this is your indication you've got a strike. This is why white flylines have become popular within the past fifteen to twenty years. The white color permits you to see the line better. The white line also is a boon to night flyfishing.

A trout fisherman who moves away from trout country can try to make the adjustment by using the same flyfishing techniques which paid off for him on his favorite rainbow, brook, and brown trout streams on his new quarry—largemouths, smallmouths, and spotted bass. He'll just need heavier leaders (6-to-12-pound) and a different selection of slightly bigger bugs. Although he might not forget trout entirely, he still can have some fun with his flyrod.

ULTRALIGHT TACKLE

Ultralight tackle is nothing more than the smaller spinning rods and reels with 2-to-6-pound line and the tiny $1/32$-to-$1/4$-ounce lures. Ultralight gear has its place in the clear lakes of the north and in some of the TVA and Army Corps of Engineers impoundments in the south. It also is good in some of the very clear rivers. A lot of bass anglers don't realize that ultralight tackle is truly a necessity in some waters. This has been proved in tournament competition during the past ten years. Some of the southern fishermen would come to a tournament at an impoundment like Smith Lake in Alabama, which has a lot of spotted bass that frequently stay deep. The guys from the swampy country in Louisiana and Florida and the heavy-line fishermen who live near impoundments such as Santee-Cooper believed at the time that 15-to-20-pound line was the standard in bass fishing and that 7-to-8-inch worms were what was needed to catch 'em.

Well, one of these tournaments—the Dixie B.A.S.S. Invitational in 1968 at Smith Lake—helped change their thinking. Bill Dance went to ultralight tackle and used 4- and 6-pound line and won that tourney. He threw small spoons and little plastic worms on a $5 1/2$-foot spinning rod to catch spotted bass from schools. Since that time there's been a bunch of ultralight-tackle fishermen. Foremost among these light-tackle buffs in the country today is probably Bill Westmorland, who was raised close to Dale Hollow, which is one of the clearest lakes on the TVA chain. Westmorland says he can't tell much differ-

Forrest Wood of Ranger Boats loves to take bass on ultralight tackle at Bull Shoals and Table Rock reservoirs, where the clear water makes bass hard to fool.

ence in the number of strikes he gets on 6-pound vs. 8-pound line, but he has found a lot of difference between 4 and 8. He says he gets many more strikes and many more bass on the 4-pound.

Even though I own ultralight tackle, I've never been one to specialize in it. I do fish it in some clear lakes. I don't like to, but the conditions force me to. For example, when I fish Table Rock or Bull Shoals, I have several small spinning rods rigged up with 4- and 6-pound line for small grubs, small jigs, and small plastic worms. These lures are particularly good for spring fish in the clear water along bluffs. All three bass species hit these lures on ultralight tackle.

In the B.A.S.S. tournament at Table Rock in 1971, John Powell won by dropping down to 10-pound line and using standard casting tackle. John never had used line that light for bass in his life, but he wasn't catching any on his 20-pound line, so he changed. I'd gone to 6-pound line and ⅛-ounce jigs and small L-2 black pork eels, and found some spawning bass beneath cedar trees in the back end of a creek. Bobby Murray and I had found them, and I had marked over 200 bass on the beds. The problem was the water was ultra-clear. I came in fifth, and the reason I didn't do any better was that the brush was so thick that nearly all of the several 4-to-5-pounders hooked went screaming off back under the bushes and behind the rocks and I failed to hold them. John also caught spawning bass, but he found his in an open cove.

Some lakes have a limited amount of cover and open, very clear water, and these are the ones I reserve for ultralight tackle. If I'm fishing a Florida lake full of stumps and lily pads, I wouldn't try to catch a big bass on 6- or 8-pound line in that water. Maybe Westmorland could, but I wouldn't even try. I think it's a proved fact that 4-pound line will get more strikes than 20-pound, but if you're fishing around heavy cover, how many big fish are you going to land on the 4-pound line?

56 Teeny Jigs on Spiderweb Line

When I fish the White River chain of lakes—Bull Shoals, Norfolk, Beaver, and Table Rock—and Lake Martin in Alabama, it's a standard for me to fish what in the Tennessee hills they call the "fly 'n' rind." This is simply a small jig and 2-to-3-inch piece of pork rind. I prefer the marabou jig because it seems to breathe more, has better action. I like to use an open hook if the water isn't too brushy and a small 2-to-2½-inch Uncle Josh split-tail pork eel. Sometimes I cut it down in length.

Jig fishing is quite a bit different from worm fishing. It requires a different way of holding the rod and reacting to the strike. It's not at all like worm fishing, where you hold the rod high and give 'em a few seconds before you set the hook. In grub fishing you mainly hold the rod low, but in jig fishing I never raise the rod to more than a 45-degree angle. I like to swim the jig and pork rind down the structure and the dropoffs and ledges. I like jigs with light wire hooks, similar to what a crappie fisherman uses with live minnows. You need to react fairly quickly to the strike and have good sensitivity. A few guys

This beautiful smallmouth fell prey to a small black jig.

have gone to graphite rods for extra sensitivity. Graphite does give more sensitivity and it seems to cast those small lures farther. Of course, with 4- and 6-pound line, there's no problem casting far enough.

One pro who isn't known for using light tackle is Jimmy Houston, but in an American Bass Fisherman tournament at Lake Oroville in California three years ago, Houston dropped down to light spinning tackle and won the tournament using a $1/32$-ounce crappie jig in that ultraclear water. I fished that tournament, and before it started, ran into Houston and asked him what he'd been up to lately. He said he'd

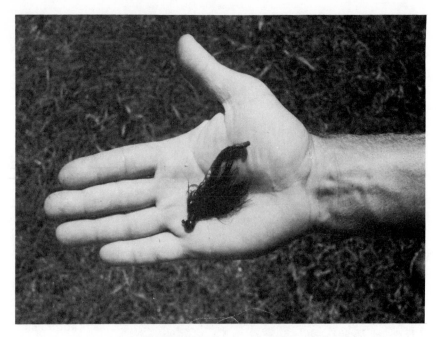

Sometimes I add an Uncle Josh 2½-inch split-tail pork rind or a small piece of plastic worm to the end of the marabou jig.

been fishing Tenkiller Lake—a lake he grew up on in Oklahoma—and had been crappie fishing. He added they'd been catching lots of crappies on little jigs and also a few bass on the jigs. When he got to Oroville, he found that several guys were using small jigs, and he decided to try his crappie jigs. He went way up one creek which has real steep ledges, and he caught almost all smallmouths. Those fish were down 4 to 10 feet on the sides of the rock ledges, particularly on the bends in the creek. Jimmy would throw his crappie jig right up to the rocks and let it sink. He was fishing fairly close to the boat and watching with Polaroids, and he said lots of times he saw the bass flash out and grab the little jig.

Ultralight fishing requires more attention than fishing with heavier bait-casting tackle. You need to be more on your toes—more alert. It's much easier to watch your 20-pound mono when you're worm fishing than it is to watch 4- or 6-pound line with a jig or grub. Again, a graphite rod is very good for ultralight fishing because of that extra sensitivity; you can feel that light peck easier. Bass often pick up the jig and rind or the grub as it's falling, and there's hardly any feel to the strike. About all you feel is a little pressure on your line. Since you're usually throwing the jig onto vertical rock where it's dropping a lot, you're swimming the bait much of the time. Of course, you can make parallel casts down the bank, and this is good, too, but often on small points, rockpiles, and ledges, you're making casts fairly straight in and letting the lure drop during a good portion of the retrieve. And that is when many of the strikes occur.

With ultralight gear you really have to readjust and feel for strikes, and this is not easy to do, especially if you're like me and do a lot of worm fishing in heavy cover with 17-to-25-pound line. Small jigs and pork rinds are very effective in cold weather, but not many guys are able to wear gloves and still feel the fish. Especially with 4-pound line, you have to adjust the drag on your spinning reel very carefully to avoid getting it too tight. I don't backwind with a spinning reel, although some guys such as Westmorland do this. I also do ultralight fishing for some saltwater species such as bonefish, barracuda, and permit, and there's no earthly way to backwind on a bonefish. In fact, if Billy Westmorland ever tried backwinding on a bonefish and the knob on his reel handle came off, it would fly off so fast that he might get killed. That handle would be revolving backward at a hundred miles an hour.

Ultralight fishing needs to be done with super-good tackle in tiptop shape, and most important is an extra-good drag on the reel. I strongly disagree with the practice of backwinding when fighting a fish. I want my drag set about two-thirds to the breaking point so it will spin freely if a bass makes a hard run.

When thinking of jigs and Kentucky bass, I'm reminded of the tournament at Bull Shoals in 1975 when I was paired one day with Johnny Morris, who owns and operates the Bass Pro Shops in Springfield, Mo. I'd found Kentucky bass 45 feet deep, and I was catching them on a 1/8-ounce jig and pork rind and 6-pound line. I'd fished with Charlie Campbell, who is better known as a Zara Spook topwater plug man, the first day of the tournament, and Charlie had shown me the pattern.

Johnny is a very good fisherman, but I got tickled at him. We would throw parallel to the bluffs and count down our jigs, then start retrieving by barely jigging the lures. Those spots would thump the jig, and Johnny would set the hook and start reeling. Here would come the fish up to within 10 feet of the top, and I noticed they'd have the pork rind but not the hook. Johnny lost seven in a row when the bass would open their mouths and the jig would pop loose.

When I got a strike, I would pause momentarily before setting the hook. If the fish got off, I'd drop the lure back again, and frequently I hadn't put enough pressure on him to scare him, and he'd strike again. The second time I'd let him take it longer, and then set the hook and have him. A couple of times when I set the hook and brought the fish up within 10 feet of the boat, I saw that he had only the pork rind, and I opened my bail. Johnny asked what I was doing, so I pointed out that the fish didn't have the hook. I could see the fish shake the bait, and then he'd finally eat it. Then I'd catch him. I caught six spotted bass that day, and Johnny caught only two or three, but he had as many if not more bass on than I did. I was letting the bass load up on the bait, whereas he was pulling them along when they didn't have the hook in their mouths.

---

57 Delicate Worming

I hate to have to worm fish with anything less than 10-pound line. With the Texas rig, I've always maintained that with any line smaller than 10-pound, it's very difficult to get the hook through the plastic and still have enough power to hook the fish solidly.

When I do use less than 10-pound line, such as in this delicate worming pattern, I modify my worm rigs drastically. If you're in open, clear water, you can fish the worm on 6-pound line with an exposed Aberdeen hook. Instead of using a large-diameter 1/0 or 2/0 hook, I'm apt to go to a No. 2 Aberdeen hook, which is nothing more than a crappie hook.

Sometimes it's necessary to rig the worm weedless for cover. Then I rig it Texas-style, but instead of going through the middle of the worm, I'll put the hook point at the side of it and make the slightest little indention into the plastic. Only a tiny slither of plastic is holding the hook point. This isn't quite as weedless as the standard Texas rig, but I'm not working this rig in heavy, heavy cover.

Charlie Brewer from Lawrenceburg, Tenn., invented what he calls the Slider and a technique called Slider fishing. He put an Aberdeen-type hook on a small, flat-bottomed jig head. The flat bottom makes the jig head slither down rather than fall straight. On the back of the

You can't set the hook reliably when the fish is headed toward you. Wait till it turns away, so that you won't just pull the bait out of its mouth.

head he uses a small-diameter 3-to-4-inch plastic worm. For years I've fished similarly by using an 1/8-ounce or even smaller slip sinker and a No. 1 or 2 hook with 6-pound line and a short worm with an exposed hook for Kentucky bass on Smith Lake and Lake Martin in Alabama. I swim the worm along the bluffs, and I was doing this back in 1965 when I was in the army stationed at Ft. Benning, Ga.

Charlie calls this method a "do-nothing" method. I'd get parallel to the rock bluff and throw out and let the worm sink about ten seconds and slowly wind it back. The two techniques are basically the same. In clear water the fish have so much vertical and horizontal visibility that this small lure attracts them from long distances.

One helpful thing which Charlie Brewer pointed out about his "do-nothing" retrieve with Sliders was the delay in setting the hook. I used to set the hook the instant I got a strike when swimming the small worm, but missed a lot of fish. When Charlie feels the pressure from the strike, he keeps reeling. Pressure from his tight line keeps the bass from being able to spit out the lure. The hook is against some part of his mouth. Finally after a few seconds the fish usually turns and goes the other way, and then is when Charlie sets the hook. The fish's mouth is away from him. When I was setting the hook with the fish facing me, it would be easy to pull the bait out of his mouth, and I'm sure that at times I did exactly that. The principle is virtually the same as described in the section on weedless lures when I talked about fishing the plastic frogs. Let them take the lure and hit them when they turn their heads and go away from you. Charlie has told me that sometimes out of ten strikes, he gets all ten fish.

FLIPPING

Going from ultralight to flipping is like switching from a powder puff to sandpaper. This is the greatest contrast in bass fishing. Flipping is a method which was originated and perfected by a couple of Californians who are friends of mine—Dee Thomas and Dave Gliebe. Actually, Thomas started it, and for several years he's used the technique to dominate bass-fishing tournaments in California and on the Western Bass Association circuit. However, he does not fish as many national tournaments as Gliebe does, and Gliebe has been very instrumental in popularizing flipping nationwide.

Gliebe has won five or six major tournaments in the past couple of years. In the past three years he's qualified for three major fish-offs—the BASS Masters Classic, the ABF's Grand Prix and the American Angler's event for qualifiers. He's one of the most consistent tournament anglers in the nation, and he relies on flipping about 70 percent of the time in tourneys. Two years ago Gliebe won three major tournaments in a row, and during those years he's won about as much money bass fishing as anyone has. In fact, he and I are the only two who ever won three major events in a row, and we both consider those feats our greatest professional accomplishments.

The concept of flipping is controversial. Several veterans say flipping has been around a long time and that they used to do it with cane poles. I disagree with them. While flipping is remotely related to using a cane pole in jiggerpoling and tule dipping, there is not the degree of line control in these latter two methods. Flipping offers precise line control for 10-to-25-foot casts. It is a controlled-cast method with usually a 7½-foot rod and always a free-spool bait-casting reel, and it offers three definite advantages. First, it offers a quiet, no-

Flipping takes fairly heavy
tackle, yet it's a surprisingly
delicate art; if done properly,
you get a pinpoint, splashless
presentation that will fool
smart trophy bass.

splash presentation. Second, it features precision accuracy. Third, it
gives you the maximum control of any size fish.

If I were teaching you how to flip, here's what I'd tell you to do:

Strip off slack line with your left hand so that you're holding
approximately 10 feet of line between the reel and the first rod guide.
The 7½-foot rod is swinging another 7 feet of line. This gives you a
total of 22 to nearly 25 feet of line from the spot where you're standing
to the spot where your bait enters the water. Now make a forward
underhand swing and let the weight of the lure pull the slack line
through your left hand. Now your line comes straight through the
guides as your lure gently drops on the target. At the completion of
the cast, the rod position is almost parallel to the water. Put the rod

To start flipping, let out about 15 feet of line—more or less depending on water depth and how long a flip you want to make. With your left hand, take line from between the reel and the first guide and hold it out to the side, leaving about 7 feet of line hanging from the rod tip.

Swing the jig back under the rod, following it slightly by lowering the rod tip, which will allow the jig to swing farther back and will also put the rod in the proper tip-down position for the next move.

As the jig starts forward, begin raising the rod tip and move your rod hand forward to increase the lure speed. At the end of the swing, give the rod tip a gentle flip to send the lure on its way.

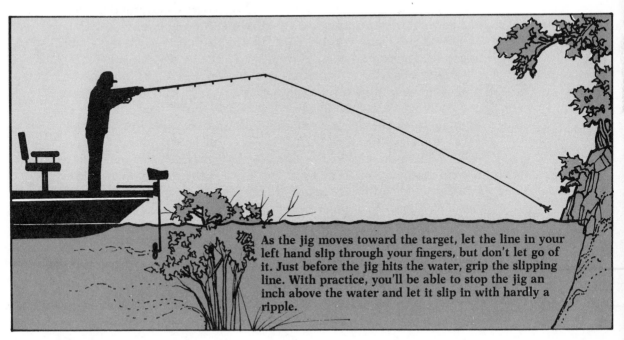

As the jig moves toward the target, let the line in your left hand slip through your fingers, but don't let go of it. Just before the jig hits the water, grip the slipping line. With practice, you'll be able to stop the jig an inch above the water and let it slip in with hardly a ripple.

butt under your right arm, and with the reel handles up, reel slowly with your left hand. When you get a strike and set the hook hard, change hands and fight the bass by reeling with your right hand.

A good flipper can put a jig or a plastic worm in a coffee cup at 22 feet. I've seen Gliebe ten times out of ten not cast a jig into a coffee cup but *lay* that jig in the cup 17 or 18 feet away. He put the jig in that cup so gently and easily that if it were water, there hardly would have been a ripple. If he had been flipping to a small hole in the lily pads and had been off target, the mechanics of flipping would have allowed him to stop the lure in midair and recall his cast and flip again. This recalling the cast is like what a flycaster is able to do when he sees he's off target. The bait-caster or spin-caster does not have this option. If he makes a bad cast and is able to stop the lure short of his target, the splash of the bait still is apt to scare the fish. Very few bait-casters can make 12-to-25-foot casts accurately. Even if they can, there is no way they can drop the lure as quietly and gently as a flipper can.

When you set the hook with a flipping rod, you're setting it with your forearm instead of your wrist. When a bass hits, slam the rod upward with your right hand while the rod butt is beneath your right arm. This gives you arm power instead of wrist power. In addition, you're holding onto the reel handle with your left hand, and this gives you added power. Flipping rods are like saltwater popping rods. They have long butts, and you can stick the rod butt into your stomach for added leverage.

If you've hooked a 7-pounder in a brushpile, all that pressure on him will cause him to come out of there in a hurry. I've flipped 6½-pounders right into the boat. I proved the power and efficiency of flipping to a dock operator, Lee Henry, on Lake Eufaula in Oklahoma. I was preparing for an American Angler tournament there, and Lee said he had a brushpile he wanted to show me. He said there was a bass in there he couldn't handle. He'd fished that place the previous two days and had his 20-pound line broken twice by a fish he never saw. One thing about no-see-'em bass I've noticed is that they generally run from 8 to 15 pounds, whereas the see-'em bass—ones you actually land—are much smaller. But those you never see, such as those 20-pounders in Florida, are much, much bigger!

I told Lee I'd show him how to flip that bass out of there and that I knew I could get him with 25-pound line and my jig with a big worm on it. He took me up this arm of the lake to where a huge tree had fallen in and a bunch of logs had drifted in on top of it. The water was

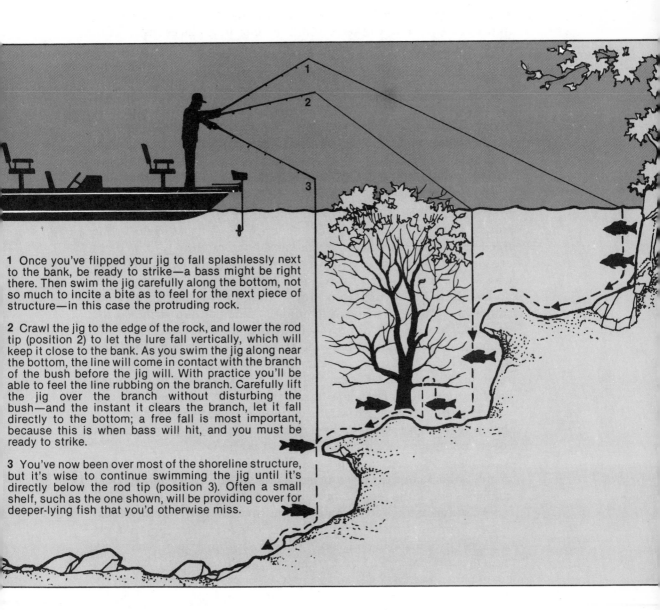

1 Once you've flipped your jig to fall splashlessly next to the bank, be ready to strike—a bass might be right there. Then swim the jig carefully along the bottom, not so much to incite a bite as to feel for the next piece of structure—in this case the protruding rock.

2 Crawl the jig to the edge of the rock, and lower the rod tip (position 2) to let the lure fall vertically, which will keep it close to the bank. As you swim the jig along near the bottom, the line will come in contact with the branch of the bush before the jig will. With practice you'll be able to feel the line rubbing on the branch. Carefully lift the jig over the branch without disturbing the bush—and the instant it clears the branch, let it fall directly to the bottom; a free fall is most important, because this is when bass will hit, and you must be ready to strike.

3 You've now been over most of the shoreline structure, but it's wise to continue swimming the jig until it's directly below the rod tip (position 3). Often a small shelf, such as the one shown, will be providing cover for deeper-lying fish that you'd otherwise miss.

about 5 feet deep, and it was a perfect flipping spot. I dropped the jig in the brushpile and worked around three or four places inside of it. We worked to the other side of it and I still hadn't had a strike in ten different spots around that tree. Finally we were drifting away from the tree when I felt a strike. I hit the fish with everything I had, and this blew him out of there 20 feet away and about 8 feet in the air. He came crashing down in the boat at Lee's feet. The bass was a 6-pounder, and I landed him the way a kid lands a bluegill with a cane pole. On the other side of the fish's mouth were scarred-up holes where he'd evidently been hooked by Lee on those two previous days.

While I don't often jerk 6-pounders through the air, it can be done with a flipping rod, which gives you an immense amount of control over the fish. Why do you need such control? Almost every lake has some type of heavy cover. Usually it's not being fished right in the thickest places. Fishermen throw all around it, but nearly all of them are unable to get their lures way back in it. Probably nobody has ever taken a worm or a jig and thrown in the thick stuff and jigged the lure up and down for any length of time. It also follows that they've not caught those bass in there which didn't come out and strike on the outside. If anyone ever did throw in there and get a strike, he wasn't equipped with a 7 1/2-foot popping rod and 20-to-40-pound line and most likely he got broken off when he hooked a big fish.

In the spring and summer of 1977, I had a 4-pound average on the bass I caught flipping in five different states. When you're jigging, you're getting bigger fish interested and annoyed, and you're also throwing into spots which others don't fish, such as into the heaviest cover, and that's were big ones are most apt to be.

Probably the biggest aspect of flipping, which seldom is talked about, is boat control. For anyone who takes up this method, boat control is one of the most important things to work on. Every flipper has a certain casting range. For example, my arms aren't quite as long as Dee Thomas' arms or Gliebe's arms. Therefore, they can flip good at 22 feet, whereas I can flip good only from 17 to 19 feet. That's my most accurate range, so I need to snake my boat around the trees and boat docks and grass beds and get in perfect position so I can put my lure in precisely where I want it. An accurate flipper can slide his lure into an inch-wide crack between two boards on a boat dock. Of course, when you throw into a spot like this, such as between two big limbs or logs, there's no way you can get the bass out through that

Flipping looks a little like shooting a flyline. You strip off about 10 feet of line between the reel and the first guide. Then you make your underhand swing and let the weight of the lure pull the line out until the lure is right on target.

tiny hole. But with the 25-pound line, you can hold him and then go in there and push the logs aside and dig around and get him out. This is another reason for the big line. A super-quiet trolling motor, such as a Minn Kota, enables you to sneak around quietly when you're getting your boat in position, too. Since you're fishing close to the bass, you need to be extra-quiet to keep from spooking them. You also need either dingy water or floating vegetation, or the bass will see you.

Sometimes I'm asked when I use a jig instead of a worm when I'm flipping. When the water's below 55 degrees, I use a jig or a jig and worm. I usually go to a plastic worm when the water is above 60 degrees. When I use the worm, I always peg the slip weight, because I'm fishing it usually in heavy cover. If you don't peg it, the worm and the weight might separate. When you peg it, you have a solid, one-piece lure which will go through cover.

I think flipping is so effective from January through March because of the jigs. As I pointed out, for some unknown reason the big 5/8-ounce jigs are the best cold-water bass lures I know of. When I had that 4-pound average while flipping in 1977, I had a bigger average from January through March. The bass I caught during those three months on my flipping stick averaged 5 pounds per fish. Later in the spring I switched to plastic worms and caught several 2- and 3-pounders.

Don't ever think you can go out and just flip all day. Seldom will this work, because there aren't that many places for a whole day's fishing. I keep my flipping rod rigged up, but I'll usually be throwing a worm or a crank bait in the more open sections of the lake. When I come up on that fallen tree or boat dock or floatsum, then I flip for a few minutes and then go on and resume casting.

---

58   Busting the Cover and Floatsum

This was a pattern I overlooked until two years ago. Dave Gliebe brought it to my attention when he won the 1977 B.A.S.S. tournament at Toledo Bend. He won it in an area with a lot of milfoil and under-water weeds. A lot of wind that spring had broken weeds loose, and they'd drifted up into piles which I call floatsum. The water was 6 to 8 feet deep below the dead weeds. The day before the tournament I'd found some of these floating islands of dead weeds, and I'd made a few casts around the edges with spinnerbaits, but I didn't catch anything.

What Gliebe did was pull up to that floatsum and lob a ⅝-ounce jig up in the air with his flipping rod. The weight of the jig coming down in that dead grass knocked a hole right through it. Then he'd sit there and jig it twenty-five to thirty times in that one hole. If he didn't get a strike, he'd reel in and jig somewhere else. He'd jig a dozen different places on a 50-foot island of floatsum, and then he'd go on to another island. The first day of the tournament he caught only four or five bass, but they were big ones. He was paired with Don Mann (Tom's brother) the second day, and they really got into 'em. Don had nine which totaled over 45 pounds, and Dave caught ten which totaled 42 pounds. Gliebe ended up winning with 83 pounds, 2 ounces for the three days.

Not long afterward, I was fishing at Lake Tenkiller in Oklahoma. Tenkiller's the clearest lake in the state, and it's known for having very deep bass. Mary Ann was along, and she was practicing for a Bass'n Gal tournament. In a cove near a boat dock was a pile of old sticks and leaves which had drifted together. I thought there would be a fish or two beneath it, so I edged the boat up close and started flipping into little pockets. I was using a ⅝-ounce jig and worm, and when I lifted the jig up and let it fall, it just stopped and quit sinking. I set the hook and caught a 4-pounder, which is a big one for Tenkiller. We started looking for more pockets of floatsum and found five or six more. Every one of them had bass beneath them. These were from 2 to 5 pounds, and we caught several.

Her tournament started the next week, and in the meantime the wind had shifted from the south to the north, and when she went back to fish that floatsum, it wasn't there. Floatsum is transient—it floats back and forth and drifts away in the wind.

In Okeechobee and Rodman Pool in Florida, nobody had figured out much how to catch bass from beneath the hyacinth patches until about two years ago. Since then I and others have discovered we can flip the patches and catch a lot of big bass. In fact, the $10\frac{1}{4}$-pounder I caught at Rodman with my father-in-law is the biggest I've ever caught flipping. They also flip the heavy vegetation a lot at West Lake Tohopekaliga (most of us call it West Lake Toho) in Florida. We use a 16- or 18-foot push pole and stick it in the hyacinths and make a little hole there by pushing the hyacinths away. We'll make four or five holes around the boat. Doing this disturbs a lot of little water shrimp

Dave Gliebe and I fish one floatsum area in the background while Al Lindner does the same in the foreground.

and freshwater crawfish in the hyacinths and creates a chum effect. Bluegills and shiners come in there to feed, and all this tends to excite the bass. Then we drop a big flipping jig or a plastic worm into those holes and jig up and down repeatedly. About one-third of the time they'll hit right away, but more often we have to jig twenty-five times before we feel that little tick as the bait is sinking. You'll see a little twitch in your line, and you have to hit 'em quick or they'll spit out the lure.

This heavy cover can be in the form of dead milfoil as at Toledo Bend, or leaves and sticks as at Tenkiller, or hyacinths as in Florida lakes. At some time or other, most every lake might have this floatsum. When it does, flip it, because that's a way to catch the big ones.

Sometimes you have to blast-cast in floatsum, such as in hyacinths when there aren't any holes and you don't have a push pole along. A blast cast is a straight overhand cast as if you're chopping wood, and you aim at a spot about 10 feet in front of you. You're coming down on the water with a lot of pressure, and this drives the lure through the vegetation. This, naturally, is not a quiet approach, but sometimes it's the only way to get through the floatsum.

59 Dabbling the Trees

This is one of the most interesting patterns I've ever encountered in Oklahoma in the late spring and early summer. Lakes such as Kerr, Hugo, Oolegah, and Eufaula are reservoirs 20,000 to 100,000 acres in size, and a lot of the coves and other areas of these lakes are full of timber. I like to find big, shallow flats adjacent to creek channels and fish in the timber along the channels. The water usually is 5 to 15 feet deep, and I frequently take a flipping rod with 20- or 25-pound line and use either a jig or a plastic worm. I look for the biggest, shadiest tree I can find along the creek channel, and this is usually an old oak or a sycamore with a big trunk. I work around the shady side and swing the lure to the base of the tree. With a good cast the bait hits the water right where it touches the tree, and there's zero splash.

Bass often are suspended in late spring and summer near the tree a few feet under the surface. The water might be 10 feet deep, but they're apt to be only 4 feet down. The lure falls down right next to the tree, and it's such a quiet presentation that bass lying there watch it tumble down. If you know the water is 10 feet deep, and the lure suddenly stops 4 feet down, *set the hook!* It most likely is a bass which stopped the bait, though it could be a limb. Regardless what stopped it, I set the hook. This will cause you to lose a few jigs and worms, but it also will catch a lot of bass.

Another kind of tree you'll find in most every lake in the country— natural lake or impoundment—is a tree which has fallen into the water. Most fishermen work topwater plugs all around it early or late, and they also throw spinnerbaits, crank baits, and worms around it, but hardly anybody sneaks up to the shady side and jigs the thickest

For dabbling the trees I like to find big, shallow flats adjacent to creek channels. Flip the lure right next to the tree, let it tumble—and if it stops, set the hook.

part of that tree. I like to flip those thickest parts when the water is dingy. Flipping doesn't work well when the water's real clear. Sometimes I'll jig one spot twenty-five or thirty times. This pays off.

60   Flipping the Docks

This is another pattern completely overlooked in many places. Many of the big natural lakes and impoundments are literally lined with boat docks. Many of the private dock owners put out brushpiles around their docks to attract crappies, and several of them have lights out on their docks to attract minnows so they can catch white bass and crappies. Some of the docks are big storage docks which offer lots of shade for bass. Many of these docks get fished, but the hard-to-get places up beneath the docks are almost totally unfished.

One advantage of flipping is that you can get to those otherwise almost inaccessible areas of the docks. You can sneak up to a dock and flip back into those dark, shady recesses and jig around where there's probably never been a lure since the dock was built. Again, I like to approach the dock from the shady side and consider the wind direction. If it's a large dock, it likely extends out over deeper water, and the bass are going to be facing the wind.

Look for such things as steps leading into the water for the benefit of swimmers. This offers a bit more underwater structure. A twig sticking out of the water often indicates that someone has put a brushpile there. If you find a dock rigged with a light, you can figure that the dock owner is a fisherman who probably has put out brush. His light probably has been on at night, and this usually attracts baitfish, which, in turn, probably have attracted several bass. Even though it's daytime and the light's not on, that dock probably will pay off better than those without lights.

Watts Bar Lake in Tennessee is typical of the older lakes where much of the cover has rotted away, and in recent years the dock pat-

Bridge and dock pilings make a pattern perfect for pinpoint flipping. Here Dee Thomas and I flip it to them.

tern has been one of the best patterns on the lake during the late-spring and summer months. This is typical of many of the older lakes I'm familiar with, particularly on the TVA chain. Grand Lake in Oklahoma has hundreds of docks and lots of brushpiles around them. Lake Sidney Lanier, near Atlanta, is a clear lake, but in the upper section in the spring when there's a little dingy water, the dock pattern is dynamite for both spotted bass and largemouths.

Lots of times the bottom of the dock is a couple of feet above the water, and when I'm flipping, I swing the lure several feet underneath the dock. If you were able to cast under there, you'd have to skip your lure, and this would be a noisy presentation which might scare the fish. When you're flipping, you can let go the slack line just as the lure clears the boards, and it will end up way back in the dark shade. This quiet presentation really pays off under there.

You don't need 20-to-30-pound line when you flip if you're fishing fairly open water. You can drop down to lighter sizes. The heavy line is needed only in heavy cover. I've even dropped down to 10-pound line in clear water.

SCHOOLING

61   Start on Top

Where I grew up in Maryland, there aren't any shad to speak of. I'd read Grits Gresham's bass book and articles about fishing in the south where they talked about schooling bass. I'd fished a lot of reservoirs in Maryland, and I just didn't understand what they were talking about because I'd never seen a school of bass breaking on the surface the way those writers talked about.

My first experience with schooling bass was when I went to Santee-Cooper for the first time in 1963. At that time Santee was more famous for its landlocked striped bass than for largemouths. I'd caught schooling stripers in Chesapeake Bay, and when I got out on Santee for the first time and saw fish breaking, I thought immediately they were stripers. I had some big Atom plugs which I'd used for stripers in Chesapeake Bay, and I tied one on and went to the schooling bass. I threw these big plugs and finally caught one fish—a black bass about 12 inches long. That caused me to think maybe these breaking fish *were* bass, something I'd never seen. Then I started throwing smaller lures, and I caught some largemouths from the schools.

In the seven years which followed, schooling bass were not an everyday occurrence at Santee, but they schooled often enough that when I was guiding, if I had a party and they wanted to catch a limit, we fished for schoolers. Since most of them were under 4 pounds and I was a trophy-bass hunter, I never messed much with the schoolers.

I've heard from reliable sources that in some of the mountain lakes, such as Fontana in North Carolina, giant bass sometimes get into the schools. I've heard that this same thing happens on the St. Johns River in Florida. Glenn Crawford, a tournament fisherman who runs Sportsman's Paradise fishing camp on the St. Johns at Welaka, tells Mary Ann and me to keep watch for any small fish breaking when

Here's Forrest Wood casting to some breaking fish with the sun low in the sky. Early and late in the day are the logical times to expect topwater activity—schooling bass breaking on the surface.

we're running up and down the river, because sometimes if you throw a swimming plug to where you saw fish breaking, you'll come up with a 5-to-10-pound bass.

Only once did I ever see this happen on the St. Johns, and that was back in February of 1973 when we were fishing with the outdoor writer Charlie Waterman, who is from Florida. Charlie had his camera out, and all of a sudden right behind us he called our attention to five or six small to medium-sized bass breaking on top within a cast of us. I threw out a Little George and let it sink to the bottom in about 15 feet of water. I cranked it one time, and a 6-to-7-pounder nailed it. I got him up to the top, but he got off. Mary Ann threw out a Little George and caught one about 5 pounds, and on my next cast I got one about 6 pounds. The fish that were breaking on top were smaller.

I've never caught many big fish from schools, but I do enjoy catching schooling bass. Toledo Bend, Sam Rayburn, and Ross Barnett are three of the best lakes for schooling bass I've ever fished. I've caught a lot of schoolers at Ross Barnett, and one time I counted ten different schools of bass surfacing at the same time.

Bobby Murray beat me by catching schooling bass on Lake Ouachita, which used to be his home lake, in May of 1972 at the Arkansas National B.A.S.S. tournament. He caught several bass on grubs, but he caught his three or four biggest fish on Bagley's large-sized 007 surface plug. When he saw a school of bass break, he ran to them and put that giant 007 on 'em. Jim Bagley discontinued that plug a few years ago, but it's a heckuva plug for schooling bass. I finished second in that tournament. I didn't bother to mess with the schooling fish because I was catching bass on plastic worms in the submerged timber. Lots of times Bobby caught only one fish out of a school, but it might be a 3- or 4-pounder. The little ones didn't hit that big lure.

62   Follow Them Down, and Get Out in Front

When you're on a shad lake in the summer, you need three different lures rigged up before you ever start across the water, because you might see a school of bass. You need a good Injured Minnow type of surface plug on one rod (other good ones include the Devils Horse, Diamond Rattler, Wounded Spook, and Tiny Torpedo). On another rod, you need an intermediate-depth lure—a running lure such as a Spot, a Swimming Minnow, or a Countdown Rapala. A crank bait will work, but I lean toward the swimming lures. Then when the school goes real deep to the thermocline level—their cruising range, which might be 25 feet deep—then you need the deep-jigging lures, such as spoons, Little Georges, weighted plastic worms, and jigs. You should have three different rods rigged up with these three types of lures.

To follow them down, I'm keeping an eye out for any surface activity while running down the lake. Anytime I see a breaking fish, I head wide open right to that spot. At Santee, a lot of my guiding was for striped bass, and I learned a technique for stopping right on the school. When you get within 50 to 75 yards from the school, you have to develop the instinct for shutting off the motor at the right time. You don't put the motor in neutral; you're running wide open, and you turn the key off. The boat then skis in toward the school, and when I'm about a cast away from the fish I cut the steering wheel to the left or right, depending on which way the wind is blowing. Since I had the boat pointed directly toward the school, this area will not receive a bit of the wake. It will go out to the sides. Turning the wheel broadsides the boat. My first cast is with a propeller-type surface plug. I have all three rods laid out and ready for schooling fish. The plugs are not tangled. If that first cast doesn't produce, I immediately grab the rod with the swimming lure and throw it and count it down.

Keep in mind that this school is cruising at 20 to 25 feet; they come up to chase shad on the surface and then go back down to their running depth. They don't spend much time in between. When they do come up, this is when they're active and really feeding and will hit. If you can get a lure to them when they're on the top or on their way up or back down, you'll get strikes. They're apt to turn off when they get back down to their cruising range, and you might see them on your locator but still have a hard time catching them. Yet even though they might not be actively feeding, some of them can be caught.

It's important to fish in the direction the fish are moving. Bass, and stripers too, follow a leader much as do ducks and geese in the air. When I tell you to get out in front of the school, it's because this way you'll likely catch the bigger fish. I've observed schools of striped bass and big largemouths in shallow water, and I've noticed the bigger fish leading the pack. I've watched this at Salt Springs and Silver Springs

I knew this one was down there because I'd figured out where he was headed; he was part of a school chasing shad that had broken water a few minutes before, and I got up ahead of him.

in Florida. And one day in one of the clear blackwater ponds at Santee, I was standing on a stump at the edge of a small ditch looking down into 6 or 7 feet of water, and along came about ten largemouths from 3 to 10 pounds. The two biggest fish were leading the pack. I didn't make a good enough cast when I threw into the school and ended up catching about a 4-pounder, one of the smaller ones, on a small spoon. Then the school swam out of sight, and the water was too deep to wade after 'em.

By applying this reasoning when the school has gone down, you can fish for and catch the bigger ones. Schools usually are moving in one direction. When they break once, they sort of leapfrog before they break again, and they keep doing this. You can plot their movements somewhat because they almost always are traveling in one direction—and that direction is the direction the shad are moving. If the baitfish are moving south, you can bet the school of bass will be traveling that way, too. Bass quite often follow a structure, such as the edge of a river channel or a timberline, as they move along

The worst thing you could do is stay behind the school. If you're throwing to the tail end of the school, you're going to be catching mostly smaller fish, and also your lure will be running the wrong way. If they're headed north and you throw north, you'll be retrieving your lure south. This is not matching the hatch. You need to be running your bait the same direction the shad and the bass are traveling, and your bait needs to be the same size and color as the baitfish. This is a prerequisite for catching schooling bass.

Normally I don't think of using live bait in schooling bass, but in certain situations I'm told it really pays off. One of Larry Mayer's favorite lakes for schooling bass is Fontana in North Carolina. This TVA impoundment lies adjacent to the great Smoky Mountains National Park. Larry says locals up there in the fall and winter throw a plain treble hook through a school of shad and snag one or two baitfish. Then they either leave the shad on the hook as they snagged it or they reel in and reposition the bait. They throw the shad directly into the school and often catch smallmouths on the live bait. He says this works when the bass are traveling under the baitfish, and at times it seems to outproduce lures five to one.

FLOWING WATERS

63 Smallmouths in the Rapids

From the time I was sixteen years old until I was twenty-three, I fished the Potomac, Susquehanna, and Shenandoah Rivers during the dog days of hot summer when the bass in our lakes and reservoirs in Maryland pretty well turned off. My favorite was the Potomac, and I fished it all the way from Paw Paw, W.Va., to Little Falls near Washington, D.C. What my companions and I found was that the hotter the weather, the more the smallmouths sought whitewater areas. The rapids put more oxygen into the water and so those areas were more

When smallmouths are really feeding, you'll find them facing the current at the heads of deep pools.

comfortable to the fish. The big smallmouths—those in the 4-pound range—were fairly rare, but we caught several in those rivers.

We waded wet with felt-soled sneakers. The Potomac is deep, and a pair of waders would do nothing more than fill up with water, and the water temperatures were 70 to over 80 degrees anyhow. About every five to fifteen miles the Potomac has a major set of rapids which extend up to a mile in length. We looked for boulders and calm places in the rapids. Most of the rapids are shallow, and we could stay almost knee-deep in a lot of them, but some of the holes are almost over your head. The devastating way to catch smallmouths in that

A string taken on floating plugs in the rapids. The lure must drift downstream to the fish; like trout, bass know how their diet should behave in the current.

river is to use live crawfish and live hellgrammites, and that's what we did if we were out for numbers of fish. With spinning tackle and a BB shot ahead of the live bait on a small hook, there's no more effective way to catch 'em.

When smallmouths are really feeding, they work at the heads of the deep pools, and they're always facing the current and are ready to pounce on anything that comes bopping by. While the live bait was more effective, the real challenge came with lures. We started off with spinners, and back when we were short on money, we'd take clams and open them up and slice strips resembling pork rind. (That way, we didn't have to buy pork rind.) We put those clam strips on Shysters

Fishing the rapids is a lot of fun—and safe enough, if you're careful. It's easy to lose your footing in that current.

and ABU Spinners, and that was our El Cheapo way of catching smallmouths. Then we gradually progressed to the epitome of man against fish—wet-wading up to our necks and throwing topwater plugs. This is a real challenge.

Smallmouths, like trout, are very conscious of the way a lure drifts. The plug should be coming downstream at all times. I don't even like to throw crosscurrent unless I absolutely have to. I prefer to start wading at the bottom of the rapids and keep working upstream at all times. I do make side casts when I find a wide pool with not a lot of moving water.

I learned one thing about feeding smallmouths from a veteran river fisherman, Orville Price from Washington, D.C. When I was working at the Atlas Sports Store in D.C., Orville used to come in there many weekends with 4-pound smallmouths. He was the champion smallmouth fisherman on the Potomac, and I kept asking him questions. Finally he invited me to fish with him, and what amazed me about him was he didn't cover much water. I'd be charging up through the rapids and casting at every rock, and at the end of the day he commented that he bet I scared ten times more bass than I caught. I'd catch as many or more than he would, but he'd have a couple of 4-pounders while my biggest was 2 1/2 pounds. He said the trick to catching big smallmouths was to be very conscious of any rocks you stepped on which moved. He maintained you should try to find a firm, flat rock which doesn't move when you step on it. You should try to step on firm pebbles softly so you don't scare any fish. I'd be tromping along and would stumble and fall and get my butt wet, but Orville waded slowly and quietly, and he never fell down. He mainly used small Dalton Specials and Tiny Torpedos. He knew the river real well, and he'd concentrate on a good hole. He'd throw up behind a boulder and let the plug float down 4 or 5 feet and make a slight twitch. Then the plug would float another 4 or 5 feet before he twitched it a second time. He also made repeated casts to the same boulder, and maybe on the fifth, eighth, or tenth cast, he'd catch the fish.

With all this in mind, I went to the Potomac one year on Labor Day with Joe Whitesell, a building contractor from College Park, Md., and we got into a good number of 3-to-4-pound smallmouths. We caught ten in that range that day. We fished the Harper's Ferry area where the Shenandoah runs into the Potomac. We started wading downstream from the old railroad depot and headed upstream to Mad Dog Rapids. We'd cast from ten to twenty times with Tiny Torpedos at the heads of the big holes, and sometimes after many casts those bigger fish would strike.

I've used these techniques in the Buffalo River in Arkansas and a few other places, and they've paid off. This same quiet approach works where you find the whitewater and work the calm holes near the rapids. Topwater baits are not the best way to catch 'em, but it's the most-fun way. One thing about the Potomac is there are several stretches of rapids which are impossible to wade. They're dangerous, and you shouldn't even consider trying to fish these places.

64   Tidewater Duck Blinds

At the 1975 BASS Masters Classic at Currituck Sound, Jack Hains overtook Paul Chamblee's lead in the final round to win, and Hains caught all four of his bass that day around duck blinds.

From 1956 to 1963 I regularly fished the tide rivers on the Eastern Shore of Maryland. Except for a few scattered patches of grass or milfoil, there was almost no other cover in these big, open flats. But since the Eastern Shore has a lot of ducks, there are a lot of duck blinds, and these blinds offer shade and cover for the bass. We could see duck blinds from long distances, and we'd run a couple of miles across a bay just to get to another duck blind. We fished from blind to blind, and this pattern paid off all year long.

Generally where a duck hunter builds a blind is on a point, and nearly every major point in those bays and flats had duck blinds. What got me started off right on the duck-blind pattern was reading the late fishing writer Joe Brooks' stories about how to fish blinds. His biggest bass ever weighed over 11 pounds and was caught on a flyrod

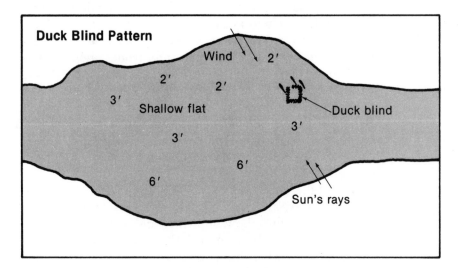

On large shallow flats, a duck blind can be prime bass cover. The fish will be facing the current—which in such a flat is generally produced more by the wind than by tidal flow—and in the shadow of the blind.

and popping bug around a duck blind, and he wrote about how you needed to sneak up on the blind and fish the shady side.

Two important factors exist in duck-blind fishing. The first is the direction the water is moving, and the second is the position of the sun. These factors position the bass. In tidewater, either the tide current or the wind current moves the water. In a lot of the shallow bays there is hardly any tide movement, but the wind influence is considerable. It pushes the water along and constantly is creating current. Tidewater largemouths are like stream smallmouths in that they're facing the current, and in the shade of the duck blinds. Here again you need to conjure up that old image of where they'll be. If there are three or four of 'em around one duck blind, they'll play leapfrog to try to keep ahead of each other, and they'll be in the shade on the upcurrent side of the blind. You need to figure out which is the upcurrent side.

One of the best of a variety of lures you can use is a plastic worm, because you can throw it past the duck blind and let the current swing your line beneath it, and you can get the worm under the blind. Joe Brooks would throw a popping bug in there and let the bug drift beneath the blind. When you do this and twitch it initially when the bug's back beneath the blind, you've got a bass if one's there. Popping bugs and topwater lures—anything you can drift beneath the blind— work real well.

---

65 Slack Water in Winter, Swift Water in Summer

Bass seek current when their metabolisms are high, and they get away from current when their metabolisms are low. One year I heard some strong reports about big bass being caught in the dead of winter from Broad Creek in Delaware. I'd been fishing swift-moving tidewater rivers up until the first ice, but after it got icy, we didn't catch much in these shallower rivers. But I'd heard that guys were breaking ice to fish Broad Creek, and Chuck Regnier from Baltimore and I went up there. We too had to break ice. Broad Creek was deep and had very little tide flow.

We put bullhead minnows on the back of small black jigs and fished the deepest holes, including one which was about 10 feet deep. We'd throw to the deepest parts and let the bait sink to the bottom,

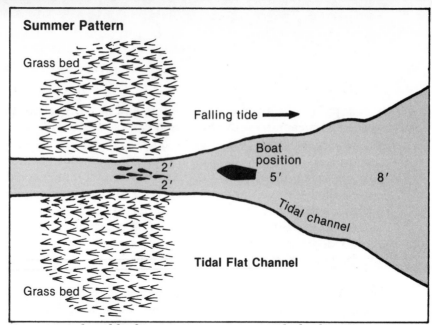

Summer Pattern

Grass bed

Falling tide →

Boat position

Tidal channel

Tidal Flat Channel

Grass bed

In summer, bass like fast-moving water, so an ideal tidewater spot is in a tidal channel through a weedbed. The channel provides structure for the fish, and in addition, if the adjacent weedbed flats are only a foot or so deep in falling water, the fish will concentrate in the slightly deeper water.

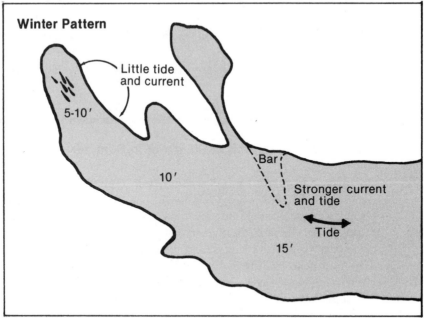

Winter Pattern

Little tide and current

5-10′

10′

Bar

Stronger current and tide

Tide

15′

In winter, bass avoid the current, so you'll find them holed up in the upper ends of tidal streams and creeks, far from any structure such as a sandbar that speeds up the flow. Winter bass are very logy and you have to work to make them notice your lure.

and slowly hop it along. Sure enough, we caught 3-to-5-pound large-mouths, and I'm convinced it was the coldest water I've ever caught bass out of. We broke ice all day, and our strikes were light. Sometimes all we'd feel was the bass swimming away slowly with the jig and minnow. But the fish didn't drop it. This was between Christmas and New Year's, and it was the most amazing cold-water bass fishing I've ever done.

The opposite of this tidewater fishing is in the summer when you have to look for structure, and this is mainly in high-current areas. It doesn't have to be a point or a dropoff, but usually it is, and here's why. An oyster bar or a bend or point often sticks out in a long deep stretch of tide river, and such a constriction increases the velocity of the water. In the hot weather, bass will lie there in that current and face upstream, and you'll catch them around oyster bars and submerged logs and points. Water current really holds fish in the summer, but it certainly doesn't in the winter. Once the water tempera-

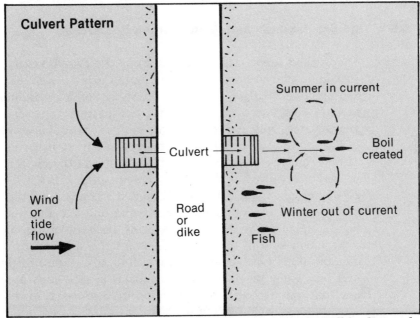

The same winter-summer difference holds true around small bridges and culverts that create a boil or eddy as the water moves through. In summer the bass will be in and around the boil, but as the temperature drops through the 50s and down into the 30s, they'll head for quiet water.

ture gets below 50 degrees, you'd better look for slack water and deep holes in the tide rivers.

Below Santee-Cooper's lower lake lies the Cooper River, and it, too, is affected by tides. The main pattern there for summer fishing is the rice breaks. Years ago during the plantation era, they diked up the entire floodplain, so that now the edges are all abandoned rice fields. Water flows in and out of these old fields on the tides. When the water is flowing in on a high tide, the only thing you can do is follow the water in and get on the inside of the rice fields and fish the current against the dike. But the best condition comes on the extreme low tides, and when the water really pours out of the fields, you can bust 'em. It's a matter of being there at the right time. Throw upcurrent and let your worm or jig work downcurrent. There are a lot of old cypress pilings on the bottom, and the real experts, like the late Howard Cotton, knew where all this stuff was. Every rice break is different because of what's on the bottom.

66   Tide Creek Bends and Feeder Creek Bonanzas

I've fished super tide creeks all along the East Coast from New Jersey and Delaware down through South Carolina, and what lots of fishermen don't realize is that this coast has some 5 million acres of tidewater bass and seemingly only 200 fishermen for every million acres of water. Our reservoir systems in this country have only about twice as many acres of water, but many times more fishermen.

This is one reason tidewater bass aren't hard to catch; they simply don't get heavy pressure. Whether you're in a tide creek in Georgia or New Jersey, that creek has bends, and the bends have the deepest water. I'm not only looking for deep water on the bends but also for irregular features, such as a tree, shelf, rock, or oyster mound. If there's much flow in the creek, I look for the spot where the slack water meets the swift water. If I can find any stretch in that bend where the water reverses itself and forms a back eddy against the bank, that spot probably is the best for finding bass. It may be only a 10-to-30-foot stretch, but it's slack water and always deep, and it's a perfect ambush point for the fish.

Tide-creek bass have a tremendous fondness for surface lures. I think they hit on the surface better than reservoir bass do. I don't know why unless it's because they're so accustomed to being in shallow water that they frequently feed at or near the top. Take Currituck Sound, for example. Of all the waters in the world, Currituck simply has to be the greatest place for a flyrod and popping bug and also for the propeller-type baits such as the Devils Horse. When I'm fishing tide creeks, I always have a Devils Horse tied on one rod, and I usually have a flyrod and bug rigged up, especially for the early-morning hours and cloudy days. In the summer I don't think you ever could go wrong by throwing a plastic worm into a back eddy right next to the bank. Hit the bank and slither the worm down into the eddy.

I can't stress enough how many acres of good bass water there are in the tide creeks compared to the small percentage of bass fishermen you'll find there. There aren't as many bass per acre in tidewaters, because some of them are too salty and some are polluted. One river might not have any bass, while the next one to it has a real good largemouth population. Pollution from some industries is being cleaned up, but some still remains. Those which are polluted could be cleaned up and good bass fishing restored when the ecology gets back in order.

One difficulty about tidewater creeks is that several of 'em are primitive and access is difficult. There are hardly any boat docking and launching facilities. In the Albemarle and Currituck Sound areas of North Carolina, you might have to run twenty miles to get back up a good tide creek. The water in some of the bays might be too salty, and you need a big boat to reach these primitive areas. I've run nearly a hundred miles in a day on Albemarle Sound and not seen another bass fisherman, and this was in the summer when you'd expect to see several of 'em.

Duck blinds, fallen trees, and boat docks are obvious patterns, but aside from those, if you're unfamiliar with tidewater bassing, another easy, obvious pattern which is very reliable is small feeder creeks on a falling tide. You couldn't get your boat in them on a rising tide because they're only a foot or so wide. I generally catch twenty times as many bass on a falling tide than on a rising tide. The bass move with the water, and when the tide's falling, they're accessible. They move out of these tiny feeder creeks. The water might be only a foot or so deep, but anchor out from the mouth and throw a topwater plug early or late in the day or a plastic worm in the daytime. If it's cold

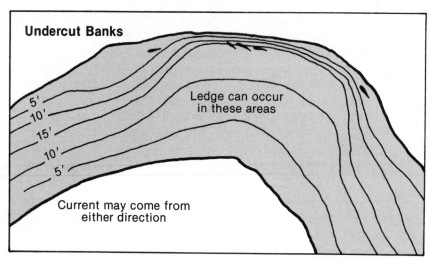

In a tidal creek, the deepest water and the steepest banks are on the outside of the sharpest and narrowest bends. At the beginning and end of a bend there may be underwater ledges, often lined with trees, brush, or exposed roots—good cover. Back eddies are also especially good.

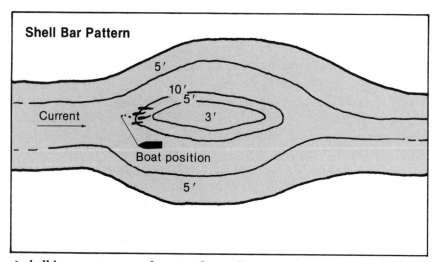

A shell bar, oyster mound, or similar underwater obstruction is excellent structure. In summer the bass will hang on the upcurrent edge, quickly moving to the other end when the tide changes. Often early and late in the day schools will break the surface, chasing baitfish; this is a great time for topwater chugging-type plugs, which you can let the current deliver to the watchful bass.

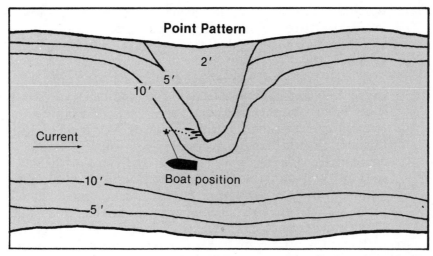

Points are easy to locate and, like shell bars, are bass feeding stations; you fish them the same way. When there are no schools breaking the surface, a No. 13 Rapala may work in depths of 2 to 5 feet, though my standard lure is a black plastic worm, 6 or 7¼ inches, with a 3/16-ounce weight.

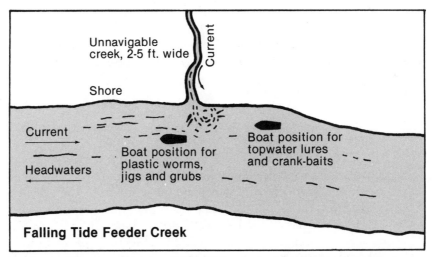

Feeder creeks are great on a falling tide—even in cold weather, because the flow from the creek may be several degrees warmer than the surrounding water, especially on a sunny day. I find a jig best in cold weather, but in summer you can cast topwater lures and crank baits early and late in the day, and drift plastic worms and grubs into the eddy any time of day. Of course, when the flow reverses, the bass depart.

weather and the water's below 55 degrees, I go to a jig. I've noticed in the Cooper River and other tidewater areas that bass really go for jigs, and they're excellent cold-water lures at the entrances to these tiny feeder creeks.

Some of Maryland's finest tide creeks flow into Fishin Bay, such as the Chicamicomico, Transquaking, and the Blackwater River. Other super tide rivers of the Eastern Shore are the Pocomoke, the upper Nanticoke, the upper Choptank, Sassafras, Still Pond Creek, and the legendary North East River. In a ten-year period starting in 1956 I fished better than 200 days on the Eastern Shore with fishing buddies such as Floyd Parks, Norman Lowery, Tom McNey, Joe Ferrell, Joe Whitesell, Pat McEvoy, Dave Emge, Chuck Regnier, Lyn Torbett, Lewis Sullivan, my brother Bobby, and a bunch of others. In fact, in 1960 I fished twenty-six consecutive weekends on the Chicamicomico with Lyn Torbett. On our last trip that year the day before Christmas we had to break ice all day. I used a No. 3 Mepps Spinner with a strip of pork rind and caught thirty bass up to 5 pounds, and many of them were over 4. Lyn caught the biggest—a 6-pounder—on a River Runt. We fished the deepest, calmest stretches we could find, particularly the deep creek bends, and we used super-slow retrieves.

HOT-WATER DISCHARGE

67   Dead-of-Winter Delight

At the outskirts of Asheville, N.C., is a suburb called Skyland which is on the shore of Lake Julian. This lake is owned by the Carolina Power and Light Company and features a hot-water discharge. Locals call the place where the hot water pours back into the lake "the hot hole," and even on the coldest days of winter they line the banks and throw various and sundry lures and catch several 4-to-8-pound largemouth bass. I've heard all about Lake Julian, but I've never fished it. I do know Julian is typical of several places in the country where there's a hot-water discharge. One way it's typical is that most of the best fishing occurs from December through February when the weather's at its coldest.

In Maryland, there's a big power plant on the Potomac River, and hot water is released in the river near White's Ferry. They have buoys

It was a cold day, as evidenced by my clothing, but hot-water discharge kept this bass active enough to jump my Fat Rap.

out where the hot water pours in, and for a quarter-to-half-mile strip, the water is much warmer than the rest of the river. I've fished this strip, and during cold weather you can catch a lot of smallmouths, largemouths, channel catfish, and just about any kind of fish in the river. We used to anchor right by the buoys and fish little jigs to catch the bass. Throughout most of the winter, there simply were hardly any other places worth fishing.

The fish are active around a hot-water discharge, obviously, because the water's from 60 to 70 degrees. These discharges from Massachusetts to Florida also attract saltwater species such as striped bass and redfish, and I've heard of places where tarpon are attracted, too. The discharges attract the fish only when the surrounding waters in the lake or river are much colder; in hot weather when the remainder of the water is warm, it's too hot for fish to hang around a hot-water discharge.

Several years ago Ray Scott and Harold Sharp of B.A.S.S., John Powell, and I fished with Bodie McDowell, a Greensboro, N.C., outdoor writer, on Lake Hyco in North Carolina. Hyco is a recirculation lake which is a tributary of Kerr Reservoir. We went up there in the winter, and when we got over near the power plant, we noticed there were not only more weeds, but they were thicker and greener and they grew up close to the surface. This was near the discharge where the water was much warmer; when we got farther away from the discharge, there were fewer weeds and we got fewer strikes. The bass hit the best closest to the warm water.

For hot-water-discharge bassing, I recommend the same lures you use on deep structure in the summer. Jigging spoons are excellent and my top choice. My second choice would be the jigs, but tailspin lures such as the Little George also are good choices. If the water's real warm, a plastic worm also works good.

NIGHT FISHING

68 Jitterbugging

There is a fraternity of fishermen who fish the Musky Jitterbug at night, and Larry Mayer and I and my old college buddy Pat McEvoy, who now lives in Atlanta, all are members. We fish it mainly in the summer in the southern states, and we pick mostly the clear natural lakes in north-central Florida. Some of our favorite night Jitterbugging lakes used to be Watermelon Pond, Lake Jackson, and Lake Miccosukee. Watermelon Pond used to have more than 7,000 acres of water, but now it's probably not more than 2,000 to 3,000 acres.

I'll never forget the night I was fishing Miccosukee with Benny Meadows of Montgomery, Ala., who is a factory representative with Lowrance Electronics. This lake is about twenty-five miles north of Tallahassee, and it's filled with lily pads, dollar weed, and sawgrass. We'd secure the side treble hooks with rubber bands above the back of the Musky Jitterbug, and we'd turn the back treble hook around so that only one hook hung down, and then we'd cut that one off. This was done to get the Jitterbug across all that vegetation without hang-

A Musky Jitterbug, modified for night fishing in messy water—middle trebles secured to the plug with a rubber band and one hook clipped off the rear treble.

ing up much; we could bring the bait right through lily pads on 40-pound line. When we did get hung up, the heavy line enabled us to snatch the plugs loose. I was using a muskie rod. The technique I've always used is to make a long cast and then start retrieving it. When you have the big lip tuned right from bending it in more of a cup shape, you can hear the rhythmic *plop . . . plop . . . plop . . . plop* as the plug wobbles across the surface.

Well, we'd caught a couple of bass when we first got started that night, but by one a.m. we hadn't had a strike in about two hours. Benny had fallen asleep in the back of my boat. He was all stretched out with his head back against the seat. I remember we'd been talking about alligators shortly before he fell asleep. I was up in the front running the trolling motor, and I was half asleep myself, mesmerized by that *plop . . . plop . . . plop* sound. The lake was very still and calm. I reeled my plug up to the rod tip, and the metal bill went *clunk* when it hit the tip. The plug and the rod tip were on the surface, and before I could lift it, a 9½-pound bass exploded on the bait. Instantly I just pulled back real hard. The fish was about half in the middle of a jump, and I lifted him right into the boat. The bass came unhooked and landed right in Banny's lap.

I don't know if you've ever been awakened at night by a 9½-pound largemouth thrashing around in your lap, but Benny must have been dreaming about alligators, because he starts screaming, *"Gator's got me! Gator! Gator!"* He was convinced a giant alligator was attacking him, and he'd managed to get one leg over the side of the boat and was ready to bail out. It was so dark I actually couldn't see what it was. I finally managed to get a flashlight on, and there was Benny hanging onto the motor and that big bass flopping around on the deck.

Night Jitterbugging requires clear water, just as regular night fishing does, and it also takes a warm night, because this is topwater fishing. It just doesn't work in the winter. The ideal water temperature is about 75 degrees. A fair amount of vegetation nearby also seems to improve the conditions. Shallow-water fish in natural lakes usually favor cover. The greatest thrills in Musky Jitterbug fishing come from the sound of the plug, the anticipation, and the explosive sound of the strike. When big bass hit at the side of the boat, they almost scare you to death.

One of the most important aspects of this fishing is having your timing correct when you get a strike. When you hear the strike and

When this one struck right next to the boat, I thought maybe it was an alligator. Night jitterbugging can be scary.

jerk hard, you're apt to miss the fish and jerk this 1¹⁄₄-ounce bait through the darkness and really injure yourself or companion. Imagine this monster plug with giant treble hooks sailing at a person's face at thirty miles an hour. Lane Eaton, a Tallahassee banker who is a good friend of mine, won't fish the Musky Jitterbug at night with anyone other than an experienced Jitterbugger because of the danger involved.

The secret is to wait until you feel the fish. Lots of times they'll bump at it or even hit it hard four or five times before they finally get it, and this is true even for big bass. There are two schools of thought on what to do when a bass hits at it and doesn't get it. Some say stop the bait for a couple seconds and then start it off again, whereas others just keep on retrieving steadily as if they hadn't had a strike. Larry Mayer is an avid Jitterbug fisherman, and he just keeps on retrieving after the strike. His biggest bass on the plug—a 9-pounder—hit a second time on a steady retrieve 10 feet away from where the fish had initially struck.

It takes more than merely a casual fisherman to go Musky Jitterbugging at night. If you're afraid of snakes and alligators, this isn't for you. Alligators definitely will hit the Jitterbug. I've hooked them on it and have had 'em up to the boat before they shook off.

Much in demand by Musky Jitterbug fans are the wooden baits which were manufactured until five or six years ago. They're much stronger than the plastic models made today. Dick Kotis, president of the Arbogast Company, which manufactures this bait, says the old ones were made out of aromatic cedar, and the wood not only got very expensive but also became hard to get. I have seven or eight wooden Musky Jitterbugs, and Larry Mayer has about that many. Every time we pull up to a boat dock and Larry beats me into the tackle shop, I tell him half the wooden Jitterbugs he finds are mine.

69 Thumping the Blade

Years ago bass fishing probably was better than it is now, and I got started early enough to get in on some of the better sport. In 1971 the L-67 Canal which drains part of the Florida Everglades was very hot. I was fishing out of the Sawgrass Recreational Camp. The water level was very low that year; southern Florida had a water shortage, and

At night you can't half see where you're throwing, but even in heavy cover a spinnerbait can get something like this in your net.

they'd drawn the water down about 2 feet throughout the Everglades. The fishing got so good that the Florida Game and Fish Commission removed the limits in some of those canals because there were so many fish packed in 'em.

I fished that canal with a spinnerbait—thumping the blade—and caught a 70-pound stringer on a pitch-black night. I had put in at the Andytown ramp and had run down along the dike to where I saw a drainage cut about 12 feet wide. There were a lot of weeds, and the first two lures I threw in got hung up. Then I realized I needed a weedless bait, and I dug into my tackle box and got a black single-bladed Zorro spinnerbait. I'd seen the area during the day and had noticed patches of hydrilla along the edge. When I cleared the hydrilla I let the bait sink, and this allowed the blade to thump its way down. On my first cast when I paused the bait, one smacked it hard, and he was about 7 pounds.

About every hundred yards down that canal was a drainage cut from the Everglades. There were miles and miles of canals with these drains, and in the low water, the fish had come down the drains into the main canal. Not all of the ones I fished paid off, but most of the deeper ones really were good. In the dark I made several bad casts into the bullrushes, but I got strikes when I cleared the hydrilla and let the bait fall. I kept the ten biggest, ranging to about 9¾ pounds, and I released a bunch more.

Back in the section on spinnerbaits I talked about bumping the stumps and also a bit about thumping the blade at night. A super time to use a spinnerbait at night is when you're fishing around heavy cover and can't really see where you're throwing. You have to throw a

With practice, you learn to feel the spinnerbait blade's hesitation when you bump a tiny limb or even come near a stump.

fairly snagless lure to keep from hanging up a lot, and a spinnerbait is one of the most weedless, snagless lures available. When you're around any shallow vegetation or heavy brush, I don't think you can beat thumping the blade with a single-spin. Again, I prefer the single blade on a ball-bearing swivel because of the pulsation from the revolving blade. Every time you even get near a bush or bump a tiny limb, you'll feel the interruption in the blade rotation. You might think it's a strike when you tick a limb, because there's often not much difference in the feel of that limb and a strike. I set the hook on any such interruption.

Keep in mind that to catch fish on spinnerbaits at night, you *must* have clear water. They won't pay off in dingy or muddy water. In clear lakes with a lot of shallow cover, you need heavy tackle. I recommend 17-to-25-pound-test line; I don't think line size makes much difference to the fish. You're bringing the bait past quickly, and he doesn't have much time to look at it. Also use a heavy casting rod.

70   Worm 'em Up

I never will forget my finest bass-fishing night ever for lunkers. That was when I wormed 'em up at night in Salt Run, Florida, and it was in September of 1959, and I was using 6-inch black plastic worms. People say, *"September? That's no time to fish Florida!"* It might seem odd, but my most successful night-fishing trips throughout the south have been in the hot summer. And this usually was when nobody else was out fishing. Come to Salt Springs (that's another name for Salt Run) in September, and you're alone! You won't see another boat on the water. This is one of the best-known fishing spots in the world. Everybody fishes it during the spawning season— January, February, and March—but come September there's nobody there. Salt Springs' water stays at a constant 74 degrees year-round, and in the summer when Lake George is hotter, it's likely several bass move up the run to the cooler water.

That night they were in the reeds in the lower section of the run. I'll never forget the circumstances. I'd met a guy named Leonard Strange, who operated a service station in Palatka, and he had some big ol' mounted bass in his station. I'd asked him where he'd caught 'em, and he said in Salt Run and that he and his companions caught their bass mostly on surface plugs.

Bobby Esposito from Maryland was with me, and Leonard went with us. We all started off using topwater plugs, and we didn't do any good. About ten-thirty that night, Leonard left us and went home. Bobby and I decided we'd fish awhile longer, and we tried other lures. Just when Leonard left, the moon started to rise. By eleven p.m. it had risen above the trees, and that's when we caught our first bass. It was a 7-pounder and came from heavy reeds down near a shell mound, which is probably the narrowest constriction in the run. We were using 20-pound line and throwing worms on weedless hooks with no weight way back into the reeds.

I caught thirteen largemouths over 6 pounds, and Bobby caught five or six more over 6, and in addition to those we broke off another twenty in that size range. We must have had forty big ones hit; it was the most big-fish strikes I've ever had at night. We finally ran out of hooks and worms and had to quit about two a.m. The worm was the only lure we could have thrown into that heavy cover.

When the water is really warm and clear, a 6-inch black plastic worm may nail them at night.

Worm fishing at night not only requires clear water, but it's a summer pattern. I've done good at night in the spring with jigs and eels and spinnerbaits, but I've always had my best worm fishing when the water's very warm.

---

71   Jiggerpoling the Monsters

Lots of people through the years have asked me what was the biggest bass I ever caught. I tell them I don't know, and they ask me what do I mean that I don't know because surely I weighed the fish. But the biggest bass I ever caught I didn't weigh. Then they ask how big it was, and I say it was 3 or 4 feet long. They ask again why I don't know, and I explain that while I did catch him, I didn't get my hands on him properly. I did have him in the boat, and I believe he was in excess of 14 pounds. My companion that night, Odell Haire of Charlotte, N.C., agrees that the bass was over 14 pounds, and Odell's the most reputable, straightforward, honest guy I ever knew at Santee-Cooper. No, I didn't weigh that fish because he jumped out of the boat. Here's how it all happened.

We were jiggerpole fishing that night. Jiggerpoling's an old, primitive way of fishing which I've heard has been outlawed in some places. It's not exactly a sporting method of catching fish, but it just might be the most effective way of catching the biggest fish in the whole lake. What I use is a 14-to-16-foot Calcutta-cane pole and a doubled piece of 108-pound-test line which hangs about 4 inches down from the tip of the pole. The line is twisted down all the way to the butt of the pole rather than tied on at the tip, because some fish break the end of the pole. If they do, you've still got them on that heavy line with the rest of the pole. I also use a huge stainless-steel treble hook or a saltwater single hook. My favorite bait is a big piece of fatback about 5 inches long, 1 inch wide, and 1/2 inch thick.

When you're jiggerpoling, the tip of the pole makes a staccato rhythmic sound on the surface. Therefore, the tip is part of the lure, and the bait trails this splashing tip by 4 or 5 inches. The fatback is wobbling and snaking along. We call this "running the jigger," and it's a lot different from merely jiggering. When you run the jigger, you run it in straight lines or big circles. When you come up to a cypress tree, willow bush, stump, or big rock, you run the bait around the

In jiggerpoling, the long cane pole is really part of the lure; you dab and poke and splash the tip with the big sloppy lure bumbling along behind.

edge of the object, with the tip of the pole hitting the object. With the bare treble hook, you get hung up a lot, but when this happens, all you have to do is pull backward on the pole and you usually can snatch loose.

The first night I ever tried a jiggerpole was at Santee, where I'd seen some guys using them. I was walking along the bank beneath a vapor light at Bill Jones' camp. Suddenly while I'm watching the lure, a big white mouth comes up and engulfs it. It was an 8-pounder, and that fish really turned me on to the possibilities of catching some hugh ones on the jiggerpole.

Odell Haire and I had heard a 14½-pounder had been caught on a jiggerpole down by Black's Camp at Santee, and we decided we were going to do some experimenting with it. We started off in a cut off the

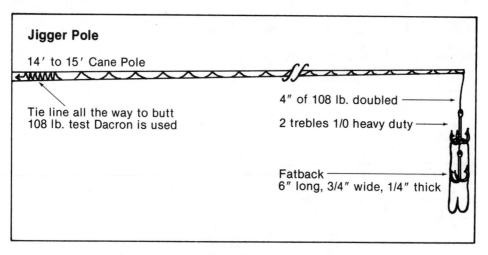

How to make a jiggerpole. The line must run all the way to the butt because a monster can break the tip right off.

Diversion Canal one night. One of us would paddle for twenty to thirty minutes and the other one would run the jigger. Then we'd switch around. We found that since we were so close to the fish, we could do far better by paddling than by running the trolling motor. It was July and the night was pitch black. We pulled up to some willow snags about 5 feet deep. When the fish hit and nearly pulled the pole out of my hand and was turning the boat halfway around, I told Odell I'd hooked a big striped bass. I didn't even think largemouth. I held on, and the fish made a big circle around the boat. When it rolled up near the surface, I told Odell to have the net ready. It never did jump the way a largemouth usually does. Odell fumbled around for the flashlight and finally found it. Instead of netting the bass, I pulled the pole back through my hands much the way you pull an anchor rope. With the tip down and the butt of the pole up in the air, I swung the fish into the boat. Odell had the light on the fish while it was in the air, and we both yelled *"Largemouth!"* at the same time. The hooks ripped out of his mouth, and the bass started flouncing around wildly. I was running a small Terry bass boat at the time. The first time he flounced, he hit the top of the driver's seat about 6 inches off the floor and his body arched across it. Then two more jumps and he went over the side. Then everything was quiet, and we could hear the bullfrogs. We just sat there looking at each other without saying much, and we finally headed on home. That fish's escape sort of ended the trip.

Shallow Structure

GREEN WILLOW TREES

"Roland, you're a deepwater-structure fisherman."

Wherever I meet fishermen, I often hear this comment. My reply is: "No, I'm a structure fisherman, but that doesn't necessarily mean I fish deepwater structure."

Most bass fishermen have come to think that structure is deepwater stuff, but that's not true. The principles of structure apply to a willow or cypress tree, a grass patch, or any object or cover even in only a foot of water. Or it could apply to a rock ledge 50 feet deep. Shallow cover is a structure condition, and the precepts of deep structure apply to shallow structure. An irregular feature is a good place to

Green willow trees are a prime example of shallow structure.

fish whether it's deep or shallow, and irregular features include those on weedlines and cypress knees sticking up in a shallow bay. An isolated feature is another precept of structure fishing. An isolated bush is better than a bush surrounded by 800 other bushes.

Wind and water currents push water, and since fish cannot swim backward, they'll lie in the current in the shade of some cover. Strong winds have a tremendous effect on shallow structure.

In this section on shallow structure, I might be talking about a cypress tree in a southern lake, whereas if you live in Minnesota or Michigan, you might not have any cypress trees. But you might be able to apply this pattern to small bushes growing in the lakes you fish. Again, if I'm talking about willow trees, you might not have any willows where you fish, but you might find some trees to which you can apply the willow pattern. There are many types of trees, bushes, and aquatic vegetation—shallow cover and shallow structure—which create patterns you can fish.

---

72 Worms in the Willows

Willow trees normally are in the older impoundments. In Oklahoma is Grand Lake, which formerly was known as Grand Lake of the Cherokees. It was built in the late 1930s with generally the same construction plan used for many of the TVA lakes, and it was designed to have a fairly constant water level. A regular summer pool generally is maintained, and consequently green willow trees have flourished in many of the flat, protected sections of the lake.

When the water is up in the willows, one of the most deadly ways to catch bass is to worm the willows. The most important thing about fishing any structure is the depth involved. There needs to be at least a foot of water in the willows, and 2 feet is better, but I believe 3 feet is perfect if the water is fairly dingy. If the water is super-clear, 4 or 5 feet probably would be better. In real muddy water, I've caught them a foot deep. These willow trees are large, for they're thirty to forty years old. Some of them are 10 inches in diameter, and they stick up 30 to 40 feet and overhang the water 10 to 15 feet. They form a giant canopy of shade for all species of fish, including carp and bluegills as well as bass on hot summer days.

Willows grow best on clay or mud bottoms in flat coves, and they

Here I'm in the willows with a bait-casting rod, but often I use spinning tackle so that I can skip-cast a worm right in under the willow canopy.

often form little patches and points. The precepts of isolation and irregular features are good keys to finding bass. Finding a windy point with willows is ideal, and I prefer it if the wind is blowing water into the willows. This is a perfect place to use plastic worms. It's a little difficult, because the back of the boat swings downwind toward the trees and you need to hold the trolling motor into the wind. You're turned around in the seat and casting toward the back of the boat. Probably the best spot is where the wind is sweeping into the farthest-out branches on the leading edge of the trees. Try to throw the worm right to that edge. Bass in current tend to leapfrog ahead of each other, and they'll be on the very upstream edge of the tree. If there's no wind, I simply look for the shadiest spot and the heaviest place in the tree and try to skip-cast the worm in there.

If the water is fairly clear, lots of times I won't use a casting rod. One of the best outfits to use for willow fishing is a spinning rod, because with it you can peg the weight and skip the worm without backlashing. With a spinning rod you can skip the worm 10 feet, whereas with a casting rod, you might skip the worm only 2 feet, and the high velocity of the cast will cause you to backlash. Willow snags aren't bad for breaking your line. A lot of the bass will wrap you up, but if you play them on the light side, I've found even 6- and 7-pounders will swim off 20 feet if you give them line. Then you can go to the willow tree, reach down with your paddle, push the line away from the tree, and hand-land them without the rod and reel. Ten-to-14-pound line should be used on the spinning outfit. However, if the bass are real tight on the tree trunk itself instead of out beneath the shady edges, then I want casting tackle and 20-pound line. If the fish goes around the main trunk, he probably will break your 10-pound line in a hurry.

One of the best willow-tree lakes I've ever fished is Kentucky Lake. Lake Barkley, which is connected to Kentucky, is a close second. Barkley has a newer crop of willow trees, but Barkley is a much younger lake. These are TVA lakes which maintain summer pools, and generally by May they have full pools up in the willows. They are fairly dingy lakes, and only about 2 feet of water is needed. Find the shade on the windy willow points back in the bay, and you'll probably find the best worm fishing for that time of year. Even though these lakes have stumps and deep-water structure, the willows attract bass. I believe that when the water gets up in the big shaded branches of willow trees, this well could be the No. 1 pattern on that lake.

---

73 Flipping the Green

For someone who wants to catch a big bass in the spring and early summer, there's probably no better way than flipping in the green willows with a regular flipping stick. In the previous pattern, I mentioned you can catch a bass on a plastic worm with 10-pound line and spinning tackle or with 20-pound line and casting tackle. But there's a certain condition when flipping with its quiet, accurate presentation—it's big advantage—will catch far more bigger bass.

This condition exists when you can stand up in the boat in the spring after the spawn and look back 15 to 20 feet beneath the willow branches and see bass suspended right below the surface. A long cast with any type of tackle usually results in scaring these fish, because the lure comes crashing up. About the only way to catch those suspended bass is with a very quiet flip. You need to make a 15-to-20-foot flip with a good 7½-foot flipping stick, 20-to-40-pound line, and prob-

All you have to do is look back in the willows, spot a suspended bass, and flip in a pegged plastic worm.

ably just a plastic worm. Peg the weight with a round toothpick and use a 1/4- or 3/16-ounce weight and a 5/0 hook. Bury that hook in a 7- or 8-inch worm.

When I see a few bass back in the branches, I figure I've spotted a pattern and there should be more up shallow. Not only does flipping give you a super-accurate, super-quiet presentation, but also you've got direct line-control the instant the worm hits the water. If you get a strike immediately, you can bust him just as quickly and blow him right out of that willow tree. With a spinning or casting rod, even if you were able to make an accurate, quiet presentation, you're often not in full contact with the lure as it sinks that initial foot or so and you don't always realize you've got a strike, because you have a little more slack than with the flipping stick. You have full control with the flipping stick, and if a fish hits, you can react much faster.

You can catch plenty of smaller ones by skipping a worm with spinning tackle, but when the 5-to-7-pounders get in those willows at Kentucky and Barkley Lakes or those Lake Mojave bass in Arizona get

You have full control with the flipping stick, and when the fish hits you know it right away and can react much faster.

into those salt cedars, you need the flipping rod to handle them. There's no way to get a 7-pound Mojave bass out of a salt cedar without a flipping stick and 30-pound line.

I can look back to our days of fishing Tridelphia Reservoir years ago in Maryland when we didn't have flipping sticks. The reservoir had plenty of willows, and we could see big bass back in them. We'd take our spinning tackle with 12- and 14-pound line and try all different kinds of ways to catch them. One of our tricks was to throw up into the willow and lower the worm down into the water. The bass would grab the worm, there was the line 20 feet up in the top of the tree, and the fish would break us off.

We could have caught those bass with flipping sticks.

STICKUPS

I've already talked about stickup fishing in relation to various baits and techniques, but there's a lot more to be said about it and some more nitty-gritty techniques to describe. Stickups in many res-

A practical warm-weather technique for landing a hawg that has wrapped your line around a stickup.

ervoirs are some of the best cover. In fact, most of the reservoirs which have been built in the U.S. in the past thirty years have at one time during their aging process had hordes of stickups. And for some reason the heavy stickups or that secondary growth would hold the majority of the bass.

Bass hold in good-sized stickups—the size of your arm—in water up to 5 feet deep on any clarity of lake almost all year long. They'll be in them even if the water is 90 degrees. My premier stickup bassing came at Santee, and I've enjoyed stickup fishing in many other lakes.

---

74 Wormers' Delight

At Santee, one of our rules of thumb was "big bass at high noon," meaning we caught most of our biggest fish from the willow stickups in the middle of the day in the hot summer. Our best hours were from ten a.m. to three p.m. I think this pattern holds true in most of the new lakes around the country. What happens is the bass feed actively

**Bright midday sun means the bass will be sticking tight to the cover—
perfect conditions for worming the stickups.**

away from cover in the early-morning and late-evening hours, and
then you can catch 'em on surface plugs and spinnerbaits all around
the shallow points where the stickups might be. But when the sun
comes out bright, the fish get tight on the cover. They'll go to the
center to tiny patches of shade no bigger than your fist and lie there
with their eyes shaded.

The wormers' delight is a standard pattern for stickup fishing. I
prefer a 5½-foot bait-casting rod, 14-to-25-pound line, and a 6-inch
plastic worm rigged Texas-style. My standard slip sinker weighs 3/16
ounce, but use a ⅛-ounce weight if the stickups are shallow and the
water's very clear. This is a spring and summer pattern which is particularly good in hot weather when water temperatures are 80 to 90
degrees on fairly new reservoirs which have a lot of stickups. I look for
stickups with the most cover and shade and, with the precepts of
structure in mind, I also look for isolated stickups and irregular features. A stickup leaning over on an angle usually is better than a vertical stickup, because it forms a longer strip of shade beneath it. In the
middle of the day with the sun high, there are spots of shade next to
angled stickups.

This stickup bass liked my plastic worm but didn't like being hauled out into the sun.

I'd rather fish a windy bank with stickups than a calm bank. In a day you can fish hundreds of stickups, and one thing I always do when I catch a bass around one is stick my rod down in the water to see how deep it is. This also tells me what kind of bottom the stickup is on. You can feel the difference between gravel, sand, rock, and mud with a graphite rod. I have seen days they were on stickups in gravel but not in mud, and such features easily could be part of the pattern. I don't say gravel is better than sand or sand is better than mud, but when you catch one off a sand bottom, you'd best look for more sand. Also consider the wind. Is it blowing on that stickup? Is it a certain type of stickup? Does it have shade?

One day on Lake Oolegah in Oklahoma, I was making a film with Don Butler, and the bass were in certain kinds of stickups. Only about one-fifth of the stickups had a certain type of bark on them, and those bass were around that type of tree. Once we were able to identify the black bark on these stickups, we easily recognized them. Out of several conditions possible, such as depth, bottom, water clarity, and current, perhaps only one or two are the reason bass are around certain stickups and not others. One day it might be current which is most important, but on another day it could be depth or shade.

75   Jigging the Shade

This is a little different from the standard stickup pattern. On the standard pattern, when you throw into the stickup you frequently get the strike as your lure is sinking. Jigging the shade is a different concept. You jig the lure because the bass aren't hitting very good. You

To jig the shade I look for a stickup with a branch over the shady side and cast over it, then lower the pegged worm into the water. This technique requires repeated jigging and heavy line.

think they're in the stickups, but you're unable to catch them by casting and letting the lure sink. You might have tried a variety of lures from topwater plugs to worms, but they wouldn't hit. Or maybe you did catch a couple, but then they quit hitting.

If the fish are still in the stickups—and occasionally you can see 'em there—then you can jig the stickups with a different type of plastic worm rig. Instead of the light 3/16-ounce slip sinker, I go to a 3/8- or 1/2-ounce size. I'll look for a stickup where the branch sticks out on the shady side, and I'll make a much longer cast over the limb and lower the pegged worm to the water to where I think the bass is. The first time I jig it, the strike likely would be out of reflex; the second and third time, he might hit out of curiosity; but after fifteen to twenty-five jigs, the worm won't move out of his territory and he gets highly provoked and grabs that intruder.

For jigging the shade, I use 20- or 25-pound-test line, a fairly heavy bait-casting rod, and a free-spool reel. Since the line is lying over a branch, you need the heavy line and the stiff rod to get the hook set properly. At times this pattern really will take bass which don't hit in the more conventional ways.

EMERGENT WEEDS

The aquatic world has all sorts of weeds, which can be broken down into two basic categories: on shallow structure are emergent weeds, and on deep structure are submergent weeds. Emergent weeds break through the surface and include bushes, reeds, lily pads, and various types of grasses. These generally are found where the water is less than 5 feet deep.

In Florida, most fishermen fish within a cast of weeds. There is very little deepwater-structure fishing done there. Okeechobee has 840,000 acres of water, and probably 250,000 acres of it is filled with weeds—emergent weeds sticking up out of the water. These weeds form basic shallow-water-structure areas, and the bass there form loose schools. I often think of my experience at Okeechobee, where I've often fished along through acres and acres of weeds and suddenly found a school of bass. There's not much difference in where you found 'em and the places you fished without getting a strike. The bottom is about the same and you're fishing the same species of grass, but you've found a school of roaming fish. At Okeechobee and in the Everglades there are a lot of shallow structures to consider, such as grass edges and different species of grass, different depths, water temperature, and wind conditions. Where you do find a school of bass, you can study the situation and usually find some feature of the pattern which is different. Probably the biggest features I've found are wind and water currents and sometimes water temperature variations. The presence of baitfish is another possibility.

76   Snaking the Grass

This is a good, valid pattern I haven't talked about. We've talked about using plastic frogs and Johnson Spoons in the grass, but this snaking pattern involves a different type of plastic worm. It was developed years ago at Lake Jackson in Florida, and one of the first ones was the Lake Jackson Special. This lake, near Tallahassee, has a

The big Lake Jackson Special is great for snaking through heavy grass like this. The J&W Hawg Hunter is a similar lure.

lot of Johnson grass, and the worm they developed to fish this grass is a 9- or 10-inch worm which is big, fat, and heavy and casts real well. It doesn't have a weight, but you can throw it with heavy casting tackle and 25-to-30-pound line. The worm also has two giant weedless hooks tied on heavy braided line and molded inside the hard plastic. The hard plastic is important, because soft plastic catches in the grass and tears when you drag it over thick weeds. The old Lake Jackson worm pulls through and bounces over every type of vegetation.

When I fish this worm, I hold my casting rod at about a 45-degree angle and snake the lure through the grass. I'm trying to emulate a snake. My first experience with this worm came in 1968, when I fished out of Red and Sam's place after I'd heard lots of reports about large-mouths in the 13-to-14-pound class being caught at Jackson. Everyone said those big ones hit the worm, and I was told the bass were back in the heavy grass. I used all the types of worms I had, and when I threw back in the grass with a weight ahead of the worm, I kept getting hung up. I caught two or three small ones and had a couple of big ones boil up, but I didn't catch much of anything.

I got back to Red and Sam's in time to see some huge bass being carried up the hill. I asked the guys what they'd caught 'em on, and they said, "Lake Jackson worms." My next question was what is a Lake Jackson worm, and they showed me one. Of course, it was different from anything I'd seen. It had that big two-hook harness and a beavertail. Consequently, I bought a couple at the tackle shop, and the second morning it was foggy and still. On my first few casts I saw some wakes heading toward the worm. On the first one that hit, I set the hook just as I would have with a Johnson Spoon and I missed him. It was a 7- or 8-pounder. I made another cast to some more grass and was snaking and skipping that big worm along, and here came another big, big bass which blew up on the worm. I struck hard and missed him. Finally the wind came up and I didn't get any more strikes, and I came in for lunch. I told Red those bass had my number, because when they hit, I struck right away and missed them. He asked me why I struck right away. I told him I thought this was like fishing a Johnson Spoon, and he reminded me I was fishing a worm.

That afternoon I went back out, and the first one which blew up on that worm, I caught. When he hit, I dropped the rod and gave him some slack, and after he moved a couple of feet, I set the hook and got him. Sure enough, he'd eaten the worm. He weighed about 9 pounds and was my first big Lake Jackson bass. I continued to follow Red's instructions, and on several trips after that I kept catching big bass on that Lake Jackson worm by snaking the grass.

A different brand name of this type of worm—the J & W Hawg Hunter, made in Jacksonville, Fla.—gained prominence in 1973 at the Florida Invitational **BASS** tournament when Bob Tyndall of Greenfield, Mo., caught a 12-pound, 13-ounce bass in that event on the St. Johns River. Tyndall not only won a bass boat for having the biggest bass in the tourney, but he also still has the distinction of catching the biggest lunker ever in a Bass Anglers Sportsman Society tourney. Tyndall caught that bass on a 13-inch Hawg Hunter. I don't know exactly where Tyndall was fishing. I've heard two different reports and both of them make sense. I do know he was on the north side of Rodman Pool, because John Powell saw him there. There were supposedly some logs there, and I went to that area about a week later and found some logs in that area, but the logs were packed with weeds and grass. I snaked that Hawg Hunter through there and did manage to catch a couple over 4 pounds, but I didn't get anything like he caught. The point is he was fishing a lot of heavy, thick cover, and he was snaking the worm on top of the cover.

This type of worm fishing is similar to topwater fishing; you see the bass swirl up and take the worm on the surface, because it's on top of the thick vegetation. Down on Lake Kissimmee and West Lake Tohopekaliga in Florida, they use a big, heavy worm which is locally manufactured and they snake it and swim it without a weight along the heavy grass. The bass really blow up on it.

Prerequisites for the snaking-the-grass pattern are similar to those for the Johnson Spoon pattern in that they hit it on top good on those calm, cloudy days or early in the morning and late in the evening.

I missed a few before I learned to give the bass enough time before I set the hook.

Such occasions are much like the good times to use surface plugs, but snaking the grass with the big worm pays off in areas with thick vegetation where you can't use a conventional surface lure. The only lures you can use in such cover are the completely weedless ones, such as the plastic frogs, Johnson Spoons, and weedless worms. You can snake the grass very slowly with the worm, whereas the Johnson Spoon needs to be moved faster.

77 Jigging the Hyacinths

Lots of times fishermen ask me how I did in a certain tournament, and I'm pleased to tell them if I did real well. After the American Bass Fisherman tournament at Lake Okeechobee in January of 1977, I told people real disgustedly that I finished second. They would ask why I was so upset about that—didn't I almost win it? My answer was heck, no, I didn't almost win it. I was beaten by *45 pounds!* Dave Gliebe won it, and he had almost 96 pounds of bass! He more than doubled anybody else's total weight! And he did it the most obvious, simple way, and the rest of us felt like dummies when it was all over.

This 10-pound-plus largemouth grabbed a worm under the hyacinths in a central Florida lake. You have to strike when the worm stops, even though most of the time it's a limb or twig rather than a fish.

Dave is a good friend of mine, and the reason I came in second was that he told me what he was doing. He told me the pattern, and I was able to capitalize on it the last day. He was running around the lake finding big patches of water hyacinths at 4-to-5-foot depths. These hyacinths had been blown up against reeds on the main lake. Right next to the reeds were small, open holes, and he'd ease up there with his trolling motor and drop his jig down into those openings next to the reeds. If that didn't work, sometimes he took his rod tip and poked down through the hyacinths and jigged the lure and let it fall back. If this didn't work, he blast-casted through the hyacinths by making sharp downward casts.

In that third round I did it a little differently. With my 18-foot push pole I'd make three or four holes a foot in diameter in the hyacinths and then take a worm and make a flip with a 7½-foot flipping stick into the hole. Dave Gliebe and I both jigged our lures repeatedly in one spot. I fished with Erwin Cole of Murfreesboro, Tenn., the last day, and we caught over 25 pounds. We caught most of our bass by jigging twenty-five to forty times in a hole. The strike came when the worm would be sinking, and it would just stop. Probably two-thirds of the time we were false-striking at limbs, twigs, and grass, but striking everytime we felt something enabled us to catch some bass we probably wouldn't have caught. The fish were simply holding onto the worm.

At West Lake Toho they do a lot of flipping in heavy grass which is fairly deep, such as from 5 to 6 feet in a lot of places. They let the wind move them along. You're almost over the bass with the boat, but it's thick and they don't know you're there. Heavier weights in the ⅜-to-½-ounce sizes are used, and a guide I know there, Bob Rohrlack from Longwood, uses two ½-ounce weights on windy days. He pegs the weights in place.

Bob also has experimented with wire line. He's tied a 5-to-6-foot piece of stainless-steel mono leader to the worm hook. He says the 30-pound wire will cut that heavy grass like a knife when he's fighting a big bass. Bob explained that the grass is so thick in some places that even 5-pound bass get wrapped up in the grass and you can't pull them out with regular monofilament, but with the steel leader you can cut the grass and get them out of it. It's a heck of a good idea, but I haven't tried it. However, I plan to do so the next time I'm flipping into deeper grass.

78   Reeds and Rushes

When I think of reeds, I think of smallmouth bass as well as large-mouths. Smallmouths frequently spawn around reeds. Lake St. Clair out of Detroit once was a lake I didn't have much confidence in. It's a good-sized lake which joins Lake Erie and Lake Huron. We fished St. Clair around Walpole Island in southern Canada. Larry Helin, the son of Charlie Helin, who manufactures the Flatfish plug, took a couple of us up there one spring, and Larry said we'd fish the reeds and rushes for spawning smallmouths. Sure enough, the smallmouths were packed up in the shallow flats. We looked for isolated clumps of reeds, and with Polaroid glasses we could see the smallmouth beds. When the water was calm and the weather was overcast, I don't think the type of lure made any difference. Larry caught 'em on the Flatfish,

My airboat blasts me through the reeds every winter on the 2.5 million acres of the Florida Everglades.

and we caught them on Tiny Torpedos, jigs, worms, and crank baits. Those smallmouths that week went absolutely bananas.

I found exactly the same pattern this past June up on the St. Lawrence Seaway. On the Canadian side I found isolated patches of reeds. I was there for a B.A.S.S. tournament, and I won it by catching largemouths in the Lake of the Isles area. When I found the smallmouths, I didn't think much about them; I figured they wouldn't win the tournament because they weren't running as big as the largemouths. They were running 2 to 3 pounds; and I didn't consider that there would be bigger smallmouths somewhere else. But Gary Wade from Greensboro, N.C., came in second in that tournament, and he was about 11 pounds behind me with some 48 pounds. What was so amazing about his fish was that he had a better than 3-pound average with smallmouths! He found his fish on Lake Ontario about two miles into the St. Lawrence River, on small patches of reeds and rushes out in the main river. He caught them on Bush Hog spinnerbaits. I have to give Gary a tremendous amount of credit for catching that many smallmouths in that 3-pound-plus size range.

Early in the morning and late in the evening I fish the reeds and rushes with a white spinnerbait.

The most fun I've ever had with this pattern came with a flyrod and popping bug up in the southern Canadian lakes. Smallmouth skyrocket when they strike during the spawning season. When a 3-to-4-pounder gets upset at a popping bug, he really blows up on it. They actually come out of the water on the strike. Largemouth seldom hit that vehemently. This flyrodding has to offer some of the supreme moments in light-tackle fishing, and it's definitely a pattern in reeds and rushes.

Early in the morning and late in the evening when I'm trying to cover a lot of water with reeds and rushes, I like a small white spinnerbait. I look for small, isolated patches. If the sun comes out bright and the fish get in the shade of these patches, I go to a plastic worm rigged Texas-style on fairly light line. Usually you find reeds and rushes in clear water and you need lighter line for worming them.

PIERS, DOCKS, AND BRIDGES

On the twenty-to-thirty-year-old lakes in the south and southwest, such as Sydney Lanier in Georgia, Watts Bar in Tennessee, and Grand Lake in Oklahoma, are a lot of piers and docks. Many people who own cottages on those lakes and have their own docks put out brushpiles to attract crappies and bluegills. During the pre-spawn period when the bass move up into shallower water, they frequently get around the piers and docks before they move to the backs of the shallow coves to spawn, and there are often some real big bass there. Then in the summer when the water has fallen and there's very little cover in the backs of the coves, the brush around the piers and docks might be the only cover in the coves, and again the bass gather around it.

In high-water periods during the summer when the water is way up in the willows and the natural brush around the shore, the brushpiles around the piers and docks tend to lose their concentrations of bass. But in low water in the summer and fall when there's very little natural cover, the piers, docks, and bridges really pay off.

Sometimes I get asked how and when I fish the bridges. A bridge support is a super spot, particularly when it's in the back of a cove or on a creek. It's super because of current and shade. Because bridges are constricted areas, there is a lot more water flow beneath them.

The best time to fish a bridge usually is during hot weather, because bass like current then, and they like to lie in the current behind a piling at the corner or at the wing wall of a bridge. The clearer the water, the more the shade will attract them. Usually I fish bridges with structure types of lures, such as grubs. Even if it's a shallow structure, the channel which goes beneath a bridge might be 20 to 30 feet deep. The bass quite often are on the bottom in deep water. Grubs, spoons, and Little Georges worked downcurrent on light line are excellent.

Bass normally lie facing the current, and to fish properly, you must fish downcurrent. In a lake like Gaston on the North Carolina and Virginia state line, the water is regulated every day. It's pumped in and pumped out. The lake level is apt to fluctuate 4 or 5 inches in a day. Maybe in the morning the water is flowing under the bridge into the cove, but in the afternoon they might be pulling water at the dam and the water flows out. In either case the bass will be facing the current right at the pilings next to the bridge. So just as if I were on a smallmouth stream, I throw my grub or spoon upcurrent and bring it along with the current. This really is important.

When there's low water and little natural cover, the piers, docks, and bridges really pay off.

Another good lure for hot summer fishing is the plastic worm. Make it crawl along those bridge supports. But make sure you work it with the current.

On a pier I look for the irregular features, keeping in mind the structure concept and trying to figure out what is the most irregular feature of the entire pier. It might be the steps built on the side of the pier for the swimmers. Maybe at the end of the pier is a double set of pilings. Generally the ends of the piers are the best.

One time Don Norton of Clinton, Miss., and I were fishing on Crescent Lake off the St. Johns River in Florida. We found a long pier which extended out about 100 yards. We fished the end of it, which was 10 to 12 feet deep, and we had only one strike and missed the fish. We started electric-motoring back along the pier and noticed a piling about every 10 feet. I was halfheartedly watching my locator, thinking the water was about all the same depth, and suddenly when we threw ahead of the boat to the next pilings, we each caught bass on our plastic worms. Both fish came from the shady side of the pilings, and when we got up there, I noticed the water went from 10 down to 3 feet. There was a natural shelf extending along that pier about halfway down it. We worked the rest of the pilings all the way back to the bank and didn't do any more good.

Then we turned the boat around and fished every piling back toward the end of the pier, and when we came to that piling right on the ledge, we each caught another bass. But we never had another strike from that spot on to the end of the pier. Almost simultaneously we looked at each other and realized there was a school of fish on that dropoff. We went back and anchored out from the dropoff and proceeded to get seven or eight more strikes from that spot where the water level changed from 3 to 10 feet. This was a structure situation with the dropoff holding the fish, and it was the most irregular feature on that pier.

---

79   Brushpile Bigmouths

Brushpiles can be fished a variety of ways. In the early spring I like shallow-running crank baits, such as a little Balsa B or a small Fat Rap, because sometimes I need to cover a lot of water to find the fish. A reflex-action bait is very good for catching big bass and covering a

Bump the dock, the stump, the
piling, and the brush with a
crank bait or spinnerbait,
making repeated casts. This bass
finally fell for a spinnerbait.

lot of docks and bridges. A spinnerbait is my second choice. If there's a
lot of heavy brush, bumping a spinnerbait through it is a good
method. Since these are reflex-action strikes, you need to bump the
cover. Bump the dock, the stump, the piling, and the brush. Make
repeated casts and keep making contact with the cover. If that 5-
pounder doesn't hit the first time out of reflex, he might hit out of
anger on the tenth cast.

Once the water really warms up, I get away from those kinds of
baits. And during the pre-spawn period there might be dingy, cool
water, and reflex-action baits work better then. When the spawning
season is over and the water is warmer and clearer, I usually use a
surface plug early and late in the day and a plastic worm during the
day when the sun is on the water. The worm is the king lure for summertime fishing in these areas.

80 Veering Is Vital

This is a very interesting technique for fishing a boat dock, particularly a floating dock supported by flotation material and secured to the bank by cables or a causeway. Beneath these docks, veering is vital. There are a variety of crank baits and swimming baits which can be "veered" up beneath places on that dock where the fish never have seen a lure. The trick to this is a matter of mechanics. Any deep-diving crank bait such as a Deep-Divin' B, a Hellbender, or a Fat Rap can be veered if you take a pair of needlenose pliers and bend the front eye slightly so that when the line is tied to the eye, it comes off about 1/16 of an inch to the left or the right. If you bend the eye to the left, you'll notice the plug veers to the right, and vice-versa. I usually bend two plugs—one to the left and the other to the right.

I want the plug to run at approximately a 45-degree angle and slice 4 to 8 feet to the left or right. The rod with the plug which veers right I put on the right side of the boat, and the one with the plug which runs to the left is on the left side. When I approach a dock, I

To put a curve in your bait, bend the eye off center a bit—to the left if you want the lure to veer right, and to the right if you want it to veer left.

throw to each side with the appropriate plug to veer off beneath the dock. I make very long casts past the object; the longer the cast the farther beneath the dock the plug will veer. If you run the plug fast enough, it will veer up and out of the water, and I have had a plug way up under the dock and then started reeling it fast and made it come up and bump the bottom of the dock. This is that old trick of bumping the object. Of course, if you ever get your plug hung up under there, you can consider it lost forever. On hard-fished lakes where the bass really are spooky, this can be a very effective pattern.

At Santee-Cooper I learned this method first by casting to big cypress trees with overhanging limbs 8 to 15 feet out and to big willow trees. Here again, veering is really vital. You can do this veering even with a shallow-running lure such as a Rapala. Such lures will veer even when they run 3 to 6 inches under the water. They'll veer as much as 5 or 6 feet on a long cast.

One time up at Grand Lake in Oklahoma, Harold Yost, who runs H&R Marine at Claremore, Okla., taught me a lesson. Harold was big on Deep Wee-R's back a few years ago when they were very popular. I didn't know it, but he had a Deep Wee-R which he'd bent the opposite way so it would run to the right. He didn't say a word about it, and the first time we fished together, he made a long cast in next to a boat dock, and I heard his plug knocking up under the dock. I noticed it had gone back under there and I thought something was wrong with his plug, but he immediately caught a fish. He caught three or four more before I realized he was veering his plug on purpose. Harold does most of my mechanic work on my boats and motors, and he's a real sneaky fisherman and a good tournament fisherman. He really put it on me that day because he had plugs which veered.

CYPRESS TREES

Cypress trees are found in lakes throughout the South, and a lot of them are fairly inaccessible to fishermen. They have big, overhanging limbs, and they're extremely difficult to cast to. When you get hung up in a cypress tree, you have to go get your lure. Even the smal limbs are extremely tough and don't break off easily. The limbs also hang low to the water. Even though they're difficult to fish, cypress trees are super ambush points and super shallow-water structure.

81 Bush-Rod Bonus

This is a mechanical type of pattern developed by a bunch of boys at Santee-Cooper. The foremost advocate of bush-rod fishing was Walt Rucker, who owns and operates a bait farm near Summerton, S.C. Walt, Billy Goff, and Joe Avin, who had fished Santee all their lives, came up with a more efficient way to cast lures under cypress trees. Their technique is extremely efficient for catching big fish.

The concept of bush-rod fishing is skipping a plastic worm back beneath the limbs. You can do this with normal spinning tackle, but the average spinning rod is capable of a maximum of 14-pound line for efficient casting. A bush rod is a modified spinning rod which enables you to cast 20-, 25-, and even 30-pound line for big bass in thick, heavy cover such as a cypress tree. This is accomplished mechanically by how the rod is set up. The rod has a one-piece blank about 5½ feet long. It needs to be short because you're often casting

This is the kind of cover the Santee-Cooper boys fish with a bush rod. Such heavy spinning equipment should work well for skipping worms into other types of cover too.

short distances. Some are only 5 feet long, and they're heavy saltwater popping-rod blanks. They use big surf-rod guides, starting with a 25-millimeter tip, which is nearly as big as the gathering guide on many spinning rods on the market today. It's a huge saltwater tip. The gathering guide is as large as 70 millimeters. This is about the largest surf guide you can buy; you can stick a silver dollar through it. The guides are Aetna guides, and they're the lightest guides available; they look like a coil of wire. The guides are double-wrapped because of the heavy lines and rough, tough fishing encountered.

The reels are light saltwater models with large-diameter spools. You can't throw 20-pound or heavier line any distance with anything less than such a reel. Such reels include the Mitchell 306 and the Quick 330. In the Zebco Cardinal series, the Cardinal 6 and 7 reels would be good.

The Santee boys use these bush rods with a pegged plastic worm. They flip and skip the worm up under the brush and cover. They use large worms, because the larger the worm, the better it skips. Since the water isn't deep, a 1/8-ounce slip sinker works well with the 7-to-9-inch worm. Too heavy a weight won't skip well, but the weight does need to be pegged.

You need to look to see where the hair roots are on the cypress tree. Most of the time these tiny roots have drifted with the current and are wrapped around the back side of the tree. The hair roots are an additional irregular feature which give the fish more shade and cover and a better ambush point. At Santee, the best cypress trees are the ones with outcrops of these hair roots and the longest branches hanging out. They are less accessible and aren't fished as much.

Walt Rucker has done so much bush-rod fishing that he's the most accurate spinning-rod caster I've ever seen. I always was amazed at his accuracy. He regularly can hit where the waterline meets the trunk of the cypress tree—the perfect cast. When he has to skip the worm, he can skip it 15 to 20 feet, but quite often he doesn't have to do this. With such accurate casting, he is able to put the worm into the water at the base of the tree trunk with a soft plop. Then the worm slithers into the water, and that is the perfect cypress-tree cast.

The bush rod can be used effectively anywhere there are extra-large bass around heavy cover. When you're dealing with 9-to-11-pound largemouths around cypress trees or any other heavy cover, you have a problem trying to get them out with conventional spinning tackle and 14-pound line. There are a lot of lakes similar to Santee where you have big bass and heavy cover. I believe the thick bull-rush places in Lake Okeechobee in Florida would be good for bush rods, and the standing-timber areas of Rodman Reservoir in Florida, and beneath the boat docks at Kentucky Lake, and certainly anywhere with thick willow trees and big bass.

82 Skin the Knees

This is another cypress-tree pattern and one which we ol' southern boys have been talking about ever since I moved to the south. Cypress knees are what they call a vestigial part of a cypress tree. Biologists never have figured out the purpose of cypress knees. Down in Lake Eloise in Florida, cypress knees grow out of the water as much as 50 feet away from the trees themselves. The knees are on the feeder roots from the main trunk. They aren't found on young cypress trees. You'll find them in the natural lakes where the cypress trees are 100 to 300 years old. (Cypress trees at Lake Eloise at Cypress Gardens have been estimated to be 500 years old.)

For some reason, bass seem to think cypress knees are among the greatest things in the world. They're perfect ambush points which frequently are overlooked by unobservant fishermen. In a southern swamp, such as in Florida or southern Georgia where there are a lot of virgin cypress trees, you really have to be careful when you're running your boat. You don't want to hit a cypress knee. It will crunch right through fiberglass and tear your motor off your boat. Probably the easiest time to fish cypress knees is when there's a little riffle or wave action, because then you can see the swirls around the knees, which are inches under the water.

I like to fish chartreuse single- or tandem-bladed spinnerbaits around cypress knees. Back in the early 1970s when the Zorro Aggravator spinnerbait was so popular, I used to come to Florida and fish Lake Eloise with Jerry Ember, a photographer at Cypress Gardens. We set up a little tournament one time with this old-timer, Dave, who was touted to be the finest fisherman on Lake Eloise. He was eighty-two years old and one of the finest fishermen in all of central Florida. He knew all of the old tricks, and years ago he had caught an 18-pound bass on a surface plug from Lake Marion in southern Florida, and he'd been written up in *Outdoor Life* for that feat. Dave had fished

Cypress knees are the feeder roots from the main trunk and are sometimes difficult to see— good bass hideouts but risky for your boat.

for bass in Cuba years before with a lot of the great names in fishing, and he'd caught hundreds of bass over 10 pounds in his many years.

An article for *Popular Mechanics* was done on this little tournament, with the gist of it being one of the new breed of bass tournament fishermen, Roland Martin, challenging one of the old-timers in bass fishing. I went to Lake Eloise a week early to do some work with Johnson Motors. The purpose of the contest with Dave was not to see which one of us would win, but to show how our techniques and methods differed and how experience and age tends to balance out the new techniques of the modern fishermen.

I'd fished throughout the week with plastic worms, and finally I got around to throwing the tandem-bladed Zorro spinnerbait, which back in 1970 was relatively new. It had chartreuse blades and was something brand-new in Florida. That week there was a bass on almost every cypress knee growing out from those big trees, and they'd seen almost every lure in Dave's big ol' tackle box. Dave's trick to catching them was to throw old-style floating-diving lures such as the floating River Runts and the Lucky 13s. He knew where the cypress knees were better than I did. But I guess the bass had grown so accustomed to seeing his lures that they'd sort of got burned out. However, the ace I had up my sleeve was that Zorro Aggravator: they'd never seen a spinnerbait. I'd cut the hook off on a spinnerbait and had gone around the lake all week. When I'd pull the bait by a cypress knee and drop it, I'd see those boils and the flashes of the bass. That week I located a dozen or so good fish. I really did my homework, because I knew the ball game was being played on Dave's home field, and since he knew Eloise much better than I did, I felt I'd really have to do good to stay up with him on both size and numbers of bass.

Meanwhile, Dave figured he didn't need any practice, because he'd been fishing the lake fifty years—in fact, he'd fished it for twenty years before I was born! The day of the contest came, and we fished together. Half the day I was to run the boat, and he would run the boat the other half. I got the morning half, and I told him I knew where some bass were. I went to the first cypress knee where I'd rolled up a 4- or 5-pounder that week. I tied on a spinnerbait and told him this was a good spot. He gave me a funny look as if he'd never caught a fish there, but he didn't say anything. I flipped out that spinnerbait and caught a 4-pounder on the first cast. Dave said, *"Uh-huh!"* but nothing else. I cranked the engine and went about a quarter of a mile down the lake and pulled up to another cypress knee. I told him there ought to be a bass on that cypress knee. Again, I'd had a strike there a couple days before, and on my first cast, *wham!*—a 3-pounder. The photographers in the other boat and Dave were saying to each other that I was predicting where I would catch a fish. They were puzzled. Finally one of the photographers said they needed a 5-pound bass for pictures. They were kidding around, and I told them I thought I could catch a 5-pounder. What I didn't tell them was that I knew where a 5-pounder was. Way out in the lake was a cypress knee with a log which had drifted up against it. I told the camera boat to move around the other side and get ready, because I was going to catch a

5-pounder on the first cast. They thought I was kidding, and they didn't get halfway set up. When I threw in, I got a strike and caught a 4½-pounder. That was my biggest one of the morning. Dave was really amazed, because I'd called the shot on three straight bass. I didn't tell him I'd fished all week without a hook and that I had them located.

Finally it was Dave's turn to run the boat and fish where he wanted to. I'd caught seven or eight, and he'd caught a couple. He went to cypress knees he'd fished for years. Some of them I'd fished

North River in North Carolina has ancient cypresses and some of the prettiest bass water anywhere.

that week and had found bass on. He was casting to every knee, and I'd wait until the boat was positioned properly, and then I'd tell him there ought to be one right over there, and I'd throw to where I'd had the strike earlier in the week and I'd catch the fish.

About three o'clock Dave turned to me and said, "I thought I knew every bass in this lake, but you're predicting where they are and you've never fished this lake." I finally admitted I'd spent a lot of time on the lake, and I conceded that I had sort of taken advantage of him. I didn't want to hurt his feelings, and I told him that the spinnerbait was a brand-new thing to the bass at Eloise and that I thought they were hitting it because they hadn't seen it before. I gave him one and told him to try it. He was a good caster and truly an expert fisherman. With my Zorro spinnerbait and him being in the front of the boat, he suddenly starts catching bass around every cypress knee. I had him fifteen bass to five with two hours left before dark, and by the time we quit he was darned near tied with me. We each caught about twenty that day. And at the end of the day, we traded some lures. He traded me two wooden Musky Jitterbugs for ten Zorro spinnerbaits.

I was back to Eloise later, and Dave told me he'd gone out the next week and caught a 12-pound bass on one of those spinnerbaits I'd traded him. Ol' Dave died three or four years ago. I'll never forget fishing with him, and I'm really glad I got to share a boat with him. He truly was a great fisherman.

The best time to skin the knees on a cypress tree is in the spring. This pattern pays off in the summer, too, but then it's more of a worm pattern. For the best action I like the water temperatures to be in the high 50s to low 60s. Then a spinnerbait is super-good. I like to find isolated knees which are deeper, and during periods of low water you can spot the deeper, isolated knees. I prefer to fish them when there is some wind, because the wind seems to make them get tighter on the cover. Then the bass get right in the little cushions behind the waves and riffles. Also consider the sun, because as with any ambush point they'll usually be in the shade. Make a long cast about 10 feet past the knee and run your spinnerbait up to the knee and then drop it right down beside it.

If you want to see some of the most picturesque bass-fishing water in the world, then go fish North Carolina's North River with its cypress trees and knees. You won't catch many largemouths over 6 pounds, but the fish are scrappy and there's a lot of 'em in that river. It's definitely got the prettiest knees of any river I've ever fished.

FALLEN TREES

83 Bass Apartments

Regardless if they're in a natural lake in Michigan, a TVA lake in Tennessee, or a lake in southern Florida, fallen trees form super shallow-water structure for bass. And just about every lake and quite a few farm ponds have fallen trees. You really need to explore them as a pattern, because quite often you can have some bass bonanzas in them. The best type of lake for a fallen-tree pattern is one which has very little cover. At Lake Sydney Lanier in Georgia, most of the bank is rock or gravel or clay, but maybe every mile or so, there's one fallen tree, and it really concentrates fish. Lanier is fairly deep, and in lakes like it, 20 feet out from the bank the water is apt to be 15 or 20 feet deep. Therefore, you have some fairly deep structure involved, too.

On lakes with points, wind and wave action erodes the bank on the point and more trees consequently fall into the water. This is true on southern reservoirs, but the situation differs in northern lakes. At Vermilion and Lac LaCroix in Minnesota are fallen trees, but they're not on the main lake. What happens is in the spring when the ice is breaking up, tons of ice sweep away fallen trees along the main shoreline. Where you'll find fallen trees in the northern lakes is behind islands in protected coves and bays where the ice can't move them.

Boat positioning is the key to fishing fallen trees. I try to line up with the trunk so the limbs extend out toward me. I don't want the limbs crotched away from me because you'll hang up more that way. I want to get where I can throw a bait to the edge of the bank and come directly down the tree trunk. Beneath the trunk itself is the most likely spot for the bass to be. Here I'm talking primarily about trees in clear water. When it's clear, you usually can't get close enough to flip, so you need to cast. Flipping the fallen trees is great in dingy water, but it's not effective when the water is clear. I try to work each side of the trunk, and usually I can tell by the wind direction and the angle of the sun which side the bass are likely to be on. Since they face the wind, they'll normally be on the upcurrent side of the tree in the shadiest, thickest portion of it.

The easiest way to fish a fallen tree is with a shallow-running bait like a spinnerbait or a crank bait. If they're striking out of reflex, the

This fallen tree all by itself may be a real concentration point for bass, especially if there's little other cover on the lake.

first cast often catches the bass. I normally start off trying to see if I can catch a quick, easy fish with a spinnerbait or a crank bait. I'm trying to bump those limbs on my retrieve, and I'm using heavy tackle unless the water is super-clear. Even then, you might need to go to 20-pound line and get fewer strikes so you can horse the bass out of a big tree, such as an oak.

I won a B.A.S.S. tournament at Watts Bar Lake in Tennessee a few years ago, and only two of the bass I caught came on the fallen-tree pattern. I'd found a shallow spinnerbait pattern way up the lake around duck blinds, and that was how I caught my limit. After getting the limit, I decided to go after big fish, so I took a large Hellbender and started throwing to the fallen trees. One of the fallen-tree fish was a 6¾-pound largemouth, and the other was a 4½-pound smallmouth. Those two fish enabled me to beat Bobby Murray, who finished second. Watts Bar has a fallen tree probably every half mile along the steep banks. It's a TVA lake on the Tennessee River, and that river has a lot of current. I stayed on the upcurrent side of those trees, and the bass were in a feeding position on the deep part of the tree.

After the water warms up from the 55-to-60-degree range which is so good for spinnerbaits, you finally get into a worm-fishing situation. A 6-inch plastic worm rigged with a fairly heavy weight pegged to the worm head probably is the king bait for fallen-tree fishing in the summer. Too small a weight will swim through the branches all right, but it won't pull down through the branches and into the deep shade as a heavier weight will do. Therefore, I like a 1/4- or 3/8-ounce weight better than the 1/8- and 3/16-ounce sizes for fallen trees. The trick with the worm is to throw into the heaviest part of the tree and jig the bait. I don't mean jig it once or twice, but fifteen or twenty times.

I've probably already mentioned that I do a lot of diving. I've skindived all over Brazil and Mexico as well as on the East and West Coasts of the U.S.A. I've been down looking around fallen trees, and I have seen as many as fifteen to twenty bass packed up in one tree. The entire school would be there. One time I was diving at Bull Shoals Lake in Arkansas, and I found a fallen tree off a point, and I estimated thirty bass under that one tree. After leaving that tree, I got back in my boat and let the place cool off for a couple of hours. Then I went back there and made a good cast to the tree and jigged the worm and caught a small bass. I kept casting back there but didn't get any more strikes. Evidently they wised up after seeing that first one get caught. I figured they were still there, but instead of putting the diving tanks back on, I decided to wait awhile and come back later. An hour after that, I returned and got an instant strike on my first cast. But again I didn't get any more on repeated casts. Out of curiosity, I put my diving tanks back on and went down for another look. I thought they were still there, and they certainly were—about twenty-five of 'em. What I think happened was that those first eager ones which hit frightened the rest of the school. Possibly I should have changed my lure and maybe I could have caught a second bass. Changing size and color or going to a different lure often triggers other bass to hit.

One of the best tricks is to find a tree with a good concentration of bass. You might catch only one each time you fish it, but you can keep going back to it every hour or so during the day and maybe catch four or five. The most bass I ever caught out of one fallen tree was at Sydney Lanier in a Project: Sports Incorporated tournament back in 1972. Bobby Murray won it, Billy Westmorland came in second, and I finished third. I went back in a cove where a guy had cut a tree on his property and had let it fall over in the water. He had cut down several big trees, but way back in the cove was a small tree. It was a hickory, and it stuck over the creek channel in 10 feet of water. I threw a purple firetail worm into that tree and caught one on the first cast. I made seven consecutive casts to that tree and caught seven consecutive bass. My partner was so busy changing worms and netting my fish that he caught only two and missed two more. I don't know how many bass were in that tree, but we caught nine and had three or four more strikes. I estimated twenty to twenty-five eager bass there.

Those bass gave me the lead in the first round, and since I had about 30 pounds I figured I could come back to that same tree and win the tournament. I went back there during the second and third rounds and never had another strike. Schools of bass do frequent fallen trees, but transient bass come and go.

84 Flippers Fare Well

In the section on flipping, I mentioned fallen trees, but I didn't discuss this pattern in detail. I've already talked about how fallen trees are great shallow-water structure in a clear lake, but in a muddy or dingy lake, you can flip these trees. You can get close enough in your boat to flip and yet not spook the bass if the water is dingy or muddy. By flipping at close range, you can get that quiet, accurate presentation which you can't get by normal casting.

When I'm looking for a fallen tree to flip, I'm thinking about boat control. I'm trying to determine the best way to sneak up there with my flipping rod and lay that first cast in there perfectly. Just as with any good spot, the first cast usually is the best one. When you have a companion along and you're approaching the tree, he's likely wanting to make a long cast with his rod and reel. Try to talk him into holding back and waiting until the two of you get up to the tree. Be sure to make that first cast count. I try to get lined up on the tree trunk so I can make a 20-to-22-foot flip and drop my bait in a foot or so of water right close to the bank. I want to bounce that worm or jig right down the trunk. Every foot or so along the tree will be a side branch. When my line comes over each side branch, I'll jig the lure up and down five

In dingy water you can get right up to a fallen tree like this and flip it.

to ten times. This quiet presentation and accurate flip when your boat is in exactly the right position really can catch a big bass. Generally when the water is dingy to muddy, the bigger bass get into the fallen trees, whereas in clearer lakes, the lunkers often stay deeper and seldom if ever get up in the trees.

In Oklahoma and Texas in the summertime when the water temperature is 90 to 95 degrees, we catch 6-, 7-, and 8-pounders beneath fallen trees. Lots of times these fish are only a foot or so deep! There is plenty of cover and structure, and the water is dingy. An isolated fallen tree is better than a whole bunch of trees close together. A fallen tree on a point or close to deep water usually is better than a tree on a shallow flat. Again, an important factor is the shady side of the tree. Hold your boat into the wind, and you're better off if it's a gentle breeze rather than a strong wind. It's hard to get close to the fish without scaring them when waves are slapping the sides of the boat. Also, run your trolling motor at the lowest possible speed, and *don't* start and stop the trolling motor, because this is likely to alert the bass. Conjure up an image of where the bass is lying because of the wind and water current, the angle of the sun, and the thickest portions of the tree. Try to locate the best potential spot, because that first cast is important.

The biggest problem with the fallen-tree pattern is that you often don't know how deep the fish is. If the bank has a sharp slope, you don't know if he's in 2 or 8 feet of water. But with a 7½-foot flipping stick and a good, accurate cast, you can work the entire tree trunk. If the tree is unusually large, you need to start on the outside and work in. If you tried to work from the bank out, you might scare the bass beneath the boat.

When you're riding down the lake and have your flipping rod along, even if it's hot summertime don't pass up a fallen tree if the water's a little dingy and there is a little wind current. Not only do trophy bass get beneath these trees, but by flipping you might be probing a spot nobody else has gotten a lure into all that week. It's possible to jig in a heavy, thick spot in that tree where nobody else has ever fished.

Deep Structure

THE VALUE OF DEEP STRUCTURE

Deep structure is for me the most difficult but most productive way to fish. It involves a series of patterns for 5-to-50-foot structures primarily on main-lake areas not often fished by the average angler. Also involved are schools and concentrations of bass. When I go to deep structure, I'm looking for the mother lode—for the way to win a tournament. I've always believed the best way to win a tournament is to find five good patterns with at least one of them being a deep-structure pattern with a school of bass.

The advantage of finding a school of deepwater fish is that they're less affected by environmental conditions. That school likely will stay there throughout a barometric change or a storm front or a change from cloudy to clear weather. They're a more stable school of fish, and they're that mythical lode. I'm talking about schools of bass like those which ten years ago were found in Alabama's Lake Eufaula.

When I think of those schools, I can't help but remember the Eufaula National B.A.S.S. tournament in July of 1969 when Rip Nunnery and Gerald Blanchard each caught their fifteen-bass daily limits, and those thirty bass weighed 197 pounds.

Out of thirteen major bass events I've won, about half of them have involved at least one deepwater pattern which produced the winning margin if not all my fish. I don't always need 50-foot structure. I might find a school 5 feet deep on a bar. I won an American Bass Fisherman tournament at Toledo Bend on a spot only 6 feet deep on the top which dropped off to 15 feet on the sides, but I was out in the middle of the lake using strictly a deepwater-structure technique. A recent tournament I fished was the National Bass Association's Florida National at Lake Okeechobee, and Hank Parker from South Carolina won it by catching his bass on a crank bait 9 to 13 feet deep on a dam abutment up the Kissimmee River. It was deep structure where he had a school of fish right in the eddy in from the current.

Structure does not have one clear-cut definition which covers it all. For example, a roadbed certainly is a different type of structure from a submerged grass line such as you might find in Okeechobee. I think of deep structure as some type of irregular feature which contrasts to the surrounding area. It's generally connected with a dropoff or some deeper-water access, but not always. The edges of pepper grass 8 feet deep in Okeechobee could be called deep structure. Because of currents or the composition of the lake bottom, the grass quits growing there and it forms the edge even though the water is still 8 feet deep. At Toledo Bend you might find a treeline in 25 feet of water with all the surrounding area 25 feet deep, but the edge of those trees are the irregular feature and form the structure. The best irregular features are those which are the most isolated. This is best exemplified by a creek channel, which bass anglers know is one of the hottest types of structure. The best part of that creek channel would be a very sharp bend out in the middle of a cove *if* that bend is the only one around and is the most irregular feature on the creek. However, if there are five other bends within 100 yards, they all will hold a few fish, and you won't find that huge concentration all in one spot.

When I look for deep structure, I'm looking for an easy way to catch a limit of bass quickly. Probably the most unique deep-structure situation I ever encountered in tournament competition was at Eufaula, Ala., in 1970. There was no cutoff practice period back then in B.A.S.S. competition, and I'd been fishing the lake for two weeks. I'd located about twenty good creek and river channel ledges. Since I didn't want to catch every bass during practice, I'd go to the ledges with a worm rigged on a hook and on another rod I'd have a worm with no hook. I wanted to see how big the bass were, so I'd catch one or two. Then I'd throw a worm with no hook in there and see how many strikes I could get. I had five holes with 5-to-6-pound largemouths, and in two or three of them I could get a strike on nearly every cast for eight to ten casts. I wasn't sure if most of these strikes were from different fish or from one real hungry, aggressive fish. There might have been only two or three fish on a ledge, but there might have been twenty-five. I had no way of knowing without catching a bunch of them.

The first day of the tournament, I went to holes which didn't have big concentrations of fish, and I caught only two or three at the most from any one spot. I had only a mediocre stringer, and part of the reason was I'd gotten paired with Curt Van Zalkenburg, and he'd never caught a bass above 8¾ pounds. The first hole I took him to, he caught one that was 8 pounds, 15 ounces, and at the second hole he got a 7-pounder, and at the third he caught a 6-pounder. This unnerved me, and I figured I'd better not take him to my best holes because he was so hot that day that he might catch everything I'd found. I figured it was better to save my two best holes for the second day, and hope my partner then wouldn't be as familiar with deep-water structure. I did manage to weigh in a 20-pound string that day, but there were so many fish caught that I was way down between twentieth and thirtieth place.

The second day I was paired with a Tennessee fisherman who was primarily a shallow-water fisherman; he'd never fished a worm much

You can't fish deep structure unless you know where it is and what the situation is like down there. Here I'm taking the water temperature, after marking the spot with a float—a necessity if you want to return to an open-water location with no landmarks to go by.

in deep water. I told him I wanted to go down and fish some 17-to-25-foot depths on the edges of the river channels. Since he didn't have the tackle or the know-how for this type of fishing, this would be the time to go to my very best hole first. I made nearly a sixty-mile run from the head of the lake all the way down to the dam, and I pulled up on the ledge and anchored the boat in the right position. I had cross-triangulated my spot and knew precisely how to line it up with some trees. The wind was blowing twenty miles an hour, the waves were 2 feet high, and the boat was swinging on the 100-foot anchor rope I had out. There was one super spot where this 15-foot bar dropped into the channel about 10 feet in diameter, and I'd caught several 6-pounders there in practice. I got one about 8½ pounds on my first cast. I screamed for him to get the net, and he netted the fish. I picked up another rod and threw in another worm and jigged it three or four times on that ledge, and I got one almost as big as the first one. My partner was just about ready to cast when I hooked that second one. He got the net and netted it. Then I caught a third fish about 7¼ pounds before he threw. I made six consecutive casts and caught six straight bass, with the smallest one 6½ pounds and the largest 8¾. He managed to make three casts and catch three, with his smallest 7¼ and his largest 8¼. Those nine bass we caught on nine casts weighed almost 60 pounds.

We continued to catch fish there, and I ended up catching twelve off that spot which totaled 54 pounds. My partner had six or seven which totaled 37 pounds. That creek ledge at 15 feet deep was the shallowest water around, and acres and acres of the surrounding water were over 20 feet deep. Also, there was a lot of secondary brush on that ledge, and the brush gave the fish the cover they needed. While the top was 15 feet deep and the bottom of the ledge about 30, the fish were just off the top from 17 to about 19 feet deep. Of all the fish I caught there, 17 feet was the magic depth. I caught over 100 pounds of bass in that tournament—the most I've ever caught in competition—but finished second behind Bill Adair of Memphis, who had 116 pounds, 6 ounces.

That pattern had a very interesting part to it. In the first part of this book I told how bass in a school often hit out of mimicry or monkey-see-monkey-do. After you catch one or two, they often wise up and get reluctant to strike. After I'd caught six in a row and my partner had caught three on three straight throws, we alerted the rest of the fish in that school. Then I did something which is a very important part of this pattern, and that was changing both the size and the color of the worm. I had been catching them on a big 8-inch blue worm with a heavy slip sinker. After making five or six unproductive casts with the blue worm, I changed to a light ¼-ounce weight and a 6-inch black worm. This gave me a slower-sinking bait which contrasted sharply to what I'd been using. On the first throw with the new worm, I caught one. My partner too switched to a black worm, and he caught one. I caught a second fish and then missed one, and finally they quit hitting the black worm. I changed again and went to a red 8-inch worm and caught a couple more. I ended up changing to five or six different colors, and caught bass on four of 'em.

Deep-structure patterns go with electronic locators or depth-finders the same as mustard goes with hot dogs. Years ago before these locators made their way to the freshwater fishing scene, men like ol' Shorty Evans from Missouri said they always quit bass fishing at the end of May and didn't go anymore until cool weather arrived in October. Back in the 1940s and '50s they caught almost all their bass along the banks, and when hot weather arrived, they often did very poorly on the banks. Shorty says he knew there were bass in deep water, but he didn't know where to go look for them. Therefore, the deep-structure pattern is relatively new to nearly all bass fishermen, with a few old-timers being the lone exceptions, as it didn't get going until depthfinders started becoming popular in the late 1950s.

As I mentioned earlier, Tommy McNey and I started getting on to deep structure in Maryland when we fished some of the old water-supply reservoirs in the Baltimore and Washington regions. I remember reading an article by Carl Lowrance and Ted Trueblood about fishing deep water. They didn't call it "structure."

Buck Perry coined that term in the 1960s. They just called it deep-water fishing, and they pointed out how trout, saltwater fish, and bass would school up in deep water. Lowrance had developed his locator, and he told how to find schools of fish. They actually were going out looking for schools of fish; they didn't emphasize looking for ledges, dropoffs, and creek channels at that time. They knew that Carl's locator would detect fish, and that was the property they stressed.

Well, the first time McNey and I ever used the locator we purchased, we thought we could take it out in the middle of Tridelphia

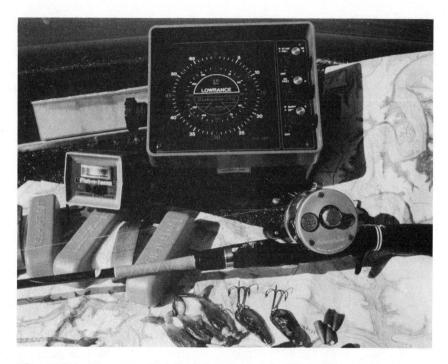

The tackle and lures may look good, but they won't do it for you without the other equipment shown—topo map, locator, temperature gauge, and marker floats.

Reservoir and see giant schools of bass and anchor there and catch dozens of 'em all day long. We didn't get a strike. By the third trip, we figured we were doing things wrong, so we decided to progress deeper gradually until we found a school of bass. We decided the best way to do this was by trolling. Our first successful trip with the locator was when we trolled small Flatfish plugs with light casting tackle. We thought 10-foot water would be a good starting point—and to this day, I don't know why we thought that—and we trolled nearly ten miles of the lake at exactly 10 feet deep. We didn't know anything about structure or what we were looking for. We didn't catch any fish, and we decided 10 feet was wrong so let's try 14 feet. We trolled a few hours out across points and back in coves while keeping at the 14-foot level. We were surprised at how the contour of the bottom ran; we hadn't realized there was so much shallow water way out in the middle. Well, the 14-foot depth didn't work either, so then we went to 20 feet. We trolled a big bunch of giant bars out in the middle, and Tommy caught one about 4 pounds on the U-20 Flatfish. We trolled back and forth, and we didn't have markers and didn't watch the locator very closely to tell what kind of a bottom we were over. Well, we ended up catching four or five bass and missed a couple in that 100-yard area. They probably all were in a 20-foot area, but we didn't have any way to line up on a spot.

At that time my father was a hydraulic engineer for the U.S. Geological Survey, and one of his jobs was building dams. The Geological Survey has the finest contour maps in the world. Dad didn't fish, but he had all these contour maps, and I'd seen them around the house. In fact, when in high school I'd worked for him part-time, surveying dam-site areas, so I knew basically what contour maps were. I suggested to Tommy that we look at my dad's maps of Tridelphia and the other reservoirs we fished, and that way we could find more bars and shoals. We looked at them, and the first thing we started noticing was all these old house foundations. We didn't know a thing in the world about fishing a house foundation or even if it would be a good spot. But we did figure nobody ever had fished them and that most of them had cellars and good places like that for bass to hide, and we thought that just maybe they'd pay off. Most of the lake bottom was clean, and we knew from our shallow-water fishing that the trick was to fish cover, so we decided to look for cover in the deep water.

We spent our next trip out on a big bar trying to find one of the house foundations, and sure enough, we found it. We saw something big rise up off the bottom, and the water got deeper where the old cellar had been. We started trolling over it. We got hung up pretty bad, but we started catching bass. The water seemed to be about the right depth—15 to 20 feet. This was our first bonanza, our first school, and we marked the spot pretty closely by lining up some trees on the bank. We kept fishing right on the house foundation, because that was exactly where the bass were. This was our first really successful trip where we had a deepwater pattern put together.

From there on, it was just a constant progression over the next three or four years of picking out pattern features such as roadbeds, house foundations, underwater islands, and creek channels and fishing them as patterns with marker buoys and the right lures.

Today, my deep-structure fishing is a very demanding, scientific challenge of searching out the most irregular features of a lake and finding big schools of fish on these places which probably seldom if ever have been fished.

Many bass fishermen who enjoy catching their fish on topwater plugs and popping bugs in shallow water don't like deep-structure fishing, and a lot of 'em never will like it. I don't recommend that anyone try to learn it unless he absolutely really wants to do it. What turns me on the most about deep water is catching ten bass in ten casts. To me, that's the epitome of bass fishing, and you certainly can do this when you find a school on deep structure.

POINTS

85 Progress Deeper

Points are the most readily found structure in any lake. Regardless of what farm pond, lake, or reservoir you're on, there has to be a point somewhere. By definition, a point is an extension of land which gradually slopes deeper. And somewhere out on that point the depth will be suitable for the bass. One of the biggest problems in structure fishing is finding the right depth for the pattern on a given day. The depth the fish are in is determined by several factors, such as amount of light, water clarity, and water temperature. Points are the easiest places to find the right depth.

Pull up to a point and start fishing at a reasonable depth, say 5 to 10 feet, and systematically fish this depth. Probably the best way to work that depth range on a point is with a crank bait, such as a Bomber or a Hellbender. If you don't catch any at this level, then you'll need to go to strictly structure lures, such as plastic worms, jigs, grubs, and spoons. When I work the 10-to-20-foot depths on the point, I usually go to a plastic worm. If I know the fish are there, a plastic worm is the best way to catch 'em, but probably the fastest way to find out if they're there is to throw a grub on spinning tackle with 8-pound line or a 1/2- or 3/4-ounce spoon on a casting rod with 14- or 17-pound line.

The advantage to structure fishing is that in schools of bass, there is almost always an eager one. No matter what lure you're using, if you throw it into the middle of a school of bass, that one eager fish usually will hit it. You might catch only the one eager bass, however.

Here, I'm fishing near a point where I had put out markers to remind myself of an underwater ledge I had found.

You can progress deeper on points on natural lakes in the north and on farm ponds the same as on southern impoundments. You can progress deeper on *any* point until you finally make contact with the fish. When I catch that first one, I'm hoping I've found a big school, but lots of times there is only one or two bass there. After catching that first one, if I make two or three more casts to that spot and don't get a strike, then I usually start changing lures to see if I can come up with something the school is more interested in. I'll also try some vertical jigging. If none of this works within five minutes or so, it's very doubtful that a school is there. The precept of schools of bass on structure is that when you find them, you can catch them, or at least get a few strikes. Very seldom will you find twenty or thirty bass in a school and not be able to get some strikes.

The point is an irregular feature itself, but remember that somewhere on the point is a key irregularity. It could be a big rock or tree stumps or a little ledge which drops another foot or so, forming cover and a subtle type of structure. I like to criss-cross a point several times. The boat won't scare the fish when they're 15 feet or deeper. I slowly idle back and forth across the point, and I've got a marker buoy handy. When I see that key irregularity on my locator, I drop the marker. The bass might not be there because the depth could be

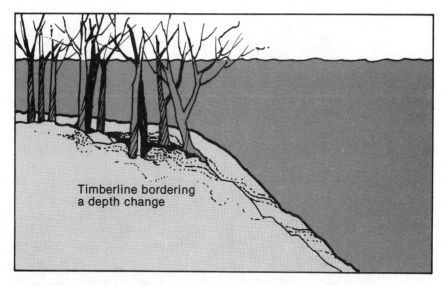

Timberline bordering
a depth change

Most timberlines have potential, but those that correspond with a change in depth are generally the best.

wrong, but that spot gives me something to key on and serves as a reference point.

Lots of people ask me how I find fish on a strange lake—one I've never been on. My approach is to go to main-lake exposed points. They're the first places to look, and I progress deeper and deeper and try to make contact with at least one fish and with luck a school of fish. Generally that establishes the pattern depth for the day. At times on Bull Shoals in Arkansas I've pulled up to a point and caught a bass or two and had a couple more strikes and then the action quit. Then I've put my diving tanks on and gone down to see what was there. Sure enough, at one depth in one general area I'd see a dozen or so bass packed up right where I was fishing. They're not always easy to catch, and it might be because they're off their feed.

86 Cast Your Bait to the Wind

The best condition I look for when I'm fishing structure and particularly points is a windy day. Lots of fishermen say they hope it's calm and clear so they can get out and fish the middle of the lake. I use

First I dress for the weather, then I cast into the wind and let my lure travel with the baitfish the bass are after—with good results.

a big 18-foot Ranger bass boat with a giant Johnson outboard and a powerful 24-volt trolling motor, and I'm able to navigate safely in open water even on windy days. And on those windy days are when I catch most of my fish on deep structure. This is particularly true on a clear lake where they're fairly hard to catch on a bright, calm day. The surface is so broken up and the light refraction is so great in the choppy water that the bass don't see as well, and there's also a lot more current involved. The wind is pushing the water and causing a current.

A school of fish is so competitive that when they're feeding they quite often get ahead of one another. One bass is feeding and another shad comes by and the second fish darts out in front of the first one to beat him to the food. They're leapfrogging each other, and the result is they all get on the upwind edge of the point. They might be 16 feet deep, but they're at 16 feet at the most upwind edge of that point.

Again, you need to match the hatch to catch them. Have your plastic worm or jig or spoon coming down with the current just the way the shad are traveling. Therefore, you need to cast *into* the wind or maybe slightly crosswind so that you can retrieve your bait with the current. This is very effective in deep-structure fishing, although a lot of fishermen don't have suitable boats to stay out there in the wind, nor do they have the casting ability to throw into the wind. Certainly it's much easier to cast with the wind at your back; many prefer to throw downwind because they can cast twice as far without a backlash. It's much more difficult to throw into the wind and to hold your boat in position when it's windy, but this is by far the most productive time for point fishing.

87   Slither the Worm, Jig the Rig

Slithering the worm or jigging the rig is a more efficient way to fish a point. Since bass on a point often are structure fish and schooled up, I want to throw a lure which is quick. I want to be able to pull up on fifteen to twenty points in a day and make just a couple of casts with something fast. If they're there, fine! Then I'll fish 'em hard. But if they're not on the point, I'll move to the next one. This is playing the percentages, just what you need to do when you're fishing points. Cover a lot of points quickly. The quickest way to fish a point is with a jigging-type lure such as a spoon, grub, or Little George. This might not be the *best* way to fish the point, but it's the *quickest* way. Here again I'm trying to capitalize on schooling bass with the hope that an eager bass will run out and grab my lure and tip me off to the presence of a big school. If I'm going down a bank and catching a bass here and there, it would require a totally different approach. I wouldn't be making those two or three quick casts and then cranking up and moving on.

When making those few casts on the point, I don't really need to catch the fish. Just a strike tells me to keep fishing that point at least a few casts more. As soon as I get a strike, I throw out a marker buoy on that spot. Lots of times the main lake points are more than 100 yards out, and the marker buoy serves as the exact reference point. Then I generally go to my most productive baits, and this means slithering the worm. When you've got a school located and you know right where they are, there's no better way to mop up on 'em than with a plastic worm. This is especially true if they're not extra-eager. If they're in the middle of a feeding frenzy right at a major solunar

Once you've located a school on a point, you can harvest them with a slithered plastic worm even when they've lost interest in the spoon or jig you found them with.

period or during a barometric change and they're simply going bananas and keep on hitting a spoon, I won't change to a worm because I can catch 'em faster on the spoon. I could get a limit in twelve to fifteen casts with the spoon, but probably no more than 5 percent of the time will they hit the spoon that good. At some time when you're fishing that school, you'll probably need to go to the worm.

Not only is the plastic worm provocative and deadly when it's slithered through the school, but it has the advantage of enticing the bigger bass better. I often catch my bigger bass on the worm. But I usually locate and catch numbers of 'em on the spoon or jig.

STANDING TIMBER

Older fishermen who grew up fishing natural lakes in states like Wisconsin, Michigan, and Maine or fishing the tidewater areas do not know personally what fishing standing timber is. This is a fairly recent phenomenon brought about by the Army Corps of Engineers. During the past thirty years, the corps has created several million acres of reservoirs. While growing up in Maryland, I never saw any bass water with standing timber except for a couple of small farm ponds. When I was in the army at Ft. Jackson in South Carolina and went to Santee-Cooper for the first time back in 1963, I had my first real experience with standing timber. I really didn't know how to handle it, because all I had with me was spinning tackle with 12- and 14-pound line and I didn't know the techniques.

Santee was my proving ground, and after I learned to master standing timber there, I fished the trees in Toledo Bend, Sam Ray-

Standing timber, a common phenomenon of manmade lakes, is productive all year long one way or another.

burn, Seminole, Ross Barnett, and many of the East Texas lakes. There are probably about twenty-five lakes in excess of 30,000 acres in the country which have a lot of standing timber. And there are several patterns connected solely with timber. They're so special that I consider them separate patterns.

Standing timber is productive all year long. Whatever the month, there's some type of pattern at some depth which will work.

88 Timberline Treat

A timberline treat goes back to the original concept of structure as being an irregular feature. Approximately 160,000 of Toledo Bend's 190,000 acres are standing timber. Every type of timber pattern known can be found on that lake. Toledo Bend probably gets more fishermen per year than any lake in the country, and in many areas of the lake are straight lines of timber. This reservoir simply has so much timber and so many bass that there probably are more schools of them than in any other lake in the world. They get on these timberlines and roam up and down. Even though the water might be 25 feet deep all along the timberline, there are some irregularities. I like to find things like a small ditch or roadbed crossing the timberline. Another irregularity is where one type of tree quits growing and another species takes over. Another potential spot is a leaning tree or a fallen tree in contrast to the standing trees. These are the types of places which might cause a roaming school to hold on for a while. They might not stay long, but they might be there long enough for you to catch several.

On other timberlines are roving schools, and their locations depend somewhat on the bait. If it's late fall and windy, maybe a big bunch of threadfin shad are moving along the timberline and the bass are there feeding on 'em. In that situation, one of the best ways to fish would be with a crank bait. At least this would be a good way to find them. Go along with your trolling motor on high in open water and throw either parallel down the treeline or else back 20 to 30 feet into the timber with any big-billed crank bait such as the Bomber or Hellbender or Fat Rap. Plugs like these bump through the timber good without hanging up much. When you find one in water deeper than 15 feet along a timberline, you'll almost always find more than one. I've

A string taken in standing timber on Toledo Bend. Usually a crank bait is the best locator, and then you can really clean up.

seen schools so big along timberlines at Toledo Bend that three of us would be limited out in thirty to forty casts apiece.

This is a good tournament pattern in a bass-club event or in national competition, and hundreds of tournaments have been won on it at Toledo Bend. The first tournament I ever fished was there in 1970, and I came in second. I jigged spoons on the creek channels, but Mike Bono of Louisiana won it with 94¼ pounds, jigging on the timberlines. His bass were suspended, but they were 40 feet deep. When a lot of timber is present, bass are suspended at intermediate depths much like schools of striped bass and crappies. You can sort of forget how deep the water is along a timberline. The pattern depth is what's important. The bass might be 18 feet deep while the water is 40 feet deep, and then you'd need to fish your lures in that 18-foot range. A lot of different lures work on the timberlines, but the crank bait probably is the best way to find them. Once you find them, then you can get over them with a worm or spoon and drop it down to the depth they're at and jig 'em up. In very heavy brush, most of my biggest bass come by jigging down the edges of the trees.

89 Points of Interest

In the section under land points, I mentioned that probably the easiest way to find fish is to find a point. This is exactly the same with timber. Probably the best way to find a concentration of bass is to find a timberline and then the point. Again, we're dealing with suspended fish and working for them at intermediate depths.

A few years ago I was fishing an ABF tournament at Lake Seminole. Through the years I've caught some 10-pound Seminole bass on big Hellbenders, and this particular time I was fishing the Hellbender on a combination deal where a bunch of grass in the Spring Creek Flats stretched out and hit cypress-tree points in the old creek bottom. The grass was in 12 feet of water, and the cypress trees were in 35 feet of water. These flats extended out to within 15 or 20 feet of the cypress trees, and they dropped into the old creek bottom. The flats had been cleared of timber, and the cypress trees were the only timber around. In the first round of the tournament I'd found these bass out there, and I had the second-biggest catch—about 30 pounds that first day. I'd caught them on the points of grass, and I figured I'd stay with that pattern.

The second day the wind blew real hard, and it was so rough I couldn't fish out there. I didn't do as well and I dropped a couple of places in the standings. On the third and final day, my first-day partner had the two pink-eyed Hellbenders I'd lent him. He asked me if I cared if he fished out where we were the first day, and I said I didn't mind as long as he didn't fish that one point of grass near the point of timber where I had caught most of my fish. I got out there, and he'd kept his word; he wasn't on that point but about 100 feet away on a

Probably the best way to find a concentration of bass is to hit the point on a timberline. If the wind is blowing baitfish toward the point, so much the better.

cypress-tree point which I hadn't been fishing. Little did I know when I got there that he had just landed a 7-pounder. He also had a 5-pounder and a couple 4-pounders. He knew I'd be asking him questions, and he told his partner that when I came over to talk with them, they should lie and just say that there were no fish there. I had fished my spot and didn't catch any, and he said they hadn't done any good either when in reality he had over 30 pounds in the boat. He didn't want to tell me they were suspended on that cypress-tree point.

I caught only a few fish that day, and he had about 35 pounds. I knew timbered points were a good pattern, but I didn't try any after he'd said he wasn't doing any good. He didn't want to steal my spot, so he'd decided to try the cypress-tree point because it looked so good. He knew the point was sort of deep, and he thought that since the wind was blowing hard, maybe those fish had moved. Plus, he saw something I didn't see—some shad out there. Seagulls were sitting in the trees, and there were so many shad being blown in that occasionally the gulls would swoop down and grab them. I simply hadn't been observant enough. If I had been watching closely, I'd have seen him catch a fish or two and I'd have seen the seagulls dipping down after the shad.

Mary Ann and I went out the next day with our son, Scott, who was only a few months old at the time. We had him all bundled up, and when we got to that spot, I caught one almost 6 pounds on my first cast. Then I got a 5, and I sat there and caught bass after bass. That had been the school of fish I'd been into that first day of the tournament. They'd simply moved from the grass point to the timber point.

This is a pattern which often works on suspended fish, and the key to it seems to be whether or not a bunch of baitfish are present. Look for a timbered point which is facing the wind. A wind blowing in on a point moves more bait and shad in there than if it's blowing away from the point. I also look for an isolated point—the only one around. If possible, I want the point to have some irregular features about its depth. A point which ends on a creek channel or has deeper-water access is also better.

---

90   Isolated Patches

Many times I've talked about isolated cover being the key to finding bass. What makes me think of isolated timber patches is the fact that some Corps of Engineers impoundments don't have solid bunches of timber. In Table Rock Lake, many areas with timber were cleared, but small patches still remain. One type of patch there is cedar trees. Cedar doesn't rot, and these trees have all their limbs and are fresh-looking even though they've been there twenty years.

Rather than find a giant stand of cedars, I like to find small clusters with two or three trees. An entire cove might have only two cedars. On a bright, sunny day, particularly when the fish are suspended and half off their feed and are looking for a place to hide in that clear water, sometimes a couple of cedars concentrate many of the bass in that cove. I've wormed these trees and run small plugs like the Speed Shad through them, but probably the most effective way I've found on Table Rock is to use a spoon. It sounds crazy to think you can get a spoon down through a cedar tree, but you can. If you really are getting hung up, you can take a pair of pliers and cut off one of the hooks.

If you pull up to a cedar tree in 7 or 8 feet of water and jig it carefully with the spoon, you might get hung up every fifth or sixth time. If that happens, just hold your rod in a horizontal position and twitch it back and forth vertically, and almost invariably you'll jig

These lonely trees may be more productive cover than a giant stand of flooded cedars.

your spoon loose. Again, these fish are suspended at an intermediate depth, and I mark my line with a felt-tip pen at the depth where the bass are.

Isolated patches are apt to pay off all year long. During the pre-spawn season in a lake without a lot of cover except the isolated timber patches, big female bass often come up to shallower water. Even though they're not ready to move into the very shallow areas, they move up and suspend themselves in isolated patches of trees. I've seen this happen many times when the water temperature is a little less than 60 degrees in the early spring. Bass of 5 to 8 pounds are lying just a foot or so deep in thick trees way out in the middle of the lake. Tommy Salisbury and I found 'em like that at Toledo Bend after three real warm days. The top 3 feet of water had warmed up 5 or 6 degrees, and one cove had a bass by every tree which was big and isolated.

---

91 Different Trees

Different trees are really the key to any successful timber fisherman. Such an angler will go into a stand of flooded timber and find a pattern. Not all the trees will be the same kind, and there will be a pattern to the type of tree he catches bass on. One year at Toledo Bend I remember that beech trees were the hot pattern. One time at Sam Rayburn, I recall we were looking exclusively for ironwood trees. We were jigging them, and the ironwoods happened to be lining the small washes and creek channels and depressions. Actually we were fishing dropoffs somewhat. We couldn't see where the dropoffs were by looking through the timber and the maps usually weren't that accurate, but by finding the ironwoods we found the structure and consequently where the fish were.

At Table Rock, many times I've gone into a stand of oak trees and found nothing but solid oaks with the exception of one cedar tree, and the bass would be around the cedar because it had a little bit more cover. Suppose you're in a pine thicket and 99 percent of the trees are pines, but they're not all the same diameter or don't all have the same number of limbs. I think the most productive tree I've ever found is a leaning tree—one which has fallen over completely or partially and is lodged in with the others. This fallen tree gives the bass horizontal running room. When the sun is out, a bass gets very little shade from a standing tree, but a leaning tree gives him a long strip of shade.

In this latter case, the species of tree might be the same, but one of them is leaning or else is bigger. At Lake Oolegah, Mary Ann and I caught more than 40 pounds of bass one day on spinnerbaits strictly by finding the biggest pecan trees. These had big limbs which had fallen off and had formed a canopy of heavy cover right at the base of the trees in fairly shallow water. The limbs which had fallen off the smaller trees were naturally smaller and had floated away.

Identify how big the tree is, what type it is, the depth of water it's in, what kind of branches, and whether it leans. Almost 90 percent of the time in any timbered reservoir, different trees offer some pattern which will pay off. Find that pattern and stick with it.

Sometimes the type of trees you're fishing in is important. Different species indicate different bottom structure, and extra-big trees and leaning trees make special cover.

ROCKS AND RIP-RAP

92 Pre-Spawn Picnic

Deep structure is a relative term. How deep is deep? It could be 5 feet or 50 feet. Many of the southern reservoirs I'm very familiar with are flatland reservoirs. They don't have many rocks, and most of the rocks you find are around the dam and the bridge abutments in the form of rip-rap. Occasionally there might be some rocks and bricks piled up from old house foundations which were torn down, but in these cases the rocks were put there by man.

As I mentioned during pre-spawn conditions, bass frequently seek the warmth of a warm cove. They also seek the warmth of a warm rock. It's amazing how much radiated energy can be put out by the

An exposed rock like this can absorb an enormous amount of heat from the sun, and spring pre-spawners may cozy right up to it.

sun and absorbed in rocks. At Santee and in other southern lakes, I've found big female bass in 50-degree water lying right in the shallow rocks 2 to 3 feet deep. This is particularly true in calm areas, such as the calm side of a bridge abutment. This most often happens where the rocks are on the north side of the lake, getting the best sun exposure from the south and the best wind protection. The female fish are in there so that radiation will help their eggs to reach maturity.

This is a pre-spawn picnic for fishermen, and it's mainly a crankbait pattern. Not many crank baits can be cast out and retrieved over 10 to 12 feet deep, and these rip-raps often hold fish from 3 to 12 feet deep. Since I'm after big pre-spawners, my favorite plugs are big ones such as the 600 Series Bombers, 900 Series Hellbenders, No. 7 Fat Raps, and big Mud Bugs. I like bright crawfish-colored lures because they're being fished in main-lake conditions, and quite often in the early spring in the southern reservoirs the main-lake areas are dingy. Dingy water normally is found in lakes such as Santee, Ross Barnett, and Seminole, and large, bright-colored crank baits which run deep are needed.

I often get parallel with the rip-rap and keep my boat in 10 feet of water if I'm using a lure which runs 10 feet deep. (If my lure runs only 7 feet down, I'll get the boat in 7 feet of water.) I want to cast at such an angle that my lure barely nicks the rip-rap four or five times on the retrieve and the angle it's diving corresponds with the angle of the rip-rap. I'm trying to keep it from diving too deep and getting hung in the crevices.

Pre-spawn bass don't crash into a lure and bust it hard. Probably the biggest trick with the retrieve is the pause, slowdown, or change-up tactic. I've fooled partners in the boat with me in tournaments by cranking the plug hard to get it down 4 to 6 feet deep, and then I stop reeling for a second and the plug starts floating back up. Big females are famous for following plugs this time of year, and when it pauses, they run into it and engulf it almost out of reflex action. On the strike when you pause the bait, you've been feeling that ounce or so of pressure from the plug and then when you resume cranking, you don't feel anything. The bass has it and is coming toward you at about the same speed you're reeling. She'll hold it for only two to three seconds and then spit it out. Anytime you have a lighter feeling, you'd better set the hook.

I use Stren fluorescent line, and that's very important in my crank-bait fishing because at times in the early spring when the water temperature's in the low 50s, I've had bass strike the lure from straight behind it. I don't feel the strike then, but I'm watching the line for any twitch or side movement. I could have hit a limb or a rock, and I'm frequently setting the hook on what are not fish. But when those twitches or side movements are fish, I'll catch ones which guys who aren't paying attention will miss.

This is almost like jigging a spoon. Many times I've seen fishermen not set the hook on crank-bait strikes. They keep retrieving and their line moves a few feet, and a huge boil comes up behind the lure. That was a big fish engulfing the lure unnoticed.

Glen Lau did an interesting thing with Homer Circle several years ago when he was doing his *Fisherman* series of films with Homer at Silver Springs and Salt Springs in Florida. Homer would be cranking a crank bait, and Glen would be filming the whole scene underwater. He's probably got ten scenes where a bass between 5 and 10 pounds came up and engulfed Homer's plug and held it for a second or two and spat it out. Glen would finish filming and would come up to the surface and ask Homer why he hadn't set the hook, and Homer would say, "Why? I didn't feel a strike." It's amazing in the spring with pre-spawn fish how many aren't detected. Many of them strike but you don't feel 'em.

Fishing rip-rap is a matter of mechanics. You need to get positioned right, and watch your line for a twitch or side movement.

HOUSE FOUNDATIONS

93 Hotspot Hotels

Mainly in the southern reservoirs, the rock and brick from house foundations is the only rock found other than the rip-rap. Big house foundations are in many flatland reservoirs, and several have much deeper water connected with them. The deeper water might be a 10-foot-deep cellar or old well. In the Piedmont sections of the country, the old houses often were on hills. If you find a good structure, such as an underwater hill, there's apt to be a house foundation holding a good school of fish.

A good contour map and a good locator are crucial in order to fish a house foundation. The U.S. Geological Survey 7½-minute map is the standard quadrangle map, and it shows more detail than any of the other maps. Before the river was dammed up and the water impounded, the government paid the landowner for his house and property, and the house was torn down. The 7½-minute quadrangle map will show virtually all the big house foundations. A big black square structure on the map usually will be a temporary building. Oblong marks on the map probably are the original house, and the barn might be big and square, and other buildings usually are shown as small squares.

Look for the old house itself. It usually was on the highest hill and is the most conspicuous structure. With a good contour map you can halfway find it, and with a good locator you can look for the double echo. When you have your locator set for a sand, clay, or gravel bottom and you get over the rock from a house foundation, which is more reflective, you'll see the double echo. I set my locator to where I'm at

Here I've located a house foundation with my depth finder and am tying on a lure to check it out.

the threshold of an echo, and what I mean by this is that the clay, gravel, or sand bottom barely starts to echo. Since rock is more reflective, it causes a strong echo when I get over it. When I find a house foundation, I throw out a marker buoy.

I can think of what Chuck Regnier and I called the "smallmouth hotel," a house foundation in Loch Raven Reservoir in Maryland. Chuck caught an 8-pound, 2-ounce smallmouth off it, and that fish held up as the state record for several years. This foundation was a very peculiar and interesting structure. It was at the end of a large shoal which extended out 300 to 400 yards from shore, and it was the only irregular feature in the area. It had walls which extended 7 to 8 feet up off the bottom, and the cellar was 8 or 9 feet deep. The bottom was about 15 feet deep, and the cellar was almost 25 feet. Every spring during pre-spawn conditions, we'd bounce big Bombers and big Waterdogs off the walls, and for about five consecutive years we caught two or three smallmouths per spring from 5½ to 6 pounds.

Probably my best house foundation ever was one of several at San-

Foundations are apt to be in deep water, and a float helps to keep the spot marked so you can return to it.

tee, and I called it *the* house foundation. It was an old plantation house in 22 feet of water. The walls came up about 4 feet, and the cellar was 7 or 8 feet deep. I anchored on it and caught stripers many times, and occasionally when I'd pull up my anchor, I brought up an old brick with it. I was using those old naval-type anchors with the ears. Some of the bricks I pulled up had dates on 'em—1780. I should have kept them, but I didn't.

This foundation was a very good trolling spot. Sometimes it had a school of stripers, while at other times there would be a school of largemouths on it, and occasionally a bunch of big channel catfish would be around it. One day I was fishing with live needlefish, and I caught three channel cats which totaled over 30 pounds. Another day we had four lures out and were trolling, and on one pass caught four rockfish which weighed 85 pounds. Once I was jigging a Hopkins Spoon, and twenty straight times I dropped down to the bottom and repeatedly jigged the lure, and I caught 20 bass, one of 'em weighing 8½ pounds. The foundation was by far the most irregular feature in the area and was way out in the center of the lower lake. It had plenty of deep water and was the only cover around. Most of the fish lay on the walls, but the catfish and some rockfish and a few largemouths were down in the cellar. I didn't want to overfish this spot, and I wouldn't fish it over once a week or every ten days, because with any school of fish, you can almost eliminate the school by fishing it hard every day and keeping a lot of fish.

Other guides knew about it. Bob George knew where it was. He's a top striper guide, but he didn't mess much with the largemouths. Linwood Thornhill probably knew about it. Actually, I found it by watching an old-timer, Sam Richardson, who guided back then but has been dead several years. He was called Catfish Sam, and he used to run a charter service out of Moncks Corner. He had about a 40-foot shrimp boat, and he'd take about ten people at a time, and they'd go live-bait fishing or trolling. The old plantation house was one of his favorite striper holes. He'd anchor on it in the spring and fish live herring, and in the summer he'd troll it with big Cisco Kid plugs and catch stripers. Time after time I'd see him out there. Although I'd crossed the area several times, I never exactly hit the house foundation. I knew a hill was out there, but I didn't know what else. One day I really checked it closely, and I found the house foundation with my locator. And from reading the history books about the area, I figured out which plantation it was.

It's amazing how seldom house foundations *ever* get fished. I'll spot them on contour maps, and I'll ask the local guides and boat-dock operators about the house foundations. Nine times out of ten, I'll hear something like, "Well, it's probably not there. When they cleared the lake, they probably bulldozed the house foundation." This is quite true if it was a temporary structure, but if it was a large house foundation with a lot of brick, rocks, or concrete and heavy structure in the cellar, it would not have been completely eradicated. Portions of it would remain. Rocks and brick would be strewn on the bottom, and the cellar still would be there. It still would be a good irregular feature and good structure for a school of bass. House foundations are still the hotspots they've always been; they're seldom fished and they're super spots for schools of fish.

SUBMERGENT WEEDS

When I think of submergent weeds, I think of good structure. I also think back on the time Jerry McKinnis and I caught a pair of 10-pound bass at Okeechobee and released 'em on film. You don't think of Okeechobee as a structure lake, but this definitely was a deep-structure situation. This was back in 1971 when the water was real low and below the weedlines. The only cover in the lake was pepper-grass, which grew out to 5 or 6 feet deep. Of course, now the lake level is up, and this grass is probably 8 or 9 feet deep.

Jerry and I had heard the bass were hitting Johnson Spoons in the peppergrass, so we drifted across big areas and threw spoons and caught a couple of bass. One day the wind quit blowing and we got out to the edge of the peppergrass. Billy Murray and my wife, Mary Ann, were with us, and when we saw the edge, we thought it would be a good place to throw plastic worms. We'd happened to come out not only on the edge of the grass but on a long point as well, and this was an added benefit. Right away we started catching 'em on worms 6 inches long with $1/8$-ounce slip sinkers. We'd throw to the edge and pull line off our reels so the worms would fall straight down beside the weeds. We'd let the worms sit on the bottom and then barely move them.

We really tore up the big fish. I've fished Okeechobee for ten or twelve straight years, but I caught more over 7 pounds on that one

Weeds are structure—you can clean up if you find the edges and the underwater points they form.

trip with Mary Ann, Jerry, and Billy than I have at any other time. We caught a 10½, a 10¼, several 8s, and a bunch of 7s. This was before I'd gotten into the film business, but Jerry had been in the business five or six years. Since we had these trophy bass we decided to really make a show-business production out of the film. We agreed to weigh 'em back at the dock and then release them right there.

Jerry had caught one of the 10s and I'd gotten the other one, and we weighed 'em on the Vances' scales back at Clewiston Marina, and then to everyone's surprise we dropped them back in the water and explained we were releasing them so they could be caught again another day. Richard Vance and the guys at the dock just about died. Never at Okeechobee had they ever seen anyone release two 10-pound bass right at the dock. For the next week, a lot of people were fishing right around the dock. A 10-pounder at Okeechobee is outstanding.

94 Edges are Everything

Edges of the weeds in the northern lakes are probably the main structure for bass. Many of the lakes in Minnesota, Wisconsin, and Michigan have deep submergent weeds. Some southern impoundments and natural lakes also have deep weeds, but submergent weed edges are primarily in the natural lakes of the north and in Florida, such as in Okeechobee. The edges really are *everything*. They're the key, and there are a lot of edges.

This one took a small Countdown Rapala fished right along the weed edge.

How do you fish them effectively to find a school of fish? Generally a 5,000-acre lake, say in Minnesota, might have twelve to fifteen miles of grass edges in the form of patches, points, and bays. You need a comprehensive system to fish these edges. The plastic worm is the top bait in such waters, but when the edges are 10 to 15 feet deep, it's time-consuming to fish worms all day to find bass. I like to use small sinking lures such as Countdown Rapalas and Spots and also deep-running crank baits and 8- or 10-pound line to find them. This is how I won the B.A.S.S. tournament on the St. Lawrence Seaway in New York in 1978. I found 'em on a small No. 7 Countdown Rapala on grass edges in the Lake of the Isles area. The grass was growing out of 15 feet of water and extended to within 2 or 3 feet of the top. When I'd find a school, there would be a few eager ones right at the edge, and they'd be shallow. After I'd catch one or two, I'd throw out a marker and go to worm fishing. I caught the 4-to-6-pounders on worms.

Another very good lure which has been highly successful in Minnesota is the Reaper. It's kind of like a grub. It has a wedge-shaped jig head which pulls through the grass fairly easily, and the Reaper body is similar to a grub except that it's 4 to 6 inches long and is designed to look like an eel. This lure is thrown over the grass and is fished like a jig. You tweak it and barely skim the top of the grass, and when you get to the edge of the grass you jig it along the edge. When it hits the bottom, hop it upward, and that's when the bass generally hit it.

In the average natural lake in the north during the summer, probably 90 percent of the bass are on the grass line in the deeper types of grass. Depending on water clarity, grass edges are of different depths. In a super-clear lake in northern Minnesota, there could be grass as deep as 20 feet. There you'd need to stay away from crank baits and use jigs and plastic worms. Near Minneapolis is Lake Minnetonka, which gets a lot of boat traffic and is much dingier. Minnetonka's grass lines run 8 to 10 feet deep depending on the water level and its clarity.

Deep in the South at Lake Seminole in southern Georgia, the Chattahoochee River might be muddying up the grass flats in the Spring Creek area, and you might find coontail moss in 2 to 3 feet of water. In dingy water, grass doesn't get enough sunlight to grow deep.

Frequently you can't see a grass edge and it's not on the contour map, so you have to use a combination of structure tricks. You can find the edge with your locator, and you need to use marker buoys to give you reference points. This is especially true if you're out hundreds of yards from shore. I like to put out three or four on a 100-to-200-yard stretch of lake, and work that edge. I might work up the edge with one lure, and come back down it with something else.

---

95 Points and Patches

Now we're talking about the real key to submergent weeds, and that is isolated features. When you find a patch of grass, this is where you can win a tournament. I think of one time when we were fishing an area of Toledo Bend with a lot of little rises and coontail moss by the ton. For some reason, pre-spawn bass on the edge of coontail moss in Toledo Bend love small red crank baits, and I was cranking one of

Down there on the bottom of that dingy water there is likely a patch of moss or grass, and if you can locate it with your spinnerbait you may have success on its edges all summer.

these red plugs. I drifted out past where I thought the moss was, and I found a small patch about 25 feet in diameter. When I cranked that lure on the edge of it, I felt the bait hit the grass. The trick here is once you feel it hit the grass, let it float up and then snatch it real hard, and it will pull free of the coontail.

Well, we sat there and fished the edge of that patch and caught a real nice bunch of pre-spawners on those small red crank baits. Here the secret was finding that isolated patch. It was the only isolated feature nearby, and it held a good school of bass.

Another good trick around points and patches in muddy water such as we often have in Oklahoma is to fish spinnerbaits. On Lake Kerr in southeastern Oklahoma there is very shallow moss. The bottom might be only 3 feet deep and the coontail grows up within 6 inches of the surface. The water is so dingy that you hardly can see the moss. A spinnerbait not only is good for the pre-spawners and spawners, but it's good in Kerr all through the summer when the water's muddy. One thing I've noticed about shallow grass and shallow moss, particularly points and patches of it, is that you'll find bass on it throughout the summer. I prefer the single-bladed spinnerbait for this type of fishing because when the blade hits the moss or weeds, you can feel the interruption a little better. Sometimes the strike feels no different from what the moss feels like, and this is when they rush the bait from behind. Another thing too is that when you have moss, you almost always have a point of it. There might not be a patch, but there usually will be a point. Use your marker buoys for a reference when you find the point.

96   Look for a Nook

The average fisherman doesn't find nooks. But they're on every grass line. They're so often overlooked because points of grass are obvious, but nooks are the opposite. They're much, much harder to find, and this is why I always stay on the outside or open-water edge of the weedlines when I can and throw in. When I'm throwing a spinnerbait or a crank bait, I can feel the grass tops, and when I come to a nook which is farther back than my markers indicate, I can throw back there and feel that I'm not in grass.

Particularly back in coves, nooks are one of the best early-spring patterns there is around grass. Since the northern coves are better for

I took this bass out of a grassy nook that I located back in a little cove.

spawning bass, you're apt to find a nook from a drain which provides the closest access to the spawning water. And such places in the backs of the warmer northern coves really hold the spawners more than any other spot I've ever seen in a natural lake. One of the best examples of this occurs at Currituck Sound, where there are a lot of big bays with milfoil. Nooks sometimes are drainage channels through the weeds, and these are highways for the fish. They're really super structures.

BARS AND SHOALS: A SUMMER PLACE

A bar or a shoal is just a shallow place out in the lake. It's not a point and is not directly connected to a point, although it might be connected by a saddle to a point. Bars and shoals are surrounded by deep water, and they're the shallowest spots in the deep water. Some fishermen simply call them "high places" out in the lake.

Virtually every type of lake in the world from mountain lakes in Utah to flatland reservoirs in the south have bars and shoals. In Utah a rock shoal might come up out of 500 feet of water. An underwater island is a bar or shoal. The TVA lakes have a lot of bars right next to the river channel because of the current. Sand, debris, and sediment are washed up over the channel during high-water conditions, and the deposit forms a bar. Sometimes you'll find sharp bars close to the river or creek channels. Another of many reasons for bars could be that a farmer piled up dirt in a certain spot through his farming practices.

Bars are mainly good in the summer, because bass at this time of year like exposed high places. In contrast, bass in the winter prefer the deep creek channels and calmer water without the wind and water movement which is associated with the bars and shoals. The most productive bars and shoals are mostly those out in the main, exposed areas of the lake, where a lot of wind sweeps the water. Consequently, the fish on a bar or shoal can seek an ambush point and wait for the baitfish to come past them.

When there's a lot of wind, the leapfrogging effect which I discussed in the section on points will occur. A school of bass on a bar or shoal can be one of the largest you'll ever find, and this is primarily true in the lakes with a lot of shad. In the wind and current, the bass keep leapfrogging ahead of each other, and they'll usually be found on

I caught this string over a "high place"—a shoal—in the middle of the lake.

the upwind or upcurrent side of the bar or shoal. If they're very actively feeding and leapfrogging, sometimes they go from 50 to 200 yards off the shoal to what I call an off-structure place. I wrote an article for Bass Master Magazine a few years ago called "Off-Structure Fishing." I talked about this same situation in which through competitive feeding, the bass end up out over deep water but straight upcurrent from the shoal. You'll see 'em on your depthfinder as suspended fish.

97   Seek Sharp Drops

The degree of the dropoff here is relative; I'm talking about the sharpest place on the bar or shoal. In a mountain lake like Bull Shoals or Table Rock, you might have a real sharp drop which goes from 2 to 30 feet off a rock ledge. But on a flat lake such as Santee-Cooper, the sharpest decline on an entire shoal might be only a 3-foot ledge.

The secret here is to get the total picture of the lake. When you find an isolated bar or shoal, you need to visualize what it might look like. Watch your depthfinder and get the total picture. Circling the structure is your first step. Determine how large it is and study the depths. Try to find smaller structures, because they're easier to fish and take less time, and the bass are more concentrated on them. A bar or shoal with a 10-foot top that is only 100 feet in diameter is much easier to fish than one with a top which extends over several acres. But no matter what size the bar or shoal, get the total picture first. Circle it and crisscross it several times to understand the total layout, and notice the rate of the dropoff and try to identify where the sharpest drop is.

One thing Paul Chamblee and I and several others do when we go to a strange lake for a tournament is to find bars and shoals and the steepest dropoffs and mark them on our maps well before the tournament. Then during the official practice, we look for fish on them. Even though the sharpest dropoff might theoretically be the best place to fish, if the wind is blowing, it might move them off that spot if it's blowing on the wrong side of the shoal. I still mark the dropoff because I figure that's where they stay most of the time, but I fish according to the wind. If the sharpest drop is upwind, I'm in pretty good shape, but if it's downwind, I'll draw a line from the drop and work straight upwind from it. For most bars and shoals, if I have the option, I'd rather be in deep water throwing to shallow water. Many bars and shoals are not very deep, and if they aren't, you might scare the fish if you have your boat in shallow and are casting to deep water. In dingy lakes, a good shoal for pre-spawners in the early spring might be only 5 feet deep. But if the water's super-clear as in Fontana Lake in the Smoky Mountains, the pattern depth might be 25 to 40 feet.

The thermocline plays a big part in what depth you'll find the bass during the summer in a lake with real clear water. I'm not necessarily talking about a true thermocline where the heaviest, most dense water in the lake is 39 degrees and is stacked up on the bottom. Most southern reservoirs don't have true thermoclines because the coldest water is higher than 39 degrees, but there is a temperature gradient—a rapid temperature change. A good temperature change is at least 1 degree per foot. Normally in the south I find a temperature drop of 2 degrees per foot. This means a 10-degree temperature change on a 5-foot drop. At Sam Rayburn, starting in April a slight temperature gradient forms about 10 feet deep. By late May, the same gradient has moved downward, because more and more warm water has warmed at the surface, which might be 75 degrees. Down about 20 feet it's about 10 degrees colder. The temperature gradient moves on down in June, July, and August to where the thermocline is 30 to 45 feet deep. This might be too deep for the bass; they aren't necessarily at the thermocline depth because if it's a dingy lake, they just don't follow it down that far. But if the water's clear, they quite often go to their

Out here in the open water you have to circle the bar and criss-cross it several times to find the sharpest dropoff.

comfort zone, and I estimate this temperature as being in the 69-to-73-degree range. If I find a thermocline in clear water, I like to fish it at about 72 degrees.

The easiest way to fish the bar or shoal is vertically. First I put out three or four markers. I use two locators—one 18 feet back at the end of the boat and the other by the trolling motor near where I'm sitting. This gives me the opportunity to pinpoint where the drop is. I have the total picture in mind and with two locators can get the exact angle of that drop. If I'm on structure deeper than 15 feet, I normally jig with a grub or a spoon if I'm trying to check it out quickly. Once I find them, there's nothing in the summer which beats the plastic worm for largemouths. If the water's less than 12 or 13 feet, I'll cast to the structure. If it's only 5 or 6 feet deep, I'll probably run a crank bait over it first just to see if I can find that one eager fish.

Quite often the bass aren't all concentrated in one spot. They often are packed up at different depths. Even if you're on a 15-foot ledge, you might get one or two of them to hit a crank bait as it's coming down the ledge. Usually they'll be the smaller, more eager ones.

ROADBEDS

98 . . . If They're Different

Roadbeds are one of the very finest structures to fish . . . if they're different. Some roadbeds simply aren't defined across the bottom of the lake, but if they're defined and have ditches on the sides and culverts where they cross creeks or are raised and are a couple feet higher than the surrounding land, they're apt to be super spots. Some are gravel, and that might be the only gravel in the surrounding area, and the shallower places of a gravel roadbed might be good spots for bass to spawn. An asphalt roadbed might be the only hard bottom around. Concrete and asphalt roads are the most improved roads. They have culverts and ditches, and their hard surfaces can readily be identified with a locator.

After I identify where a roadbed is with the aid of a contour map, I set my locator for the threshold of an echo and pick it up on the locator by the echo on the reflecting surface of gravel contrasting with a mud bottom or asphalt or concrete contrasting with a gravel or sand bottom. Then I look for the most different spot on the roadbed—the most irregular feature on this irregular feature. If it's at the right depth, the best place on it is where it crosses a creek, drain, or small river channel. On an improved road will be at least a culvert and possibly a bridge. Most culverts and most bridges are reinforced with concrete or steel, and when you pass over that spot, you'll get a very definite echo on your locator if you have it set as I mentioned.

If the road is straight—and most roads are fairly straight—I'll put out a couple of markers and troll it with my electric motor. This is the easiest way to fish it. One of the best tricks for a 1/4-to-1/2-mile section of roadbed is to stay on the edge of the road where the deeper ditch is.

I followed the roadbed and picked up this bass along a line of fenceposts I had identified with my locator.

I cross it several times to determine which is the deeper ditch. I use a 3/8-ounce sinker ahead of a plastic worm on 14-pound line if there's not a lot of brush. If there's a lot of brush and stickups, I might go to a 25-pound line and a 1/2-to-3/4-ounce weight. In the hot summer, you can move the worm faster on the bottom by trolling it than by any other way. I discussed how to do this in the section on worm trolling. I can cover a lot of roadbed quickly this way, and I'll try to cover both edges of it.

Sometimes I stop right where the culvert is and then make casts over into the creek channel. Quite often I find scattered fish along the roadbed, but the big concentration is at the culvert or the bridge. Any kind of bend or curve in the road is better than the straight road. You'll notice if you look closely on a contour map that some roads are bordered by a fence, and the fence might still be there. Watch your locator to see if there are any fenceposts down there.

Roadbeds can be good all year. In the colder weather the fish will likely be in the deepest portions of the roadbed, such as around the bridges and culverts. The opposite often is true in the summer, when they'll usually be shallower on any high spots, but the bass also might be in the creek channels around the culverts then, too.

Most of the larger Army Corps of Engineers lakes and several of the TVA impoundments were created in fairly well-populated areas with plenty of roadbeds. Toledo Bend and Sam Rayburn have hundreds of roadbeds. Every reservoir over 20,000 acres that I've ever fished has roadbeds. At Santee quite a few roads were built through swampy areas, and these roads were built up 5 to even 10 feet above bottom. These high ridges are super structures, particularly in hot weather.

RIVER AND CREEK CHANNELS: BASS FOR ALL SEASONS

Now we're down to the nitty-gritty—one of my favorite, most productive types of fishing. I catch more bass and bigger bass and have more success in tournament competition, guiding, and just plain fun fishing on river and creek channels. My background is fishing mostly shallower lakes and reservoirs, and creek channels are predominant in these waters because they represent the major type of structure.

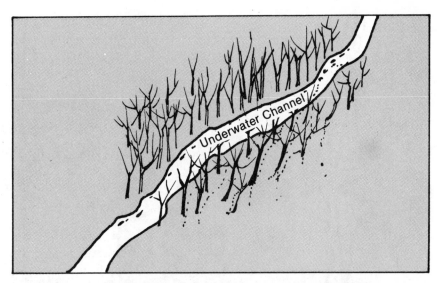

Channels or creeks running through wooded areas are prime bass territory. Look for sharp turns or intersections with other channels.

Creek channels aren't particularly good in the very deep lakes. In an extremely deep lake such as Powell in Utah, creek channels aren't any good at all because they're all too deep and too inaccessible.

In a large lowland reservoir like Lake Murray in South Carolina or Toledo Bend, Rayburn, and Palestine in Texas, coves stretch for two to four miles with water from 5 to 25 feet deep. The creeks have very little slope to them, and their channels are mostly the right depth. My biggest bass come from such places. The main advantage of fishing them is that you can find schools of bass all year round at some depth. In early spring, pre-spawners use these creeks as highways from deep water and come up them to spawn. Before they go on the beds, they find their holding depth, which might be 5 to 8 feet deep if the water's dingy. Invariably they find stumps along the channel. Usually there is a lot of heavy timber along the creeks because they once bordered farmers' fields. In a large, flat, shallow cove, the creek channel has the most cover in the form of stumps, brush, and cover, and it is the most irregular feature. It is the area that contrasts most with the bottom, and it provides access to deep water.

Creek channels are good in the hottest periods of summer as well as in the dead of winter. Bass use them as migration routes to go

Creek channels are highways for bass; you can find fish in them all year.

deeper and deeper during the temperature extremes. Creek channels also are super spots in farm ponds and mill ponds which are fed by creeks. Ponds which were formed on creeks that were dammed up can be viewed as miniature impoundments, and the same creek-channel principles hold true on them.

---

99   Outside Bends: The Ultimate Find

Outside bends in creek channels are one of the most consistent patterns I've ever known of. Ninety percent of the time when you find bass on a creek channel, they'll be on the bends. One of the reasons is that creek channel bends are a little bit shallower than the straight stretches, and this is because before the lake was impounded, high water washed up over the bank on the bends during flood conditions, and deposited sand, mud, and debris there. This made the bends sort of like small bluffs. Many of these bends are found in the TVA chain lakes. This is another example of an irregular feature.

With their small blufflike banks, outside bends have the shallowest water right next to the deepest water. Almost always the bends on any river or creek have the deepest water. Therefore, the greatest depth contrast will be on the outside bends.

In the summer when I'm fishing an outside bend, I like to stay in the creek channel. It's a great advantage to have two locators—front and rear—when you're fishing a bend because this shows you where the shallow and deep edges are, and it gives you pinpoint accuracy, particularly when you're jigging or making short casts with plastic worms. You must know where that edge is, and you cannot be accurate with one locator. I'm always throwing from deep water to shallow water in the summer because the bass likely will be on top of the shallowest spot there or on the very edge of the channel. I use either a plastic worm or a spoon or grub, depending on what lure pattern is working best. I'm working it from the shallower top on down the dropoff. On some of these bends, especially in the newer reservoirs, there are so many roots sticking out and so much brush that if you tried to retrieve from deep to shallow water, you'd get hung up repeatedly. If the outside bend is less than 10 feet deep, I'll likely hit it a lick or two with a crank bait to start with, but usually in the summer they might be down as far as 20 feet, and this would call for a deep-structure lure.

If the bottom is clean and free of any cover, as might be the case in an old reservoir, I sometimes position my boat in the shallow water and throw to deep water. Sometimes in lakes like Ouachita in Arkansas, coming up the drop is fairly productive. But primarily I like to have that plastic worm falling down the dropoff and dropping off the stumps, branches, and roots. So many times the strike comes when the lure is falling down, and you can get it to fall down only when it's coming off the ledge. If the water is clear and it's a bright day, the bass might be barely over the lip of the creek channel. Kentucky or spotted bass are famous for this on creek channels. They'll be slightly down the drop, although not on the bottom. When the lure comes tumbling down, that's when they hit it. The idea is to make it tumble down on their noses.

In the winter, creek bends sometimes pay off in another way. The bass often seek the deepest water in the bend because it's the deepest place in the area. This is January and February fishing when water

I found an outside bend in a creek channel, jigged it, and this was the payoff.

temperatures are 40 to 45 degrees and the weather's really been cold. To catch them when they're on the very bottom of the channel is primarily a jigging game. Use a spoon, grub, or small jig and get directly over the top of 'em. Try to spot them on your locator, and get right over where you think they are. Jig close to the bottom, and don't pull your lure high. When the water is very cold, jigging the bait 6 inches off the bottom works much better than pulling it 3 feet off the bottom. (In the summer when the water's warm, I'll jig the bait sometimes 3 and 4 feet high.) Bass in water this cold usually are very difficult to catch.

Until this past year I had a 7,000-gallon aquarium at my home in Broken Arrow, Okla. When the water temperature got down below 45 degrees, my bass would get beneath the logs in the deepest part of the aquarium and just lie beneath the cover. At times there would be 15 to 20 bass all packed in one spot and touching each other. I hadn't fed 'em for a long time but they weren't hungry. Their metabolisms were so low they just didn't think about feeding. The first time I dropped a jig and a spoon in there on them, I actually snagged a couple of them in the side when I jigged it. They acted as if they were almost asleep. After jigging the spoon twenty to thirty times in the same spot, three or four bass finally got their eyes focused on the lure and eased toward it. After about ten more jigs, one of 'em almost in slow motion opened his mouth and nipped very carefully at the lure. A strike like this is almost impossible to feel; you almost have to guess at it. Watch your line for the slightest little tick, and then set the hook.

---

100   Irregularities Ideal, Isolation the Key

When you're fishing a creek channel, as I've said before, you need to look for the most irregular feature on that creek. It could be a bridge or a tree lying across the creek, a brushpile, a cluster of stumps, a big boulder, or an old fencerow. A bridge would be shown on your contour map, but any natural obstruction won't be shown. A logjam at the bend of a creek might be imbedded in the mud, but it won't be on the map. When a farmer has a ravine, he often dumps rocks and logs he's cleared from his fields in it. When he did this twenty years before the lake was impounded, Farmer John thought only about clearing his fields and filling in the ravine. He didn't realize he was putting down structure for schools of bass to get around a quarter of a century later.

There might not be any feature like this on some creek channels, but if there is, it would be the most irregular feature you'll find. You have to consider all the possibilities. The creek might have an old car body in it. I've fished creeks where I kept seeing these extremely reflective surfaces on my locator, and I didn't know what they were. I kept jigging around and finally guessed they were old cars. I found one for certain at Toledo Bend. I saw this reflective surface on the screen and didn't know what it was, but five years later during a period of low water, I was in that creek and could see the top of the old car. I'd been catching fish there, too. At Lake Millwood in Arkansas, there's an old schoolbus along one of the creek channels, and as amusing as it might sound, that's a good place to fish. We call it "the old schoolbus hole."

An imbedded log on the bend of
a creek is the kind of irregularity
that holds bass like a magnet.

Any of these places—man-made or natural—which are full of
cover and very irregular are the key to finding concentrations of bass.
Isolation, too, is an important part of it. All through this book, I've
stressed isolation. At the risk of being repetitious I'll say it again: find
the most isolated cover and structure. I like to find an isolated creek
channel. When I look at a contour map, I'm looking for the widest
cove and widest creek channel I can find. The wide coves usually are
better than the small, narrow coves. The narrow cove does have a
creek channel, but in the wide cove there is more dead, unproductive
water, and therefore the creek channel is more isolated and becomes
more of a key. Another factor about isolation is that if you're in an

area where the creek has two or three branches, splits, or bends, it wouldn't be quite as good as if there were only one bend and no branches. Too much of the same type of cover tends to scatter out the bass, and this is the same with creek channels as it is with stumps, rocks, weeds, and points.

Irregularities are really a locator game, and isolation can be determined only by getting the total picture of the lake. You not only need to keep looking at your contour map and your locator, but you need to keep piecing together the total picture. Make a mental image of the area you're going to fish. Ol' Bill Dance said years ago, and he's proved it to be very successful, that he does most of his best fishing when he takes a section of a lake, such as a five-mile section, and concentrates on only that section. He tries to identify every type of cover and bottom and creek bend and get the total picture of that five-mile area so he knows every single feature and structure there. Doing what he said will provide you with five or six pattern possibilities to draw from.

Jerry McKinnis and I caught these 10-pounders on isolated patches of peppergrass in Lake Okeechobee—and caused quite a fuss when we released them from the dock.

101 Vertical Drops Spell Victory

Many times in the older reservoirs when I'm out looking for creek channels, I'll find a lot of places where mud, sand, and silt have filled in much of the channel. But particularly in the creek-bend areas, there are still some sections with good vertical drops which haven't been silted in. At Santee-Cooper, wind and wave action on some bars and shoals made those places the most vertical drops in the area, but most of the vertical drops are on creek channels. Some lakes, such as Eufaula in Alabama, have very deep channels. When you look around the lake, you notice huge ravines 10 to 15 feet deep coming into the lake. They continue out and form very deep dropoffs. Regardless of how much siltation occurs, those deep channels will never fill in completely.

But in lakes such as Santee, there is so much wind and muddy water moving around that erosion has filled in many of the creek

Ron Gentzen of Tulsa and I heft three bass weighing 32 pounds, caught off a vertical drop in Lake Zaza, September 1978.

channels, which were never deep to start with. Very few vertical drops exist there on the creek channels, but there are some. There are some really good ones in the Santee River. Again, look at your contour map and find the creek bends. That's where to start looking for vertical drops. Creek bends are undercut. Before the lake was built, the bends usually had bluff-type banks and much deeper and more vertical drops than anywhere else on the creeks.

I normally jig vertical drops. They're usually not very big places, and the fewer you find, usually the better they are. They're more isolated and more irregular and offer a bigger contrast with the surrounding lake bottom, and they often hold bigger concentrations of bass. Vertical drops pay off in both summer and winter, and most of the time I jig them with a spoon. Look for vertical drops and jig them, and when you find a school of bass, you're apt to catch your biggest bass ever. This is where you easily might drop your lure to the bottom ten times and catch ten good bass. Once you've located them with the spoon, you might find that they quit hitting it after you've caught a couple. Then go to a good-sized plastic worm, 7, 8, or even 9 inches long, and try to catch a great big bass. Learn how to cross-triangulate that spot, and you'll have a honey hole which might be good for years to come.

I hope you find a good many honey holes over the years, and I hope my 101 bass-catching secrets will help you to reap their full rewards. I also hope that in the process you'll develop quite a few secrets of your own—or maybe you have already. Don't forget to share them with me. After all, the exchange of knowledge is what provides us all with good bassin'.